GEGE AKUTAMI

What to do...?

GEGE AKUTAMI published a few short
works before starting *Jujutsu Kaisen*, which began
serialization in *Weekly Shonen Jump* in 2018.

JUJUTSU KAISEN

VOLUME 11
SHONEN JUMP MANGA EDITION

BY GEGE AKUTAMI

TOUCH-UP ART & LETTERING Snir Aharon
DESIGN Joy Zhang
EDITOR John Bae
CONSULTING EDITOR Erika Onabe

JUJUTSU KAISEN © 2018 by Gege Akutami
All rights reserved.
First published in Japan in 2018 by SHUEISHA Inc., Tokyo.
English translation rights arranged by SHUEISHA Inc.

The stories, characters and incidents mentioned
in this publication are entirely fictional.

Printed in the U.S.A.

Published by VIZ Media, LLC
P.O. Box 77010
San Francisco, CA 94107

10 9 8 7 6 5 4 3 2 1
First printing, August 2021

PARENTAL ADVISORY
JUJUTSU KAISEN is rated T+ for Older Teen
and is recommended for ages 16 and up. This
volume contains fantasy violence.

JUJUTSU KAISEN

11

THE SHIBUYA INCIDENT
—GATE OPEN—

STORY AND ART BY GEGE AKUTAMI

JUJUTSU KAISEN
CAST OF CHARACTERS

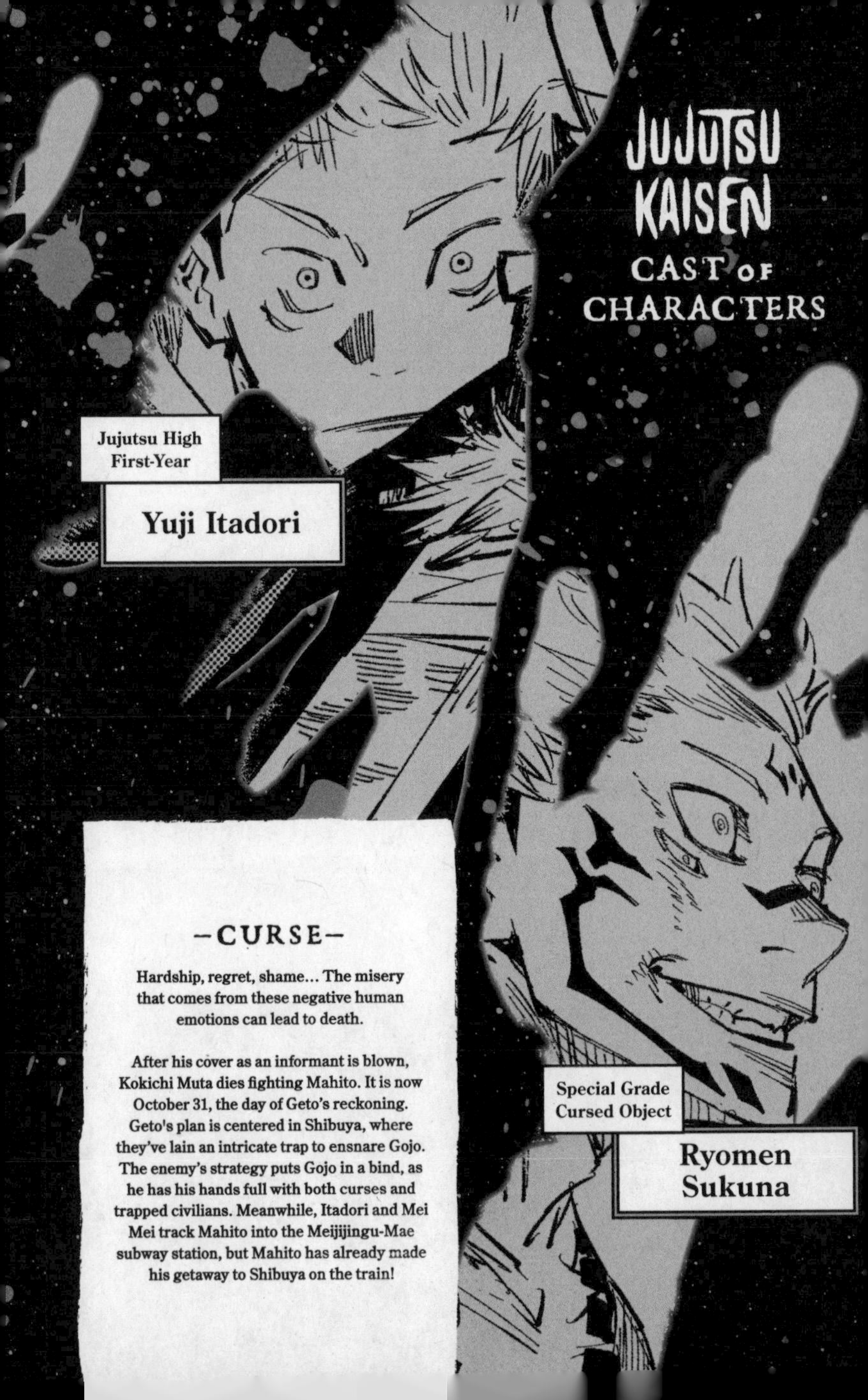
Jujutsu High First-Year
Yuji Itadori
Special Grade Cursed Object
Ryomen Sukuna

—CURSE—

Hardship, regret, shame... The misery that comes from these negative human emotions can lead to death.

After his cover as an informant is blown, Kokichi Muta dies fighting Mahito. It is now October 31, the day of Geto's reckoning. Geto's plan is centered in Shibuya, where they've lain an intricate trap to ensnare Gojo. The enemy's strategy puts Gojo in a bind, as he has his hands full with both curses and trapped civilians. Meanwhile, Itadori and Mei Mei track Mahito into the Meijijingu-Mae subway station, but Mahito has already made his getaway to Shibuya on the train!

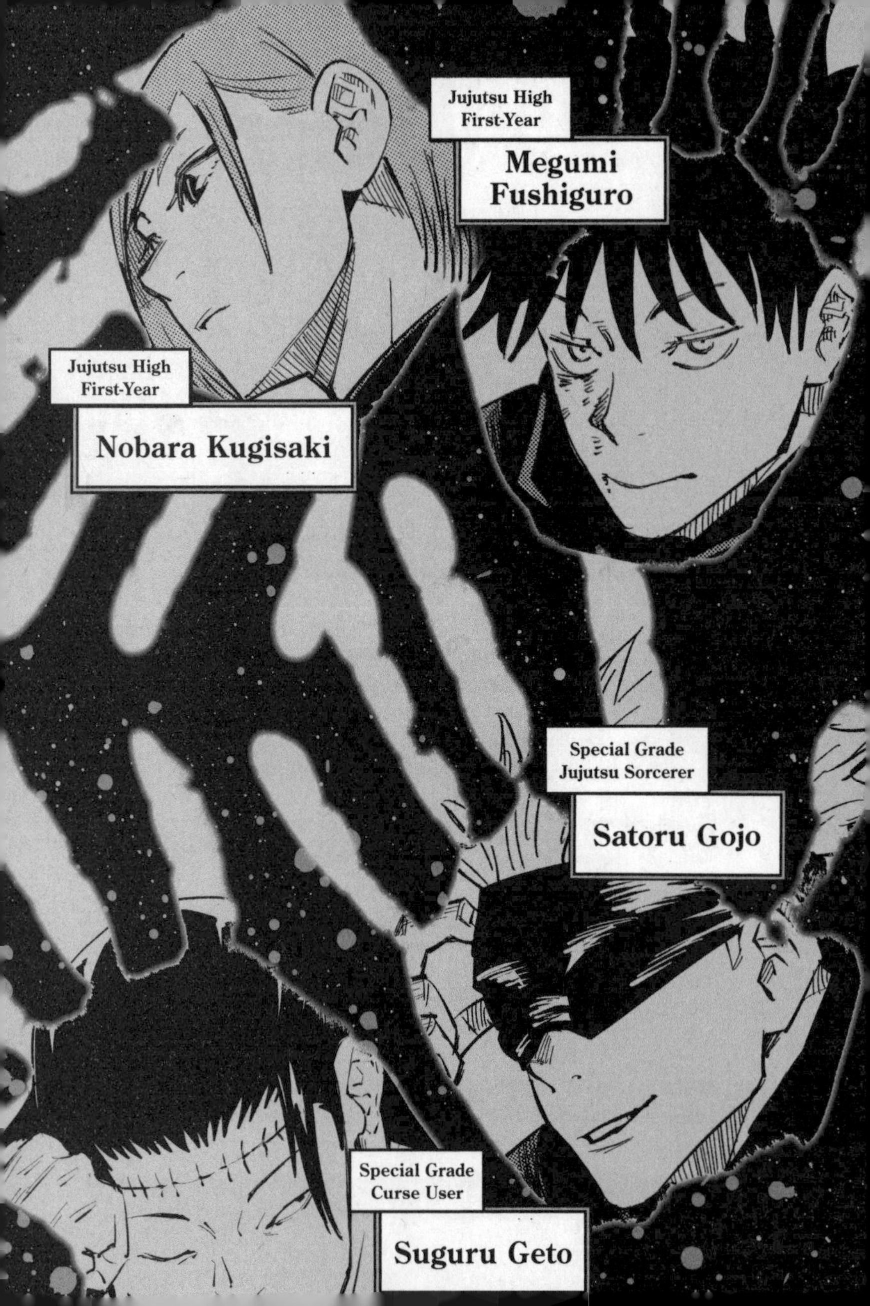
Jujutsu High First-Year
Megumi Fushiguro
Jujutsu High First-Year
Nobara Kugisaki
Special Grade Jujutsu Sorcerer
Satoru Gojo
Special Grade Curse User
Suguru Geto

JUJUTSU KAISEN

11

THE SHIBUYA INCIDENT —GATE OPEN—

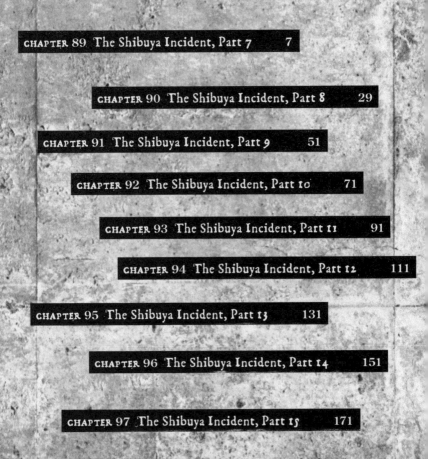

Chapter 89: The Shibuya Incident, Part 7

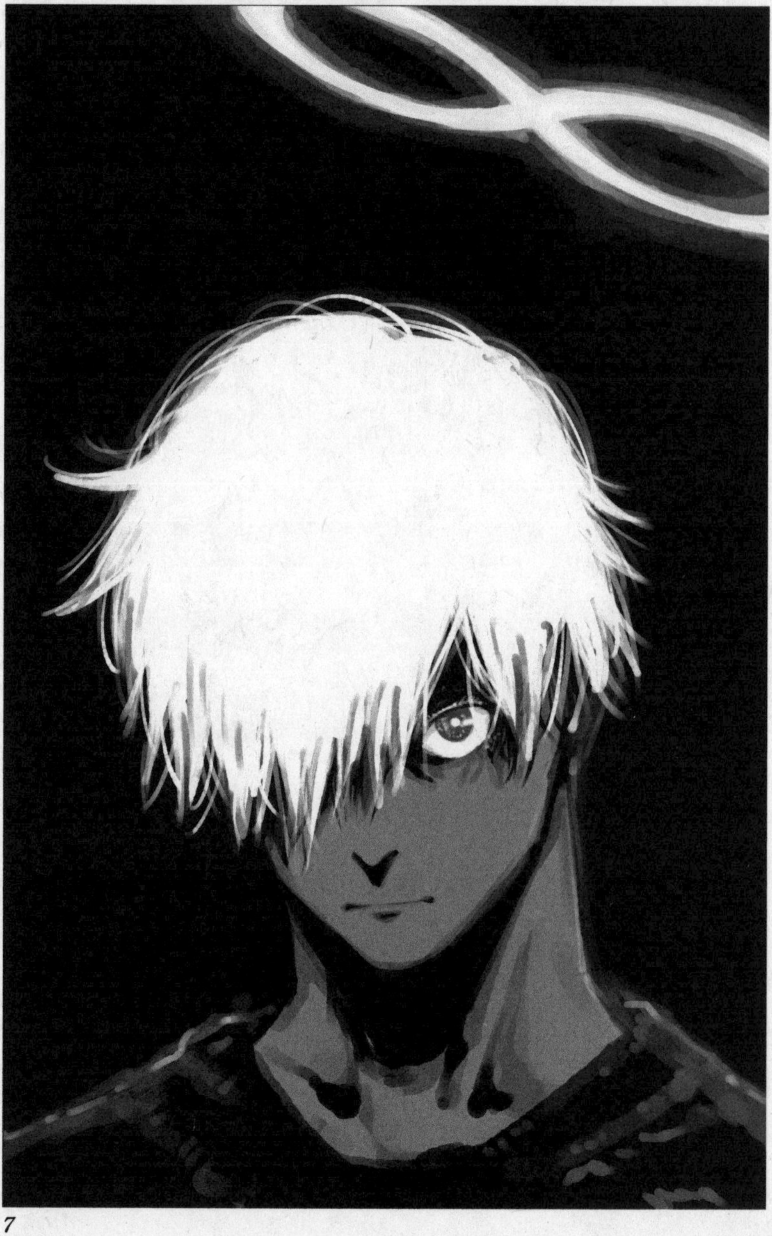

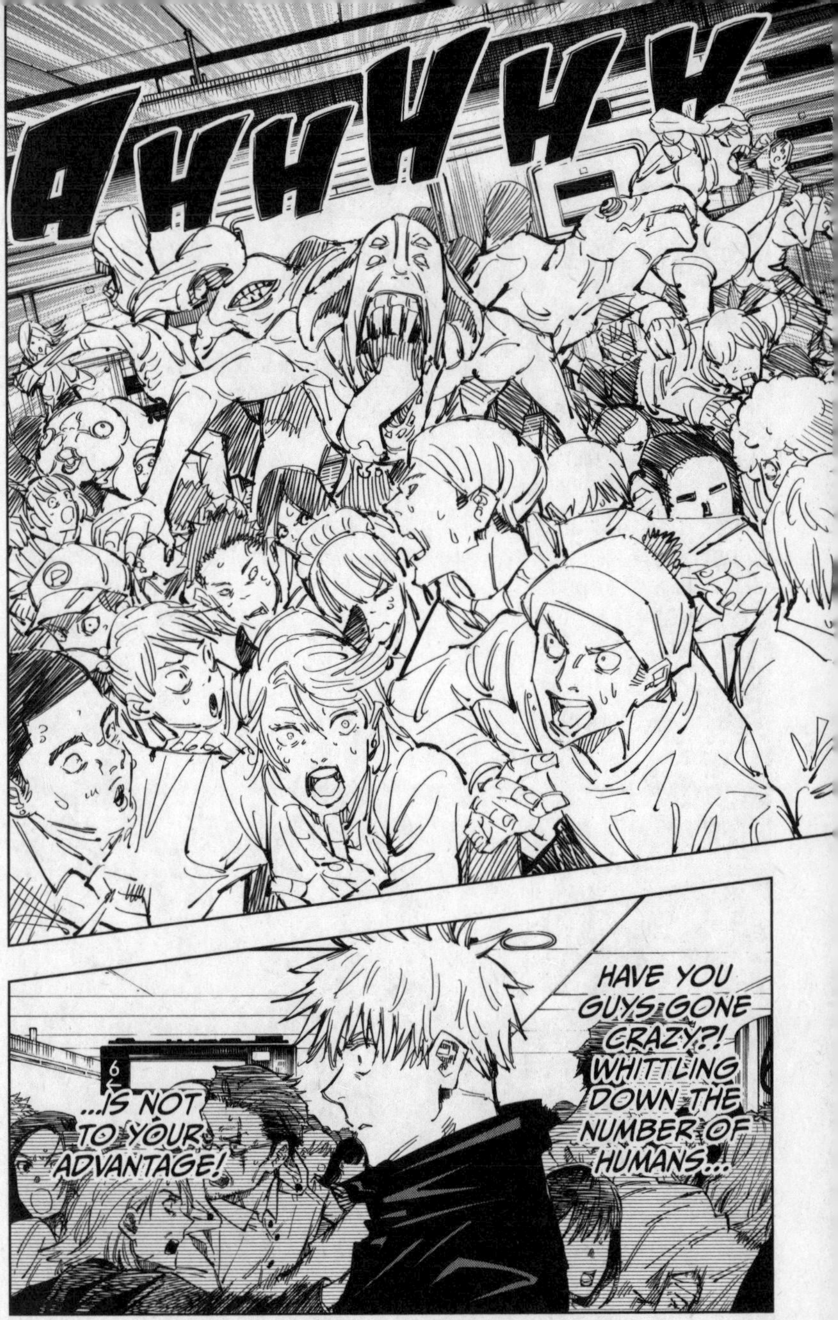
AHHHHH-
HAVE YOU GUYS GONE CRAZY?! WHITTLING DOWN THE NUMBER OF HUMANS...
...IS NOT TO YOUR ADVANTAGE!

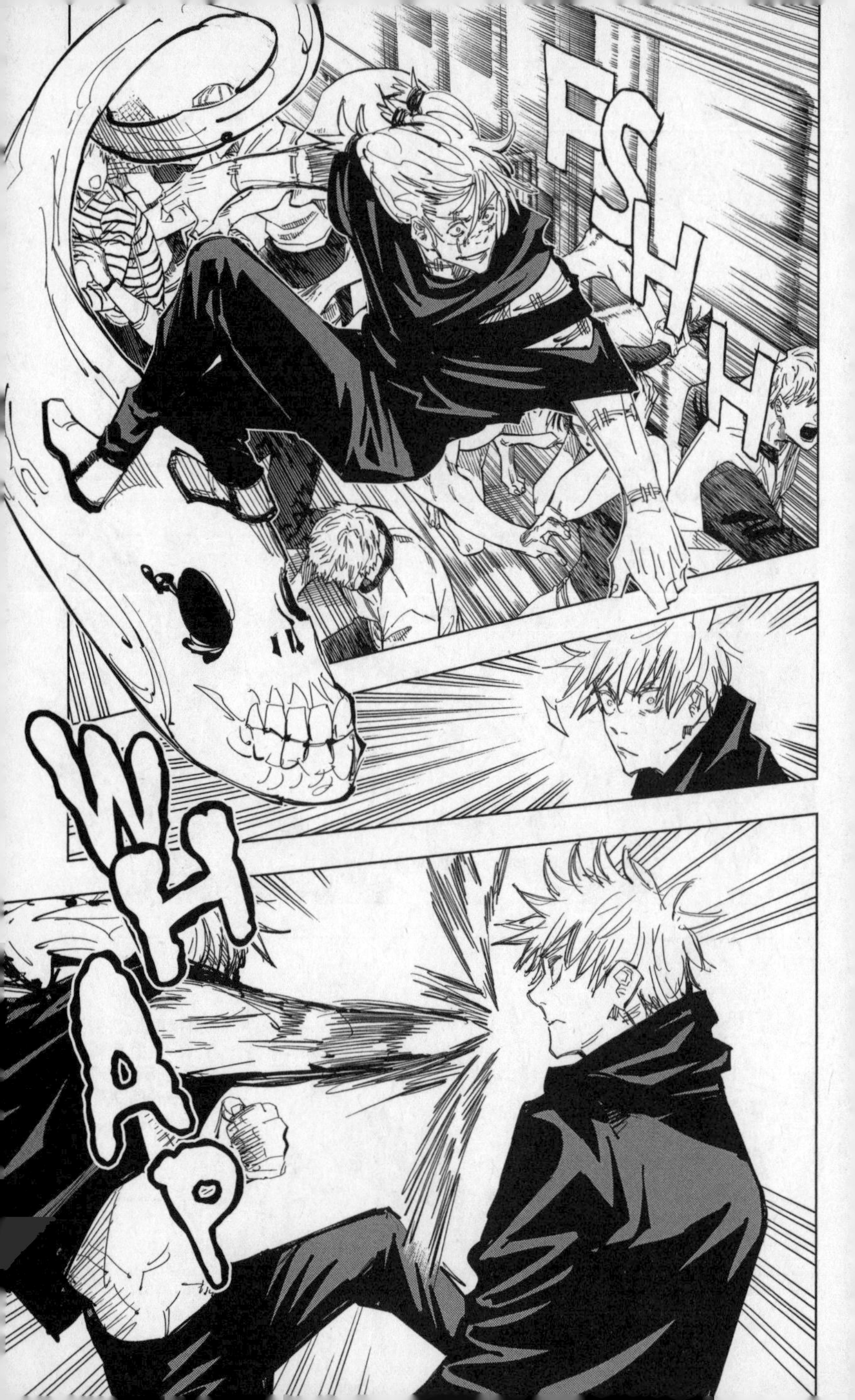
FSHH
WHAP

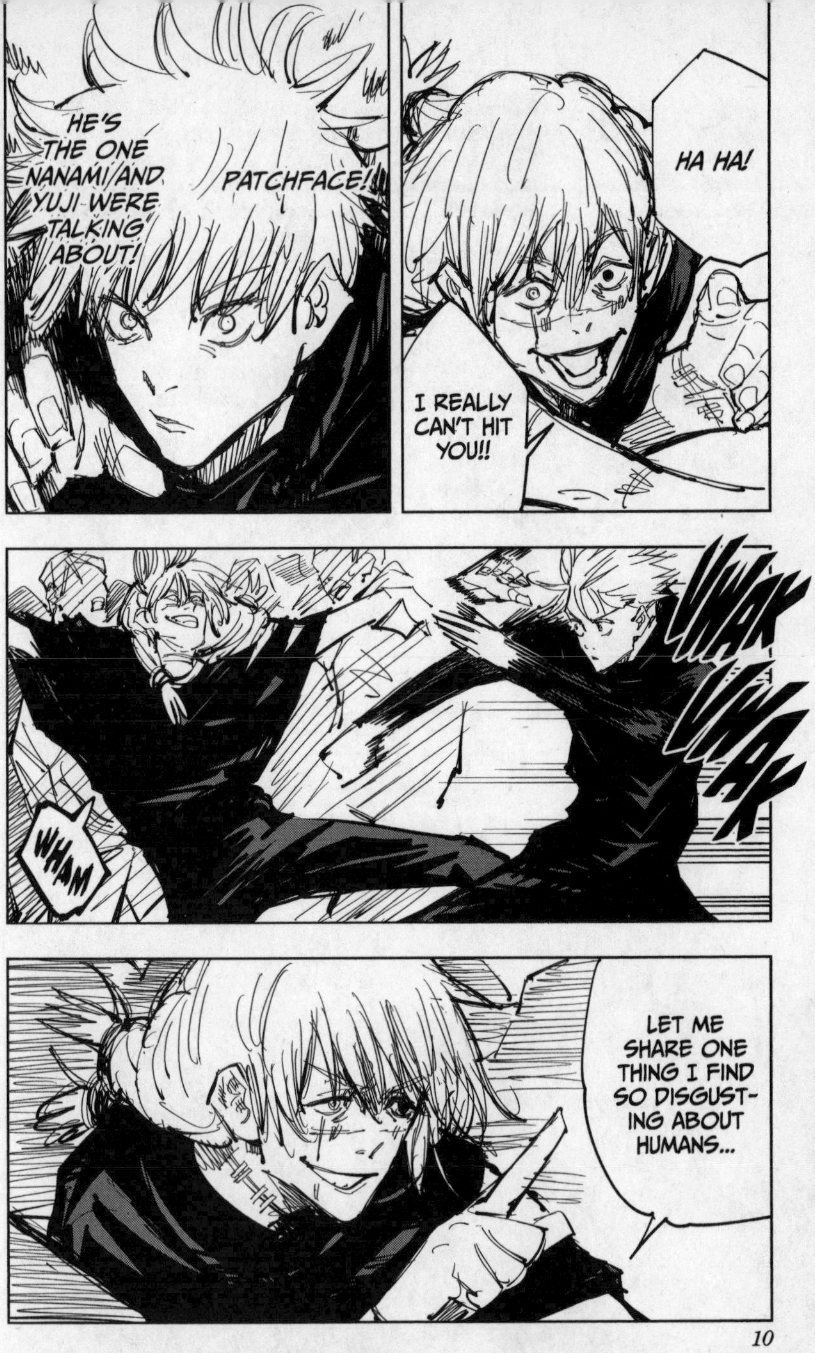
HA HA!
I REALLY CAN'T HIT YOU!!
PATCHFACE!
HE'S THE ONE NANAMI AND YUJI WERE TALKING ABOUT!
WHAK
WHAK
WHAK
WHAM
LET ME SHARE ONE THING I FIND SO DISGUST-ING ABOUT HUMANS...

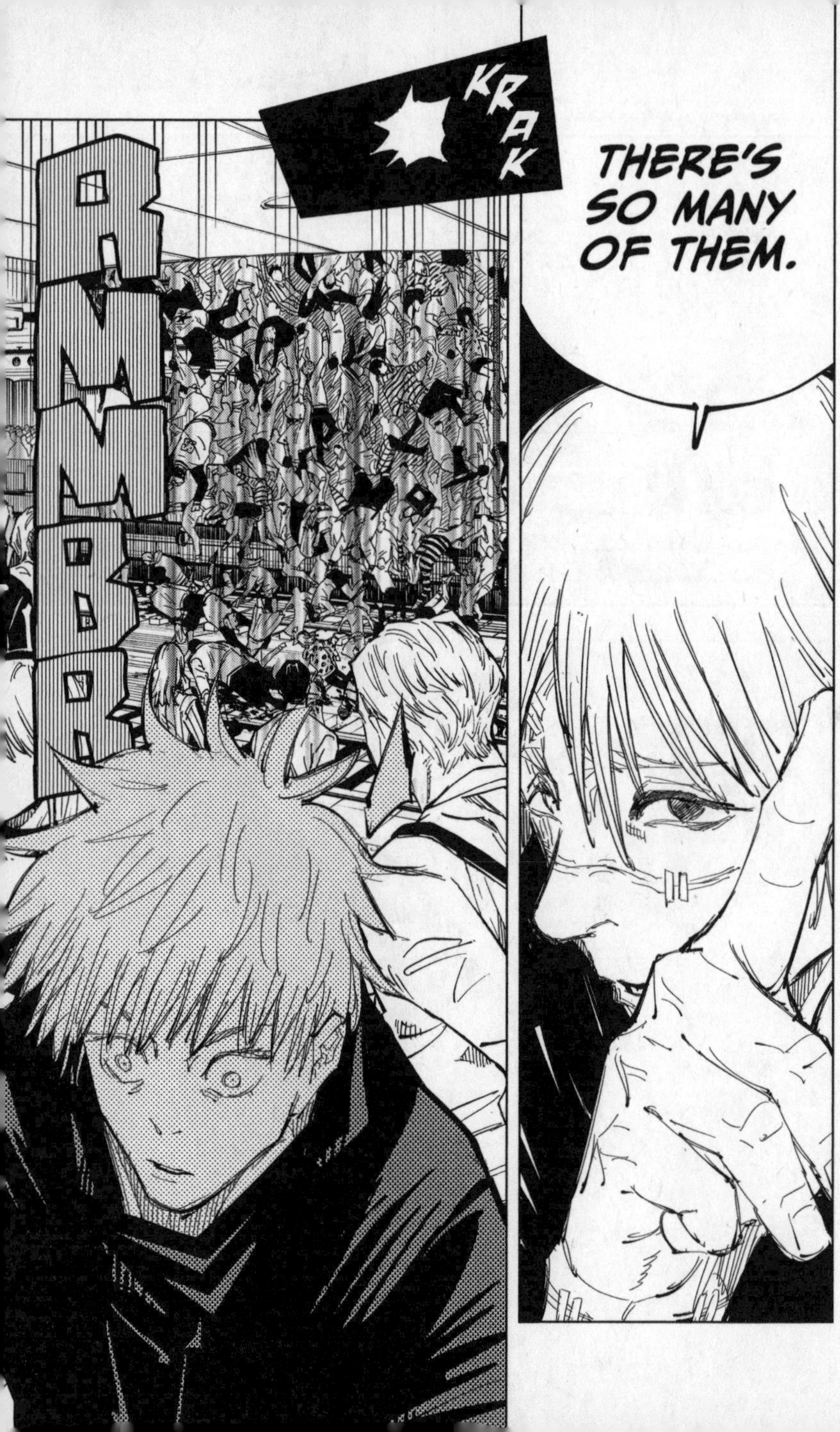
THERE'S SO MANY OF THEM.
KRAK

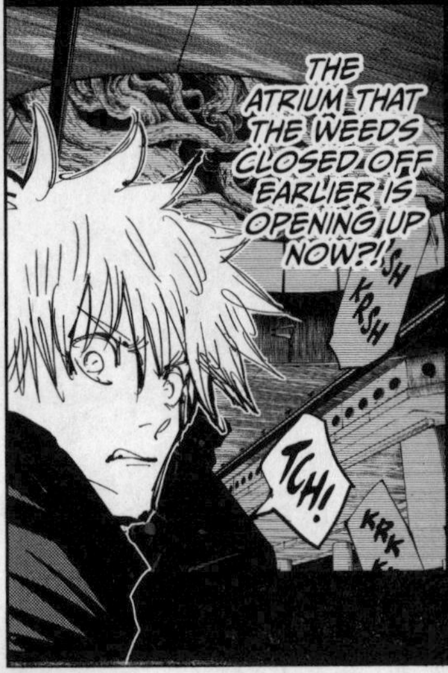
THE ATRIUM THAT THE WEEDS CLOSED OFF EARLIER IS OPENING UP NOW?!
SH KRSH
TCH!
KRK
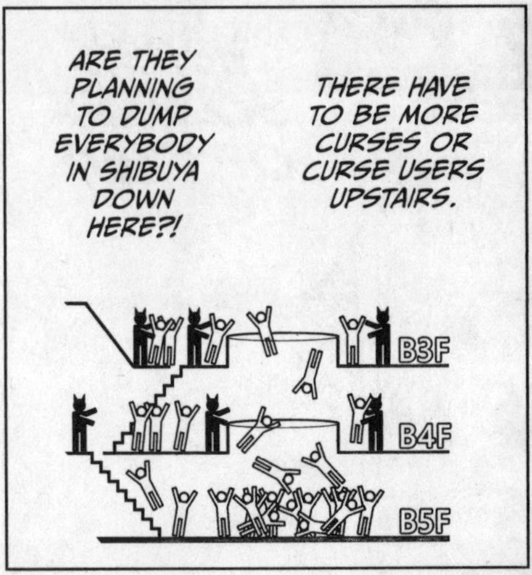
THERE HAVE TO BE MORE CURSES OR CURSE USERS UPSTAIRS.
ARE THEY PLANNING TO DUMP EVERYBODY IN SHIBUYA DOWN HERE?!
B3F
B4F
B5F
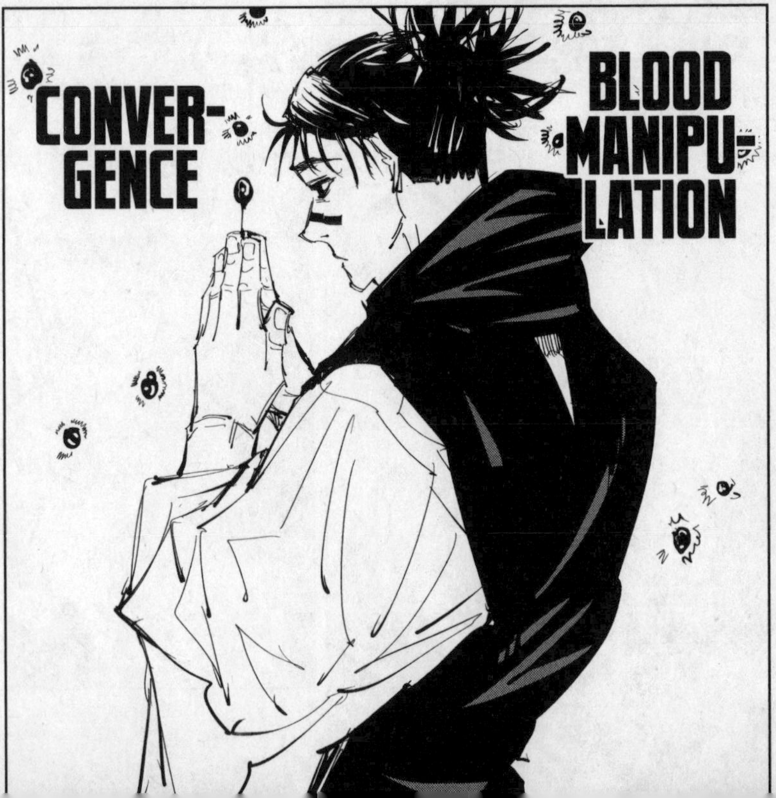
BLOOD MANIPU-LATION
CONVER-GENCE

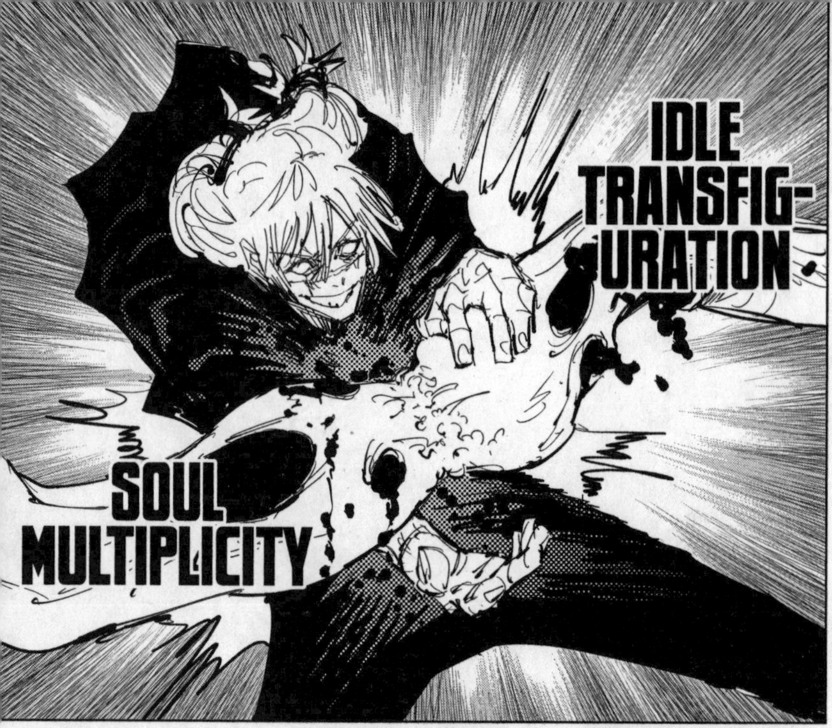
IDLE TRANSFIG-URATION
SOUL MULTIPLICITY

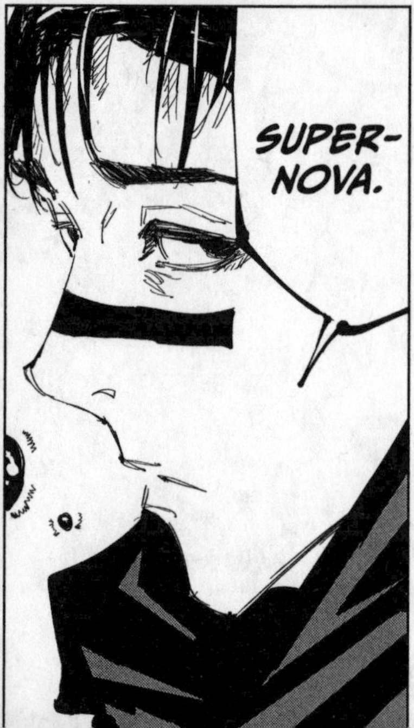
SUPER-NOVA.

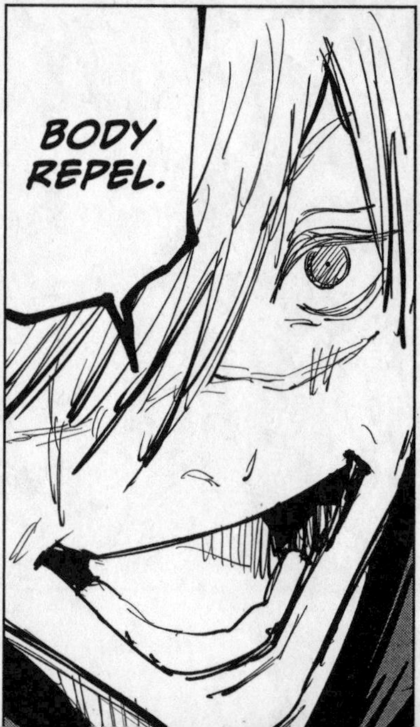
BODY REPEL.

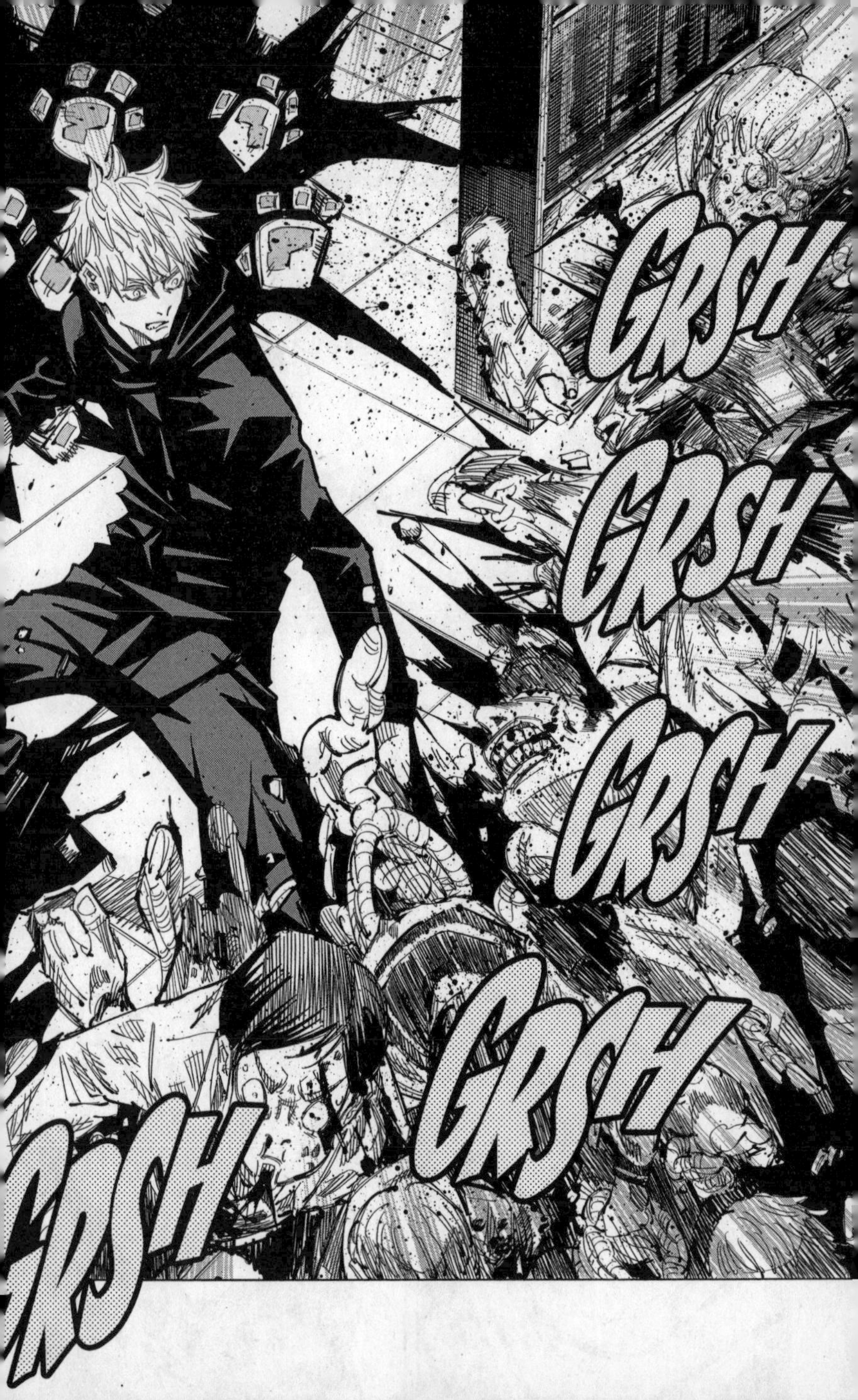
CRSH
CRSH
CRSH
CRSH

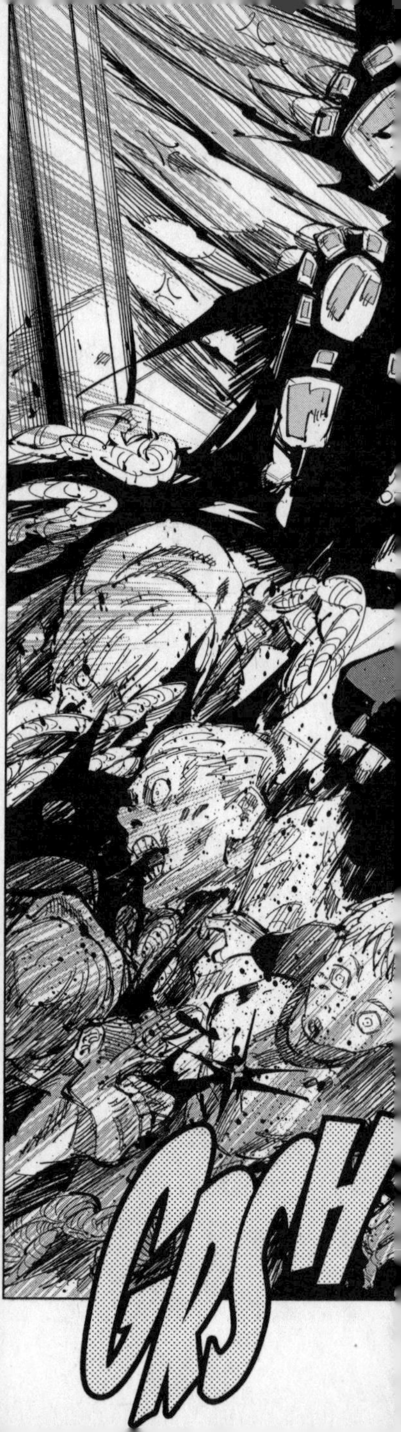
GASH!
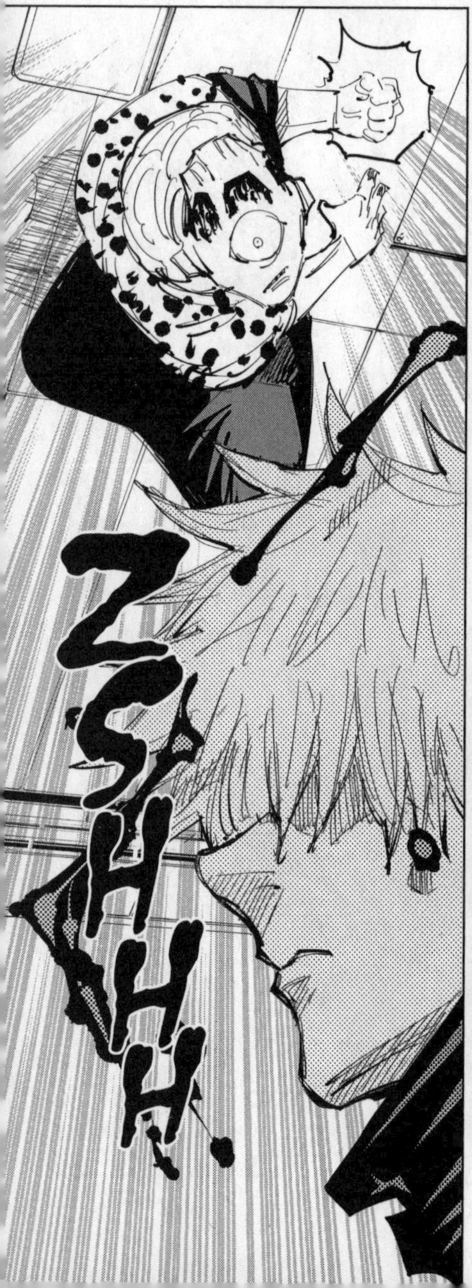
ZSHHH!

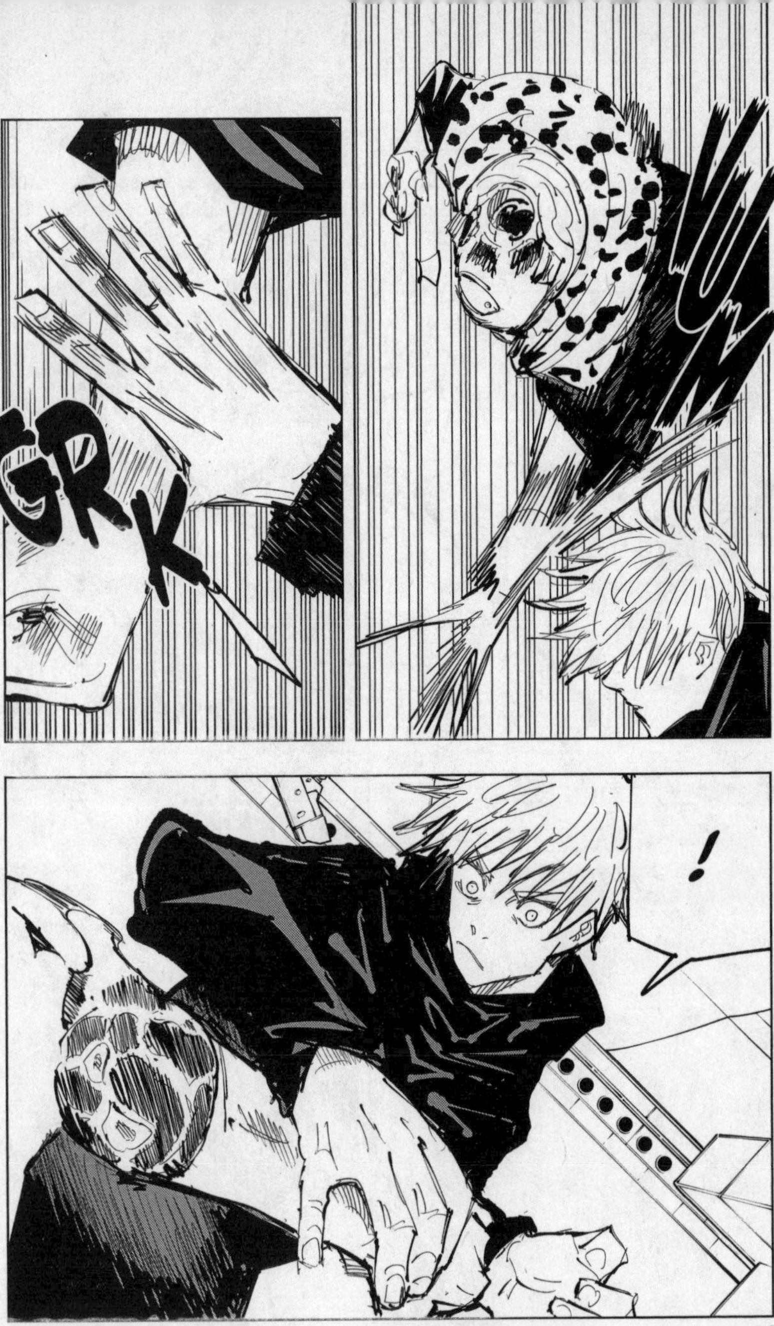
GRK
!

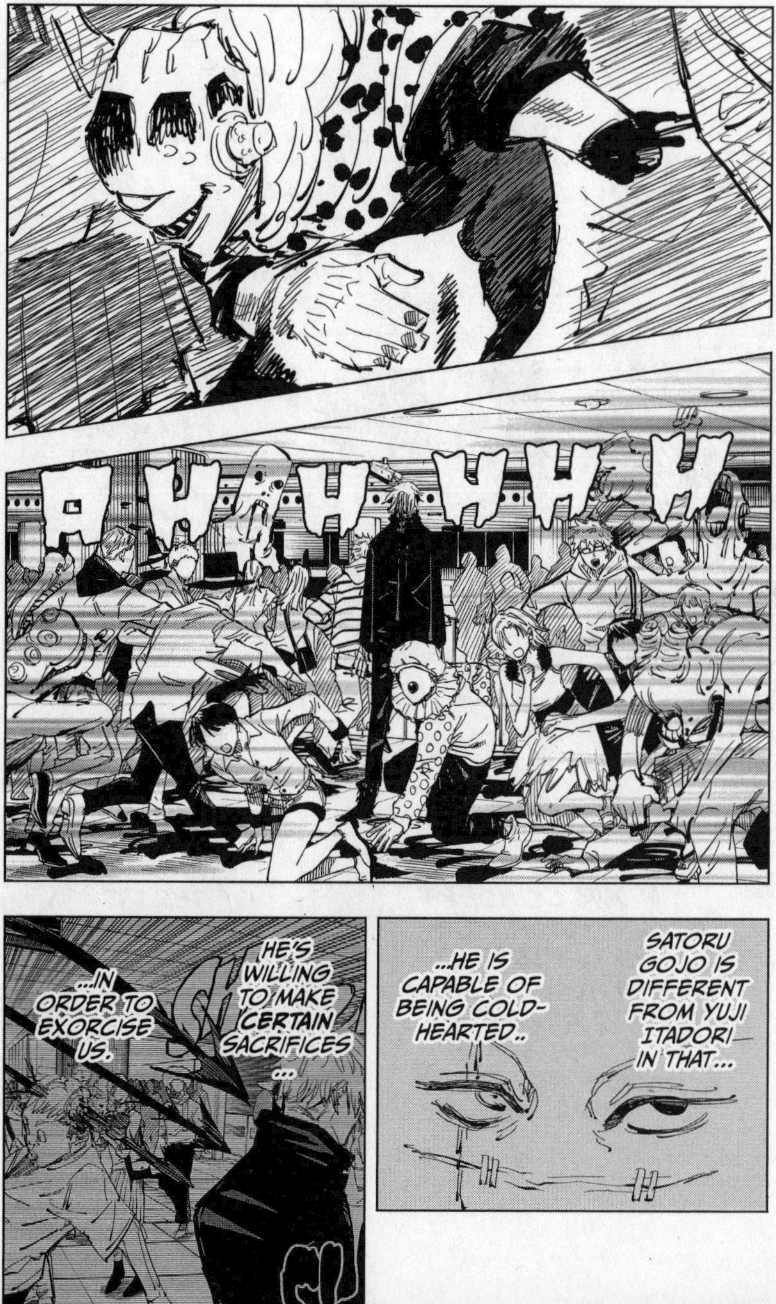
AHHHHHH
SATORU GOJO IS DIFFERENT FROM YUJI ITADORI IN THAT...
...HE IS CAPABLE OF BEING COLD-HEARTED..
HE'S WILLING TO MAKE CERTAIN SACRIFICES...
...IN ORDER TO EXORCISE US.

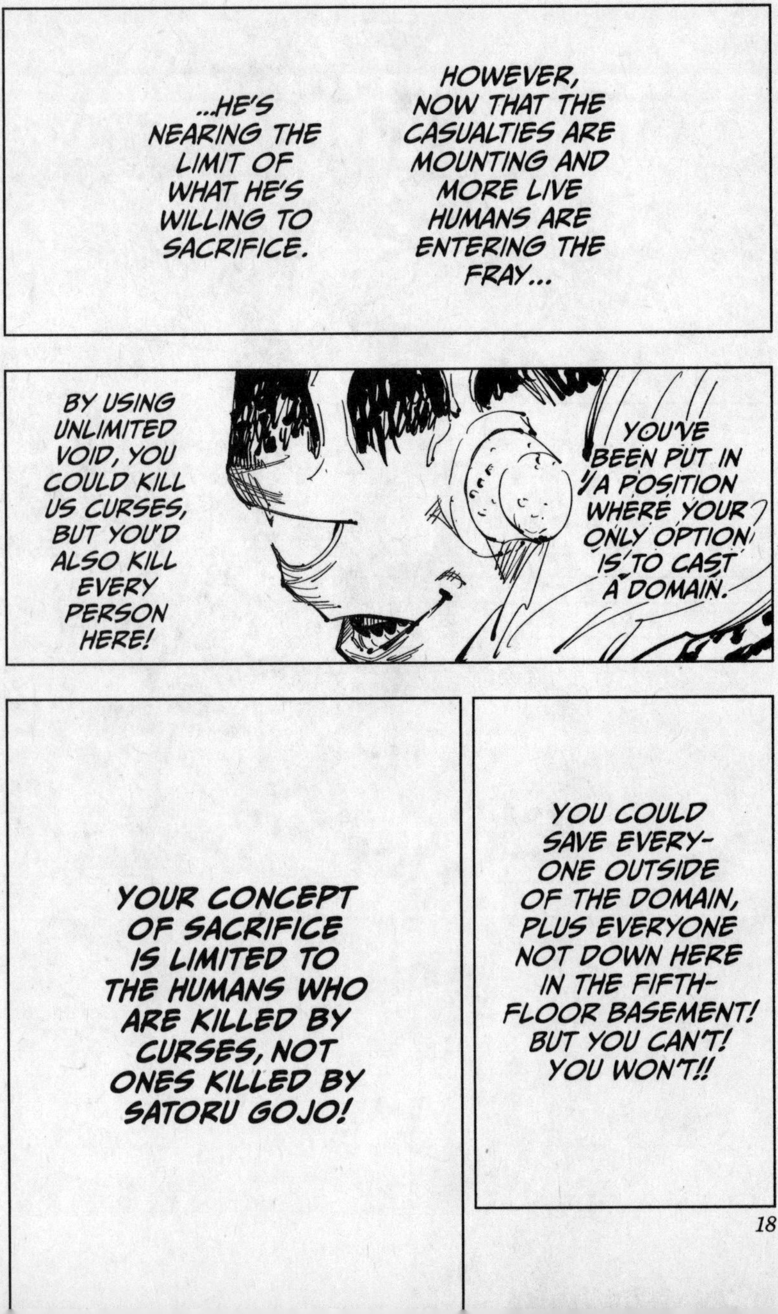
HOWEVER, NOW THAT THE CASUALTIES ARE MOUNTING AND MORE LIVE HUMANS ARE ENTERING THE FRAY...
...HE'S NEARING THE LIMIT OF WHAT HE'S WILLING TO SACRIFICE.
YOU'VE BEEN PUT IN A POSITION WHERE YOUR ONLY OPTION IS TO CAST A DOMAIN.
BY USING UNLIMITED VOID, YOU COULD KILL US CURSES, BUT YOU'D ALSO KILL EVERY PERSON HERE!
YOU COULD SAVE EVERY-ONE OUTSIDE OF THE DOMAIN, PLUS EVERYONE NOT DOWN HERE IN THE FIFTH-FLOOR BASEMENT! BUT YOU CAN'T! YOU WON'T!!
YOUR CONCEPT OF SACRIFICE IS LIMITED TO THE HUMANS WHO ARE KILLED BY CURSES, NOT ONES KILLED BY SATORU GOJO!

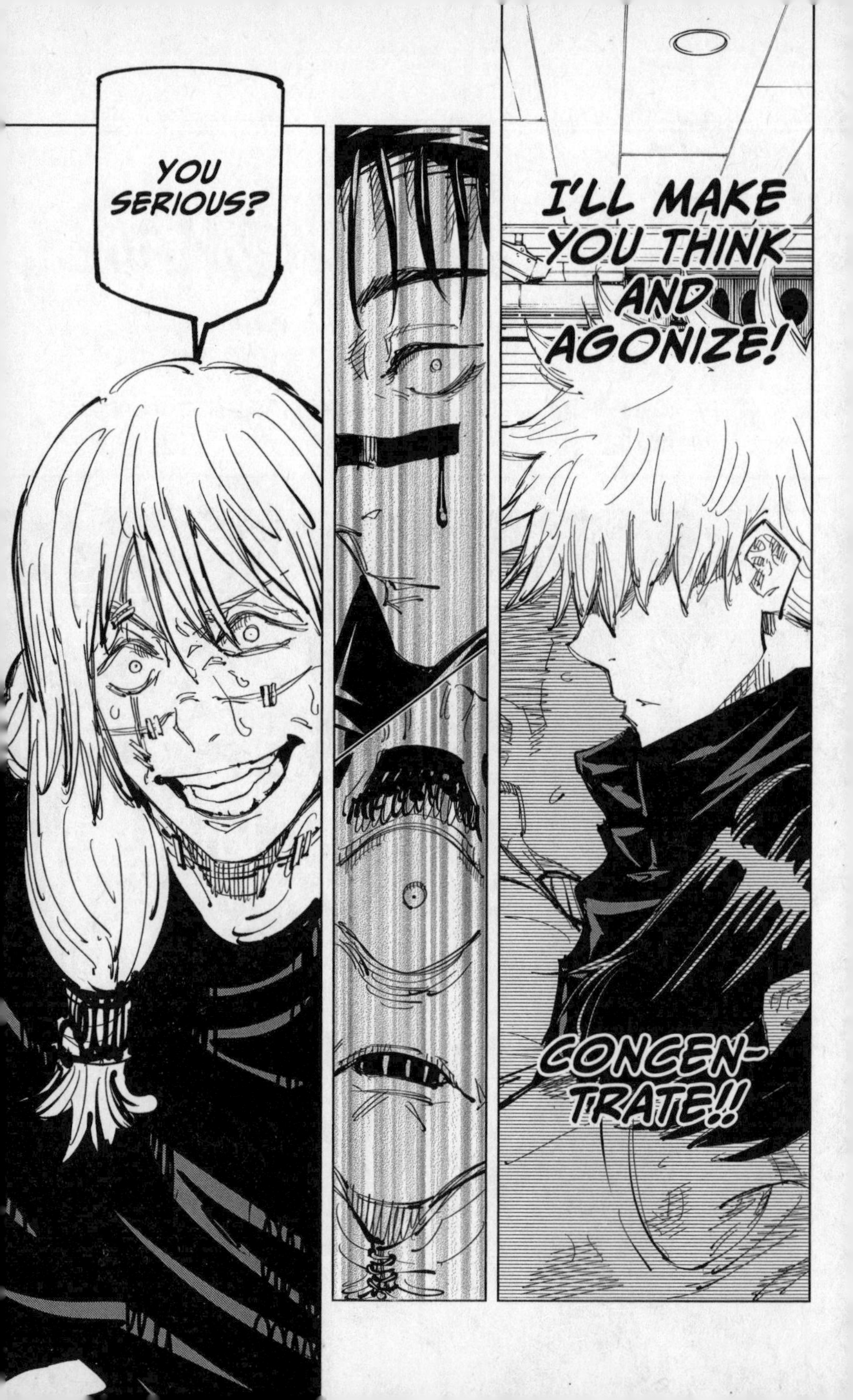
I'LL MAKE YOU THINK AND AGONIZE!
CONCEN-TRATE!!
YOU SERIOUS?

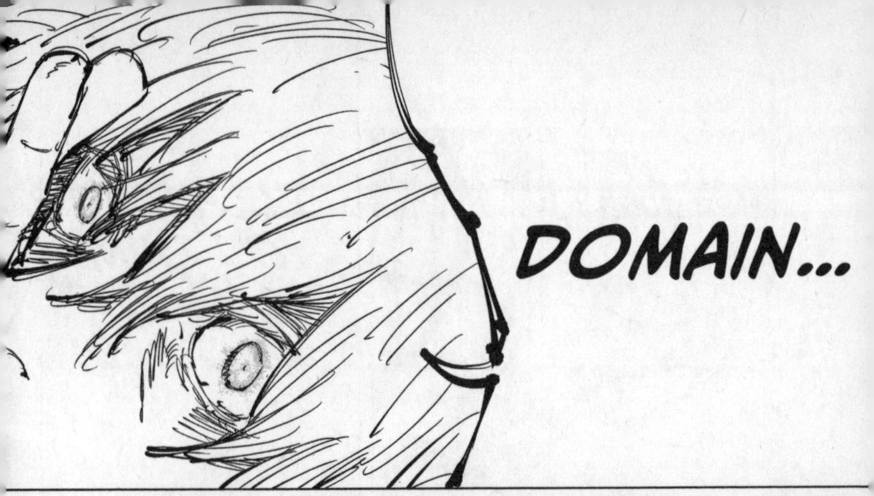
DOMAIN...
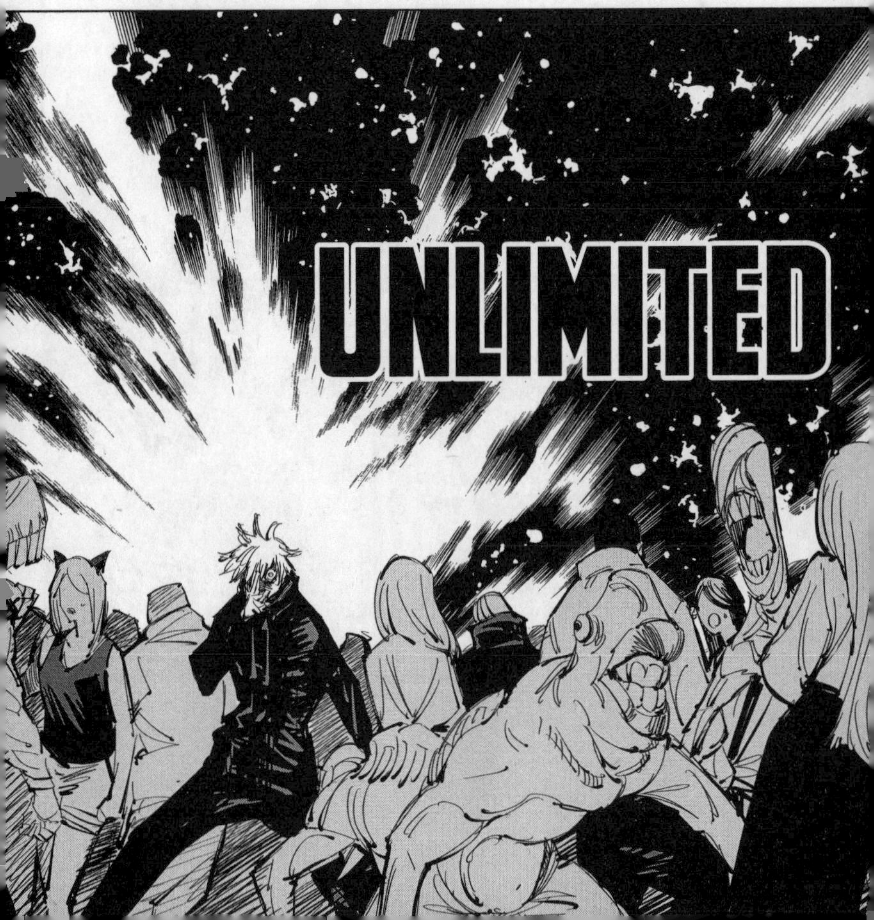
UNLIMITED

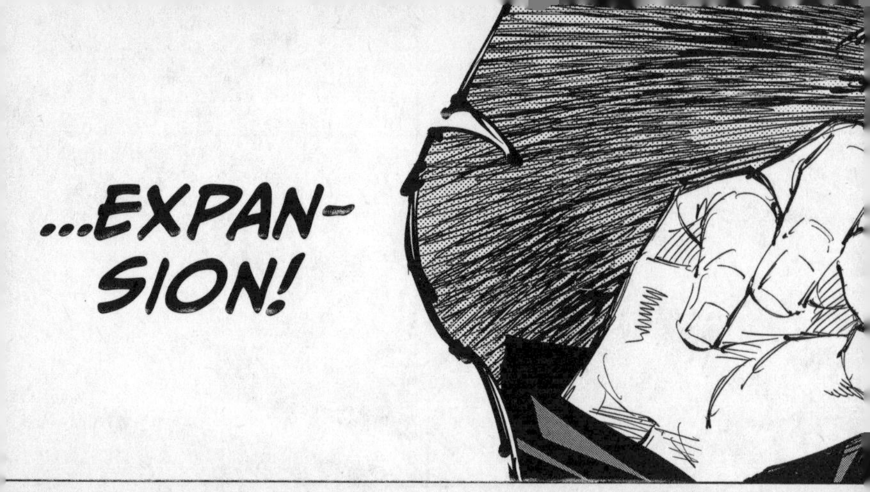
...EXPAN-
SION!
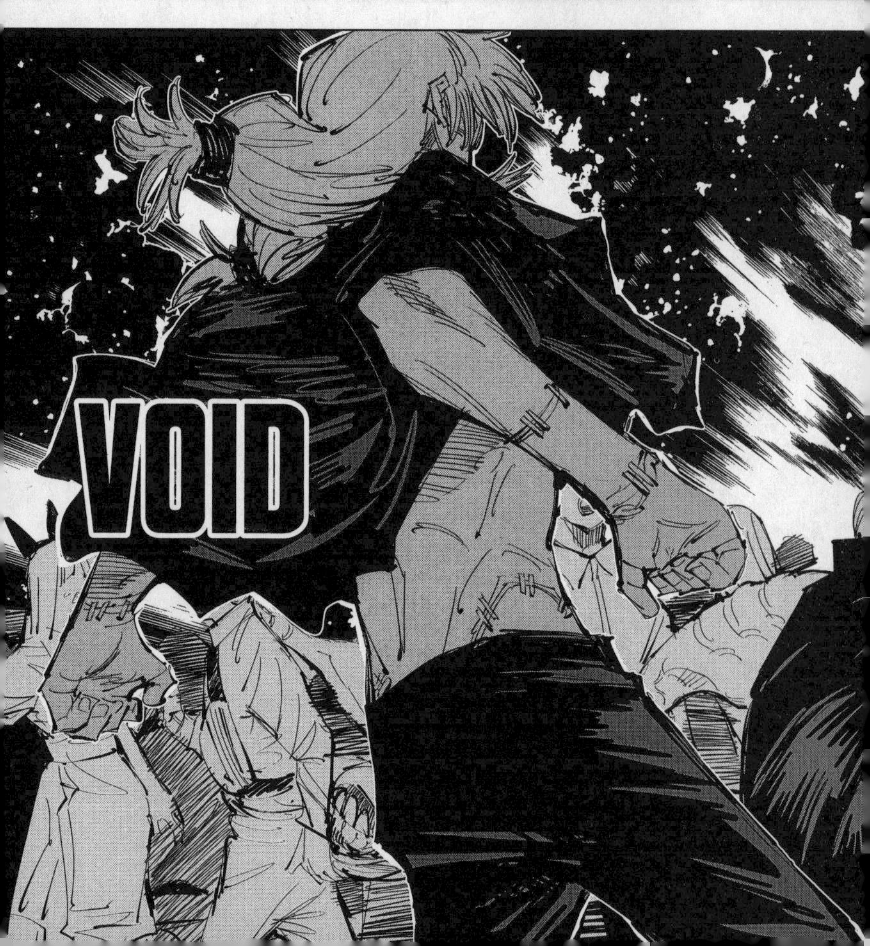
VOID

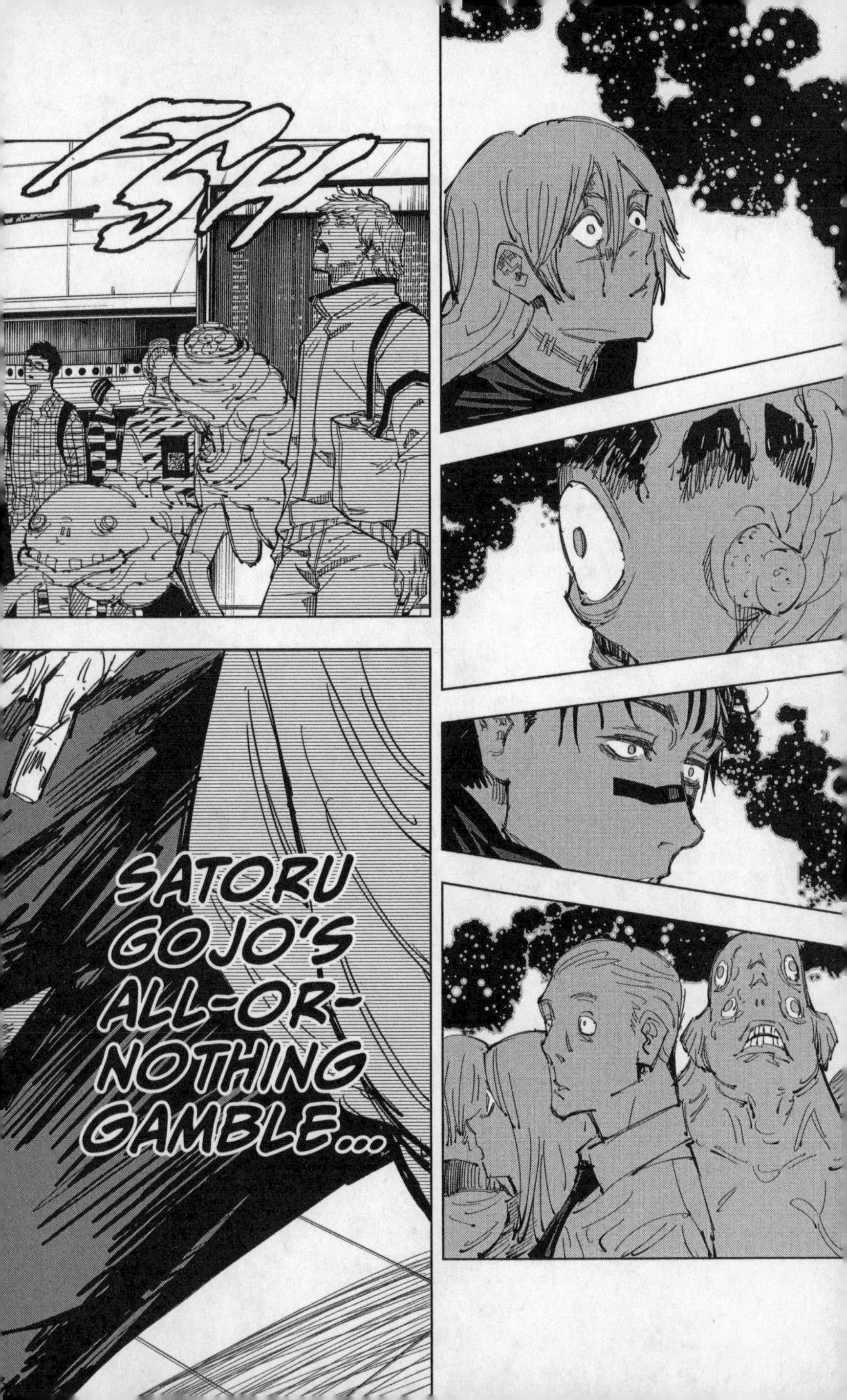
FSH
SATORU GOJO'S ALL-OR-NOTHING GAMBLE...

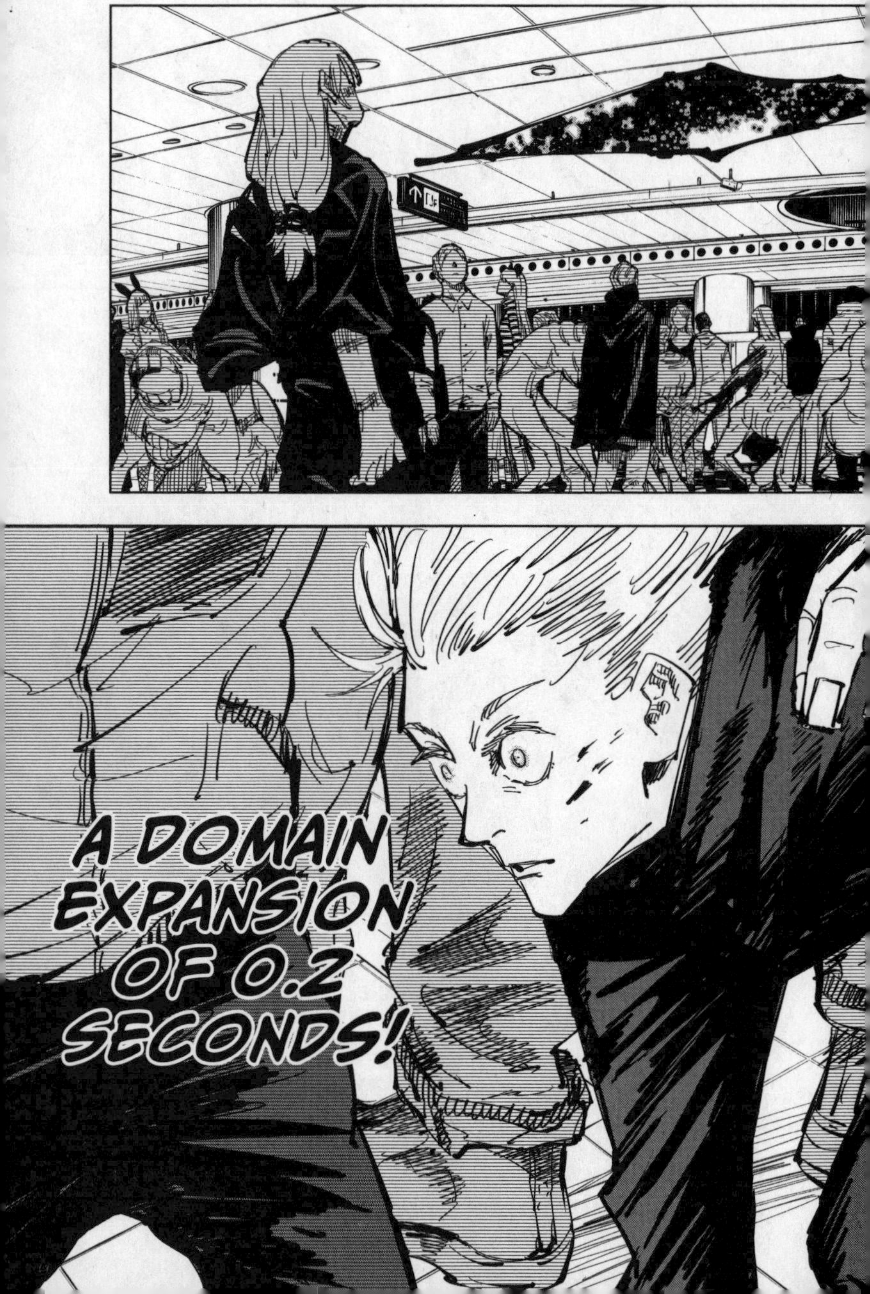
A DOMAIN EXPANSION OF 0.2 SECONDS!

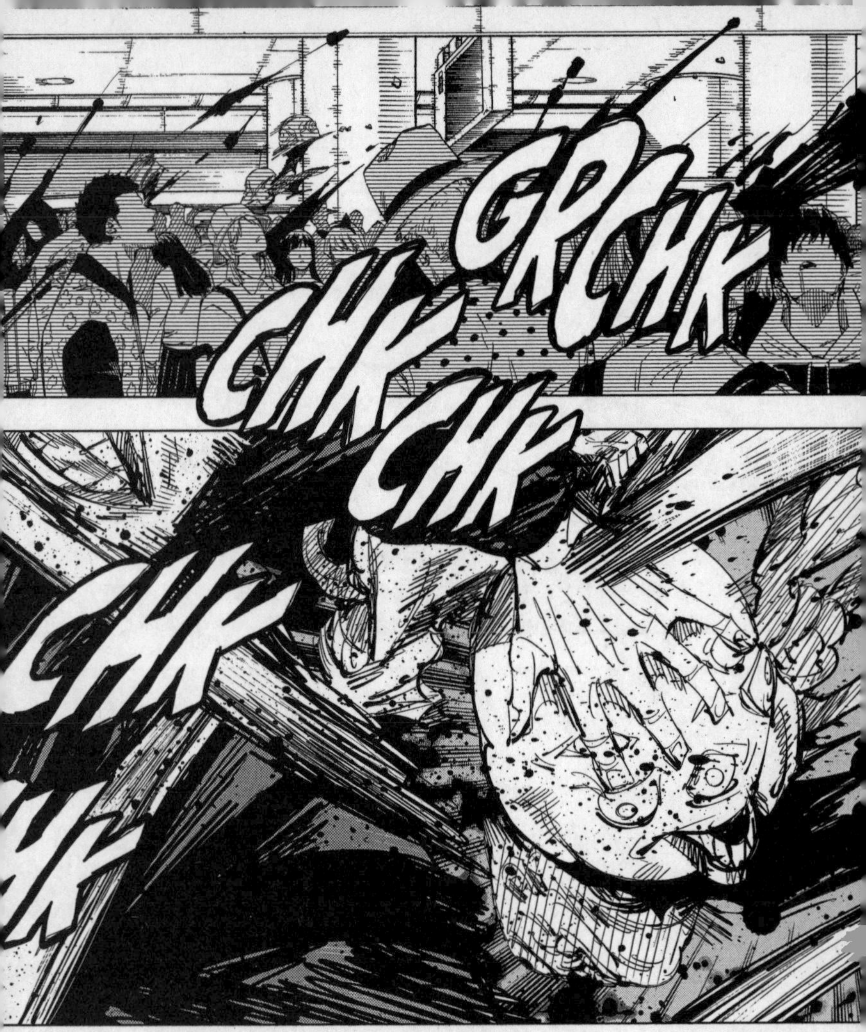
GRCHK
CHK
CHK
CHK
CHK

ALTHOUGH THIS IS JUST A ROUGH ESTIMATE, THE AMOUNT OF INFORMATION THAT FLOODED THE BRAINS OF THE NON-SORCERERS, INCLUDING THOSE TRANSFIGURED HUMANS, WAS ABOUT A HALF YEAR'S WORTH. EVERYONE WAS LEFT STANDING, UNCONSCIOUS.

GOJO CONJECTURED THAT A NON-SORCERER COULD WITH-STAND 0.2 SECONDS INSIDE THE DOMAIN WITHOUT SUFFERNG LASTING EFFECTS.

THE TIME WAS JUST A GUESS.

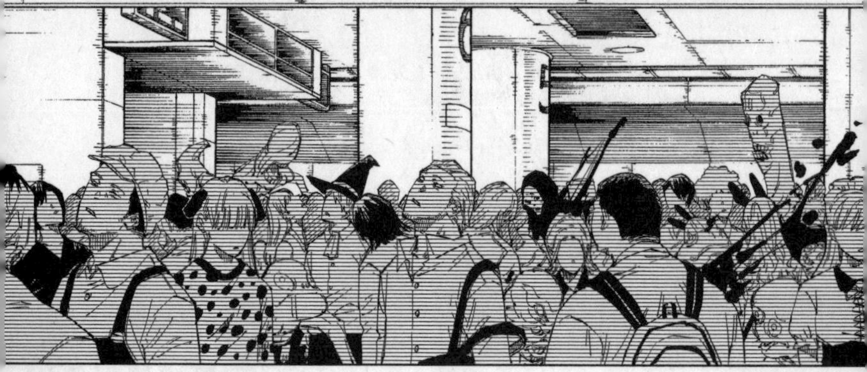

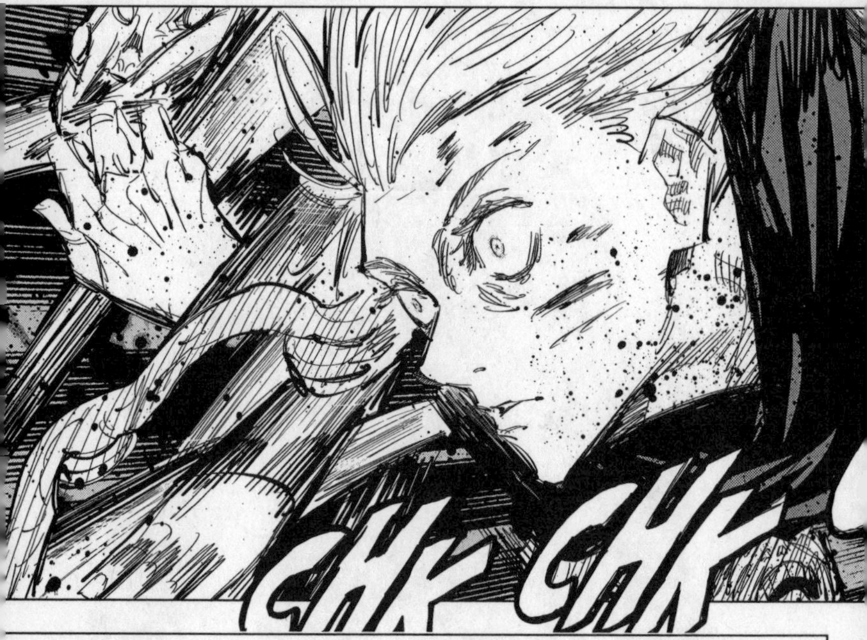
CHK CHK

IN THE AFTERMATH, THE HUMANS AT B5F WHO SURVIVED WOULD BE REHABILITATED AND ABLE TO REJOIN SOCIETY TWO MONTHS LATER.

SIMPLY SPEAKING, THIS LEVEL OF UNLIMITED VOID...

...COULD ALLOW THE SPECIAL GRADE CURSES TO AWAKEN AT ANY MOMENT.

TAKING INTO CONSIDERATION A COUNTER-ATTACK, THE TARGETS WOULD BE NARROWED DOWN TO TRANSFIGURED HUMANS.

THE APPROXIMATELY 1,000 TRANSFIGURED HUMANS WHO HAD BEEN RELEASED WITHIN B5F OF THE FUKUTOSHIN LINE WOULD BE ANNIHILATED 299 SECONDS...

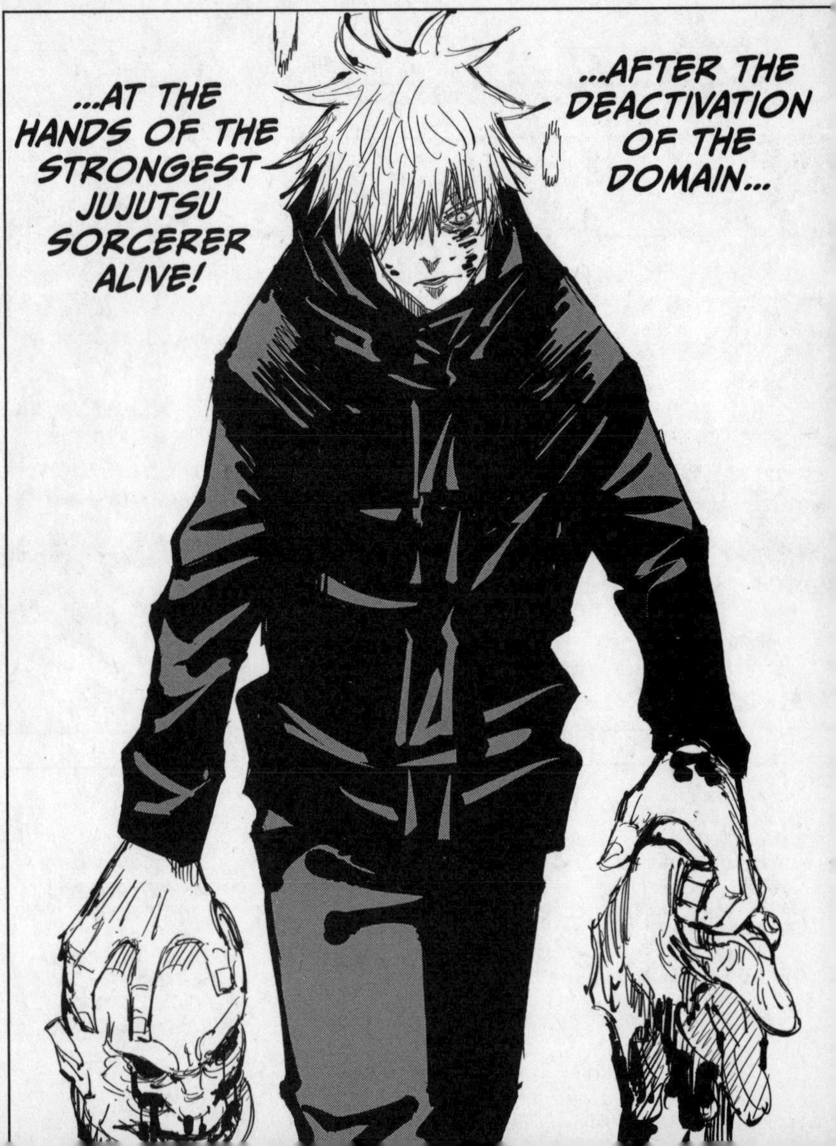
...AFTER THE DEACTIVATION OF THE DOMAIN...
...AT THE HANDS OF THE STRONGEST JUJUTSU SORCERER ALIVE!

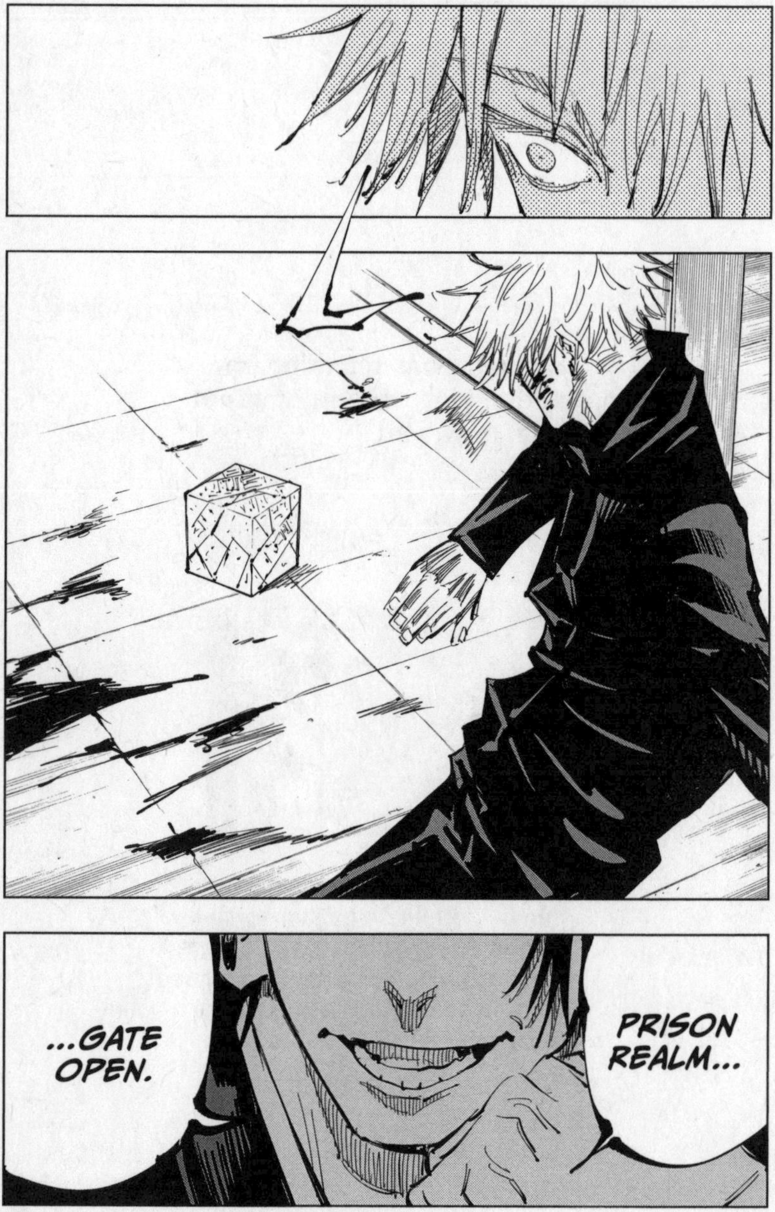
PRISON REALM...
...GATE OPEN.

Scenes I was planning on addressing but forgot about until now, part 1

• Phasing through walls

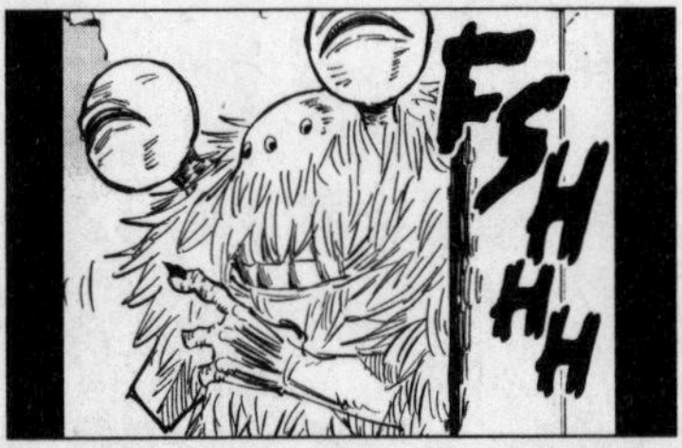
FSHHHH

Phasing through walls is an ability that can be performed by those with low cursed energy, specifically low-grade cursed spirits. Sorcerers and cursed spirits who possess a substantial amount of cursed energy cannot do this.

CHAPTER 90: THE SHIBUYA INCIDENT, PART 8

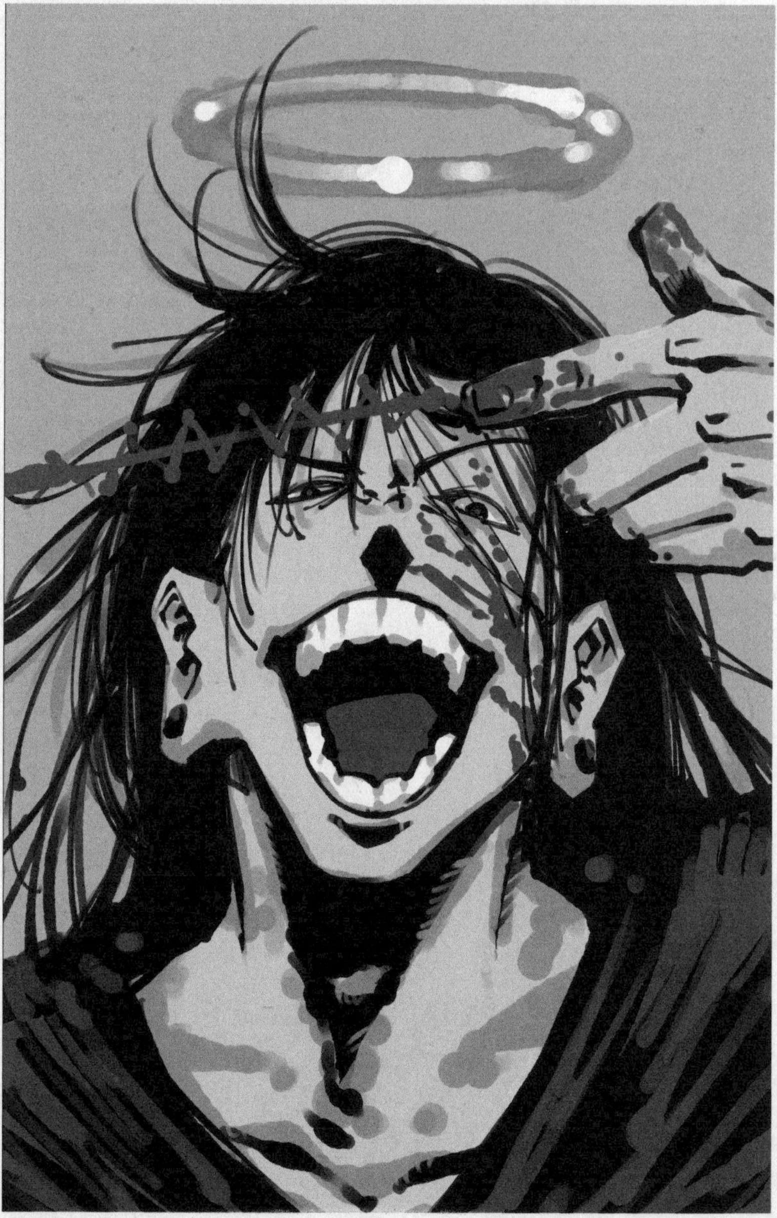

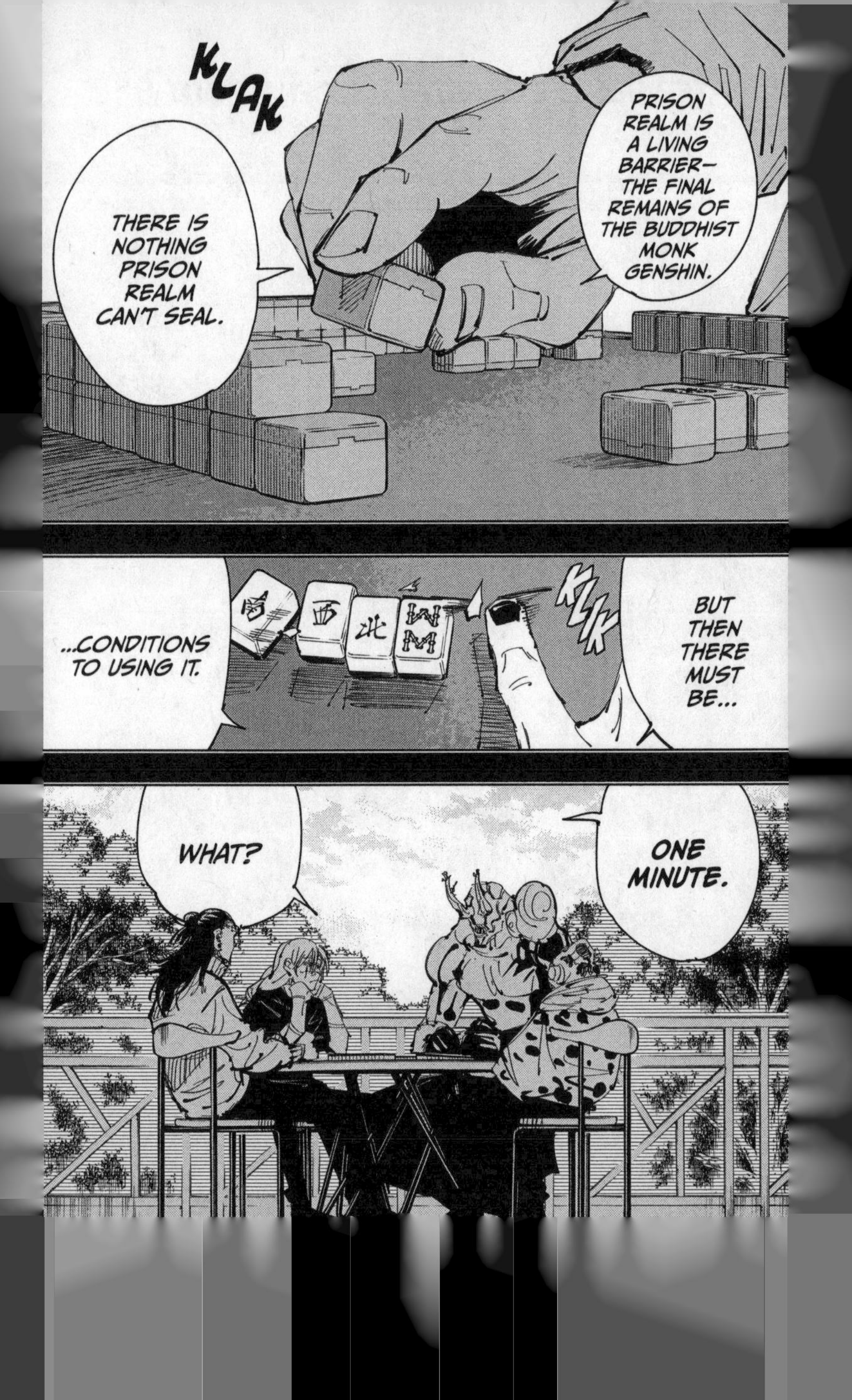
KLAK
PRISON REALM IS A LIVING BARRIER—THE FINAL REMAINS OF THE BUDDHIST MONK GENSHIN.
THERE IS NOTHING PRISON REALM CAN'T SEAL.
KLIK
BUT THEN THERE MUST BE...
...CONDITIONS TO USING IT.
WHAT?
ONE MINUTE.

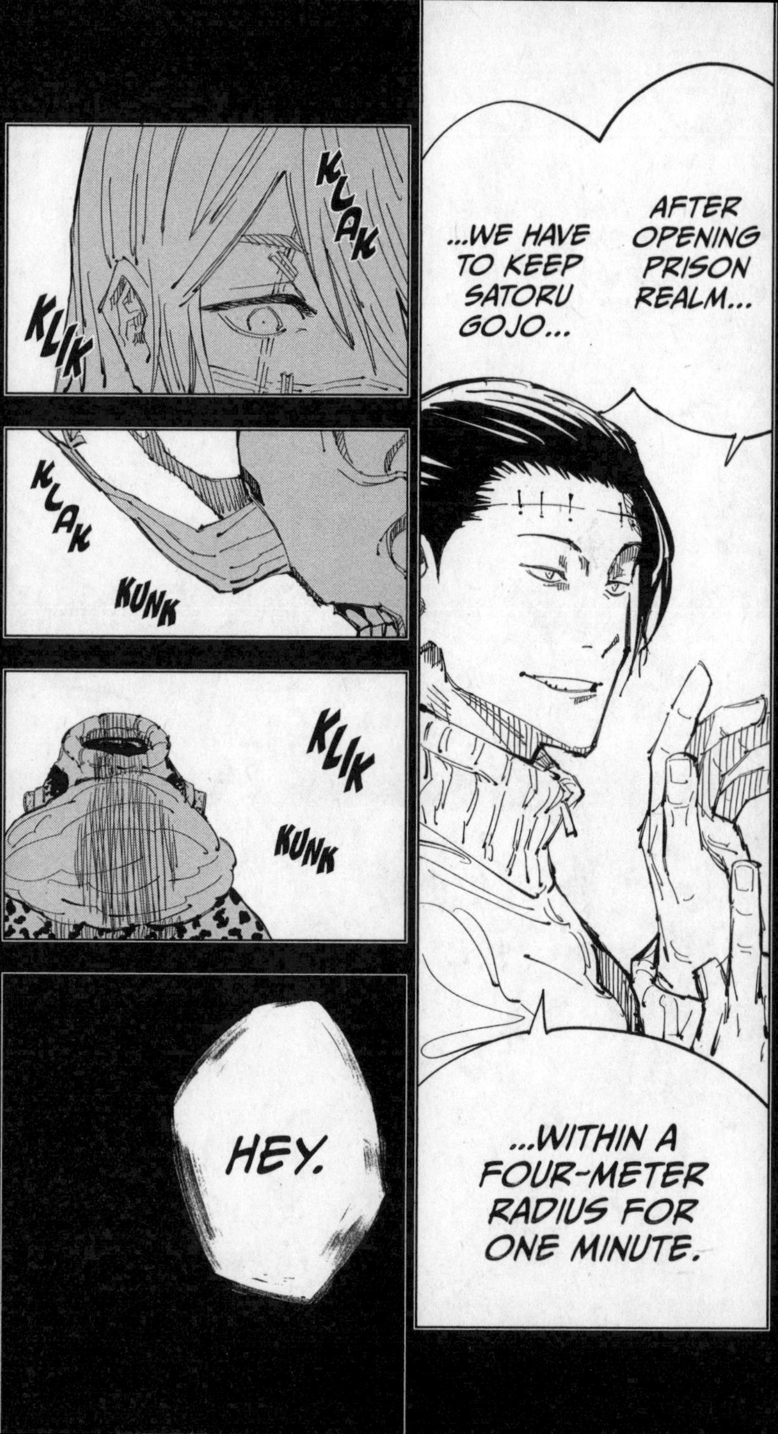
AFTER OPENING PRISON REALM...
...WE HAVE TO KEEP SATORU GOJO...
...WITHIN A FOUR-METER RADIUS FOR ONE MINUTE.
KLAK
KLIK
KLAK
KUNK
KLIK
KUNK
HEY.

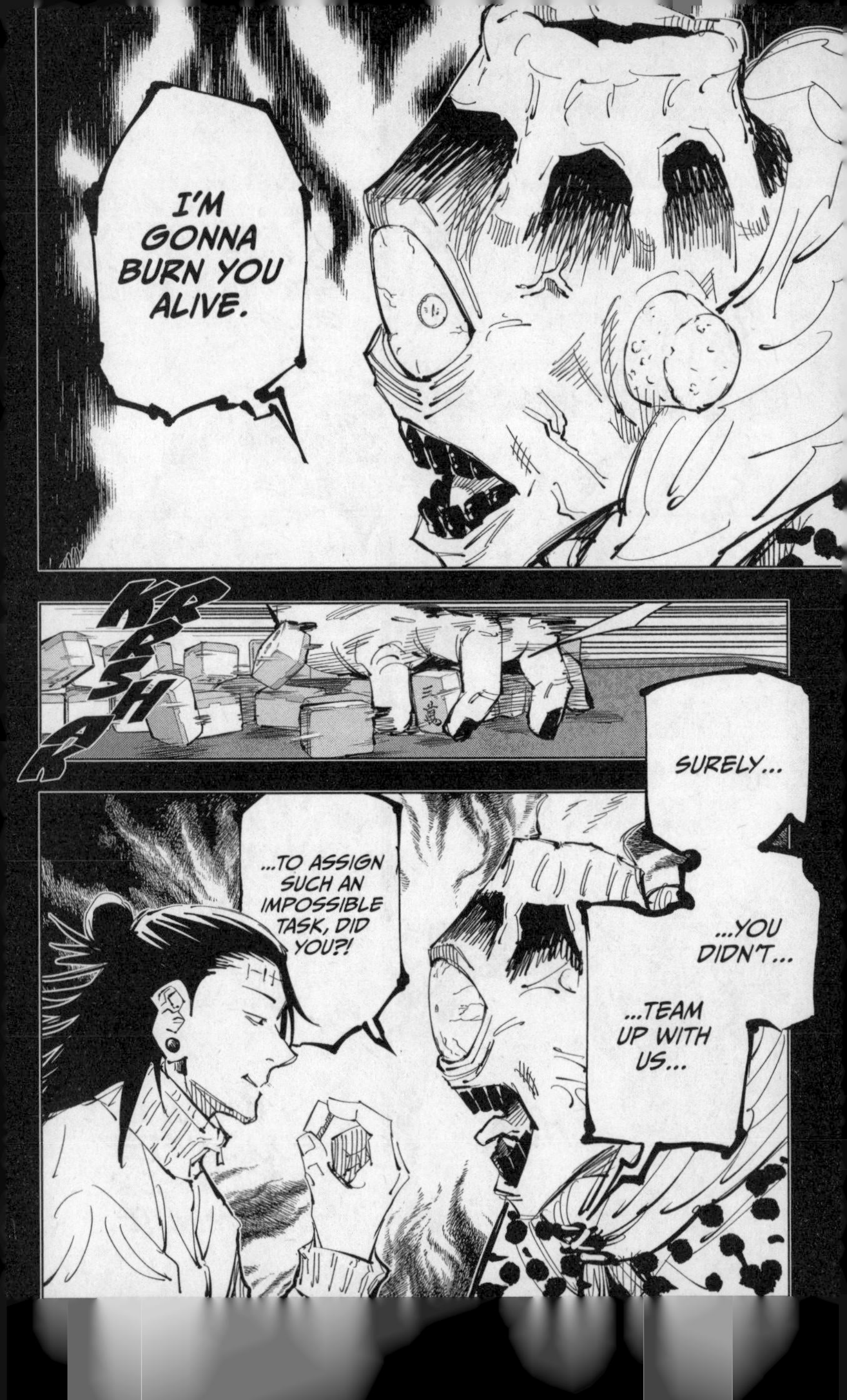
I'M GONNA BURN YOU ALIVE.
KRRSHAK
SURELY...
...YOU DIDN'T...
...TEAM UP WITH US...
...TO ASSIGN SUCH AN IMPOSSIBLE TASK, DID YOU?!

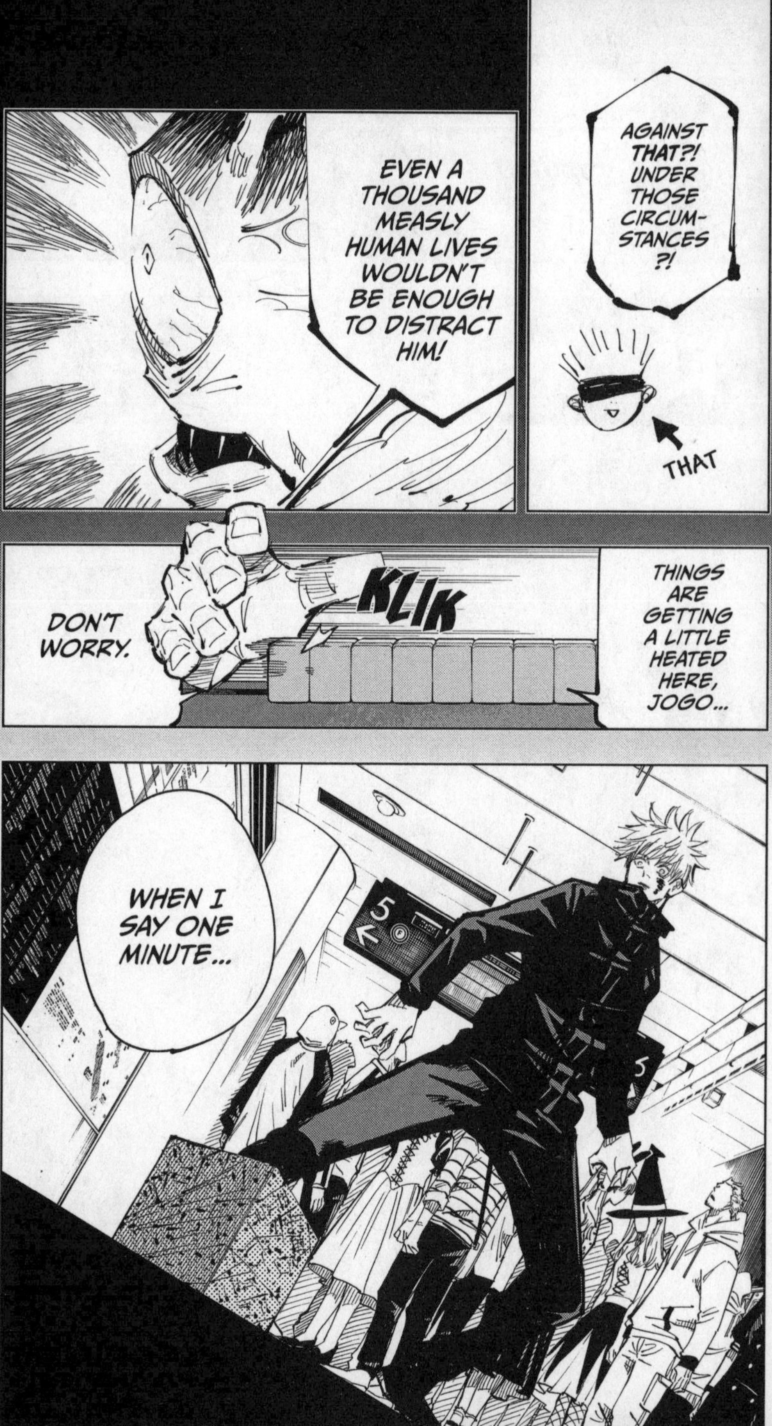
AGAINST THAT?! UNDER THOSE CIRCUM-STANCES ?!
THAT
EVEN A THOUSAND MEASLY HUMAN LIVES WOULDN'T BE ENOUGH TO DISTRACT HIM!
THINGS ARE GETTING A LITTLE HEATED HERE, JOGO...
KLIK
DON'T WORRY.
WHEN I SAY ONE MINUTE...

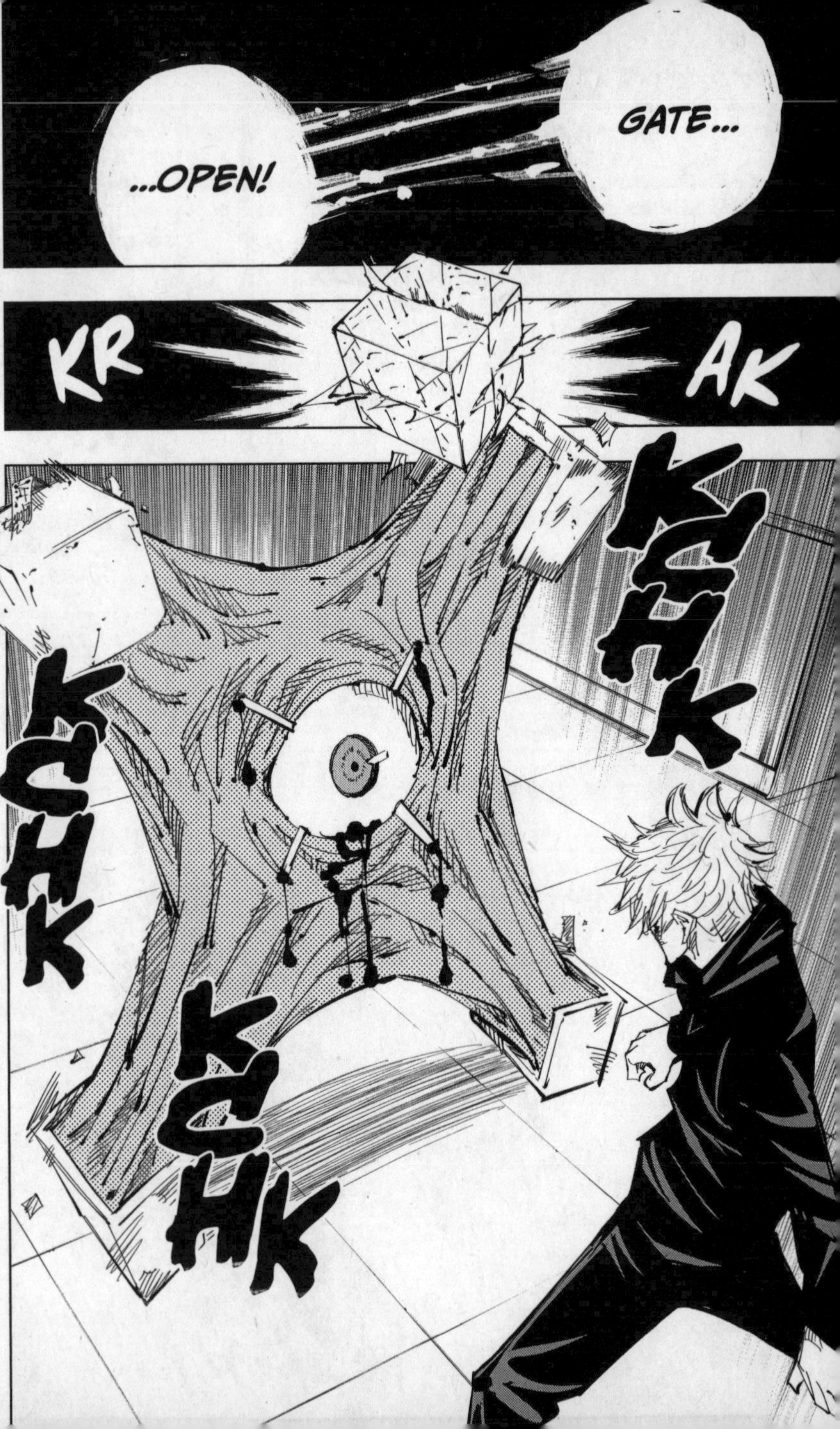
GATE...
...OPEN!
KR AK
KCHK
KCHK
KCHK

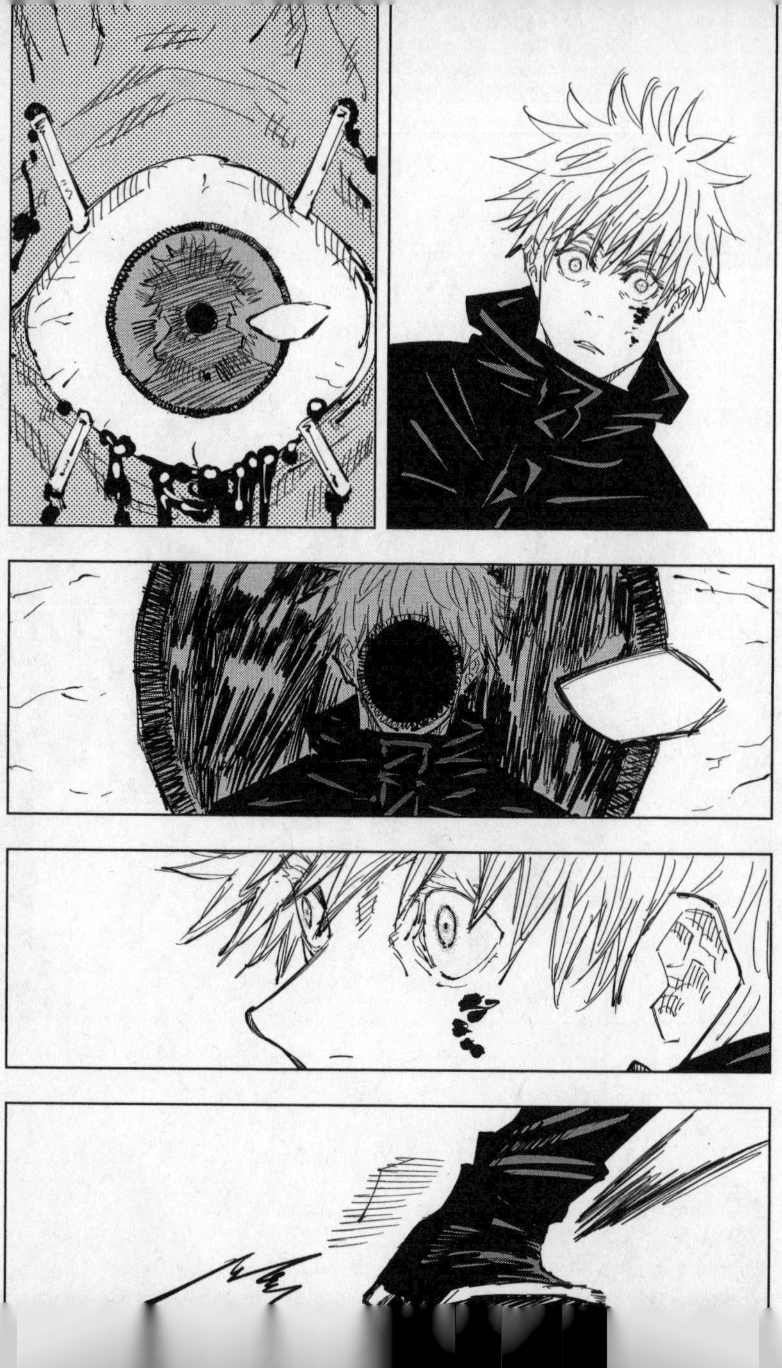

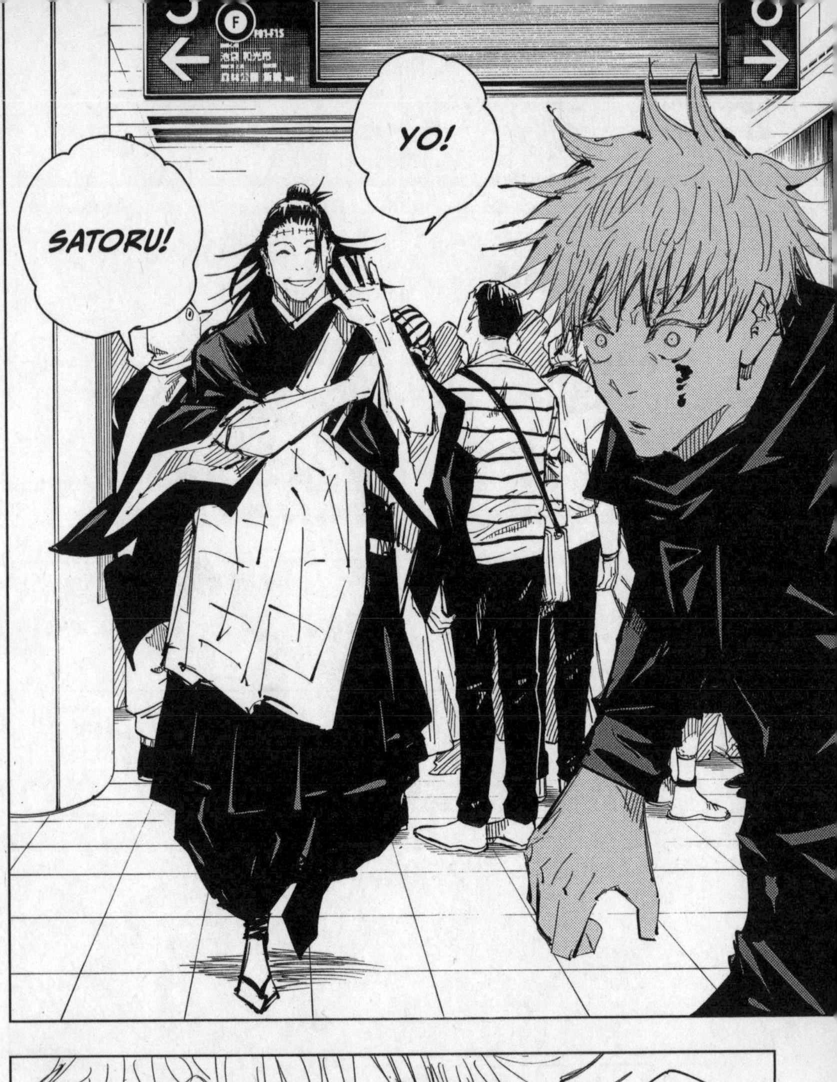
YO!
SATORU!
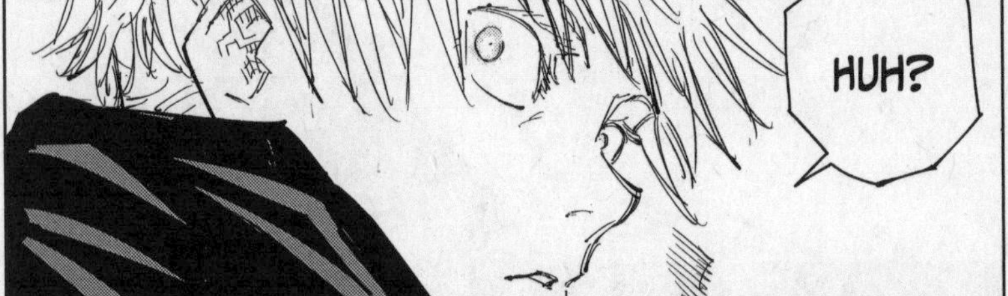
HUH?

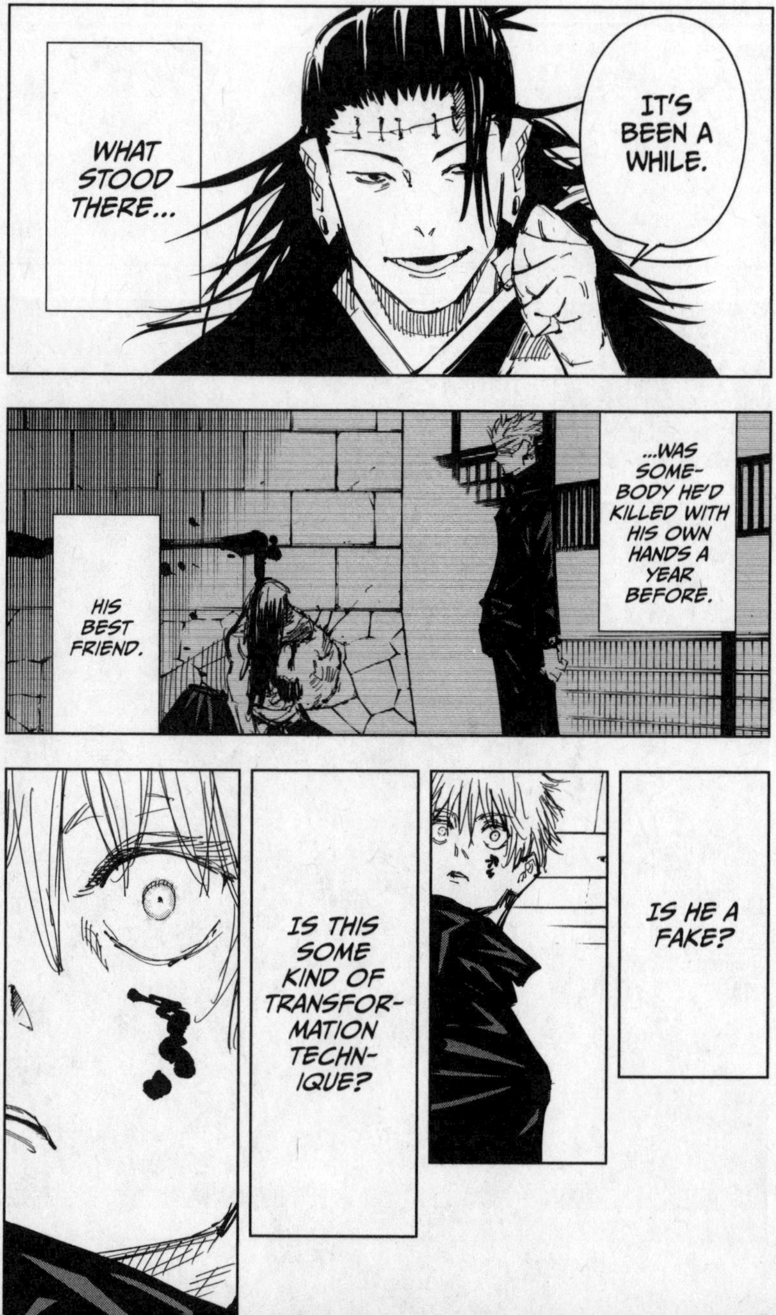
IT'S BEEN A WHILE.
WHAT STOOD THERE...
...WAS SOMEBODY HE'D KILLED WITH HIS OWN HANDS A YEAR BEFORE.
HIS BEST FRIEND.
IS HE A FAKE?
IS THIS SOME KIND OF TRANSFORMATION TECHNIQUE?

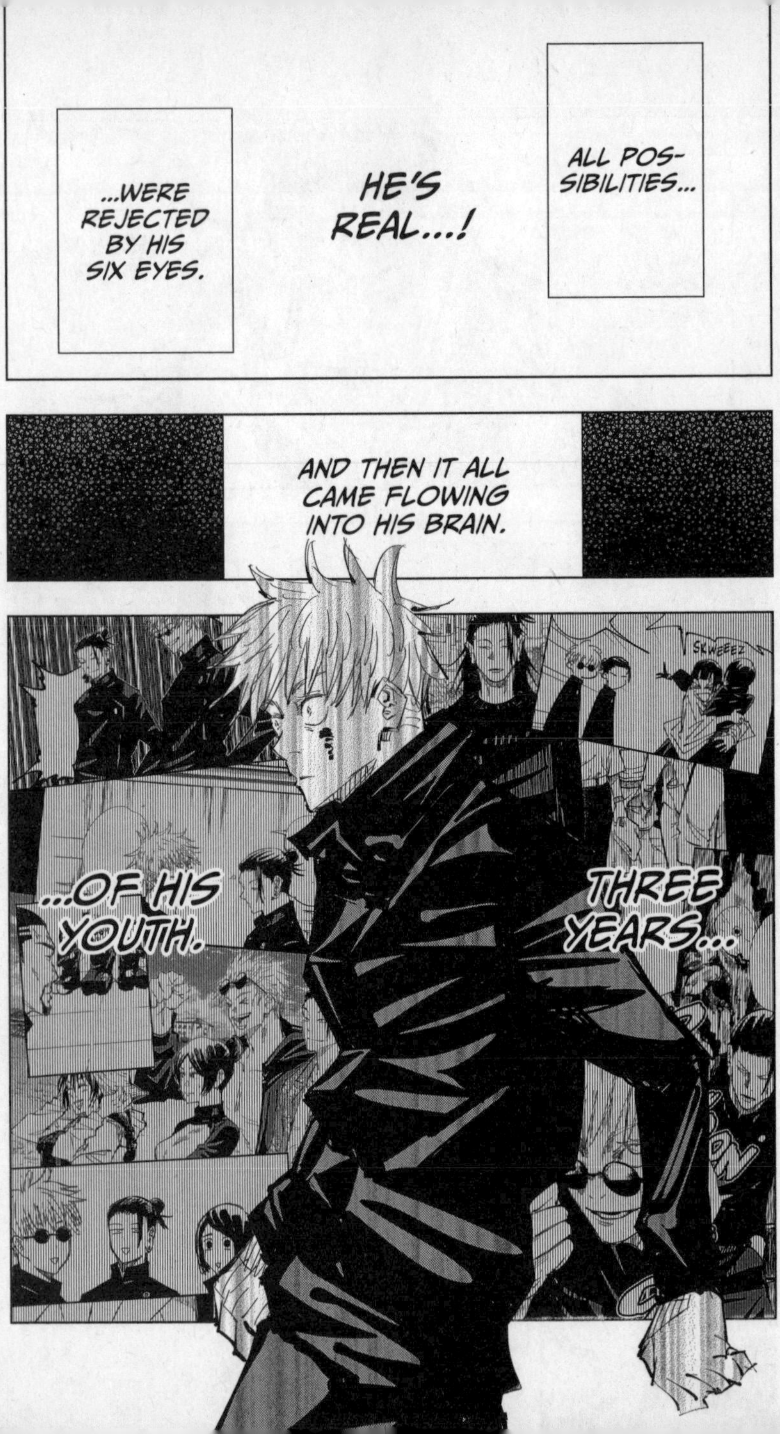
ALL POS-
SIBILITIES...
HE'S
REAL...!
...WERE
REJECTED
BY HIS
SIX EYES.
AND THEN IT ALL
CAME FLOWING
INTO HIS BRAIN.
SKWEEEZ
THREE
YEARS...
...OF HIS
YOUTH.

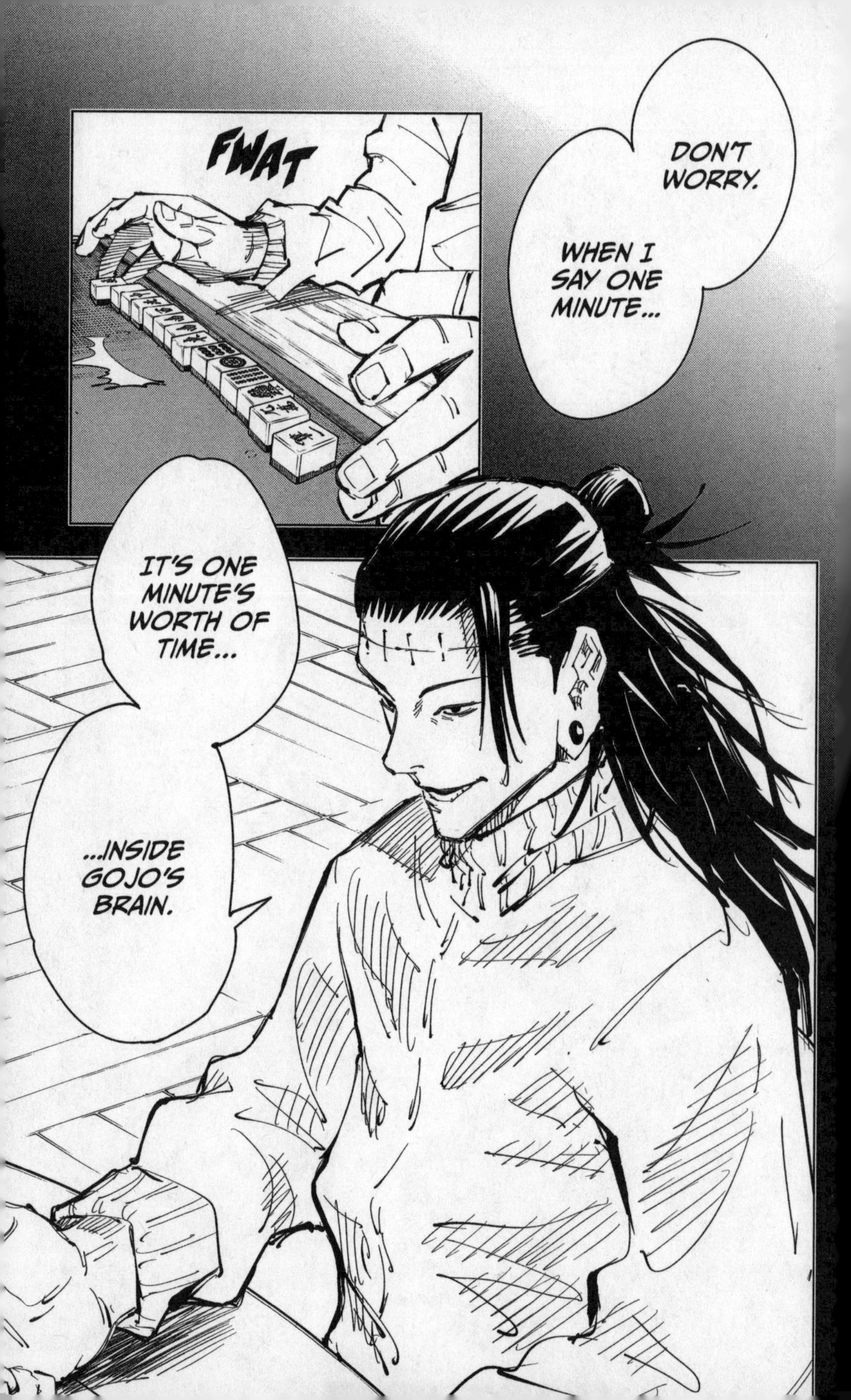
DON'T WORRY.
WHEN I SAY ONE MINUTE...
FWAT
IT'S ONE MINUTE'S WORTH OF TIME...
...INSIDE GOJO'S BRAIN.

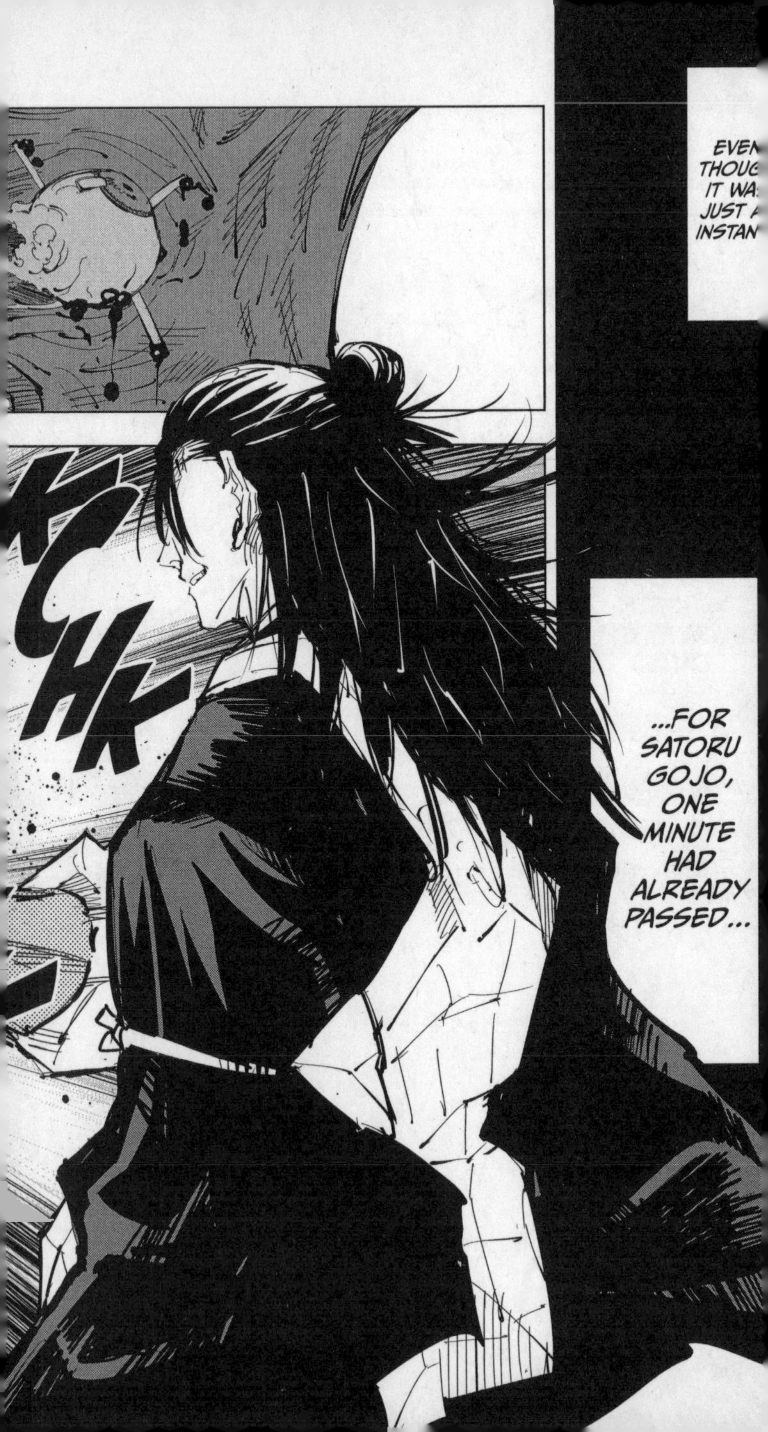
EVEN THOUG IT WA JUST A INSTAN
...FOR SATORU GOJO, ONE MINUTE HAD ALREADY PASSED...
CHK

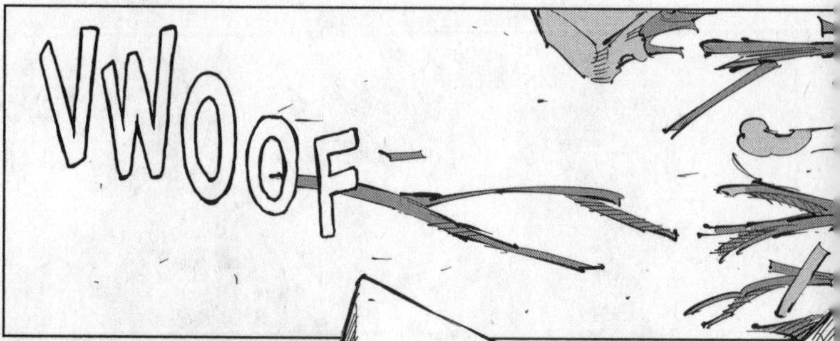
VWOOF
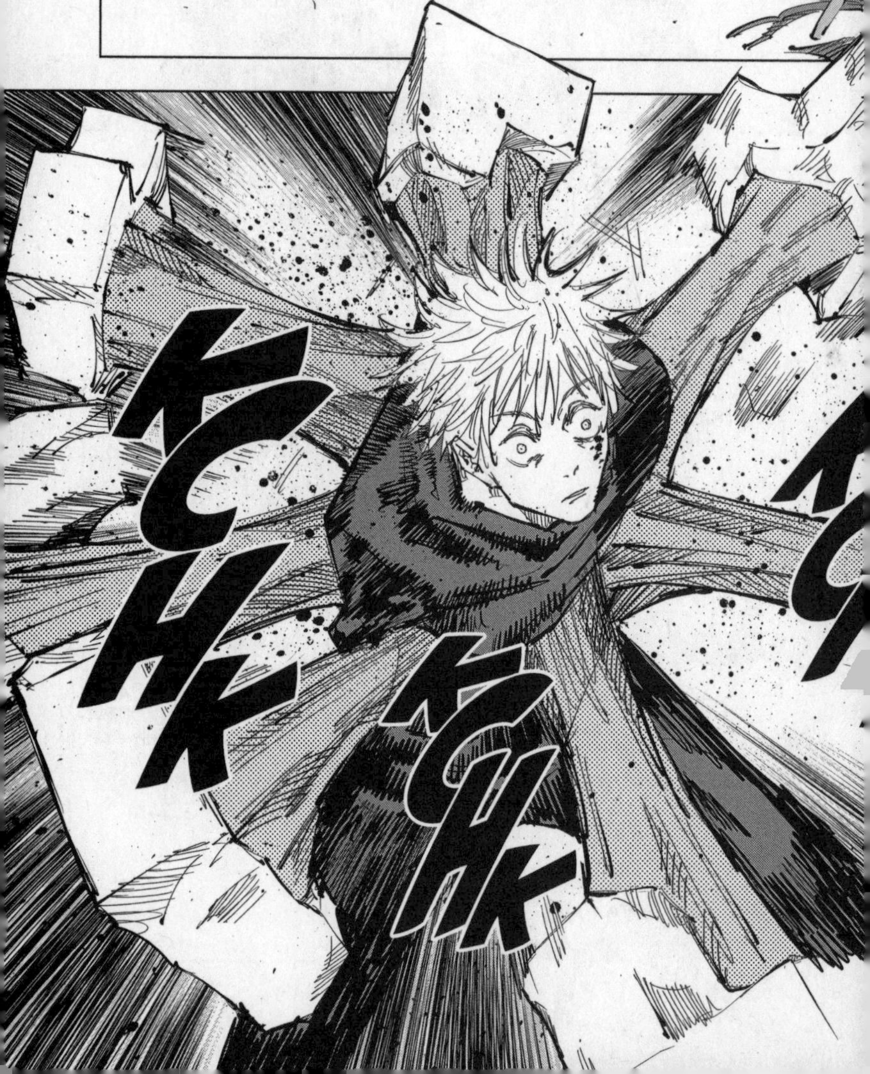
KCHK
KCHK

TCH!
DAMMIT! THEY GOT ME!!
C'MON NOW, SATORU.
ARE YOU LETTING YOUR MIND WANDER DURING A FIGHT?
I CAN'T FEEL ANY CURSED ENERGY IN MY BODY. I CAN'T MOVE A MUSCLE EITHER.
THIS IS CHECK-MATE...
SO...

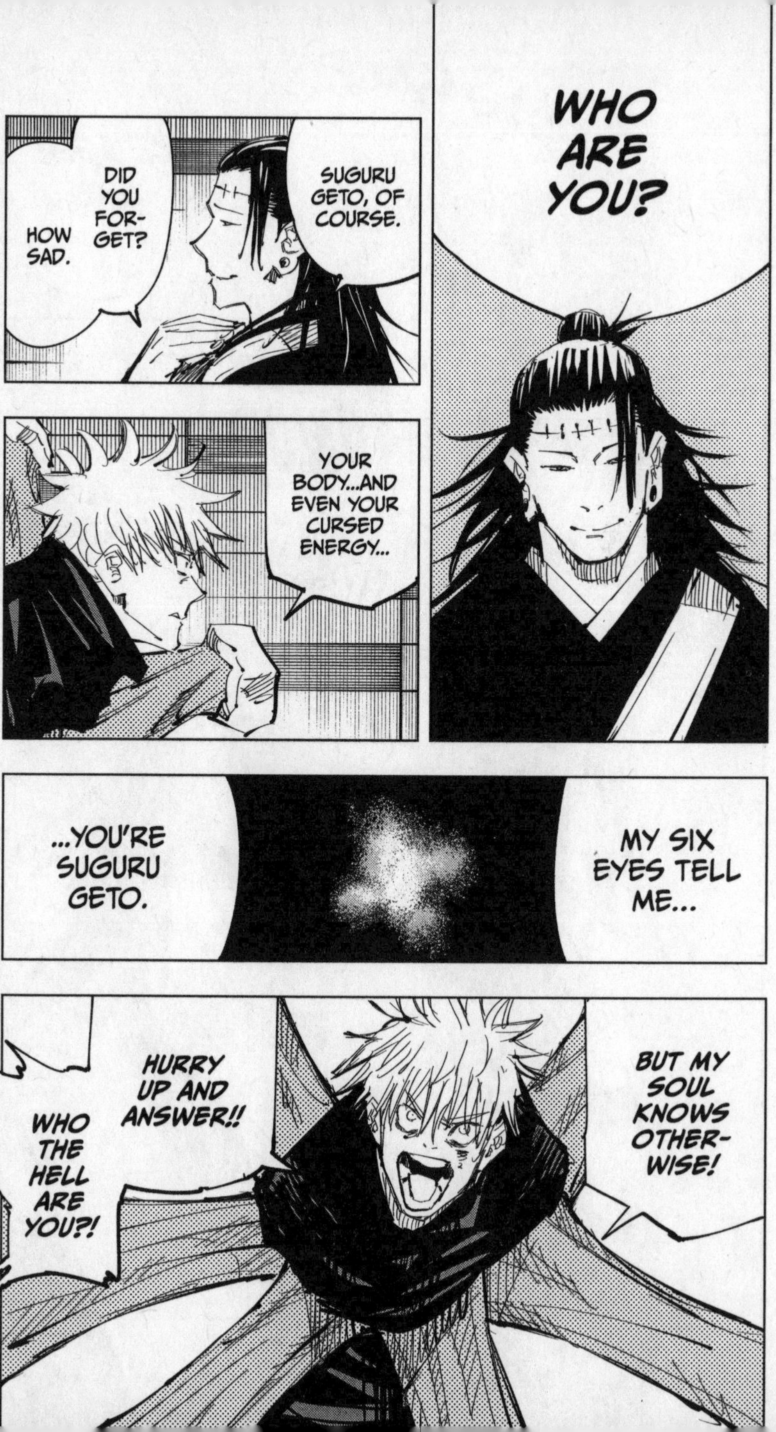
WHO ARE YOU?
SUGURU GETO, OF COURSE.
DID YOU FOR-GET?
HOW SAD.
YOUR BODY...AND EVEN YOUR CURSED ENERGY...
MY SIX EYES TELL ME...
...YOU'RE SUGURU GETO.
BUT MY SOUL KNOWS OTHER-WISE!
HURRY UP AND ANSWER!!
WHO THE HELL ARE YOU?!

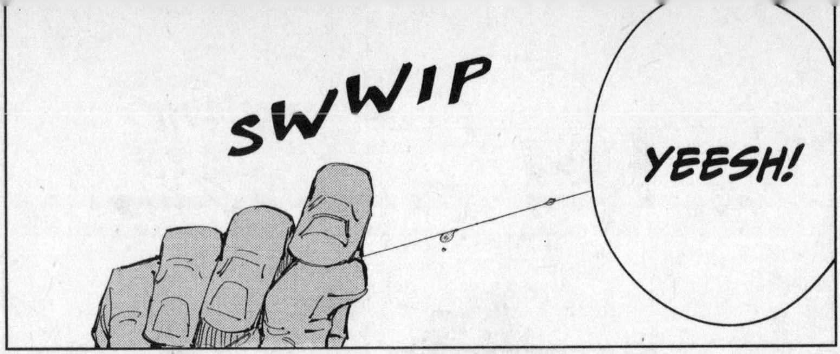
YEESH!
SWWIP
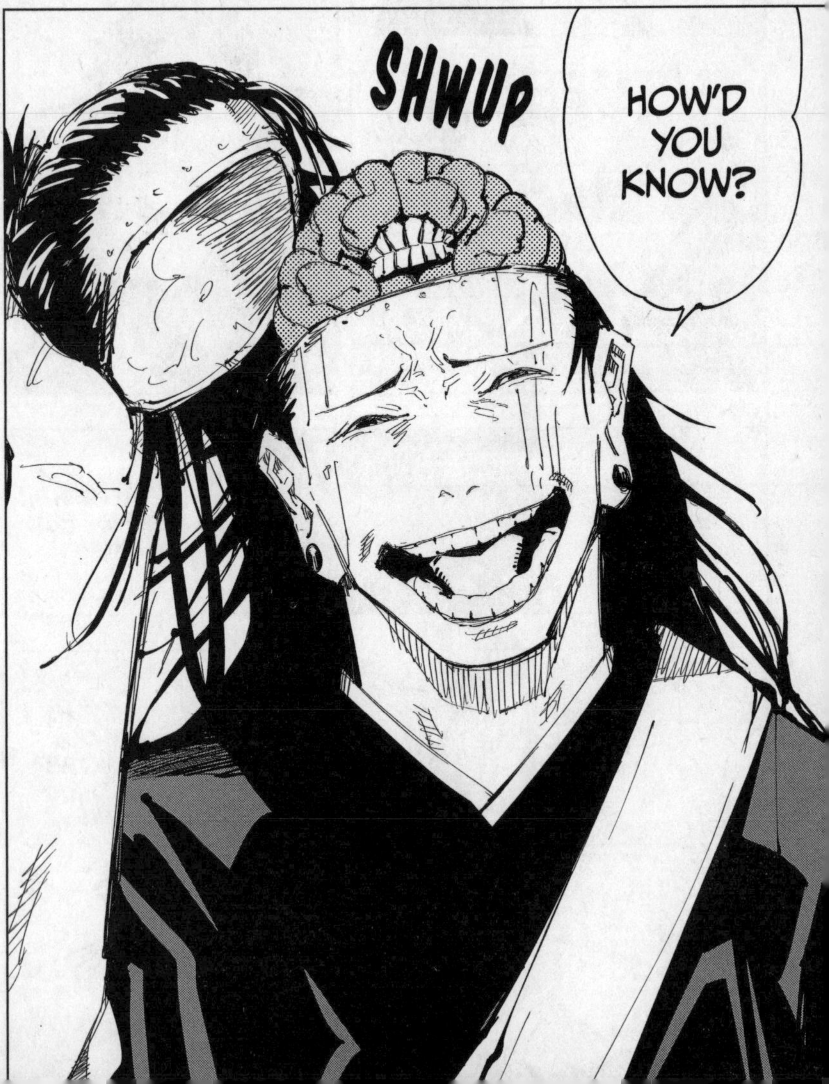
HOW'D YOU KNOW?
SHWUP

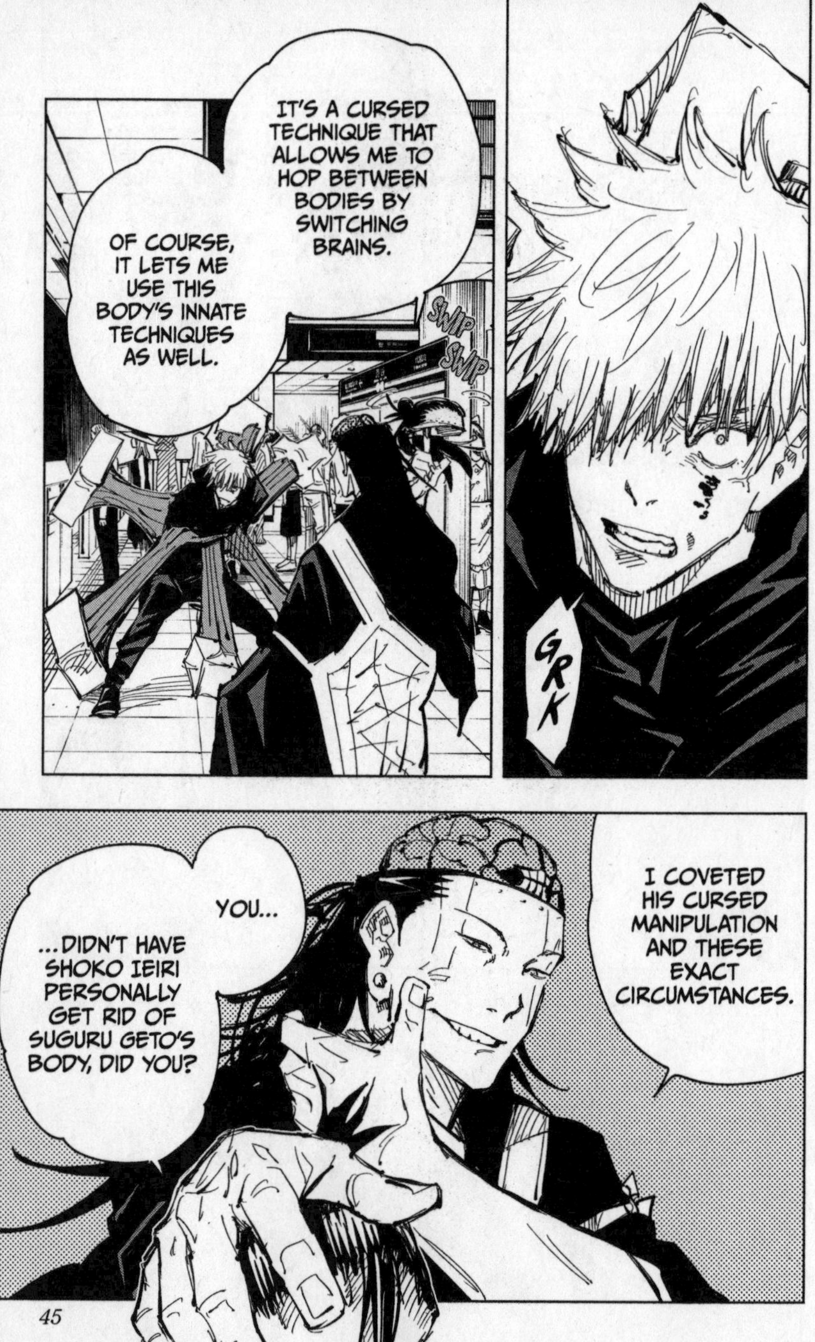
GRK
IT'S A CURSED TECHNIQUE THAT ALLOWS ME TO HOP BETWEEN BODIES BY SWITCHING BRAINS.
OF COURSE, IT LETS ME USE THIS BODY'S INNATE TECHNIQUES AS WELL.
SWIP
SWIP
I COVETED HIS CURSED MANIPULATION AND THESE EXACT CIRCUMSTANCES.
YOU...
...DIDN'T HAVE SHOKO IEIRI PERSONALLY GET RID OF SUGURU GETO'S BODY, DID YOU?

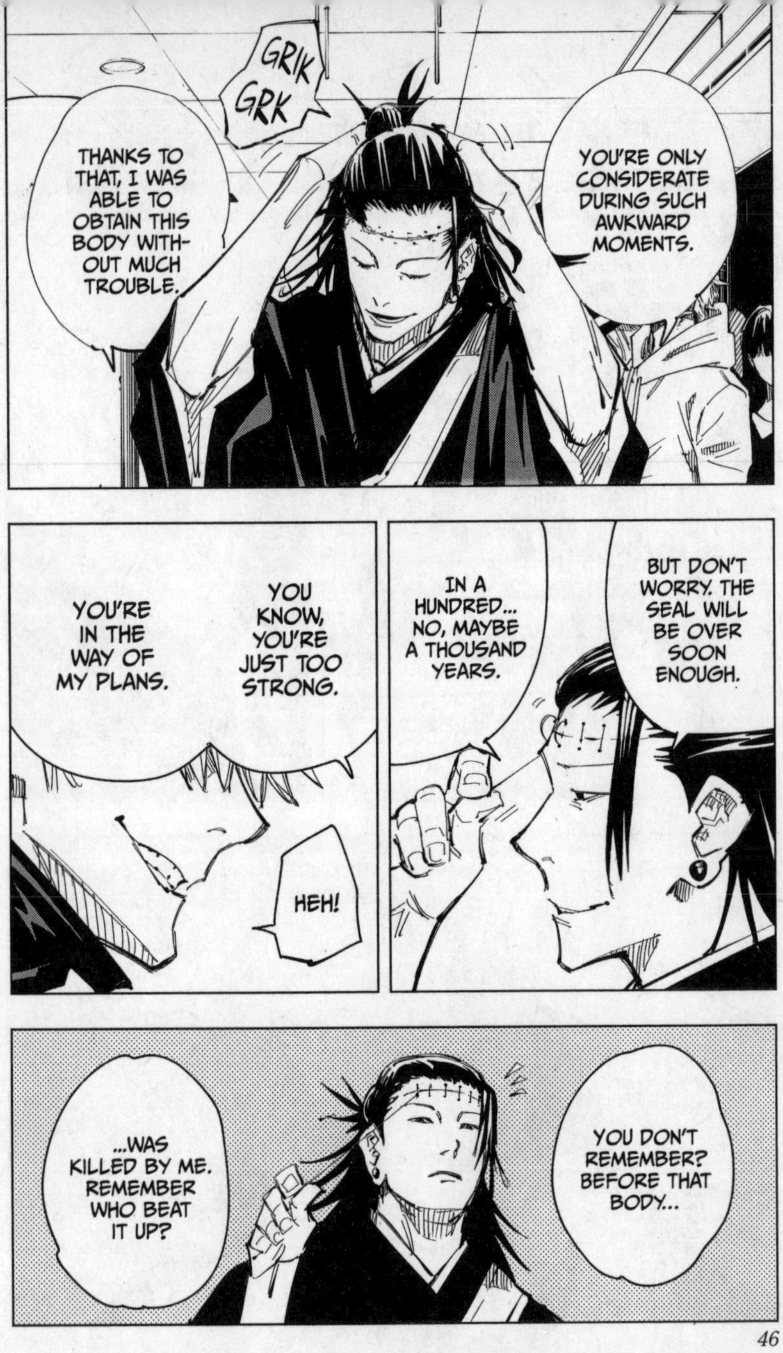
YOU'RE ONLY CONSIDERATE DURING SUCH AWKWARD MOMENTS.
GRIK GRK
THANKS TO THAT, I WAS ABLE TO OBTAIN THIS BODY WITH-OUT MUCH TROUBLE.
BUT DON'T WORRY. THE SEAL WILL BE OVER SOON ENOUGH.
IN A HUNDRED... NO, MAYBE A THOUSAND YEARS.
YOU KNOW, YOU'RE JUST TOO STRONG.
YOU'RE IN THE WAY OF MY PLANS.
HEH!
YOU DON'T REMEMBER? BEFORE THAT BODY...
...WAS KILLED BY ME. REMEMBER WHO BEAT IT UP?

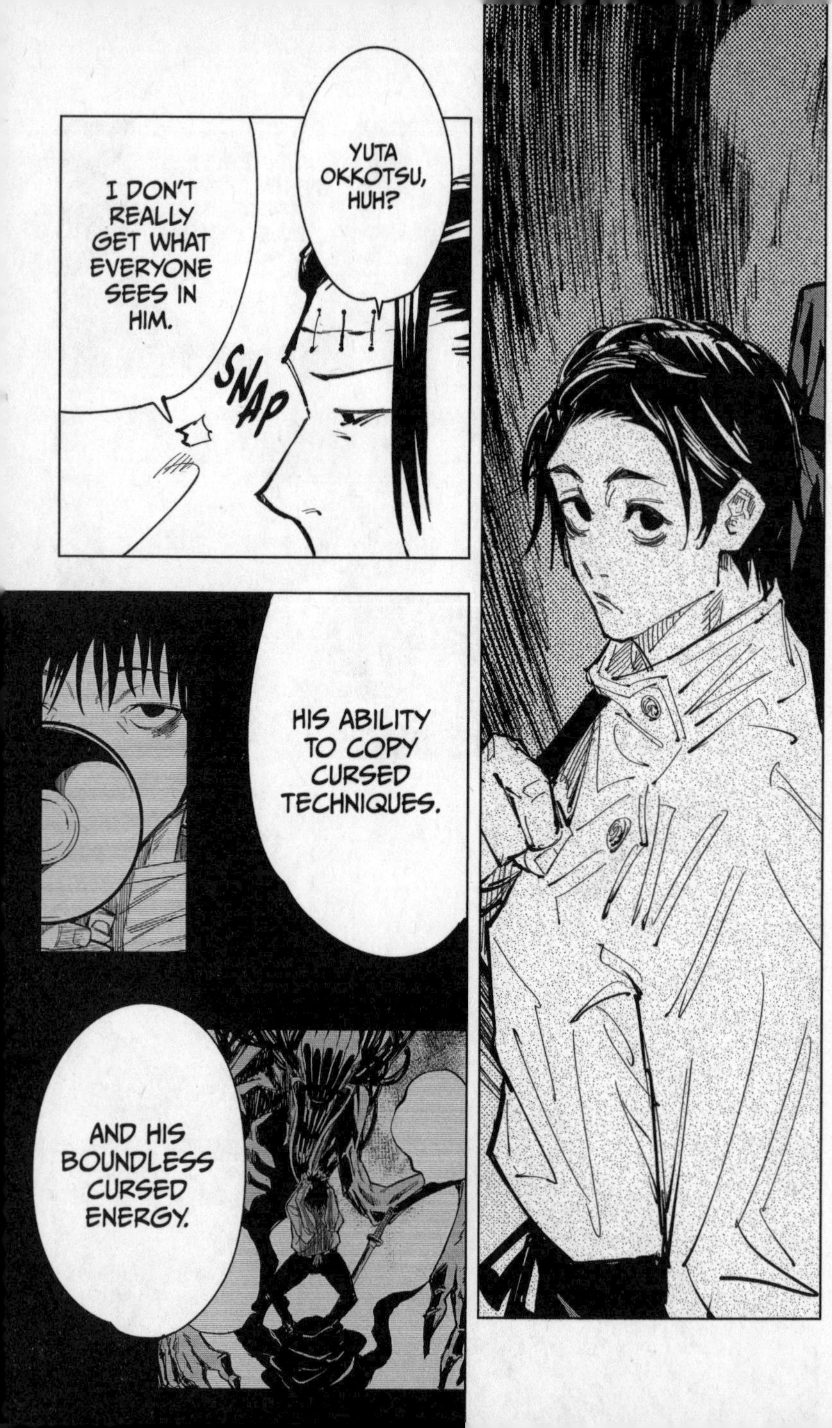
YUTA OKKOTSU, HUH?
I DON'T REALLY GET WHAT EVERYONE SEES IN HIM.
SNAP
HIS ABILITY TO COPY CURSED TECHNIQUES.
AND HIS BOUNDLESS CURSED ENERGY.

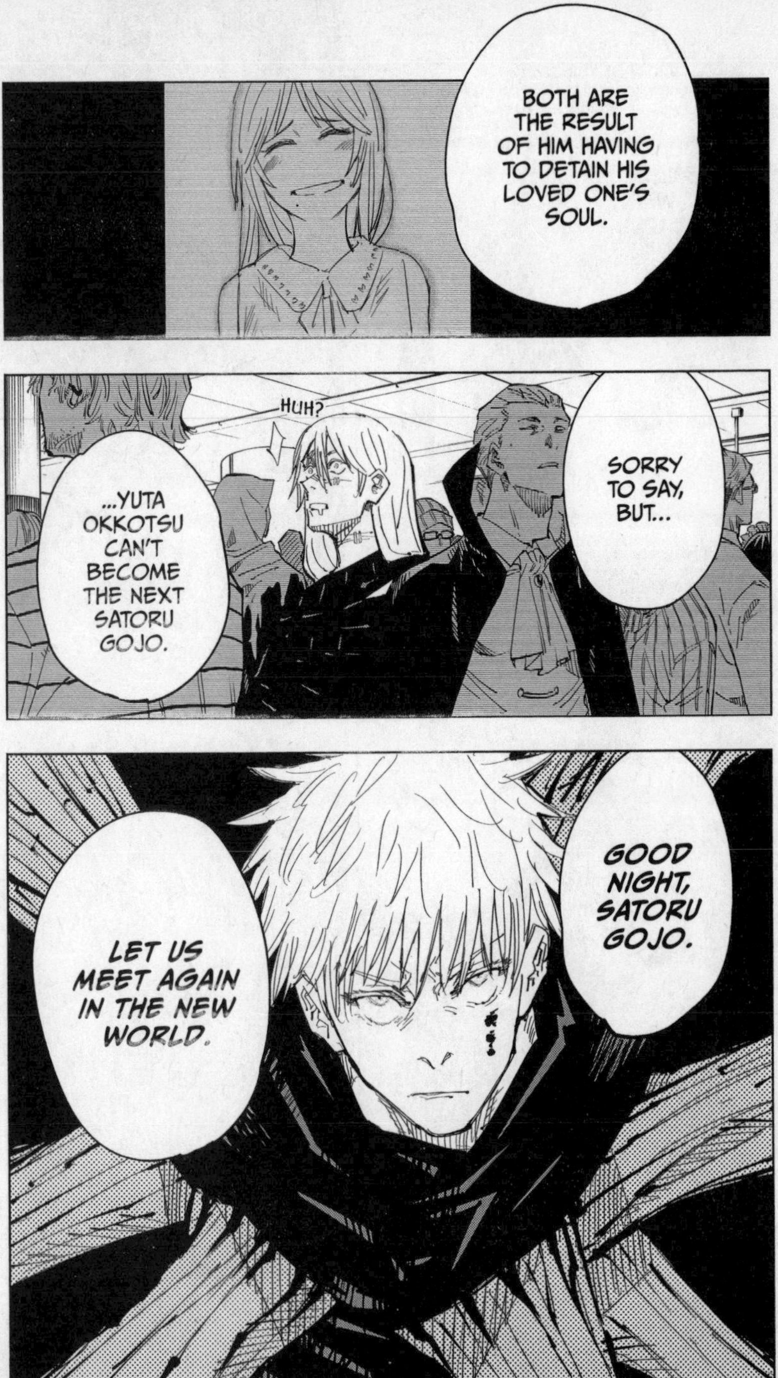
BOTH ARE THE RESULT OF HIM HAVING TO DETAIN HIS LOVED ONE'S SOUL.
SORRY TO SAY, BUT...
HUH?
...YUTA OKKOTSU CAN'T BECOME THE NEXT SATORU GOJO.
GOOD NIGHT, SATORU GOJO.
LET US MEET AGAIN IN THE NEW WORLD.

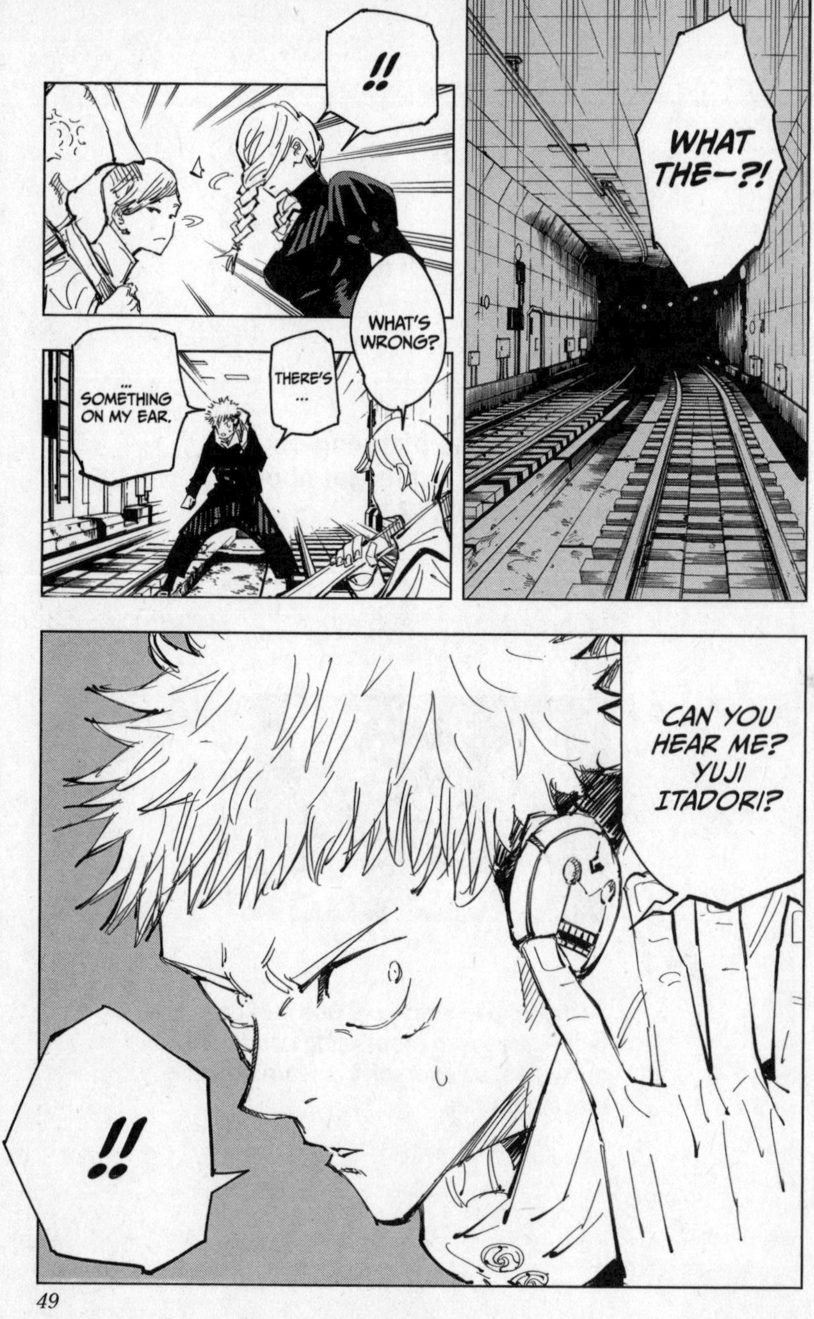
WHAT THE—?!
!!
WHAT'S WRONG?
THERE'S ...
... SOMETHING ON MY EAR.
CAN YOU HEAR ME? YUJI ITADORI?
!!

Scenes I was planning on addressing but forgot about until now, part 2

• Cursed spirits at play

Some jujutsu sorcerers use cursed techniques with preexisting conditions and rules, so everyone is learning while playing games.

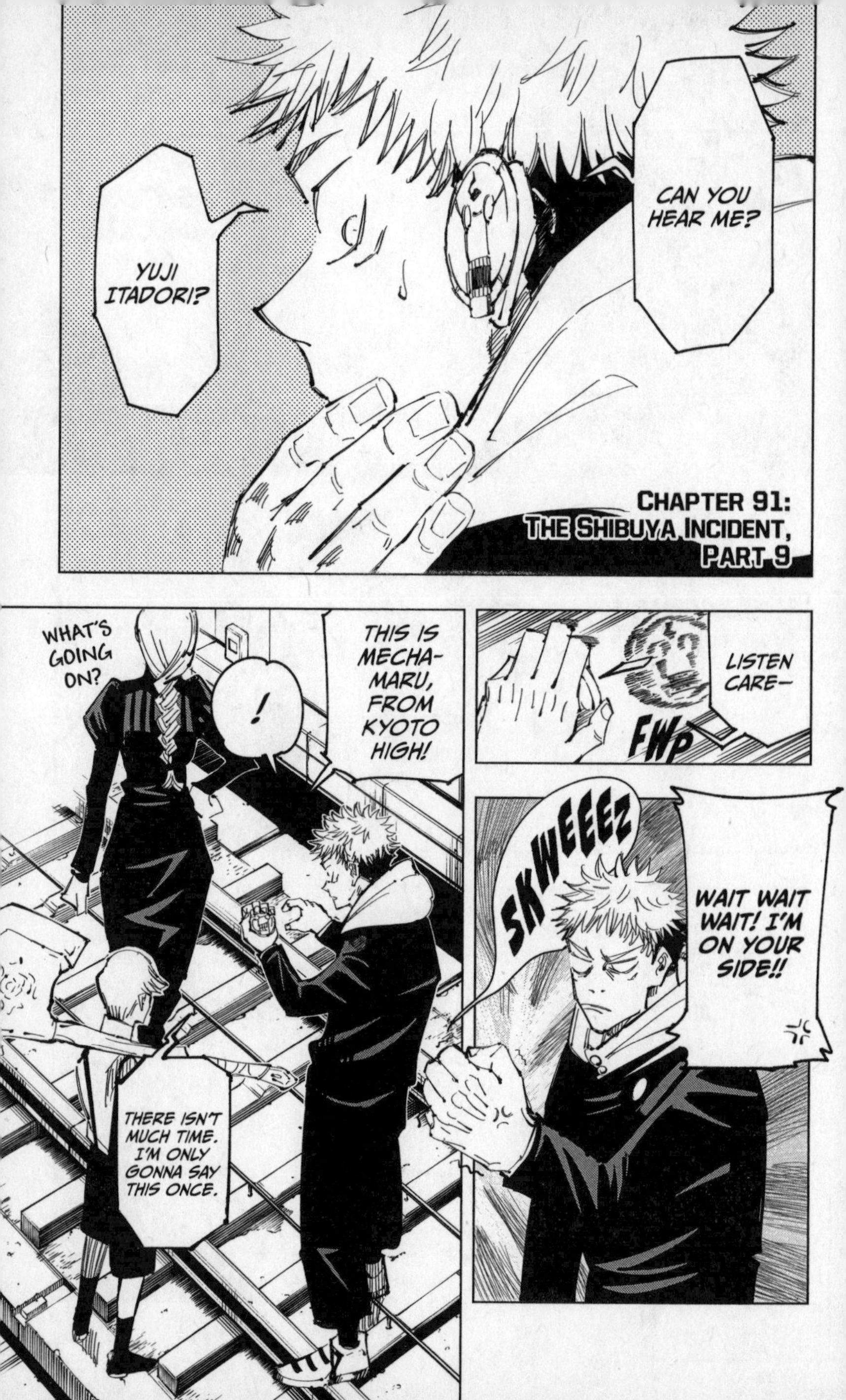
CAN YOU HEAR ME?
YUJI ITADORI?
CHAPTER 91: THE SHIBUYA INCIDENT, PART 9
LISTEN CARE-
FWP
SKWEEEZ
WAIT WAIT WAIT! I'M ON YOUR SIDE!!
THIS IS MECHA-MARU, FROM KYOTO HIGH!
!
WHAT'S GOING ON?
THERE ISN'T MUCH TIME. I'M ONLY GONNA SAY THIS ONCE.

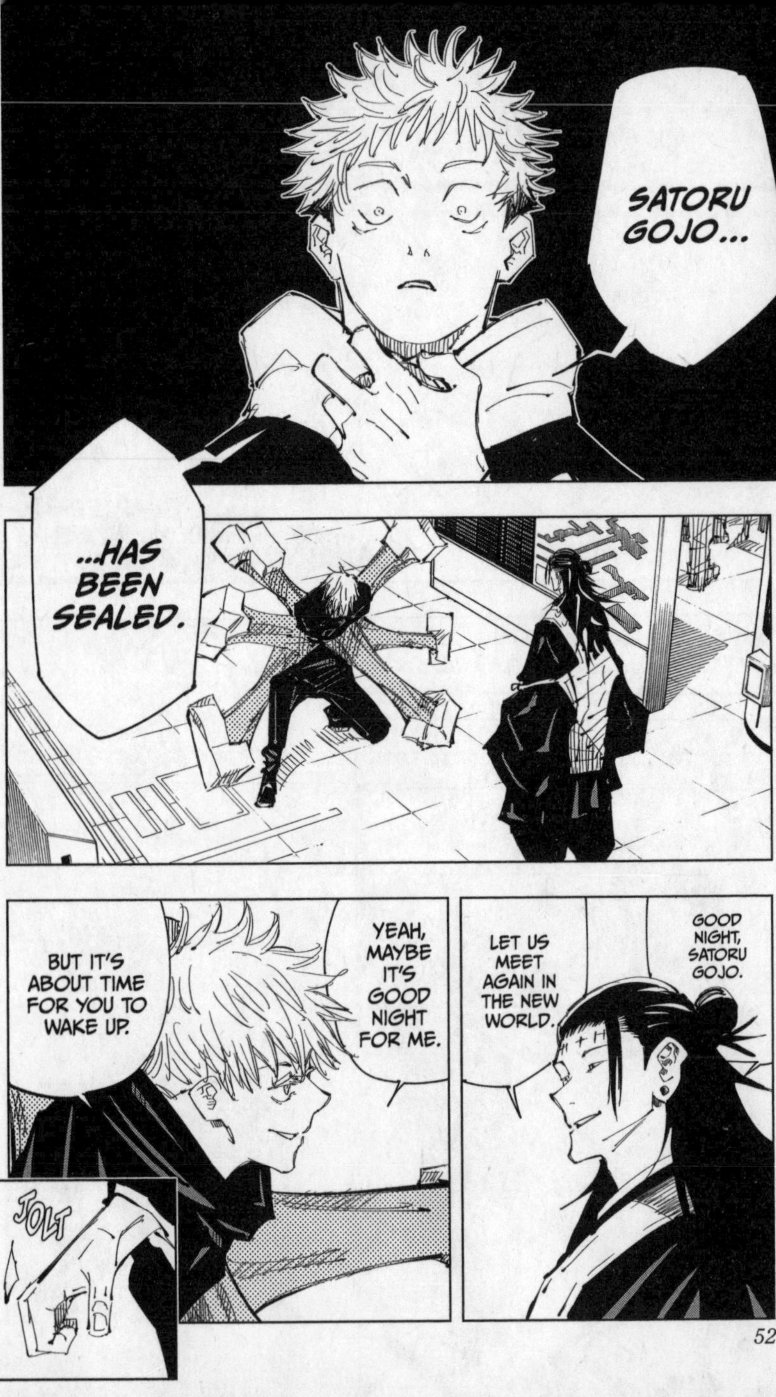
SATORU GOJO...
...HAS BEEN SEALED.
GOOD NIGHT, SATORU GOJO.
LET US MEET AGAIN IN THE NEW WORLD.
YEAH, MAYBE IT'S GOOD NIGHT FOR ME.
BUT IT'S ABOUT TIME FOR YOU TO WAKE UP.
JOLT

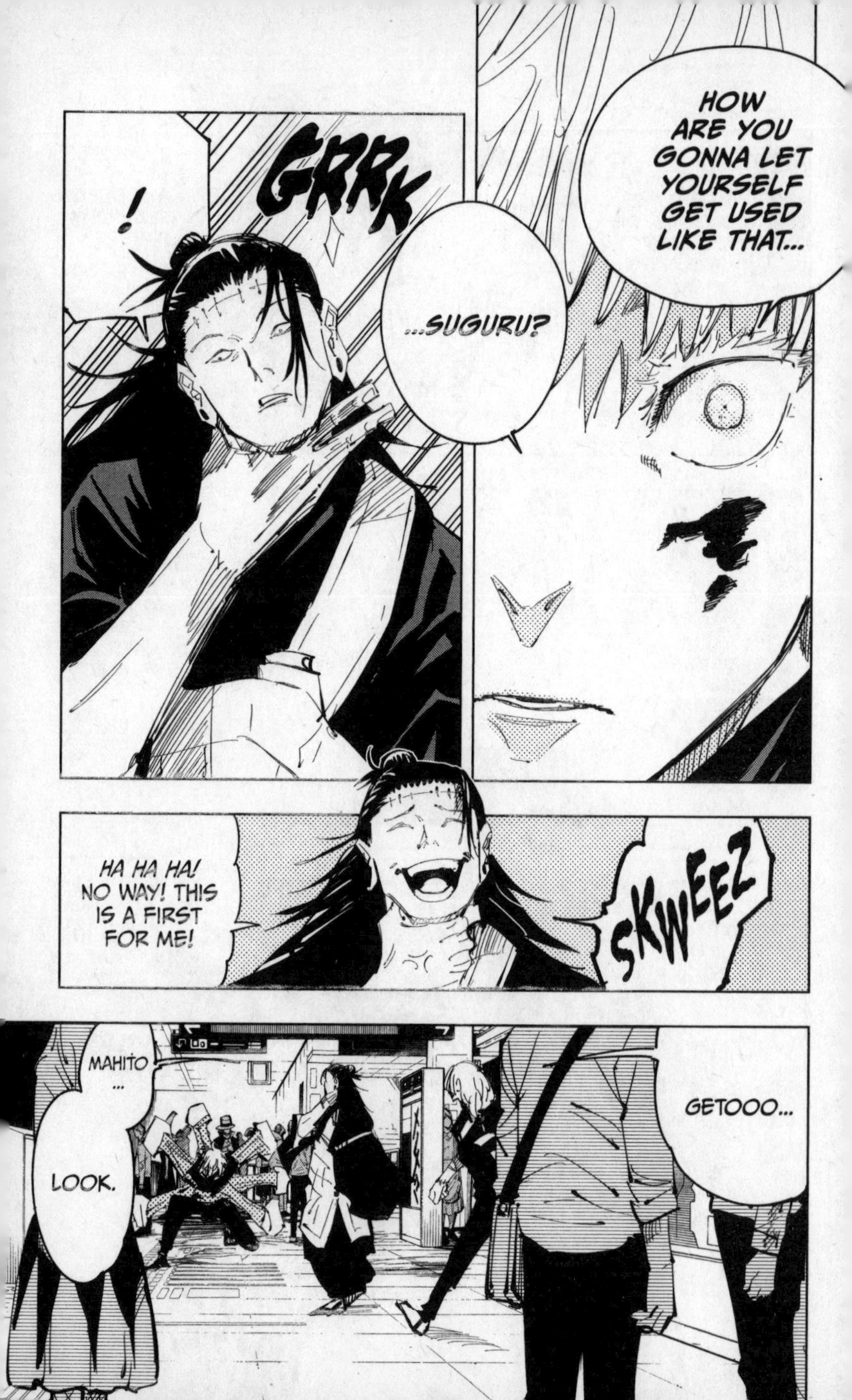
HOW ARE YOU GONNA LET YOURSELF GET USED LIKE THAT...
...SUGURU?
GRRK
!
SKWEEZ
HA HA HA! NO WAY! THIS IS A FIRST FOR ME!
GETOOO...
MAHITO...
LOOK.

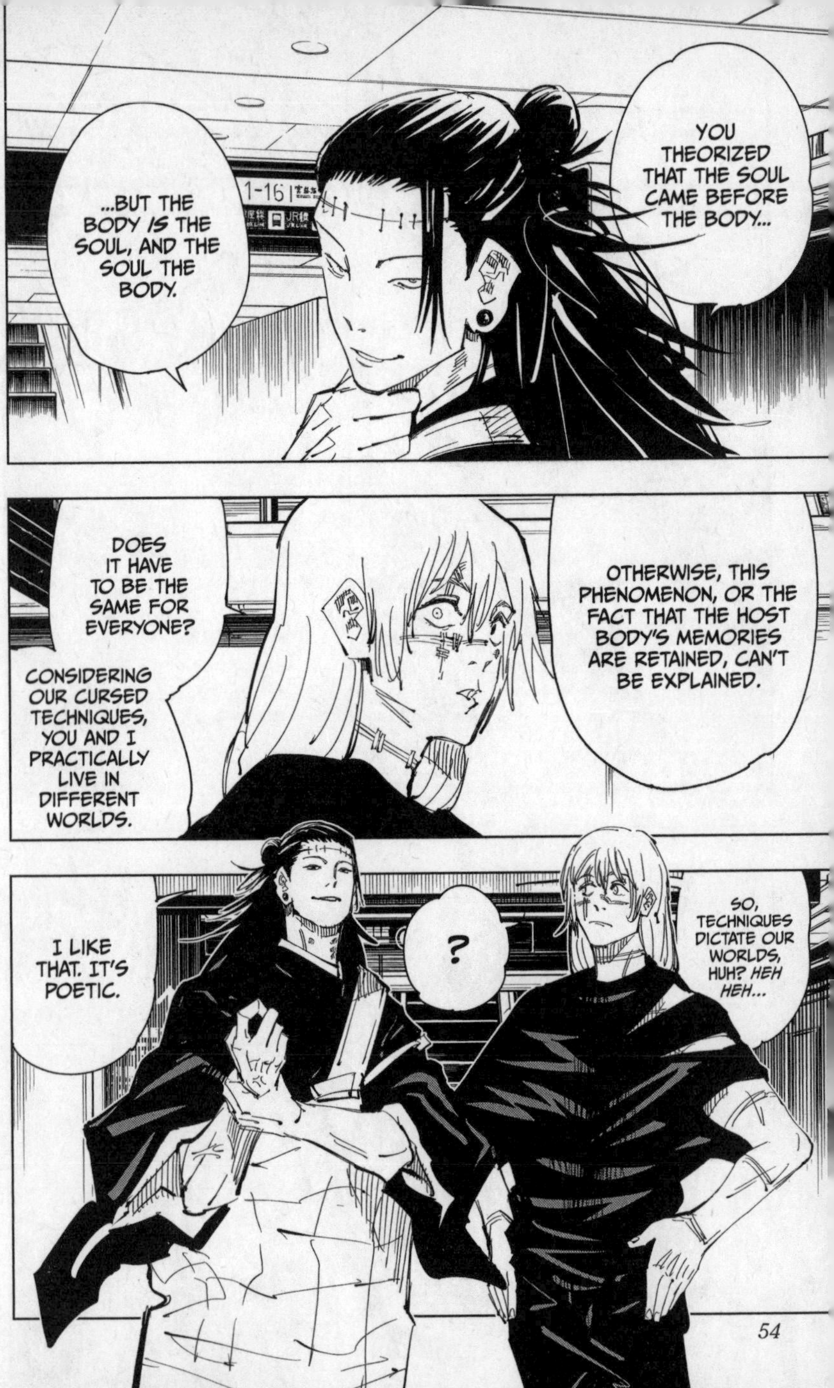
YOU THEORIZED THAT THE SOUL CAME BEFORE THE BODY...
...BUT THE BODY *IS* THE SOUL, AND THE SOUL THE BODY.
OTHERWISE, THIS PHENOMENON, OR THE FACT THAT THE HOST BODY'S MEMORIES ARE RETAINED, CAN'T BE EXPLAINED.
DOES IT HAVE TO BE THE SAME FOR EVERYONE?
CONSIDERING OUR CURSED TECHNIQUES, YOU AND I PRACTICALLY LIVE IN DIFFERENT WORLDS.
SO, TECHNIQUES DICTATE OUR WORLDS, HUH? *HEH HEH...*
?
I LIKE THAT. IT'S POETIC.

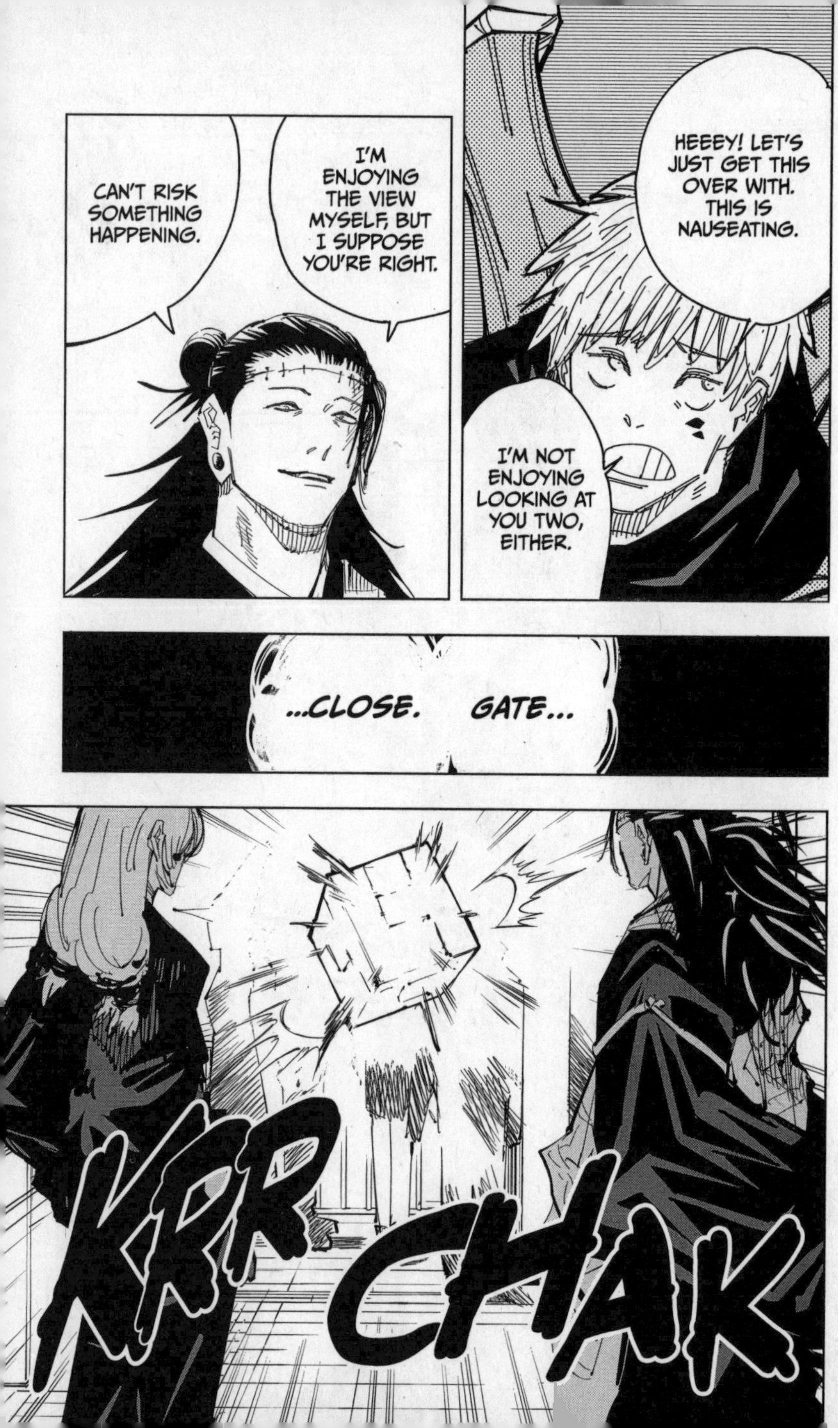
HEEEY! LET'S JUST GET THIS OVER WITH. THIS IS NAUSEATING.
I'M NOT ENJOYING LOOKING AT YOU TWO, EITHER.
I'M ENJOYING THE VIEW MYSELF, BUT I SUPPOSE YOU'RE RIGHT.
CAN'T RISK SOMETHING HAPPENING.
GATE...
...CLOSE.
KRR CHAK

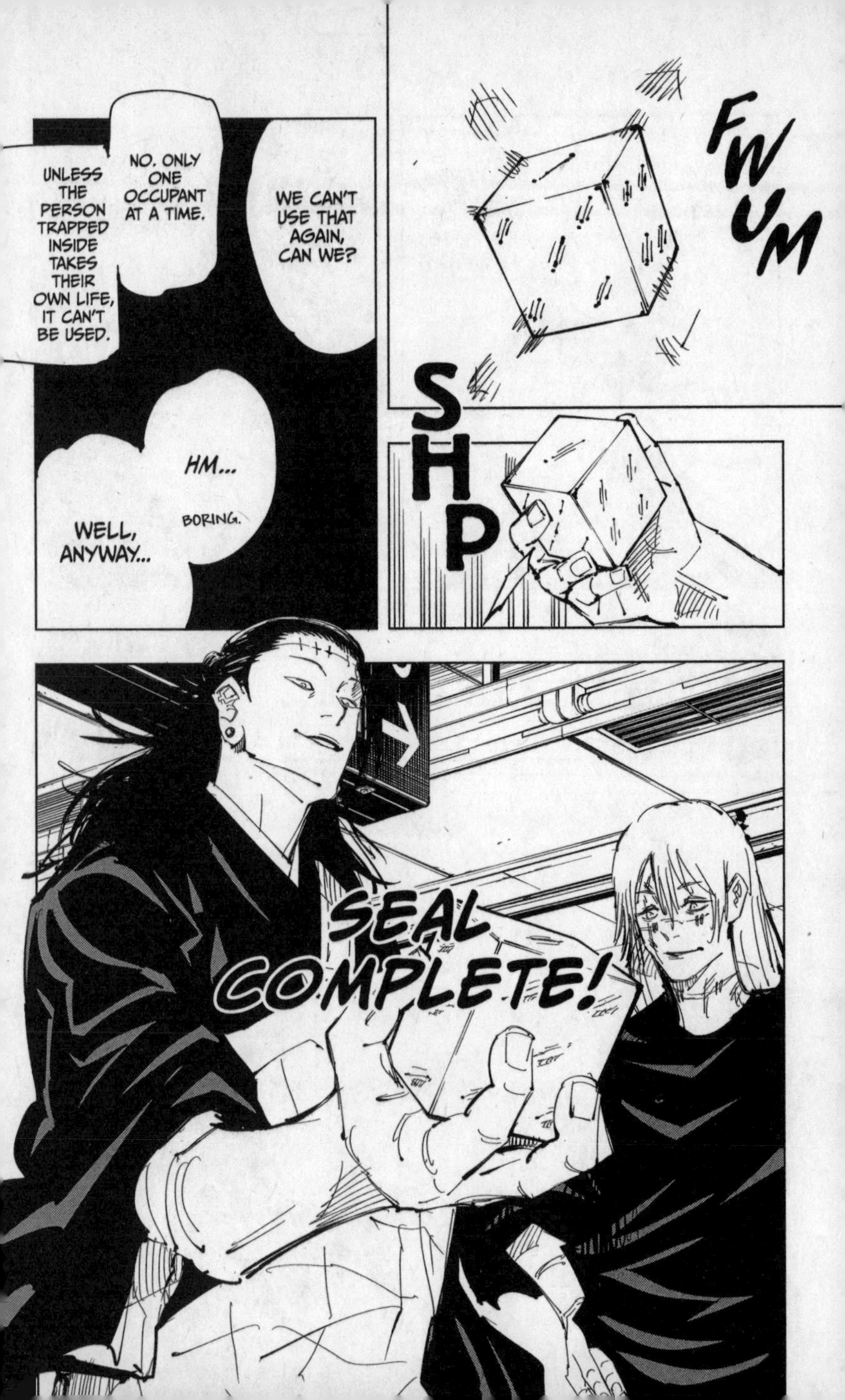
FWUM
SHP
WE CAN'T USE THAT AGAIN, CAN WE?
NO. ONLY ONE OCCUPANT AT A TIME.
UNLESS THE PERSON TRAPPED INSIDE TAKES THEIR OWN LIFE, IT CAN'T BE USED.
HM...
BORING.
WELL, ANYWAY...
SEAL COMPLETE!

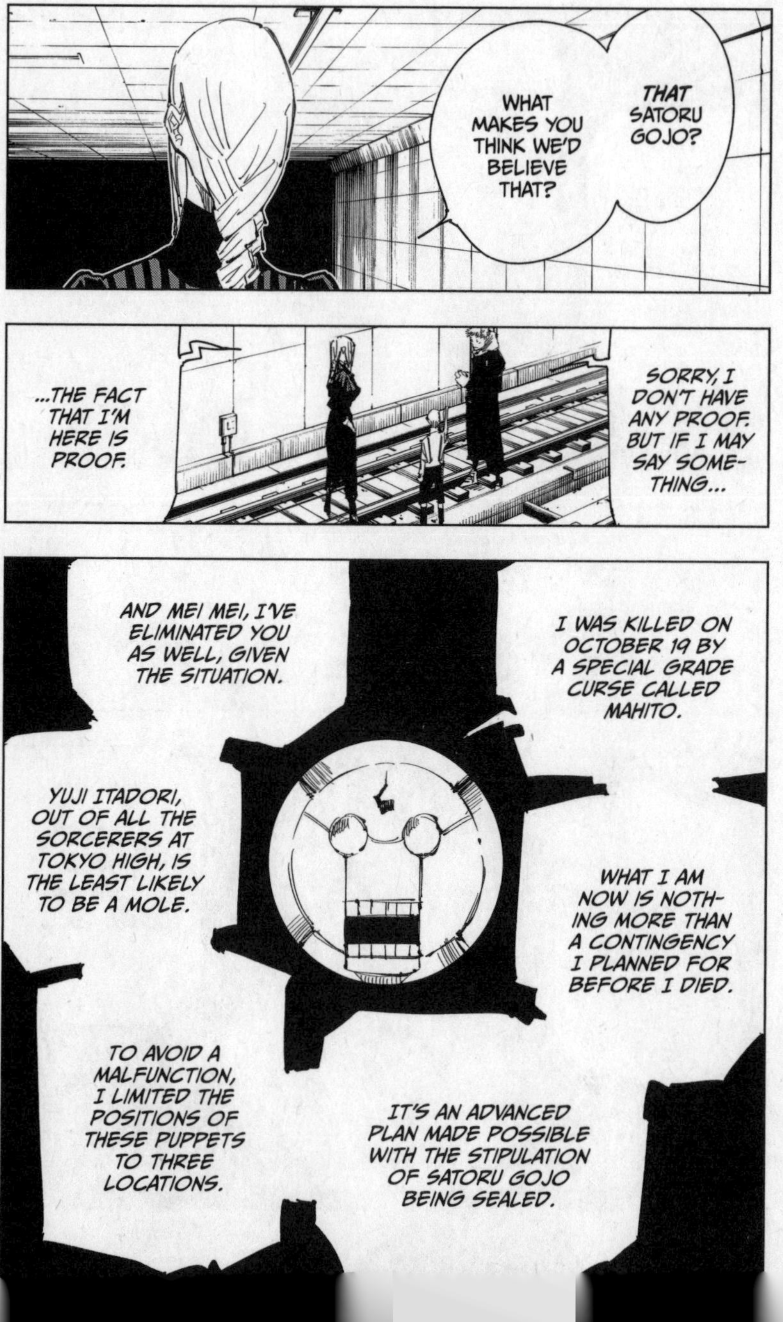
THAT SATORU GOJO?
WHAT MAKES YOU THINK WE'D BELIEVE THAT?
SORRY, I DON'T HAVE ANY PROOF. BUT IF I MAY SAY SOME-THING...
...THE FACT THAT I'M HERE IS PROOF.
I WAS KILLED ON OCTOBER 19 BY A SPECIAL GRADE CURSE CALLED MAHITO.
WHAT I AM NOW IS NOTH-ING MORE THAN A CONTINGENCY I PLANNED FOR BEFORE I DIED.
IT'S AN ADVANCED PLAN MADE POSSIBLE WITH THE STIPULATION OF SATORU GOJO BEING SEALED.
TO AVOID A MALFUNCTION, I LIMITED THE POSITIONS OF THESE PUPPETS TO THREE LOCATIONS.
YUJI ITADORI, OUT OF ALL THE SORCERERS AT TOKYO HIGH, IS THE LEAST LIKELY TO BE A MOLE.
AND MEI MEI, I'VE ELIMINATED YOU AS WELL, GIVEN THE SITUATION.

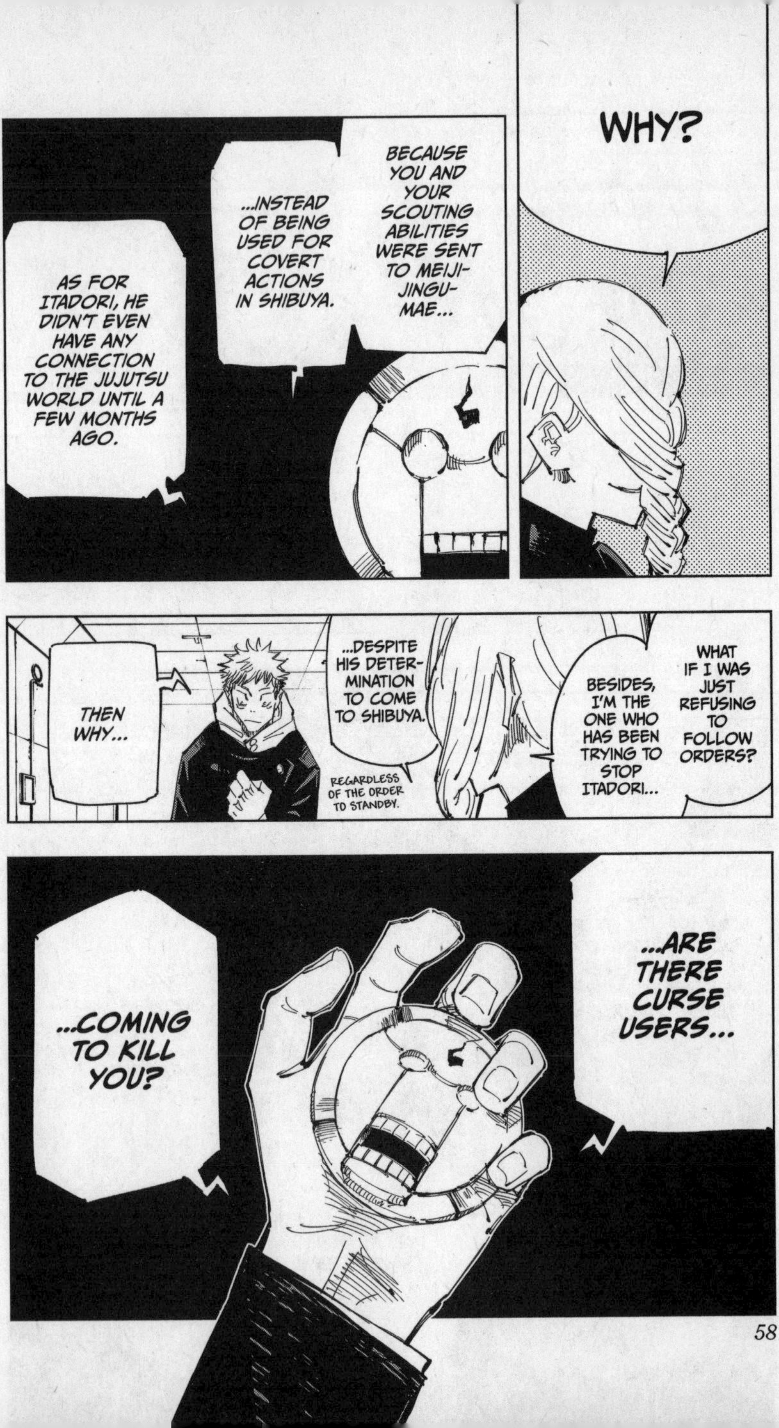
WHY?
BECAUSE YOU AND YOUR SCOUTING ABILITIES WERE SENT TO MEIJI-JINGU-MAE...
...INSTEAD OF BEING USED FOR COVERT ACTIONS IN SHIBUYA.
AS FOR ITADORI, HE DIDN'T EVEN HAVE ANY CONNECTION TO THE JUJUTSU WORLD UNTIL A FEW MONTHS AGO.
WHAT IF I WAS JUST REFUSING TO FOLLOW ORDERS?
BESIDES, I'M THE ONE WHO HAS BEEN TRYING TO STOP ITADORI...
...DESPITE HIS DETERMINATION TO COME TO SHIBUYA.
REGARDLESS OF THE ORDER TO STANDBY.
THEN WHY...
...ARE THERE CURSE USERS...
...COMING TO KILL YOU?

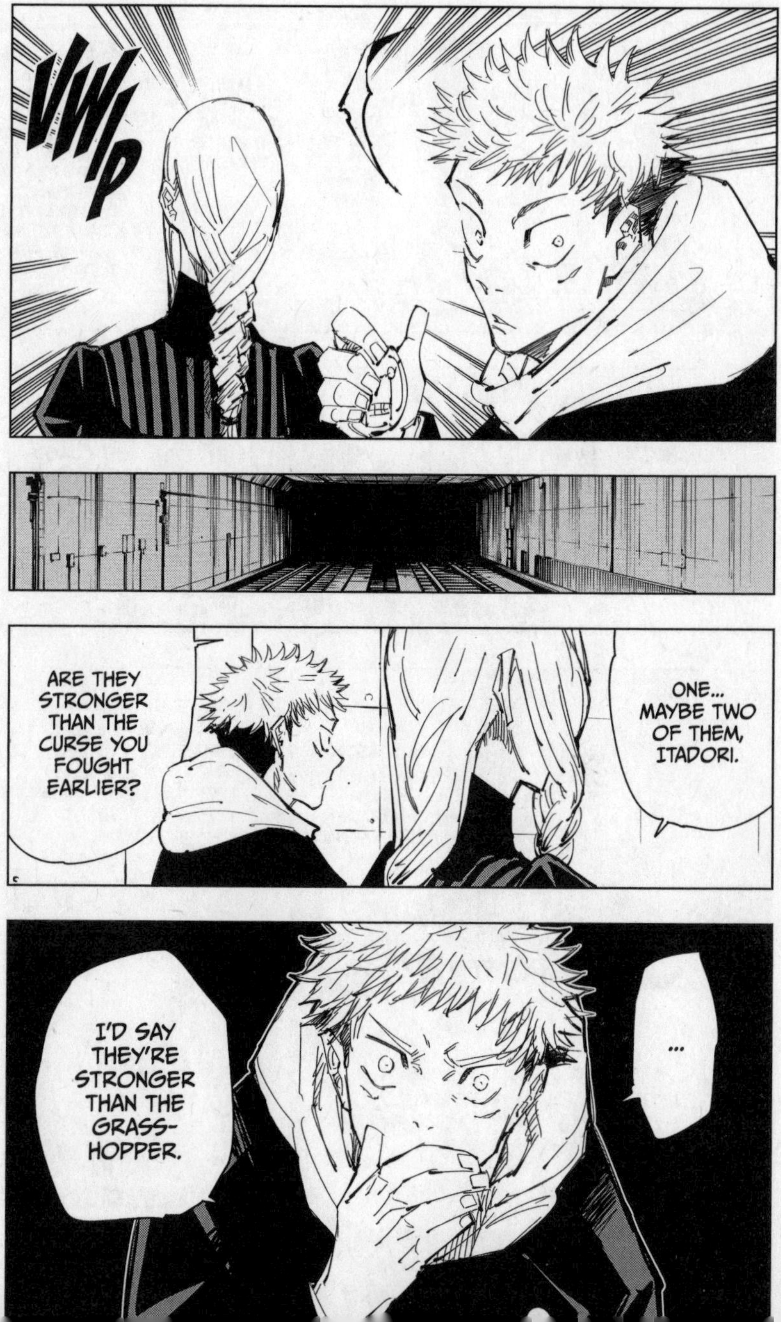
VWIP
ONE... MAYBE TWO OF THEM, ITADORI.
ARE THEY STRONGER THAN THE CURSE YOU FOUGHT EARLIER?
...
I'D SAY THEY'RE STRONGER THAN THE GRASS-HOPPER.

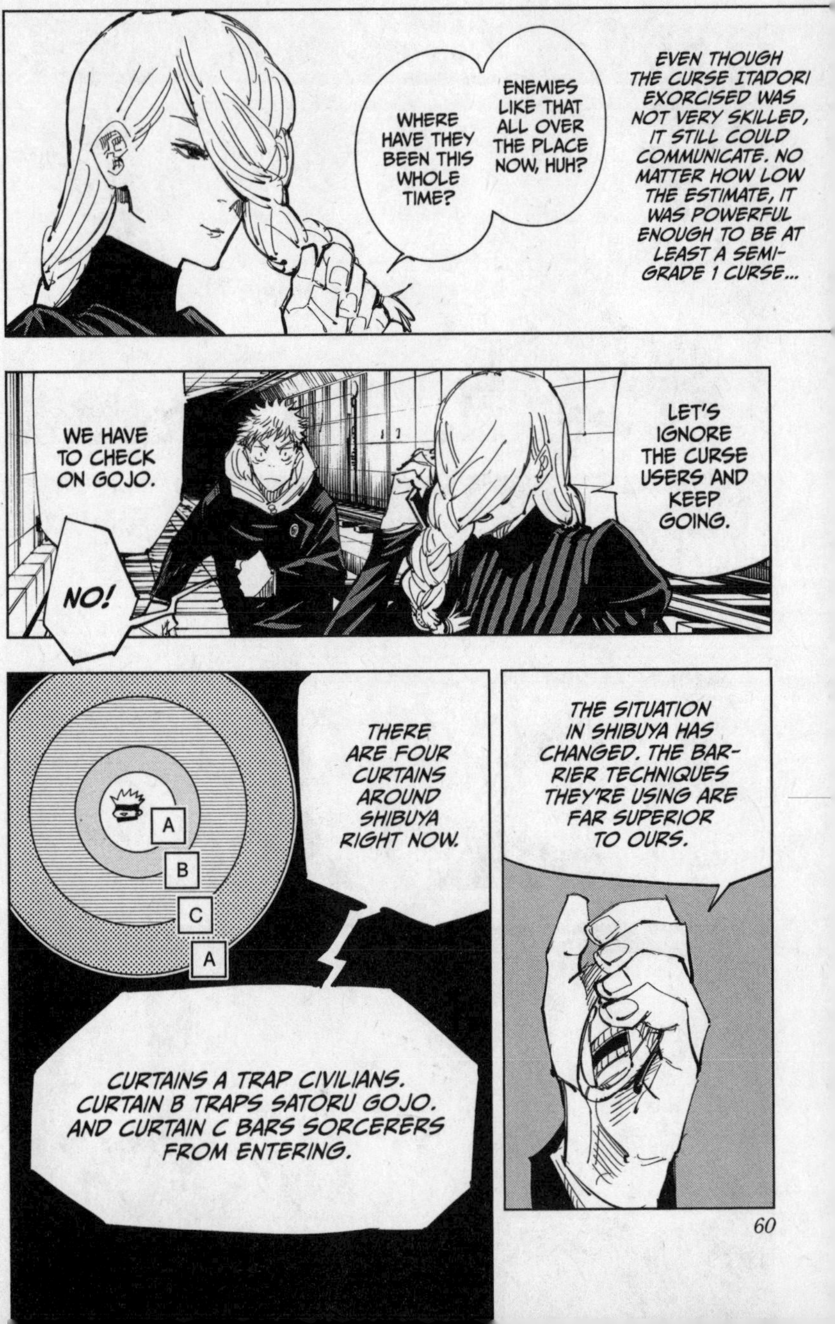
EVEN THOUGH THE CURSE ITADORI EXORCISED WAS NOT VERY SKILLED, IT STILL COULD COMMUNICATE. NO MATTER HOW LOW THE ESTIMATE, IT WAS POWERFUL ENOUGH TO BE AT LEAST A SEMI-GRADE 1 CURSE...
ENEMIES LIKE THAT ALL OVER THE PLACE NOW, HUH?
WHERE HAVE THEY BEEN THIS WHOLE TIME?
LET'S IGNORE THE CURSE USERS AND KEEP GOING.
WE HAVE TO CHECK ON GOJO.
NO!
THE SITUATION IN SHIBUYA HAS CHANGED. THE BARRIER TECHNIQUES THEY'RE USING ARE FAR SUPERIOR TO OURS.
THERE ARE FOUR CURTAINS AROUND SHIBUYA RIGHT NOW.
A
B
C
A
CURTAINS A TRAP CIVILIANS. CURTAIN B TRAPS SATORU GOJO. AND CURTAIN C BARS SORCERERS FROM ENTERING.

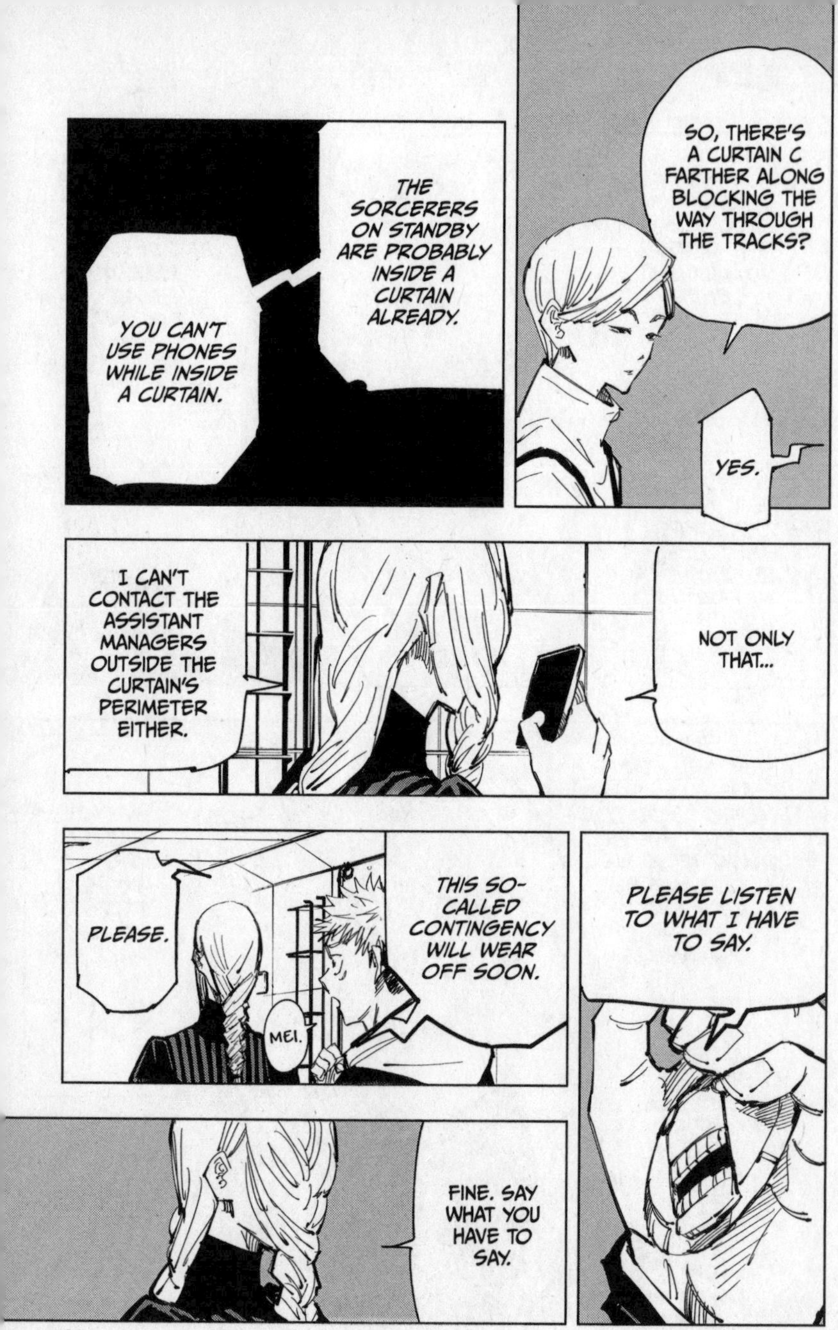
SO, THERE'S A CURTAIN C FARTHER ALONG BLOCKING THE WAY THROUGH THE TRACKS?
YES.
THE SORCERERS ON STANDBY ARE PROBABLY INSIDE A CURTAIN ALREADY.
YOU CAN'T USE PHONES WHILE INSIDE A CURTAIN.
NOT ONLY THAT...
I CAN'T CONTACT THE ASSISTANT MANAGERS OUTSIDE THE CURTAIN'S PERIMETER EITHER.
PLEASE LISTEN TO WHAT I HAVE TO SAY.
THIS SO-CALLED CONTINGENCY WILL WEAR OFF SOON.
MEI.
PLEASE.
FINE. SAY WHAT YOU HAVE TO SAY.

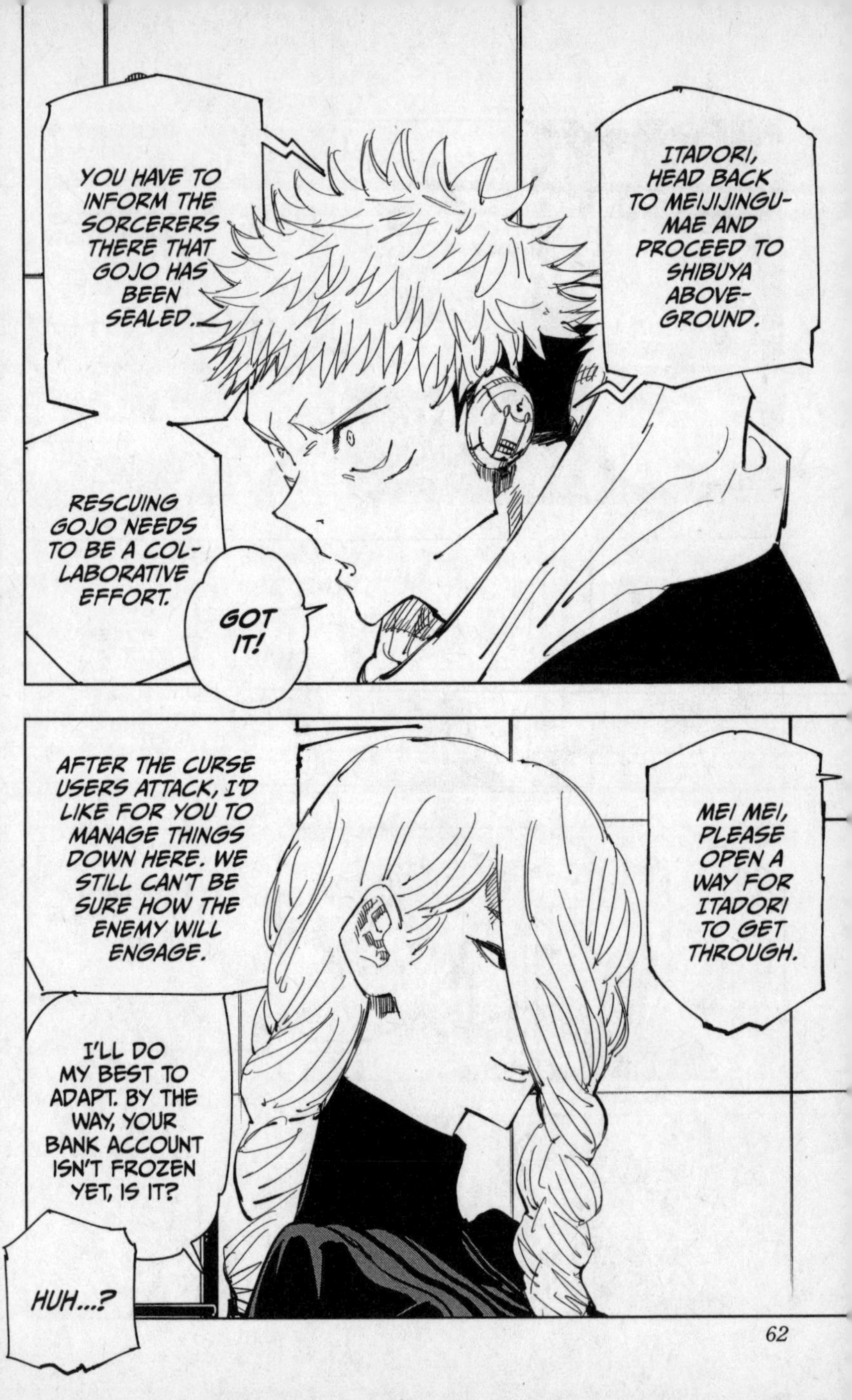
ITADORI, HEAD BACK TO MEIJIJINGU-MAE AND PROCEED TO SHIBUYA ABOVE-GROUND.
YOU HAVE TO INFORM THE SORCERERS THERE THAT GOJO HAS BEEN SEALED...
RESCUING GOJO NEEDS TO BE A COL-LABORATIVE EFFORT.
GOT IT!
MEI MEI, PLEASE OPEN A WAY FOR ITADORI TO GET THROUGH.
AFTER THE CURSE USERS ATTACK, I'D LIKE FOR YOU TO MANAGE THINGS DOWN HERE. WE STILL CAN'T BE SURE HOW THE ENEMY WILL ENGAGE.
I'LL DO MY BEST TO ADAPT. BY THE WAY, YOUR BANK ACCOUNT ISN'T FROZEN YET, IS IT?
HUH...?

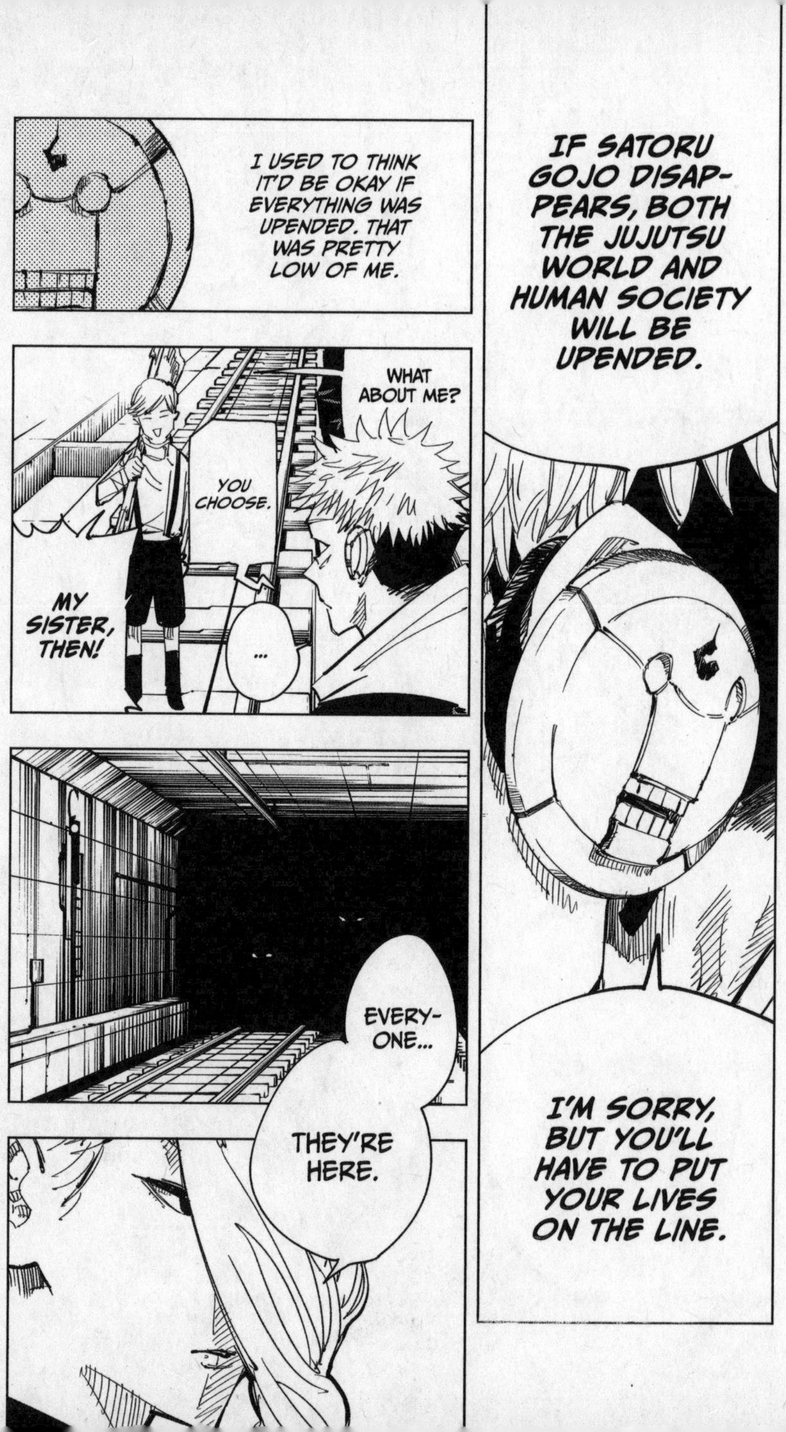
IF SATORU GOJO DISAPPEARS, BOTH THE JUJUTSU WORLD AND HUMAN SOCIETY WILL BE UPENDED.
I'M SORRY, BUT YOU'LL HAVE TO PUT YOUR LIVES ON THE LINE.
I USED TO THINK IT'D BE OKAY IF EVERYTHING WAS UPENDED. THAT WAS PRETTY LOW OF ME.
WHAT ABOUT ME?
YOU CHOOSE.
...
MY SISTER, THEN!
EVERY-ONE...
THEY'RE HERE.

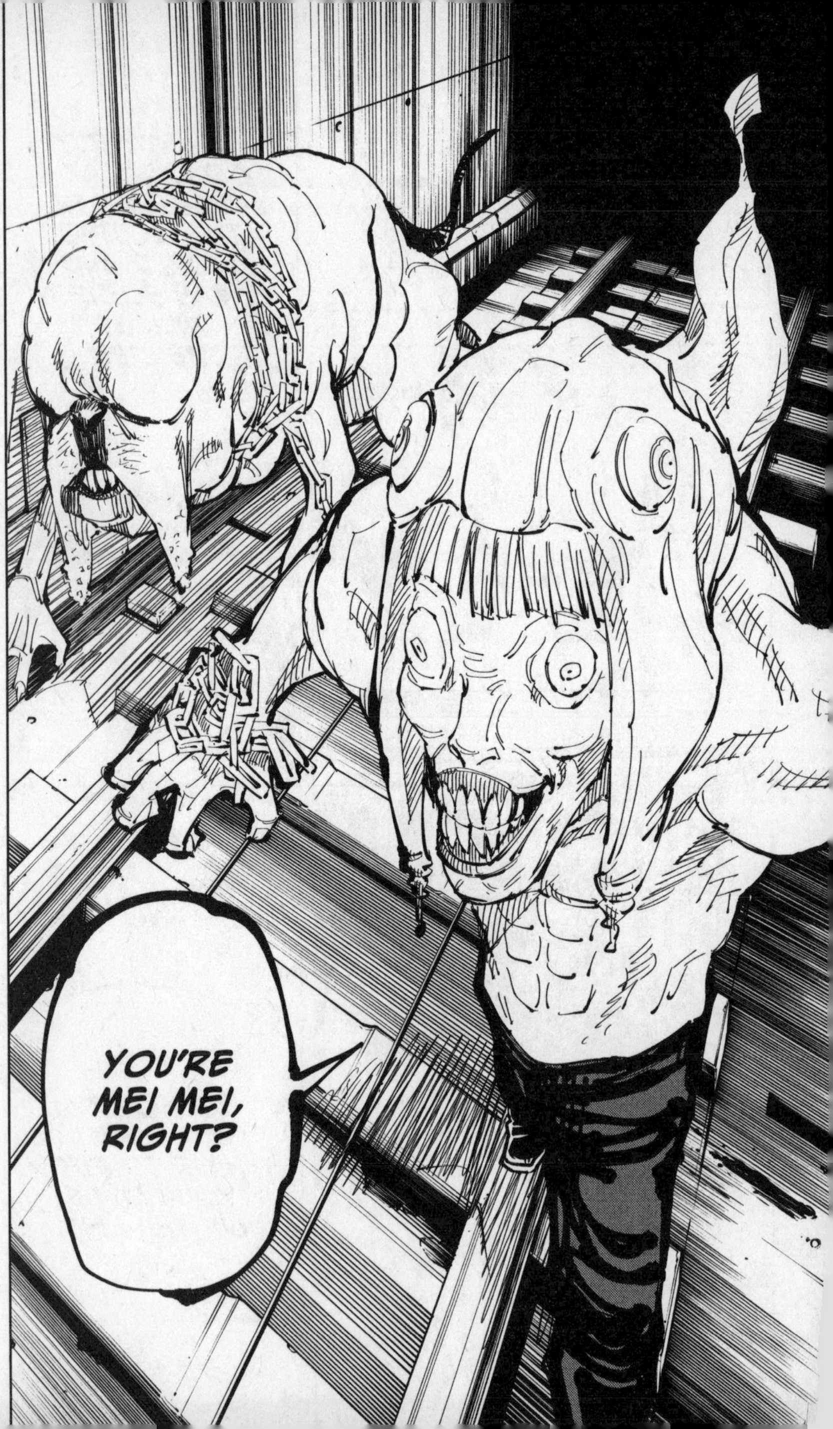
YOU'RE MEI MEI, RIGHT?

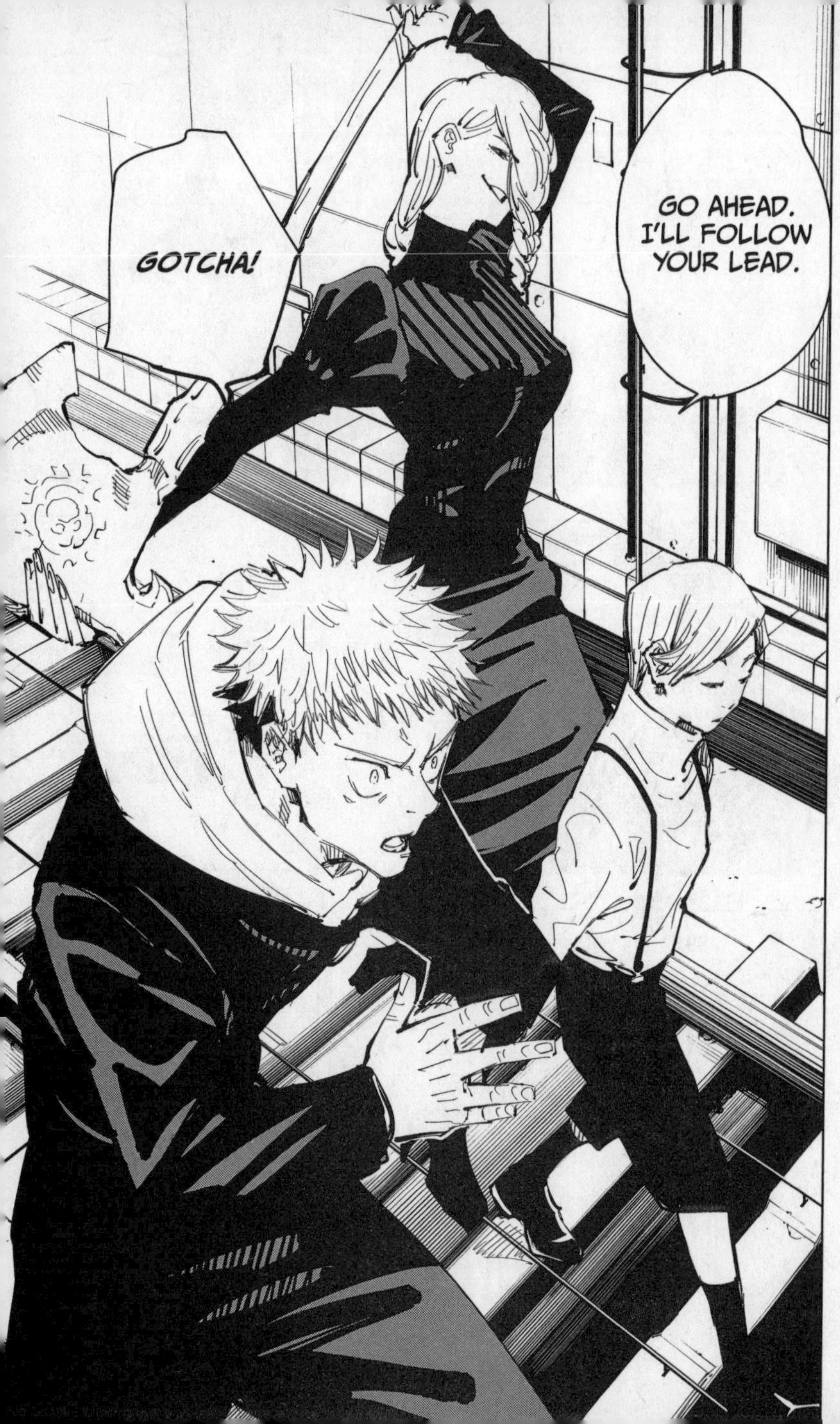
GO AHEAD. I'LL FOLLOW YOUR LEAD.
GOTCHA!

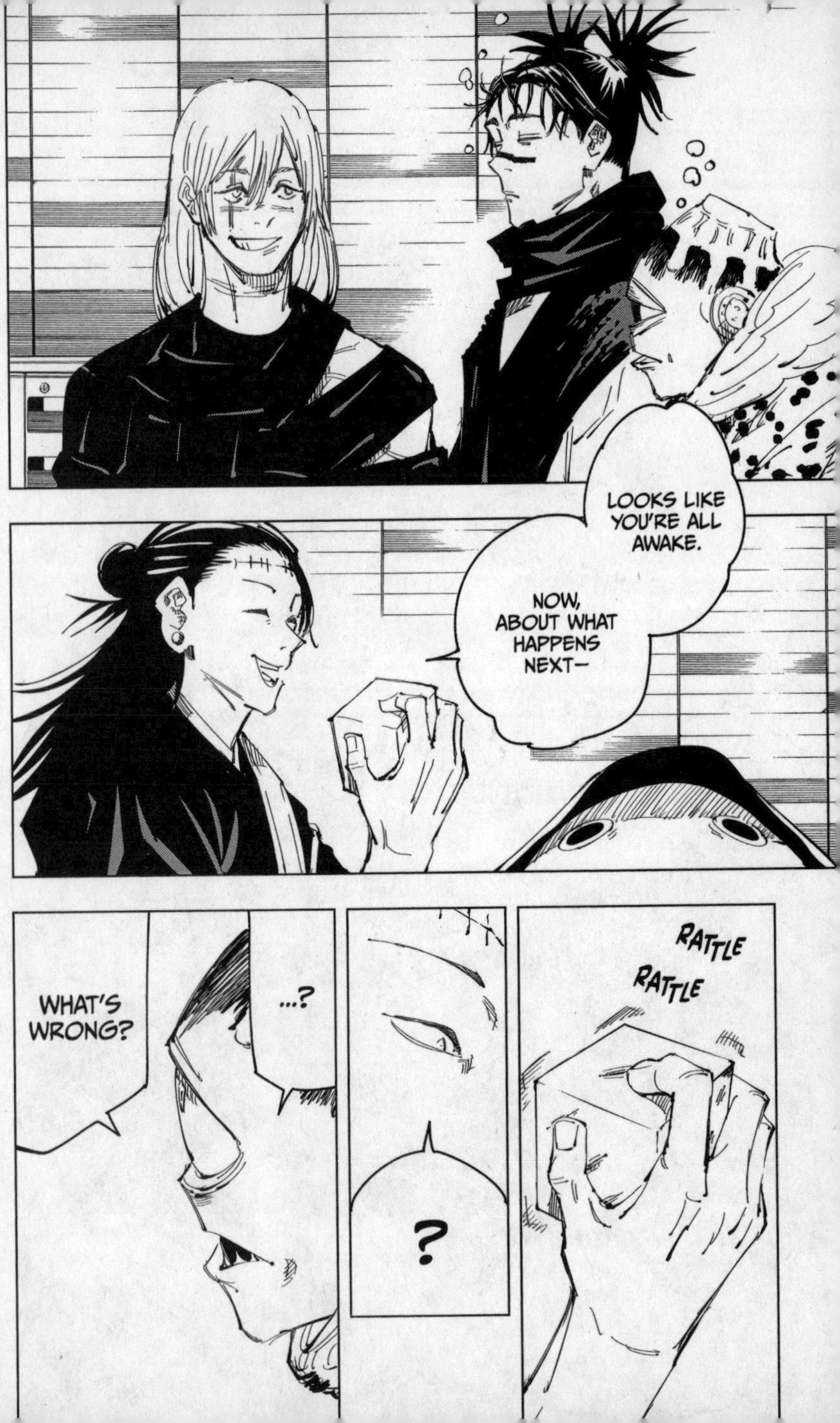
LOOKS LIKE YOU'RE ALL AWAKE.
NOW, ABOUT WHAT HAPPENS NEXT–
RATTLE RATTLE
?
...?
WHAT'S WRONG?

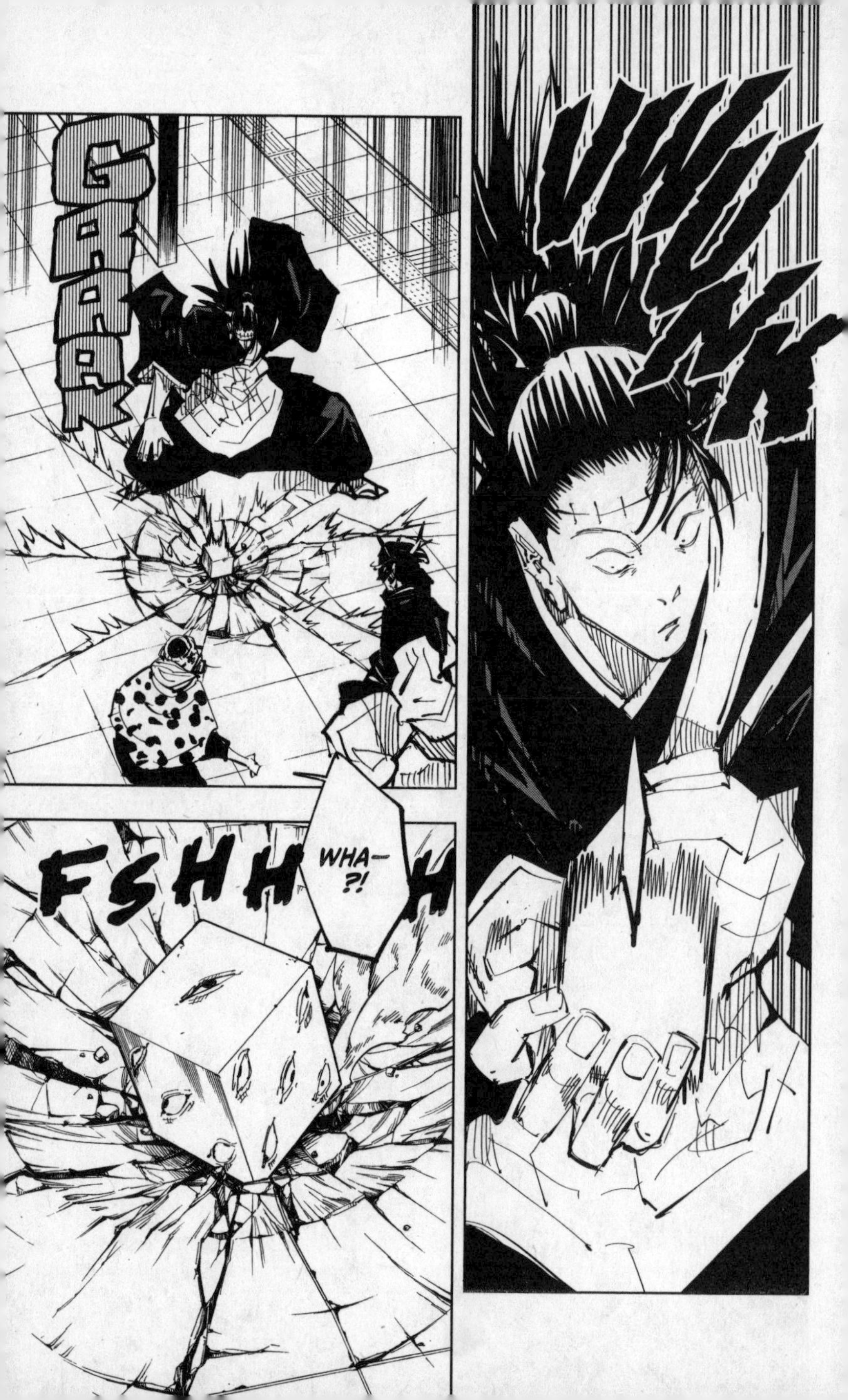
GAAR
FSHHH
WHA-?!

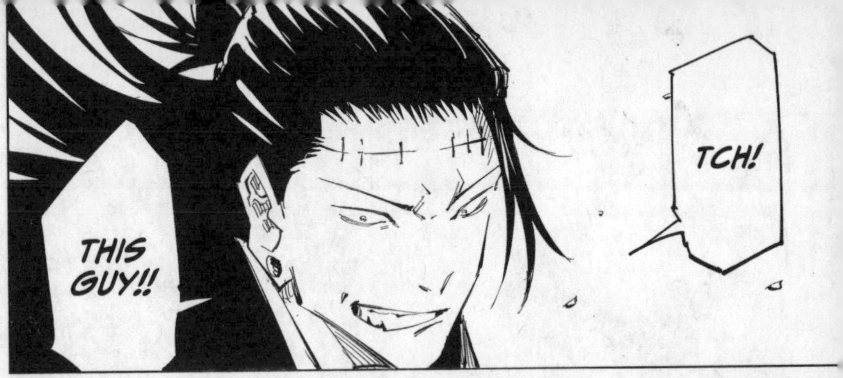
TCH!
THIS GUY!!

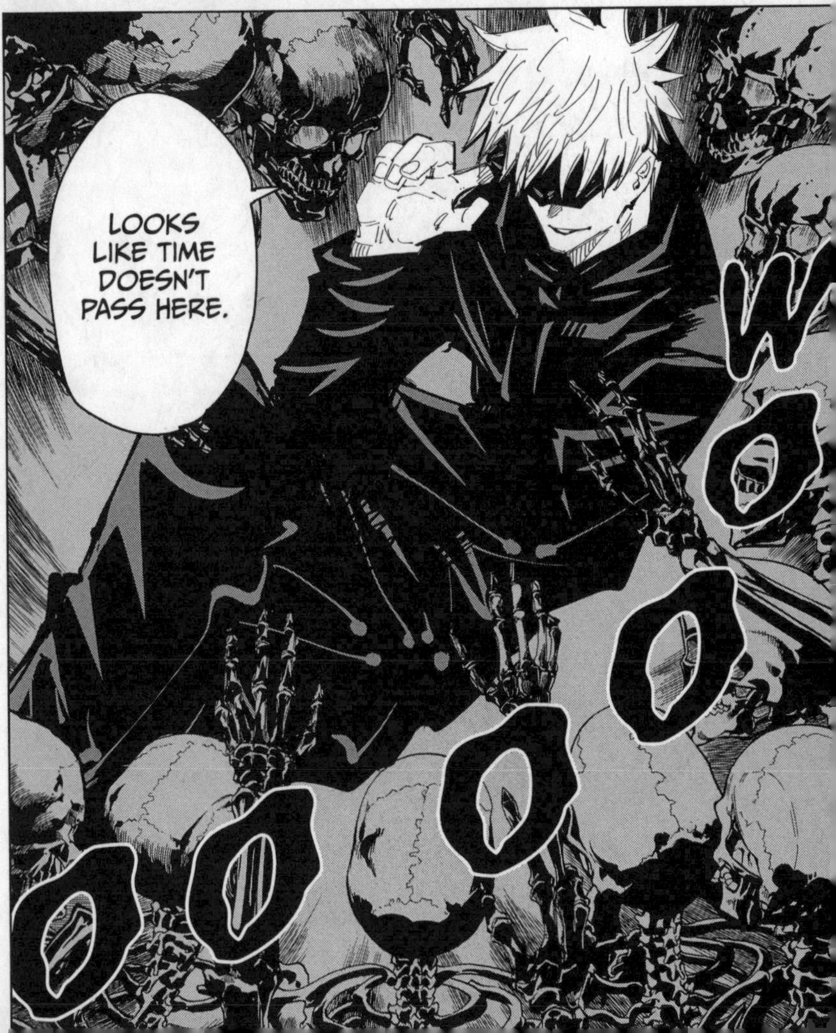
LOOKS LIKE TIME DOESN'T PASS HERE.
WOOOOO

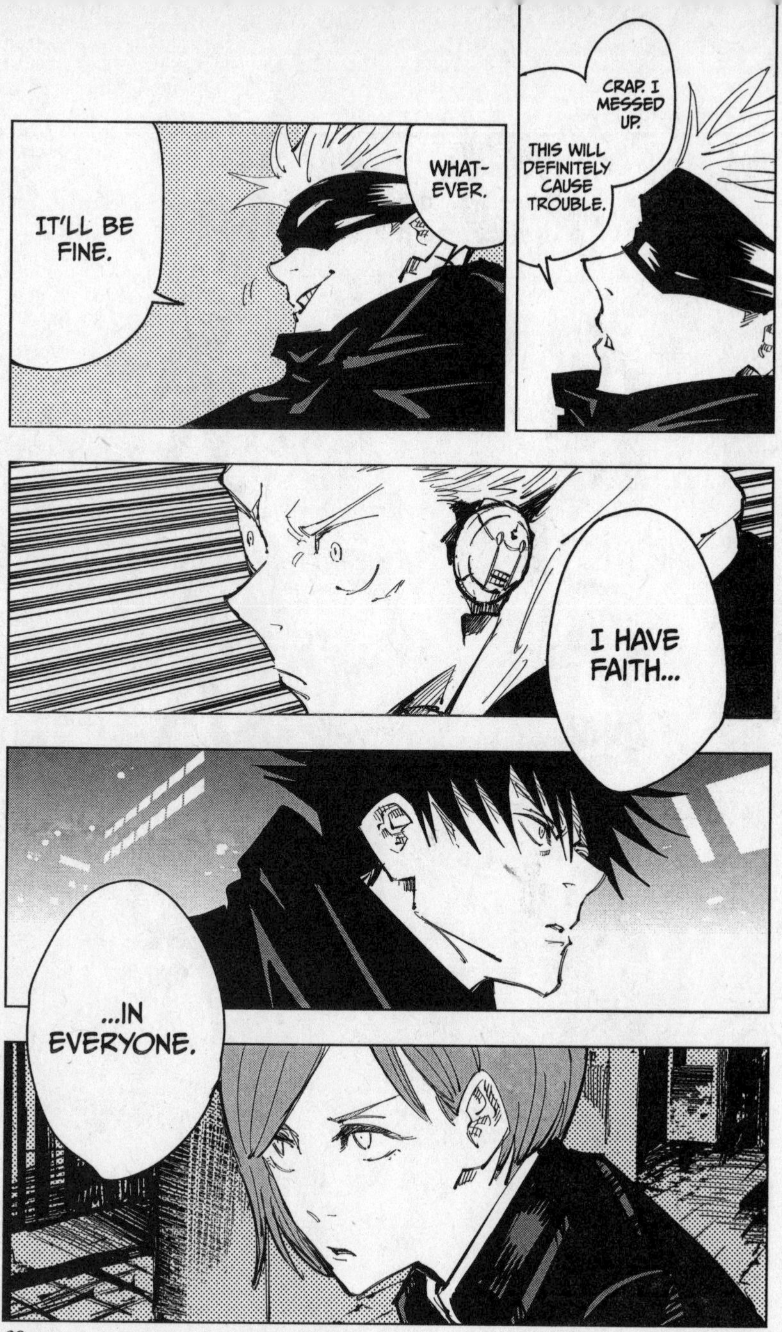
CRAP. I MESSED UP.
THIS WILL DEFINITELY CAUSE TROUBLE.
WHAT-EVER.
IT'LL BE FINE.
I HAVE FAITH...
...IN EVERYONE.

HOW TO USE PRISON REALM

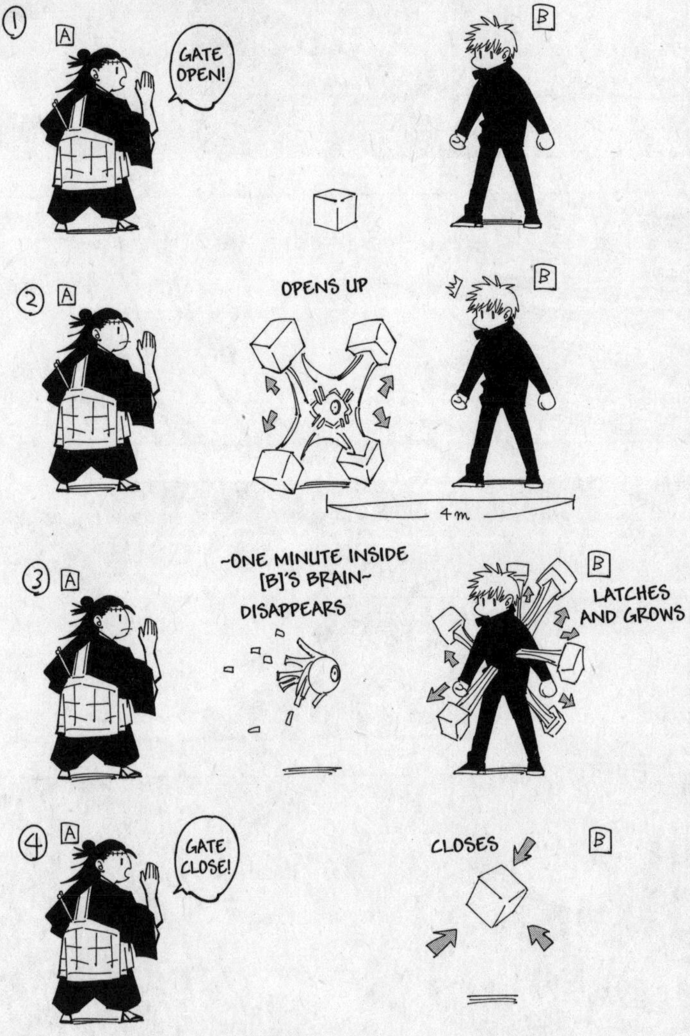

①
A
GATE OPEN!
B
②
A
OPENS UP
B
4m
③
A
~ONE MINUTE INSIDE [B]'S BRAIN~
DISAPPEARS
B
LATCHES AND GROWS
④
A
GATE CLOSE!
CLOSES
B

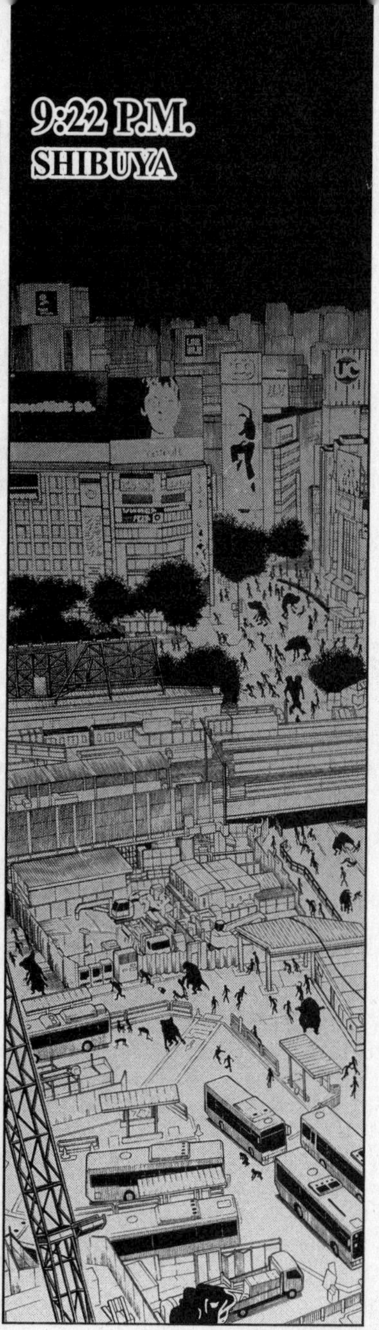
9:22 P.M.
SHIBUYA

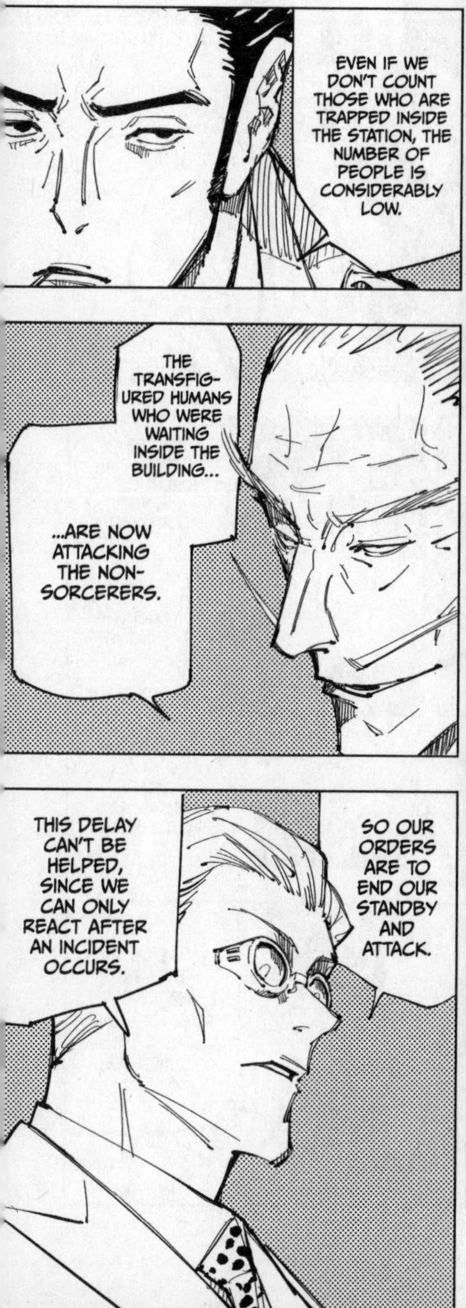
EVEN IF WE DON'T COUNT THOSE WHO ARE TRAPPED INSIDE THE STATION, THE NUMBER OF PEOPLE IS CONSIDERABLY LOW.
THE TRANSFIG-URED HUMANS WHO WERE WAITING INSIDE THE BUILDING...
...ARE NOW ATTACKING THE NON-SORCERERS.
SO OUR ORDERS ARE TO END OUR STANDBY AND ATTACK.
THIS DELAY CAN'T BE HELPED, SINCE WE CAN ONLY REACT AFTER AN INCIDENT OCCURS.

CHAPTER 92: THE SHIBUYA INCIDENT, PART 10

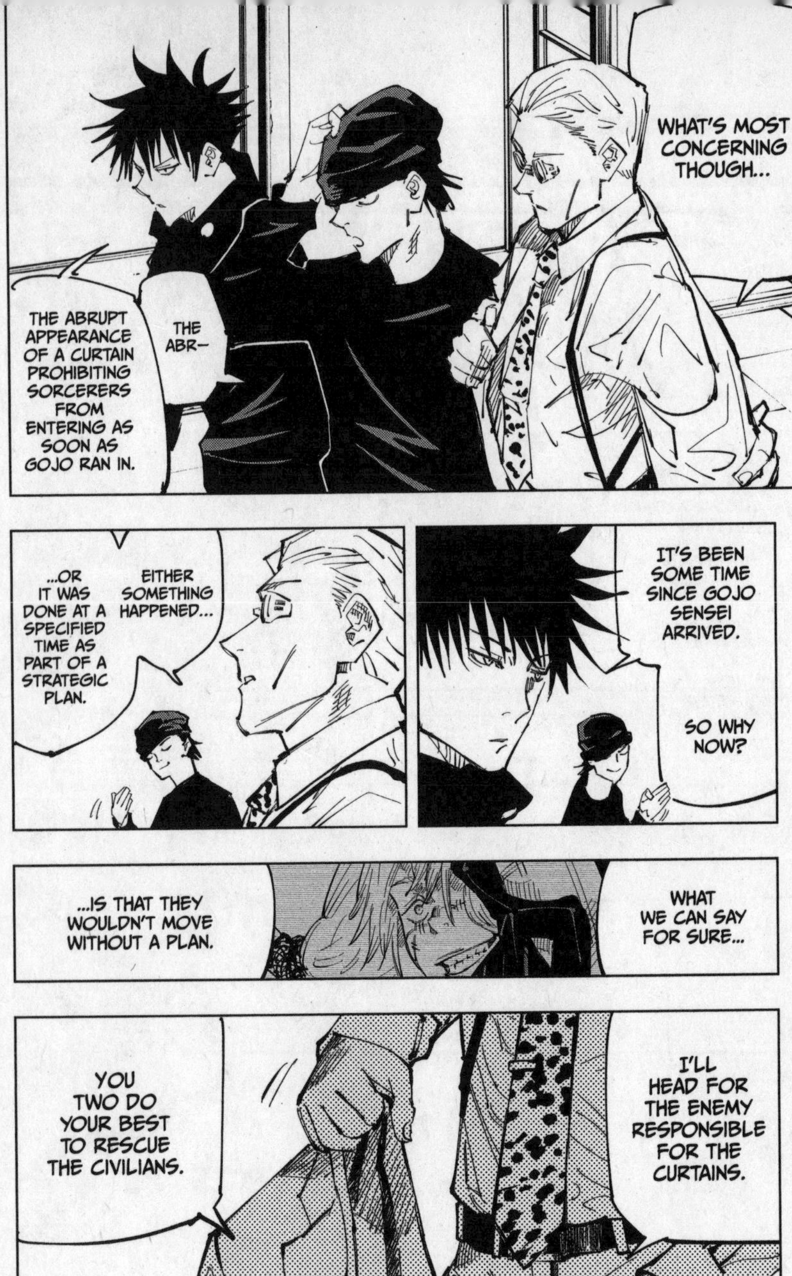
WHAT'S MOST CONCERNING THOUGH...
THE ABR—
THE ABRUPT APPEARANCE OF A CURTAIN PROHIBITING SORCERERS FROM ENTERING AS SOON AS GOJO RAN IN.
IT'S BEEN SOME TIME SINCE GOJO SENSEI ARRIVED.
SO WHY NOW?
EITHER SOMETHING HAPPENED...
...OR IT WAS DONE AT A SPECIFIED TIME AS PART OF A STRATEGIC PLAN.
WHAT WE CAN SAY FOR SURE...
...IS THAT THEY WOULDN'T MOVE WITHOUT A PLAN.
I'LL HEAD FOR THE ENEMY RESPONSIBLE FOR THE CURTAINS.
YOU TWO DO YOUR BEST TO RESCUE THE CIVILIANS.

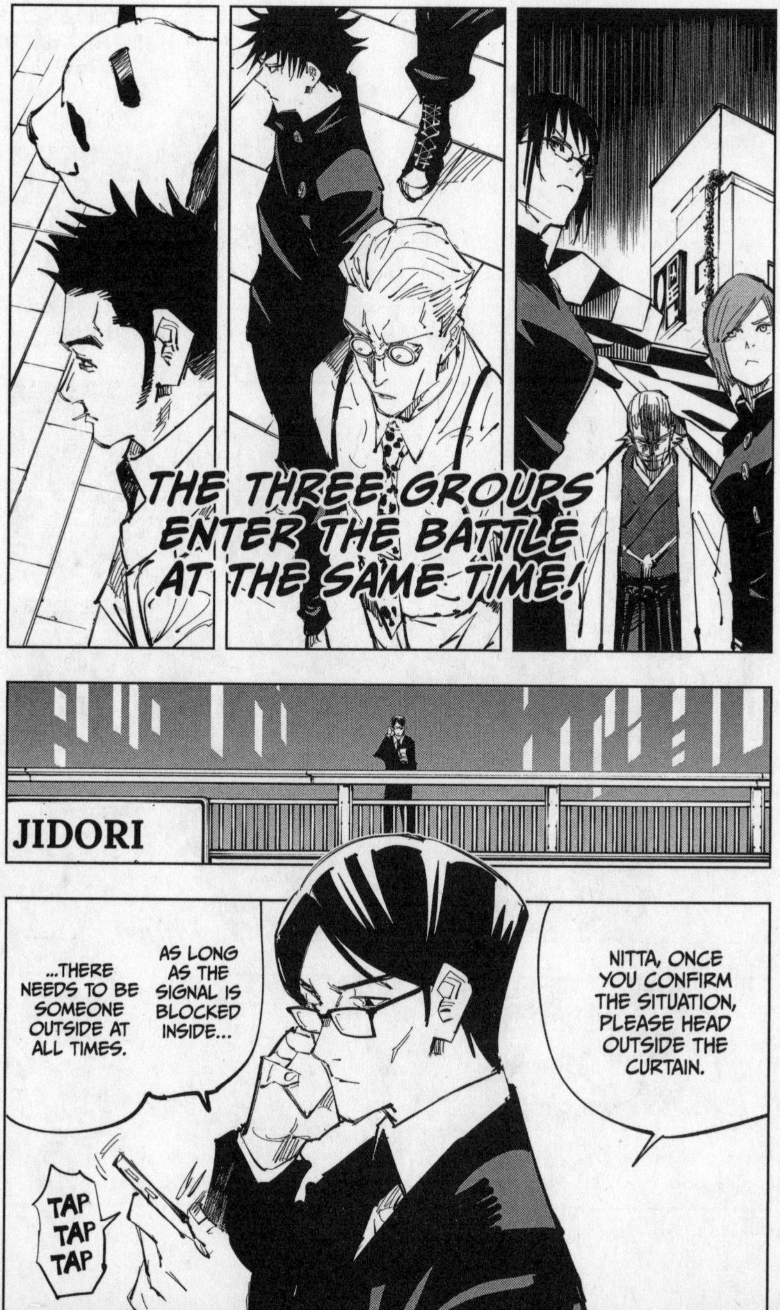
THE THREE GROUPS ENTER THE BATTLE AT THE SAME TIME!
JIDORI
NITTA, ONCE YOU CONFIRM THE SITUATION, PLEASE HEAD OUTSIDE THE CURTAIN.
AS LONG AS THE SIGNAL IS BLOCKED INSIDE...
...THERE NEEDS TO BE SOMEONE OUTSIDE AT ALL TIMES.
TAP TAP TAP

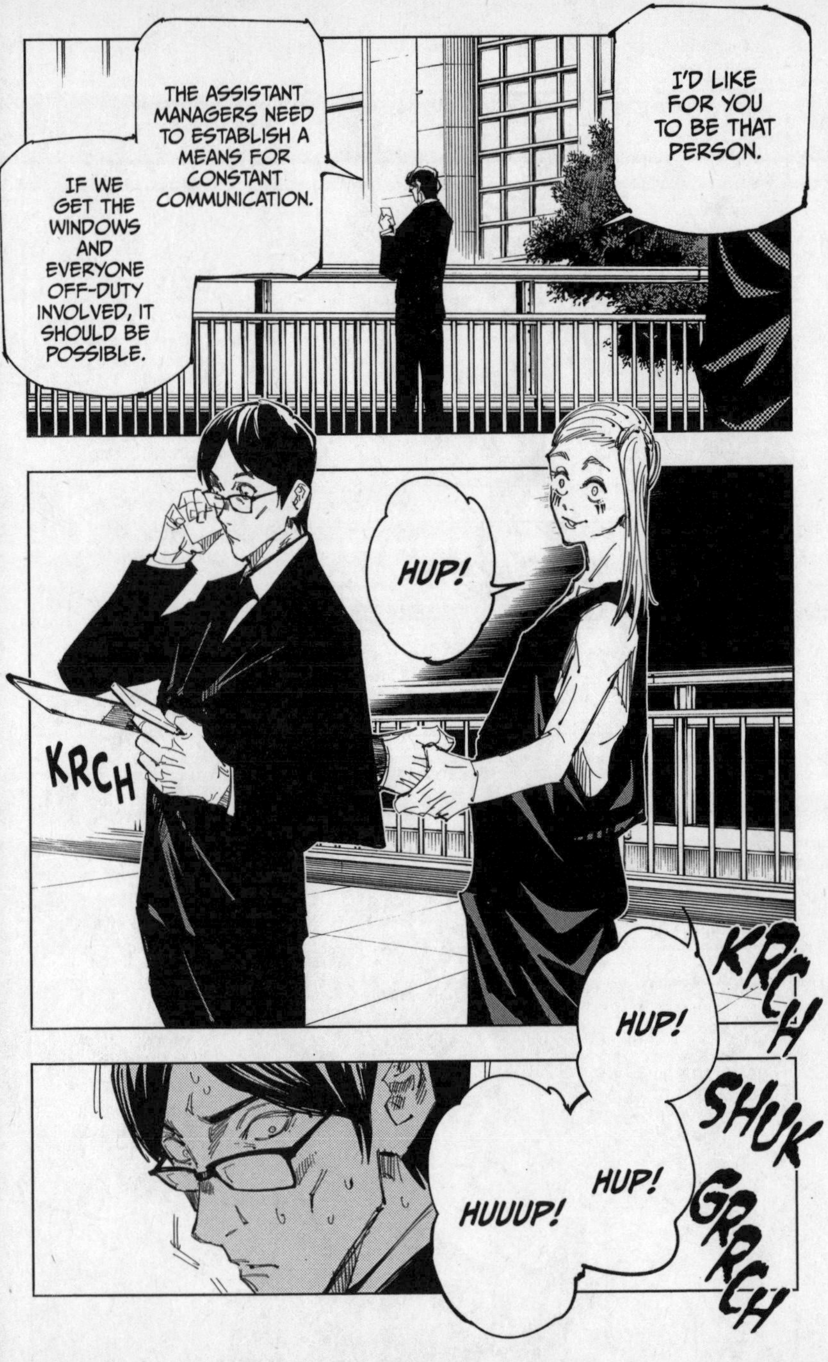
I'D LIKE FOR YOU TO BE THAT PERSON.
THE ASSISTANT MANAGERS NEED TO ESTABLISH A MEANS FOR CONSTANT COMMUNICATION.
IF WE GET THE WINDOWS AND EVERYONE OFF-DUTY INVOLVED, IT SHOULD BE POSSIBLE.
HUP!
KRCH
HUP!
KRCH
SHUK
GRRCH
HUP!
HUUUP!

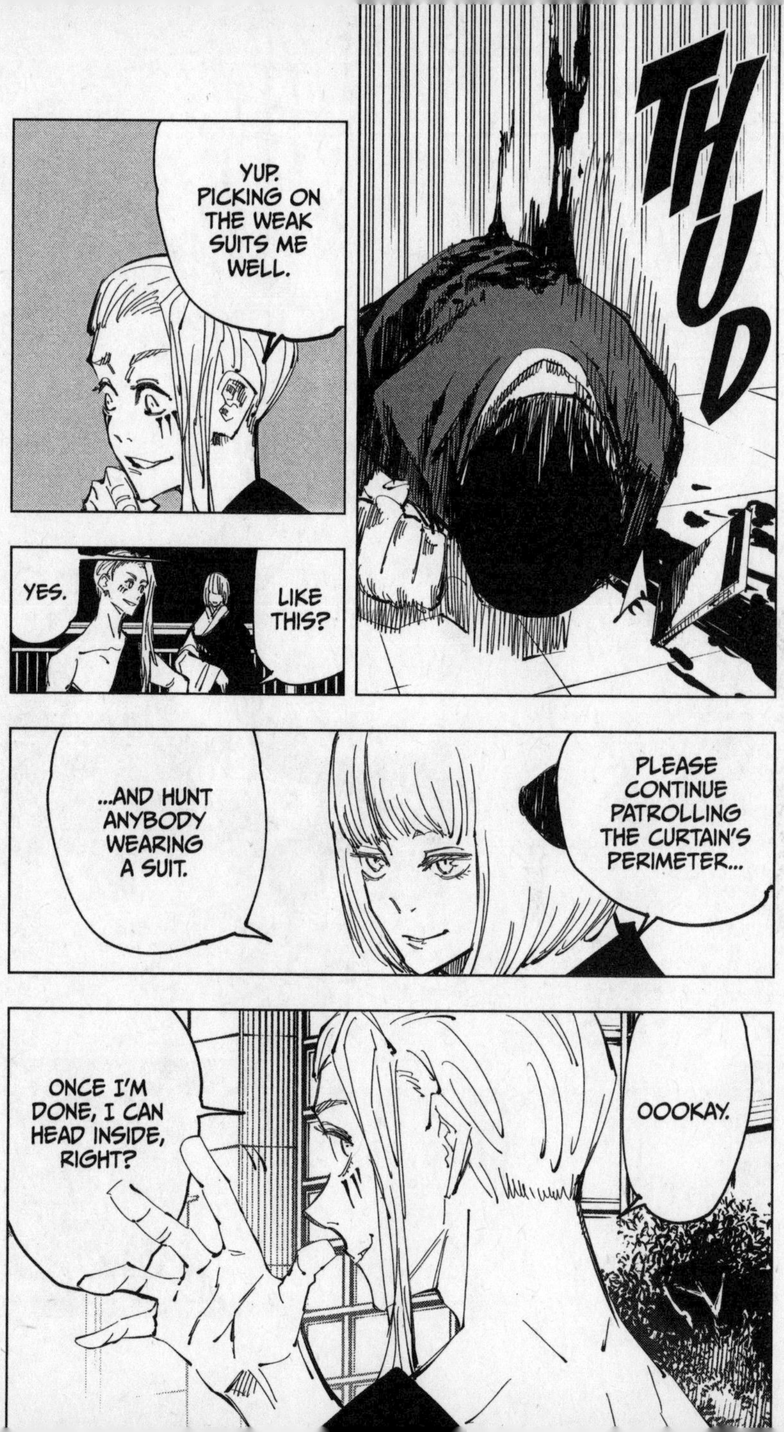
THUD
YUP. PICKING ON THE WEAK SUITS ME WELL.
LIKE THIS?
YES.
PLEASE CONTINUE PATROLLING THE CURTAIN'S PERIMETER...
...AND HUNT ANYBODY WEARING A SUIT.
OOOKAY.
ONCE I'M DONE, I CAN HEAD INSIDE, RIGHT?

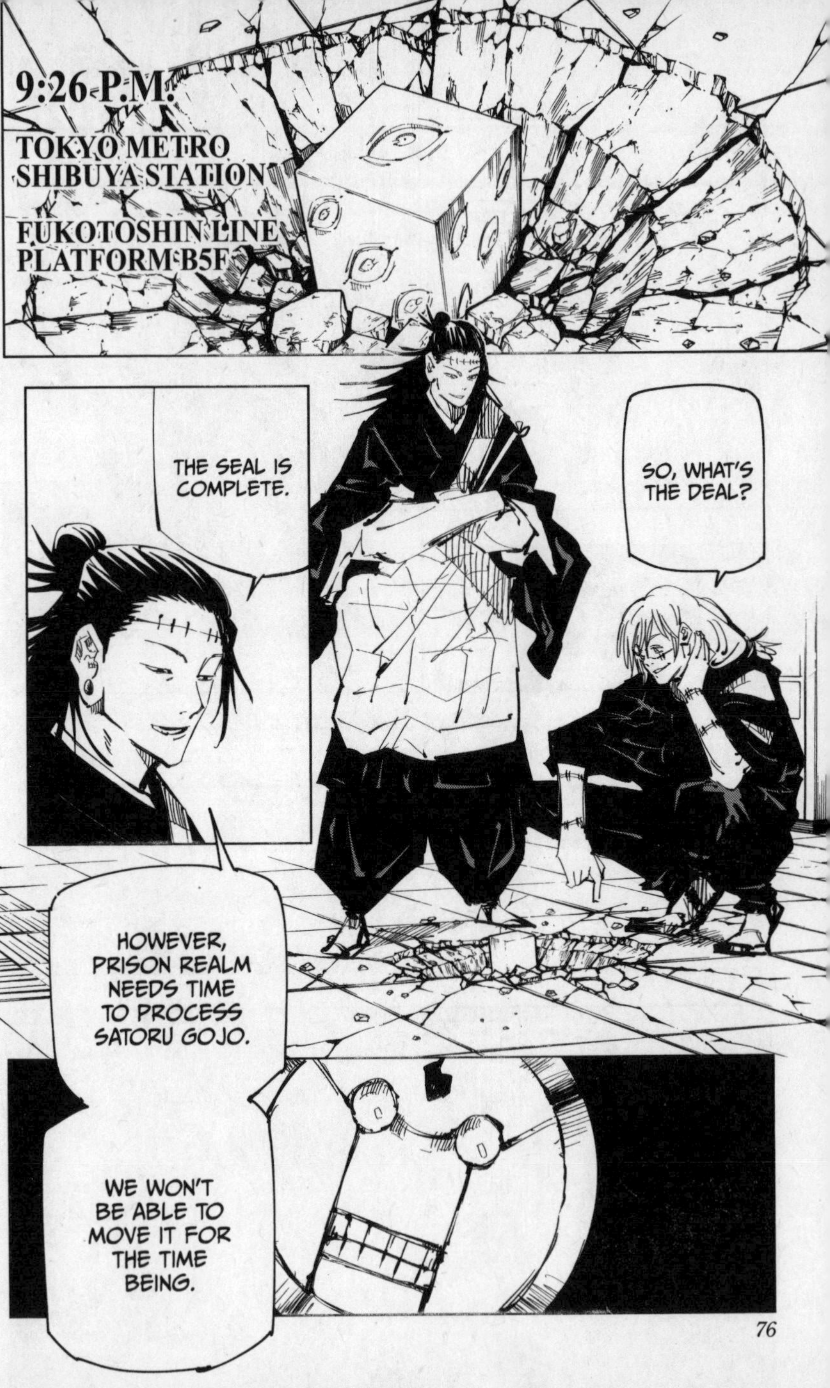
9:26 P.M.
TOKYO METRO SHIBUYA STATION
FUKOTOSHIN LINE PLATFORM B5F
SO, WHAT'S THE DEAL?
THE SEAL IS COMPLETE.
HOWEVER, PRISON REALM NEEDS TIME TO PROCESS SATORU GOJO.
WE WON'T BE ABLE TO MOVE IT FOR THE TIME BEING.

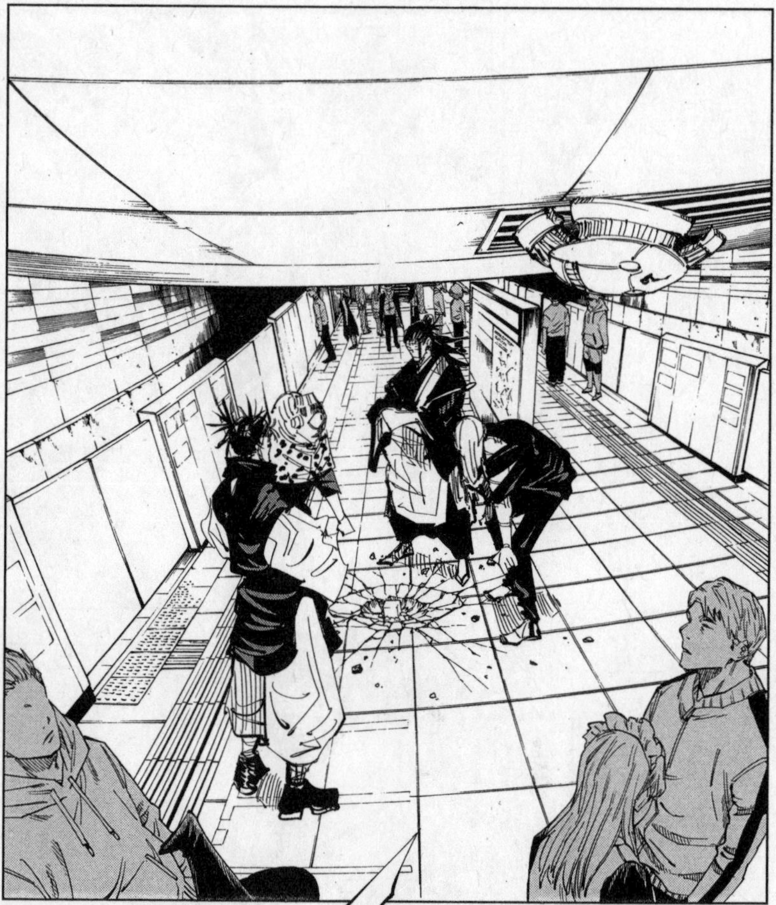
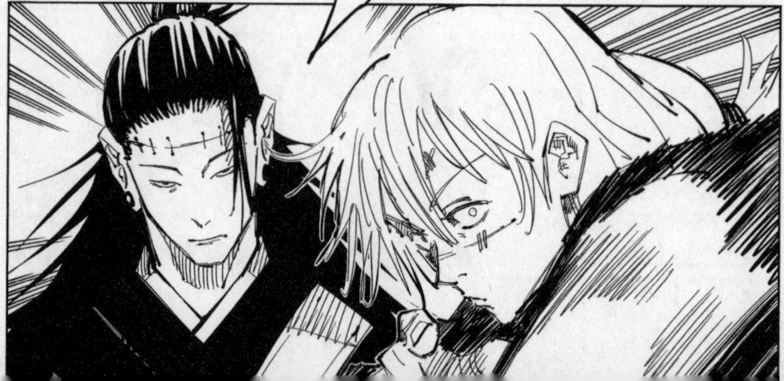

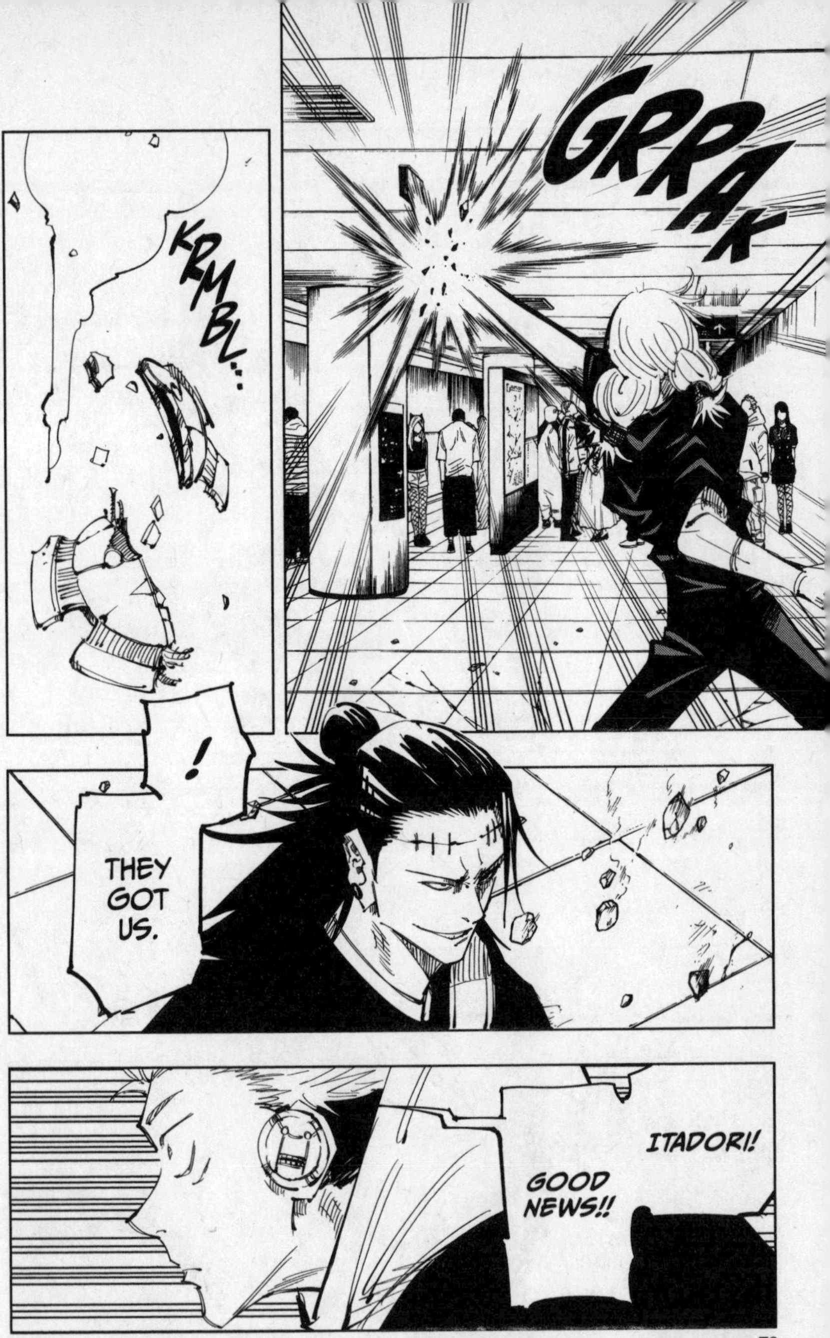
GRRAK
KRMBL...
!
THEY GOT US.
ITADORI!
GOOD NEWS!!

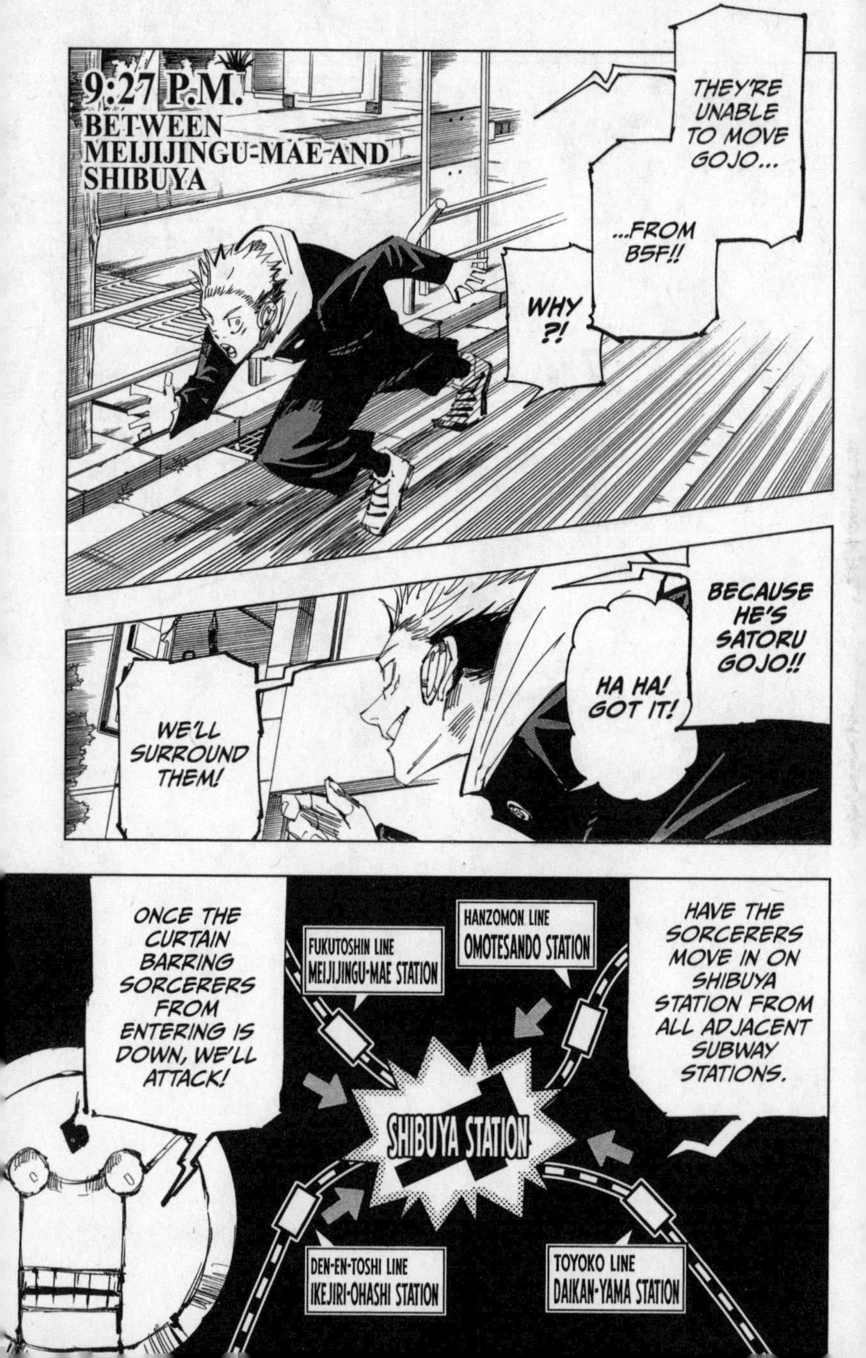
THEY'RE UNABLE TO MOVE GOJO...
...FROM B5F!!
9:27 P.M.
BETWEEN MEIJIJINGU-MAE AND SHIBUYA
WHY?!
BECAUSE HE'S SATORU GOJO!!
HA HA! GOT IT!
WE'LL SURROUND THEM!
HAVE THE SORCERERS MOVE IN ON SHIBUYA STATION FROM ALL ADJACENT SUBWAY STATIONS.
HANZOMON LINE OMOTESANDO STATION
FUKUTOSHIN LINE MEIJIJINGU-MAE STATION
SHIBUYA STATION
TOYOKO LINE DAIKAN-YAMA STATION
DEN-EN-TOSHI LINE IKEJIRI-OHASHI STATION
ONCE THE CURTAIN BARRING SORCERERS FROM ENTERING IS DOWN, WE'LL ATTACK!

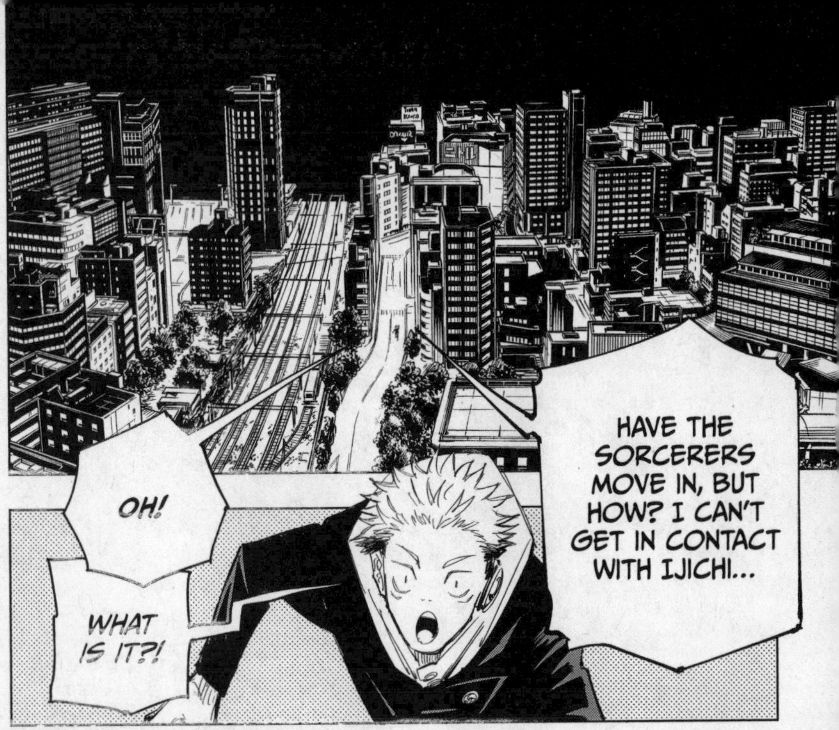
HAVE THE SORCERERS MOVE IN, BUT HOW? I CAN'T GET IN CONTACT WITH IJICHI...
OH!
WHAT IS IT?!
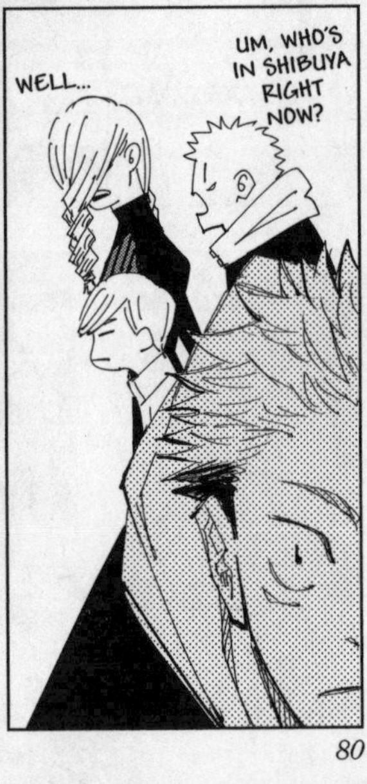
UM, WHO'S IN SHIBUYA RIGHT NOW?
WELL...
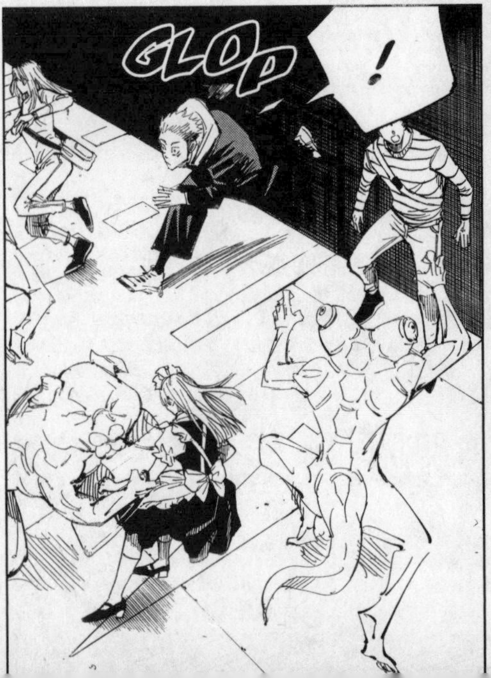
!
GLOP

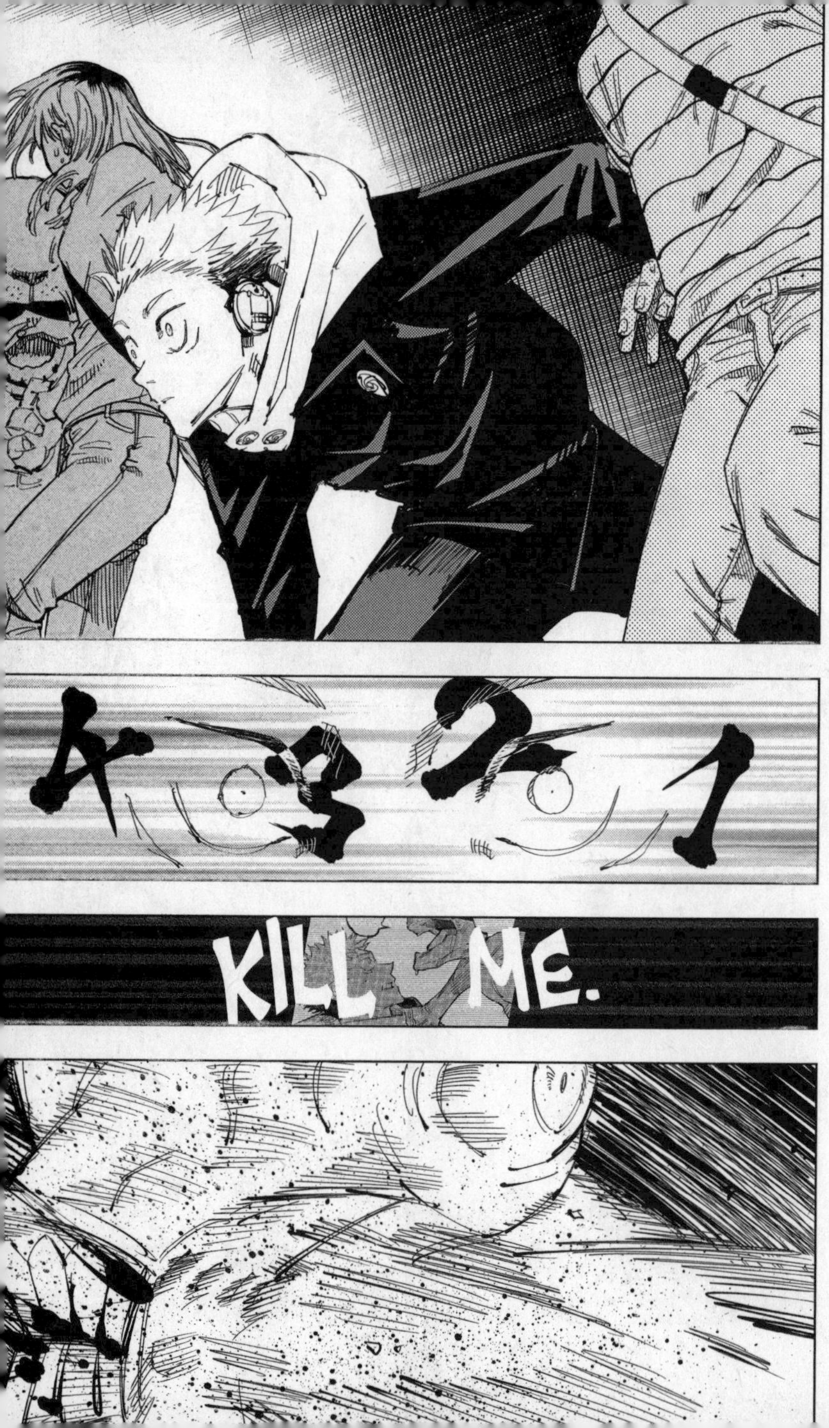
4 3 2 1
KILL ME.

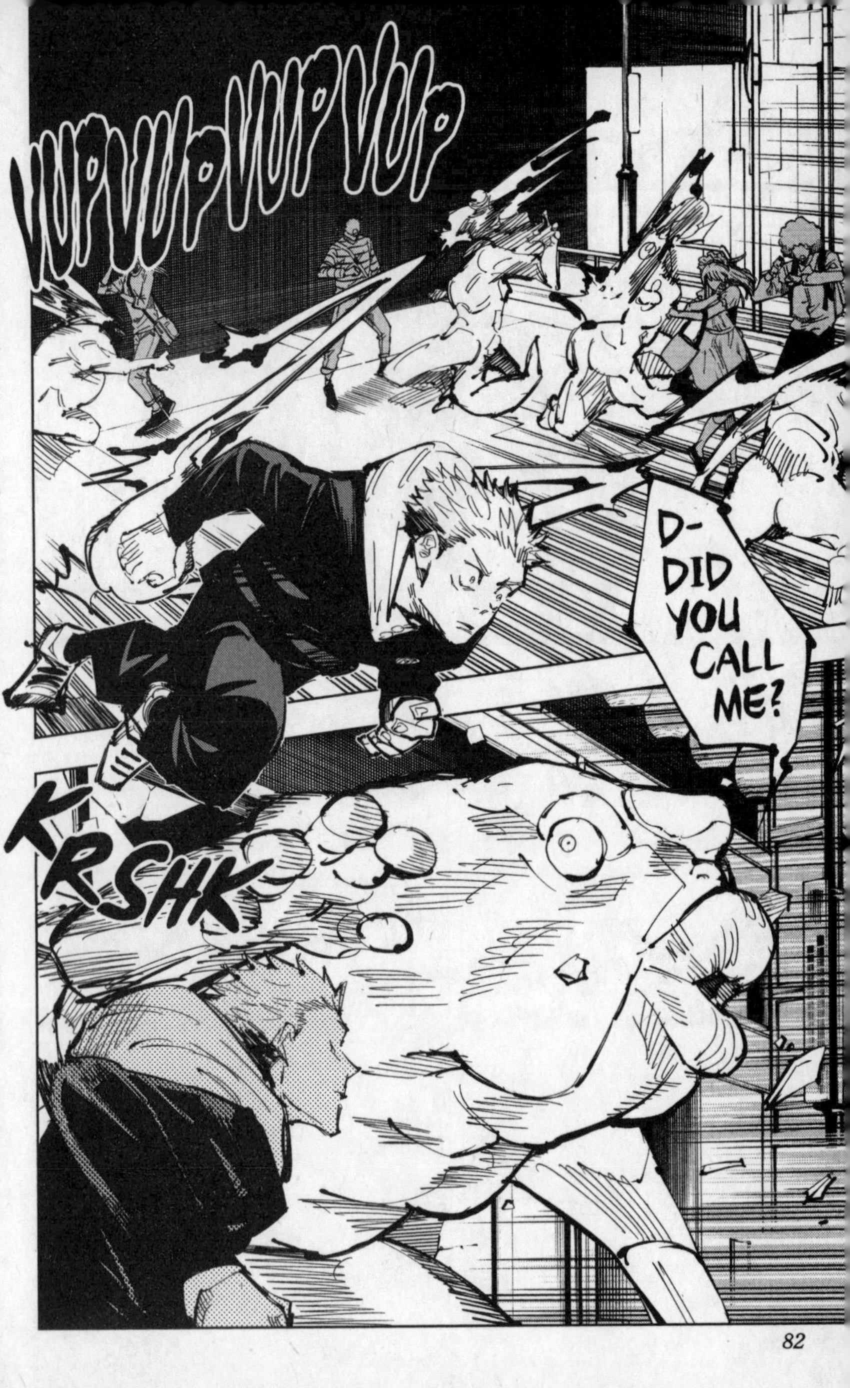
VUP VUP VUP VUP
D-DID YOU CALL ME?
KRSHK

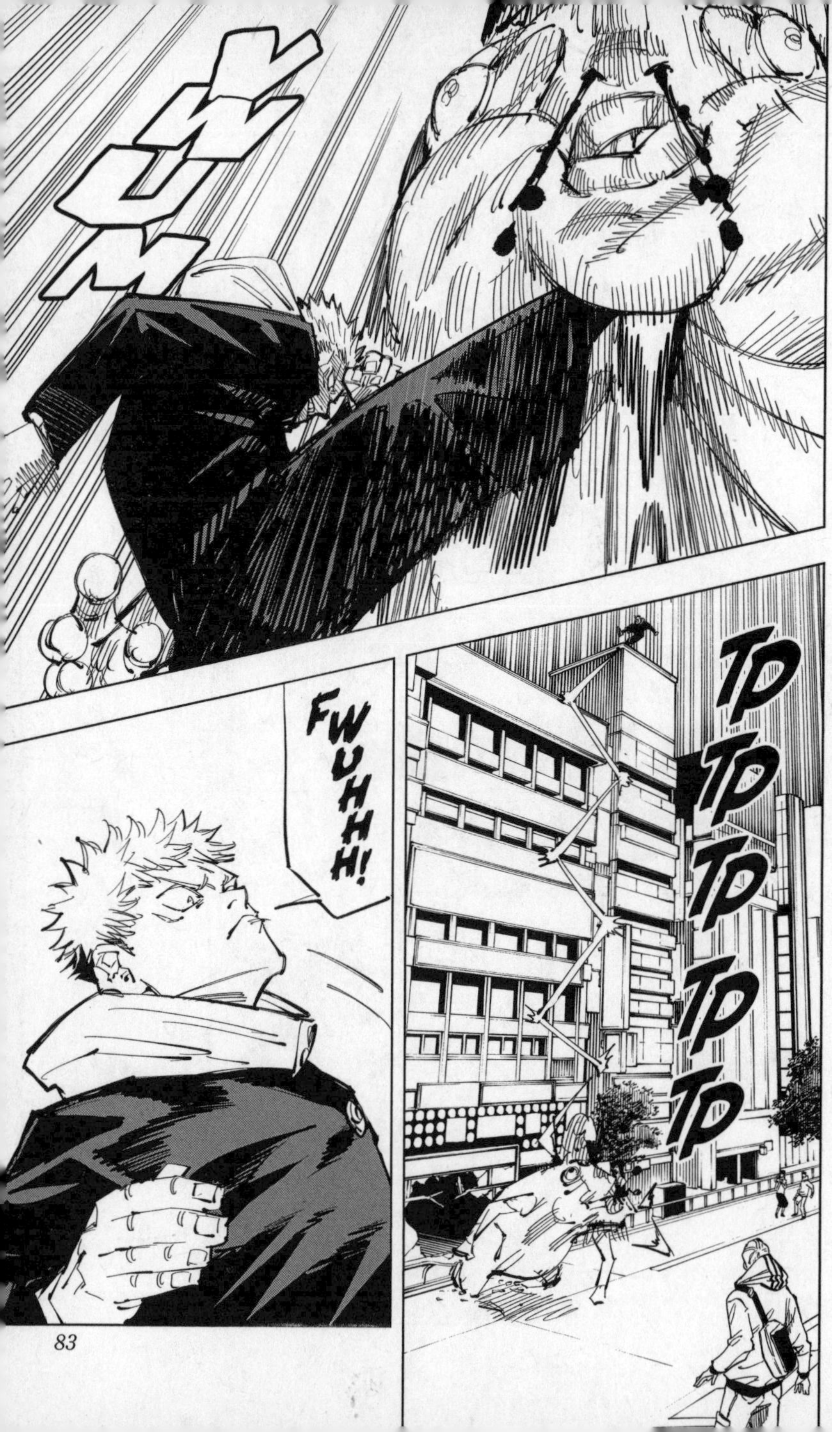
VWUM
TP TP TP TP TP TP
FWUHHH!

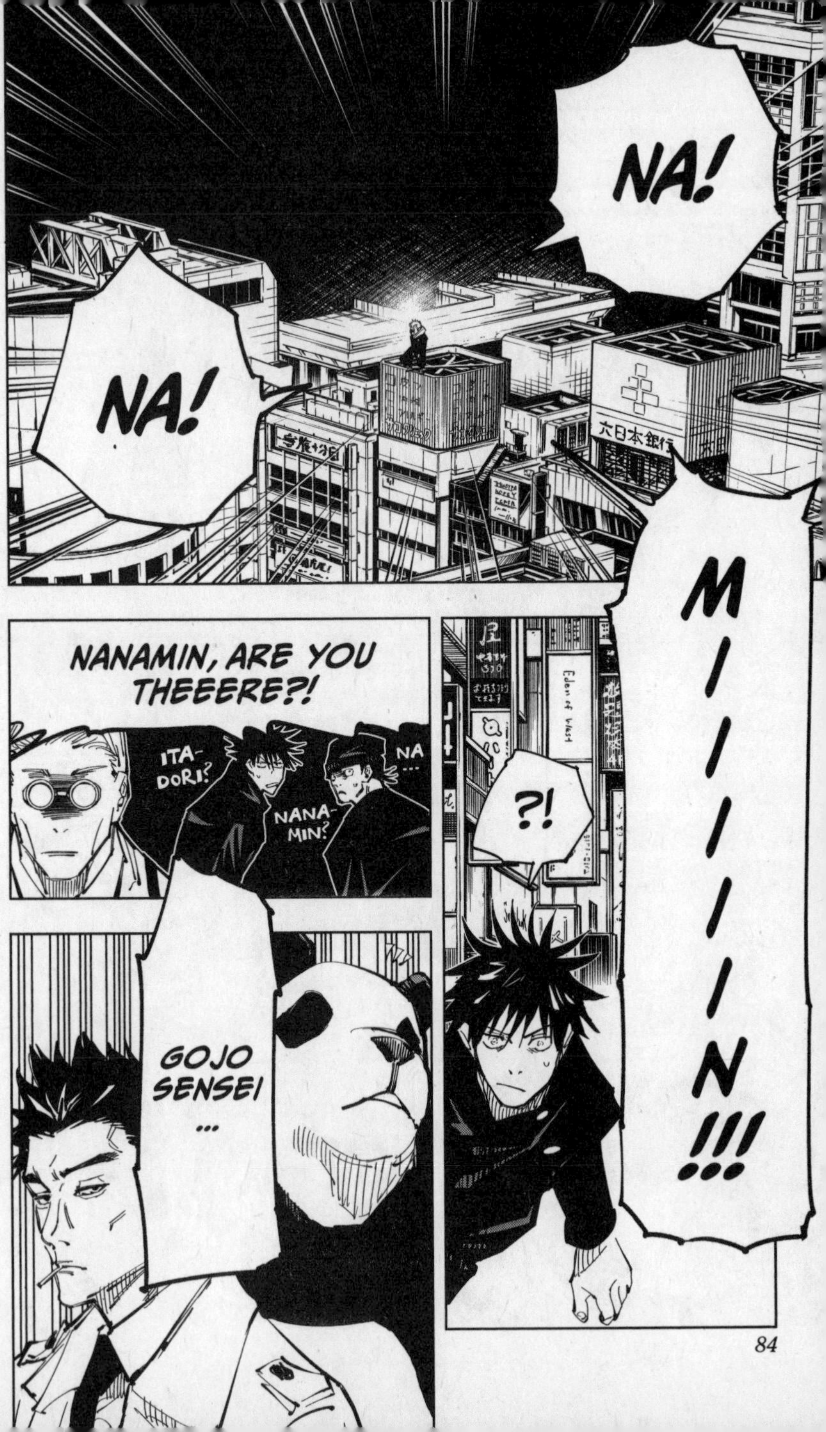
NA!
NA!
MIIIIIN!!!
?!
NANAMIN, ARE YOU THEEERE?!
NA...
NANAMIN?
ITADORI?
GOJO SENSEI...

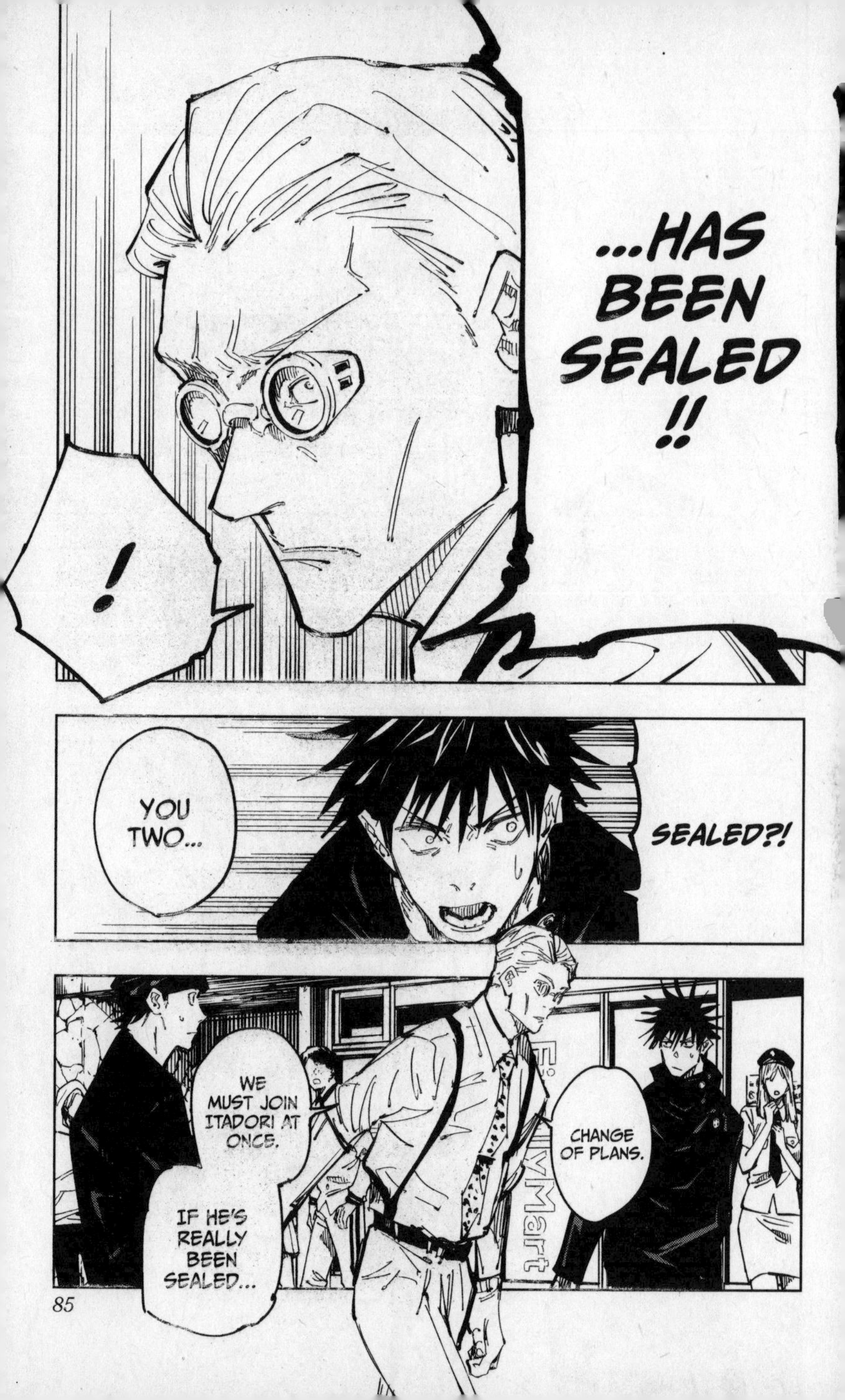
...HAS BEEN SEALED!!
!
SEALED?!
YOU TWO...
CHANGE OF PLANS.
WE MUST JOIN ITADORI AT ONCE.
IF HE'S REALLY BEEN SEALED...

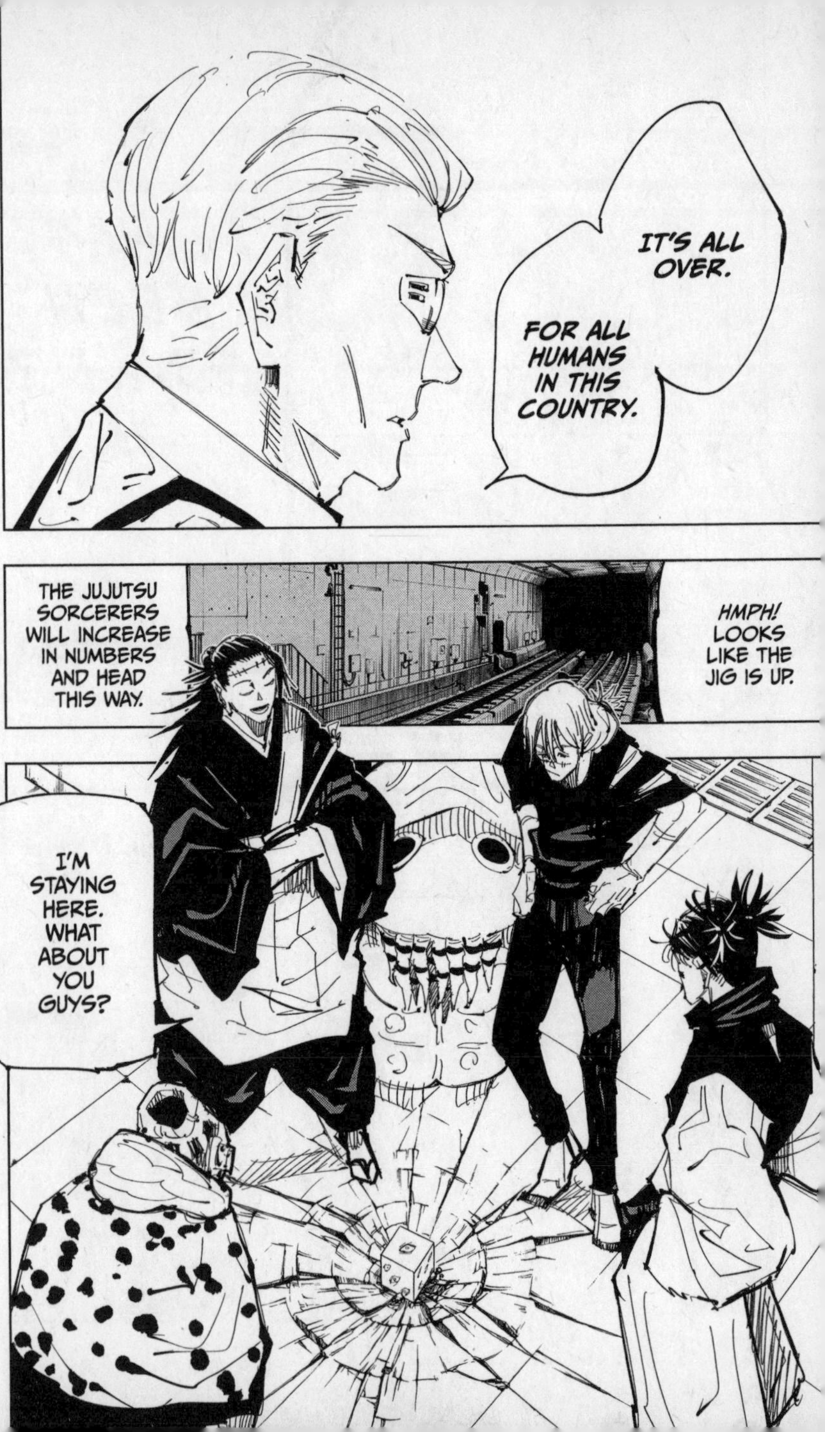
IT'S ALL OVER.
FOR ALL HUMANS IN THIS COUNTRY.
HMPH! LOOKS LIKE THE JIG IS UP.
THE JUJUTSU SORCERERS WILL INCREASE IN NUMBERS AND HEAD THIS WAY.
I'M STAYING HERE. WHAT ABOUT YOU GUYS?

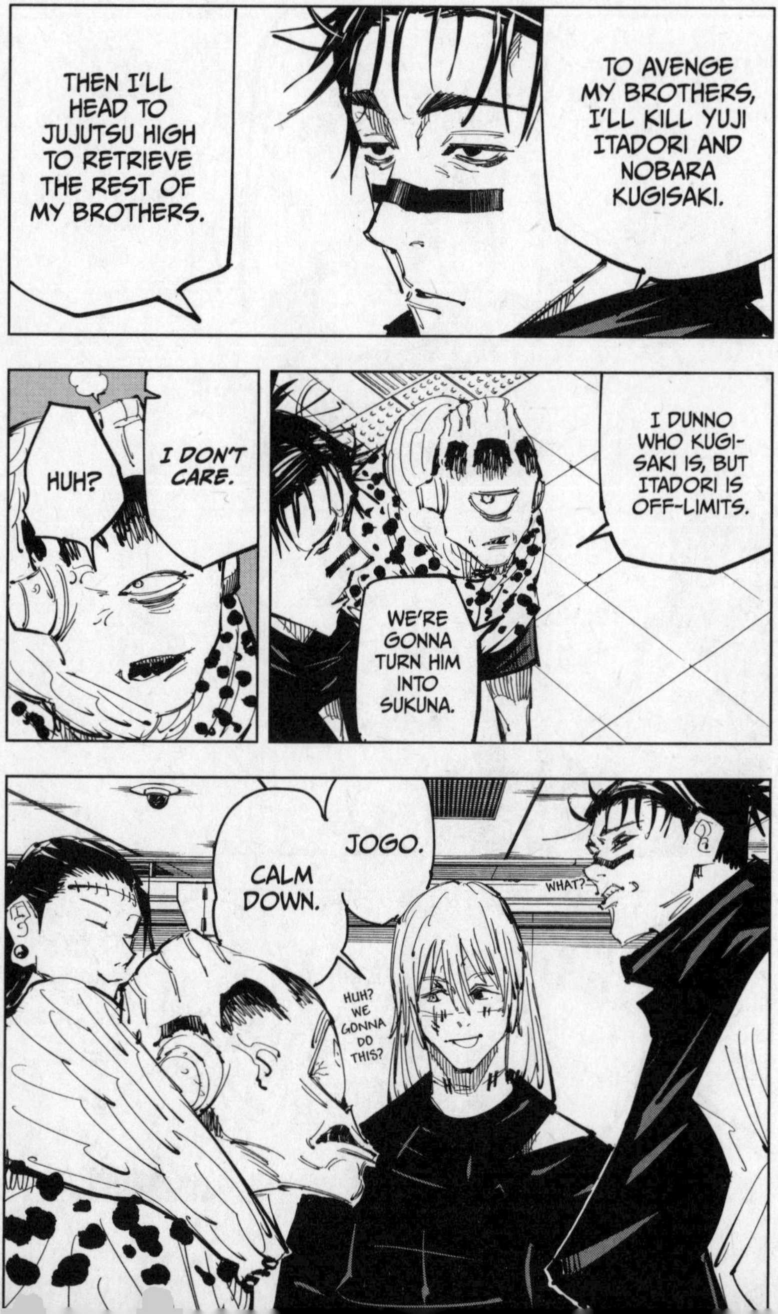
TO AVENGE MY BROTHERS, I'LL KILL YUJI ITADORI AND NOBARA KUGISAKI.
THEN I'LL HEAD TO JUJUTSU HIGH TO RETRIEVE THE REST OF MY BROTHERS.
I DUNNO WHO KUGI-SAKI IS, BUT ITADORI IS OFF-LIMITS.
WE'RE GONNA TURN HIM INTO SUKUNA.
I DON'T CARE.
HUH?
JOGO.
CALM DOWN.
WHAT?
HUH? WE GONNA DO THIS?

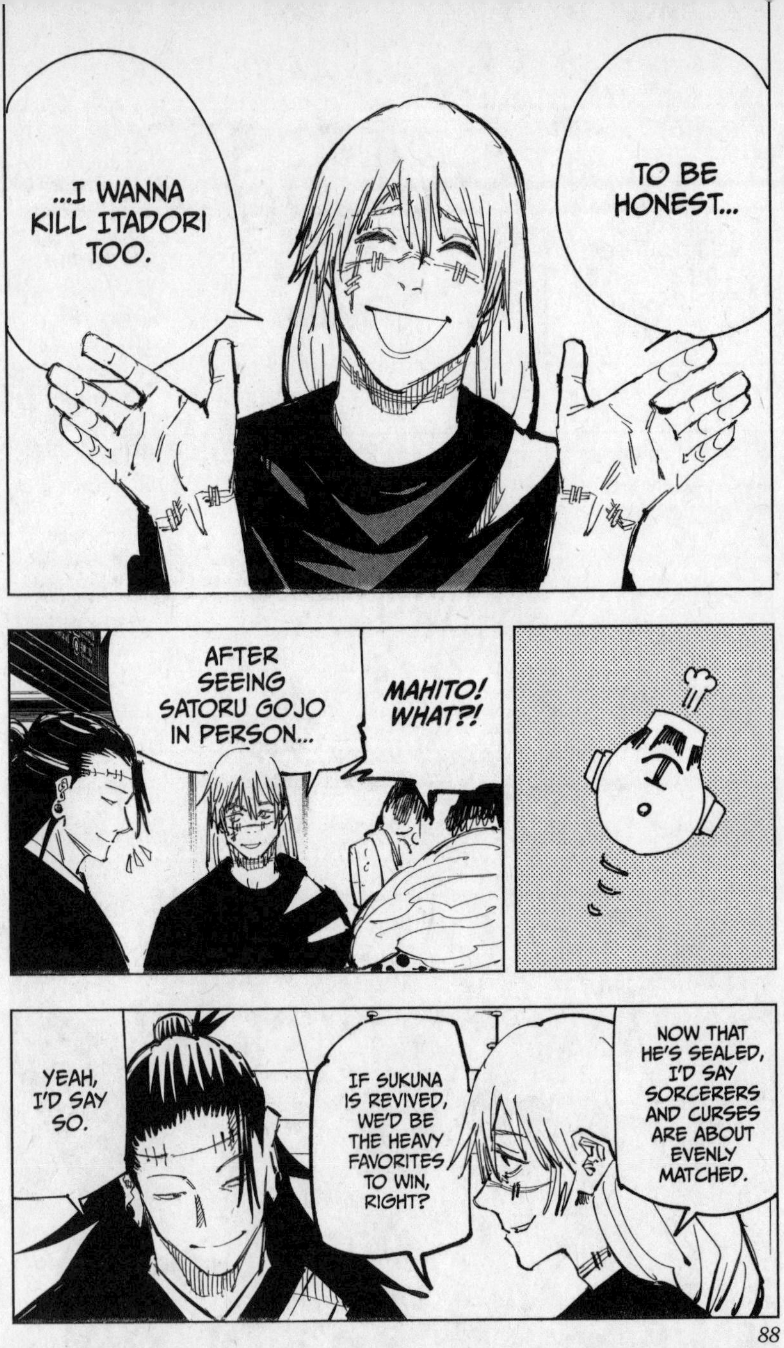
TO BE HONEST...
...I WANNA KILL ITADORI TOO.
MAHITO! WHAT?!
AFTER SEEING SATORU GOJO IN PERSON...
NOW THAT HE'S SEALED, I'D SAY SORCERERS AND CURSES ARE ABOUT EVENLY MATCHED.
IF SUKUNA IS REVIVED, WE'D BE THE HEAVY FAVORITES TO WIN, RIGHT?
YEAH, I'D SAY SO.

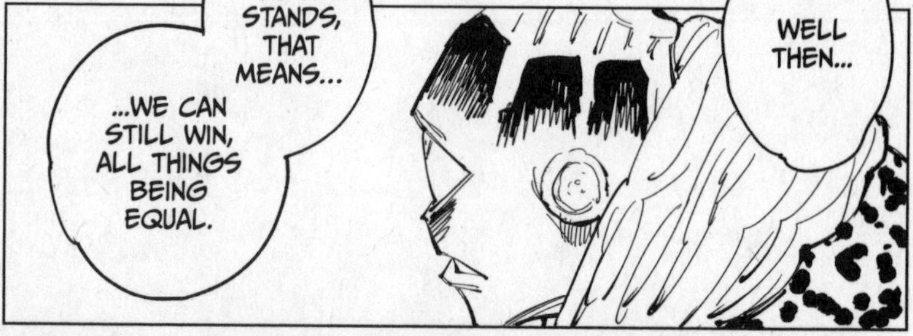
WELL THEN...
AS IT STANDS, THAT MEANS...
...WE CAN STILL WIN, ALL THINGS BEING EQUAL.
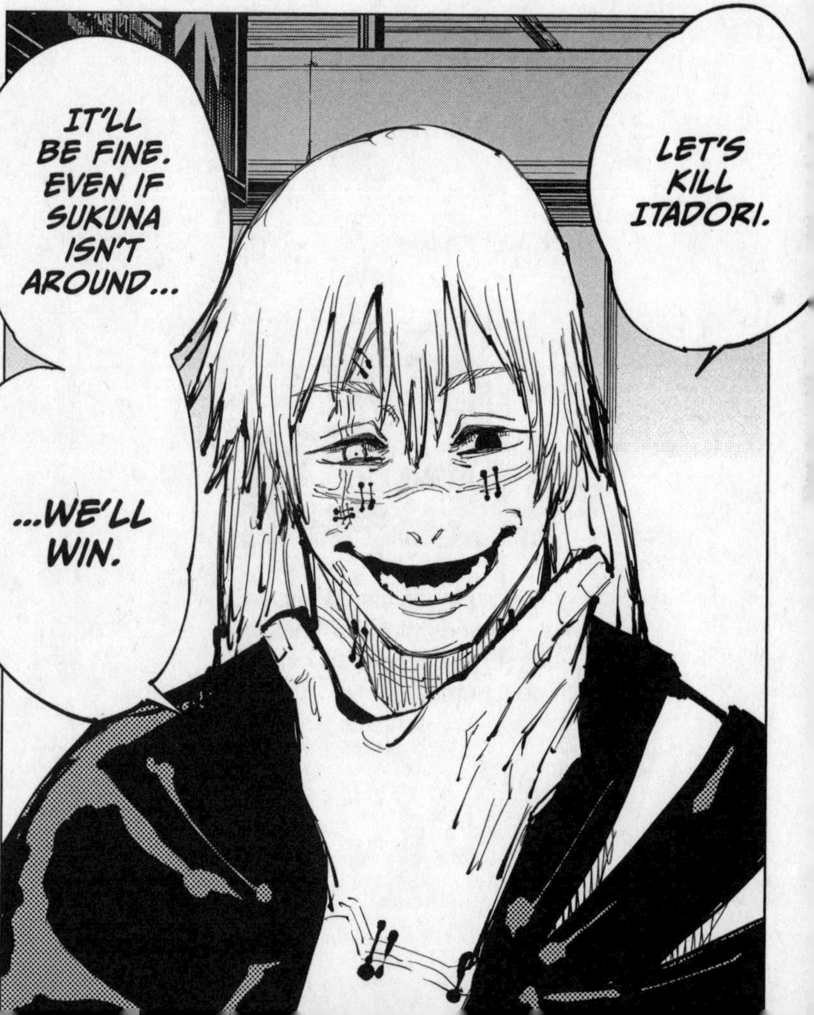
LET'S KILL ITADORI.
IT'LL BE FINE. EVEN IF SUKUNA ISN'T AROUND...
...WE'LL WIN.

Scenes I was planning on addressing but forgot about until now, part 3

• Subway routes

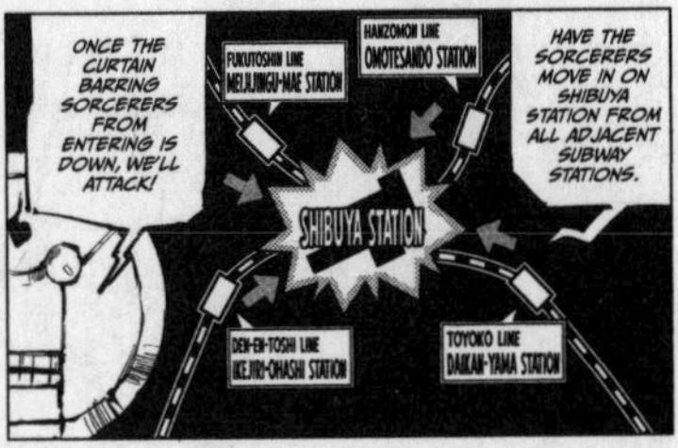
HAVE THE SORCERERS MOVE IN ON SHIBUYA STATION FROM ALL ADJACENT SUBWAY STATIONS.
HANZOMON LINE OMOTESANDO STATION
FUKUTOSHIN LINE MEIJIJINGU-MAE STATION
SHIBUYA STATION
TOYOKO LINE DAIKAN-YAMA STATION
DEN-EN-TOSHI LINE IKEJIRI-OHASHI STATION
ONCE THE CURTAIN BARRING SORCERERS FROM ENTERING IS DOWN, WE'LL ATTACK!

The Ginza Line is also a subway line, but it goes through Shibuya Station aboveground, so I didn't include it here.

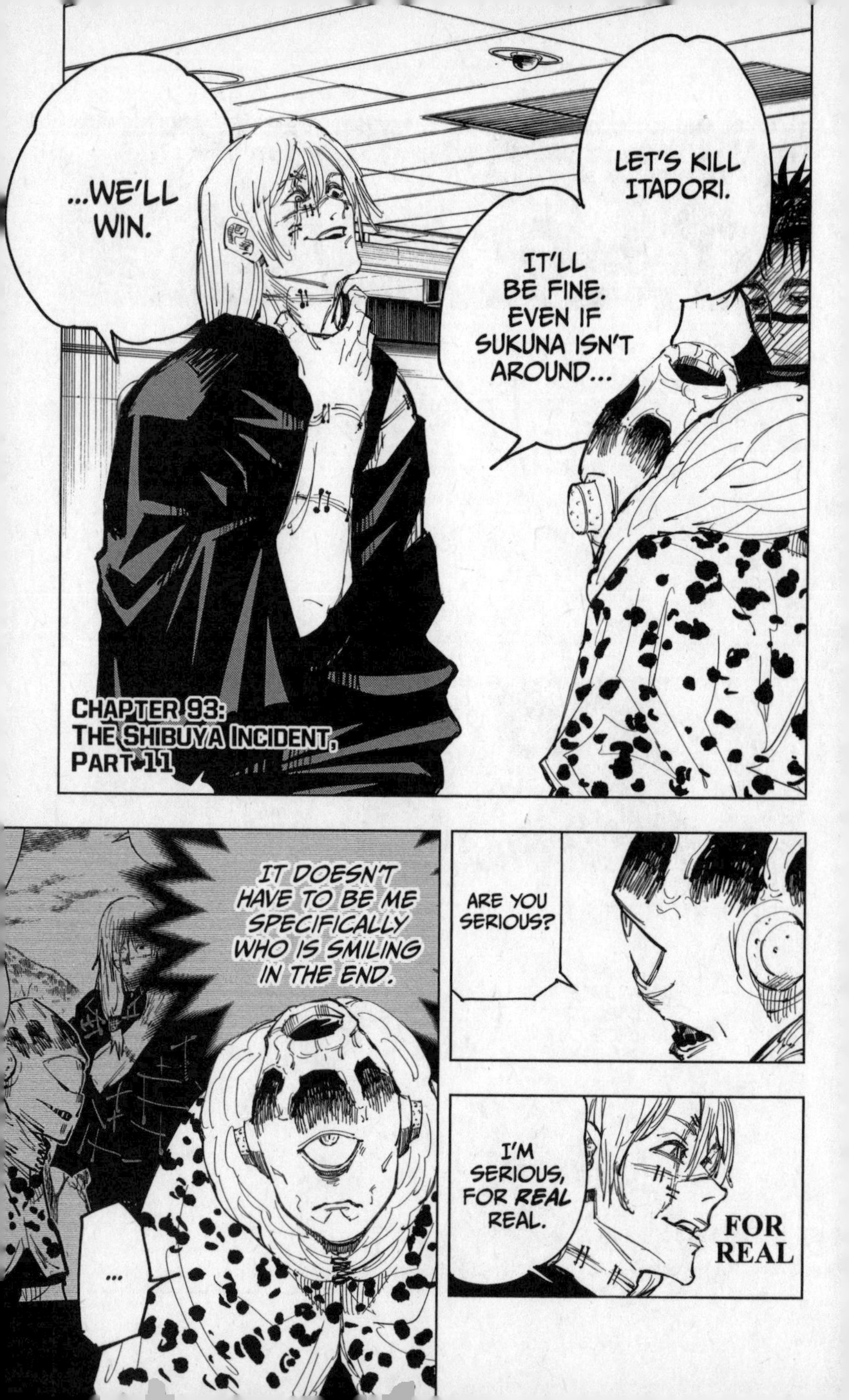
LET'S KILL ITADORI.
IT'LL BE FINE. EVEN IF SUKUNA ISN'T AROUND...
...WE'LL WIN.
CHAPTER 93: THE SHIBUYA INCIDENT, PART 11
ARE YOU SERIOUS?
I'M SERIOUS, FOR REAL REAL.
FOR REAL
IT DOESN'T HAVE TO BE ME SPECIFICALLY WHO IS SMILING IN THE END.
...

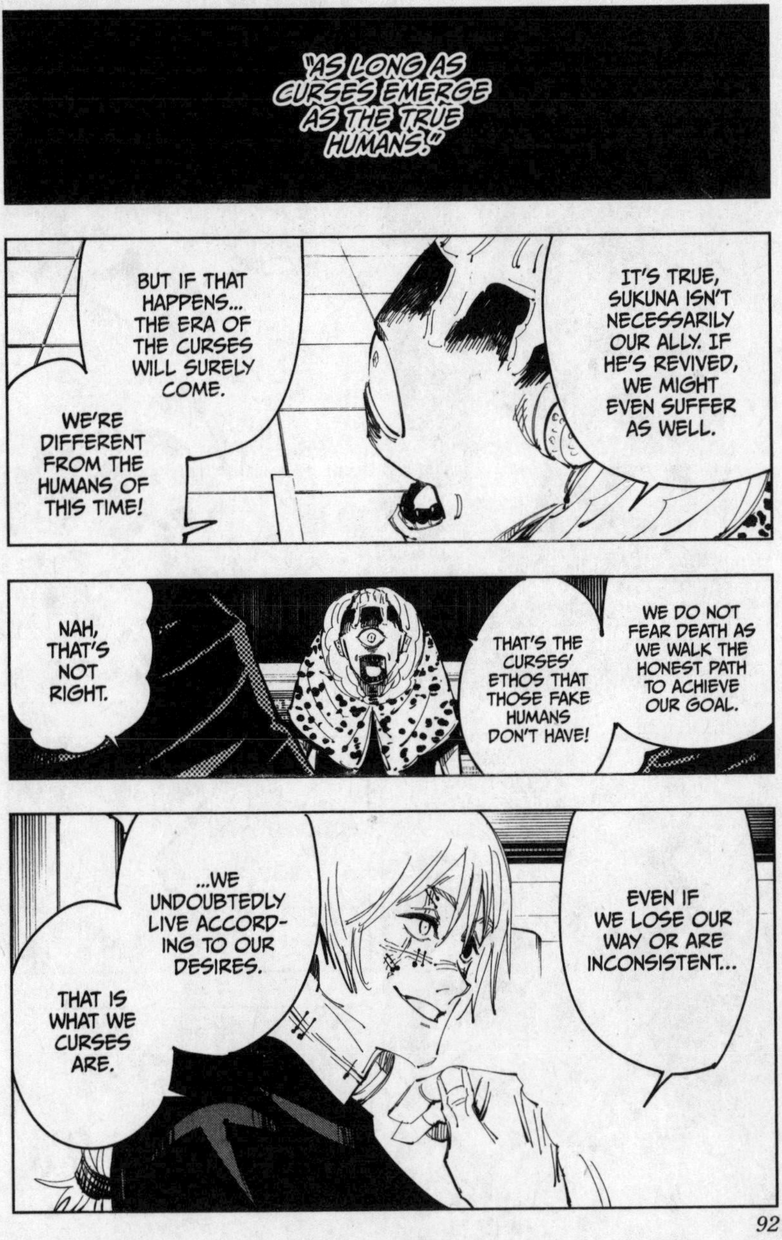
"AS LONG AS CURSES EMERGE AS THE TRUE HUMANS."
IT'S TRUE, SUKUNA ISN'T NECESSARILY OUR ALLY. IF HE'S REVIVED, WE MIGHT EVEN SUFFER AS WELL.
BUT IF THAT HAPPENS... THE ERA OF THE CURSES WILL SURELY COME.
WE'RE DIFFERENT FROM THE HUMANS OF THIS TIME!
WE DO NOT FEAR DEATH AS WE WALK THE HONEST PATH TO ACHIEVE OUR GOAL.
THAT'S THE CURSES' ETHOS THAT THOSE FAKE HUMANS DON'T HAVE!
NAH, THAT'S NOT RIGHT.
EVEN IF WE LOSE OUR WAY OR ARE INCONSISTENT...
...WE UNDOUBTEDLY LIVE ACCORD-ING TO OUR DESIRES.
THAT IS WHAT WE CURSES ARE.

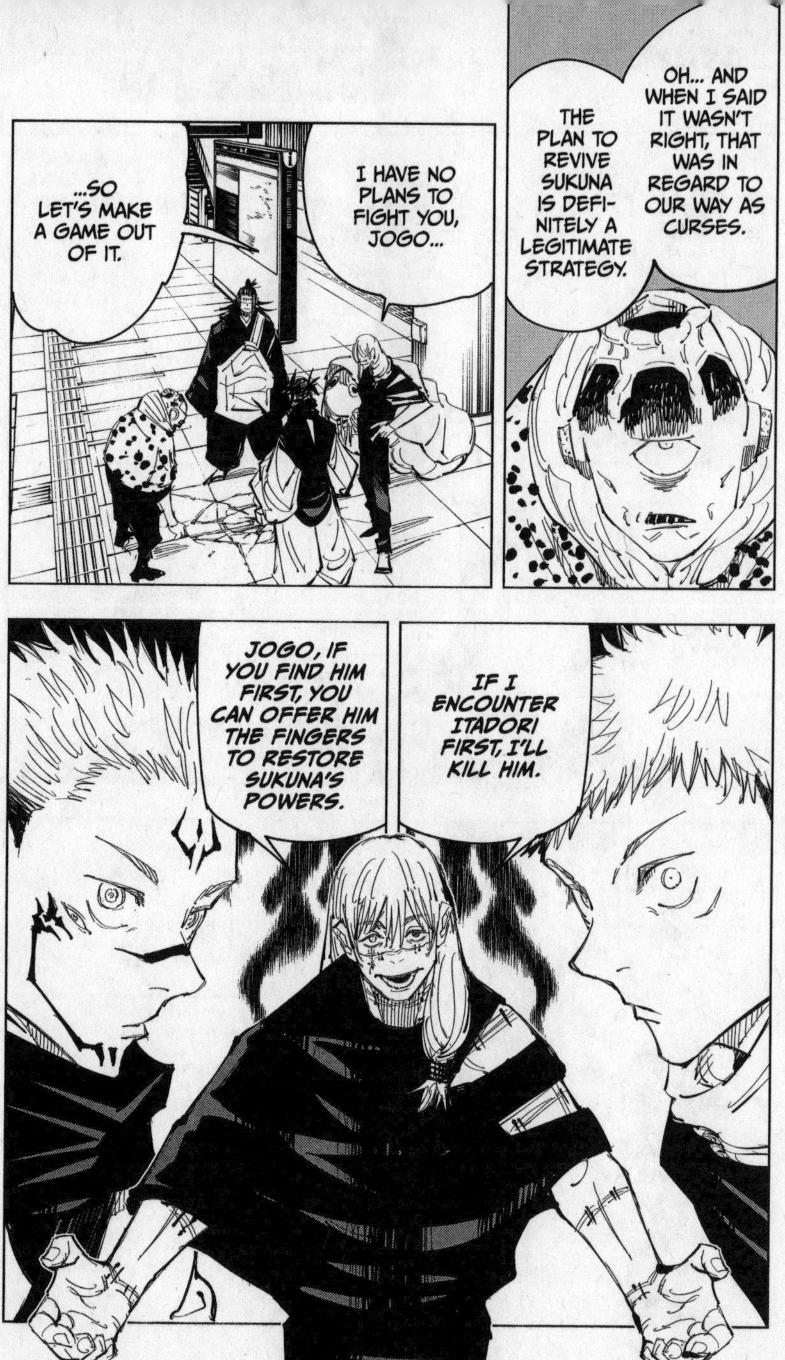
OH... AND WHEN I SAID IT WASN'T RIGHT, THAT WAS IN REGARD TO OUR WAY AS CURSES.
THE PLAN TO REVIVE SUKUNA IS DEFI- NITELY A LEGITIMATE STRATEGY.
I HAVE NO PLANS TO FIGHT YOU, JOGO...
...SO LET'S MAKE A GAME OUT OF IT.
IF I ENCOUNTER ITADORI FIRST, I'LL KILL HIM.
JOGO, IF YOU FIND HIM FIRST, YOU CAN OFFER HIM THE FINGERS TO RESTORE SUKUNA'S POWERS.

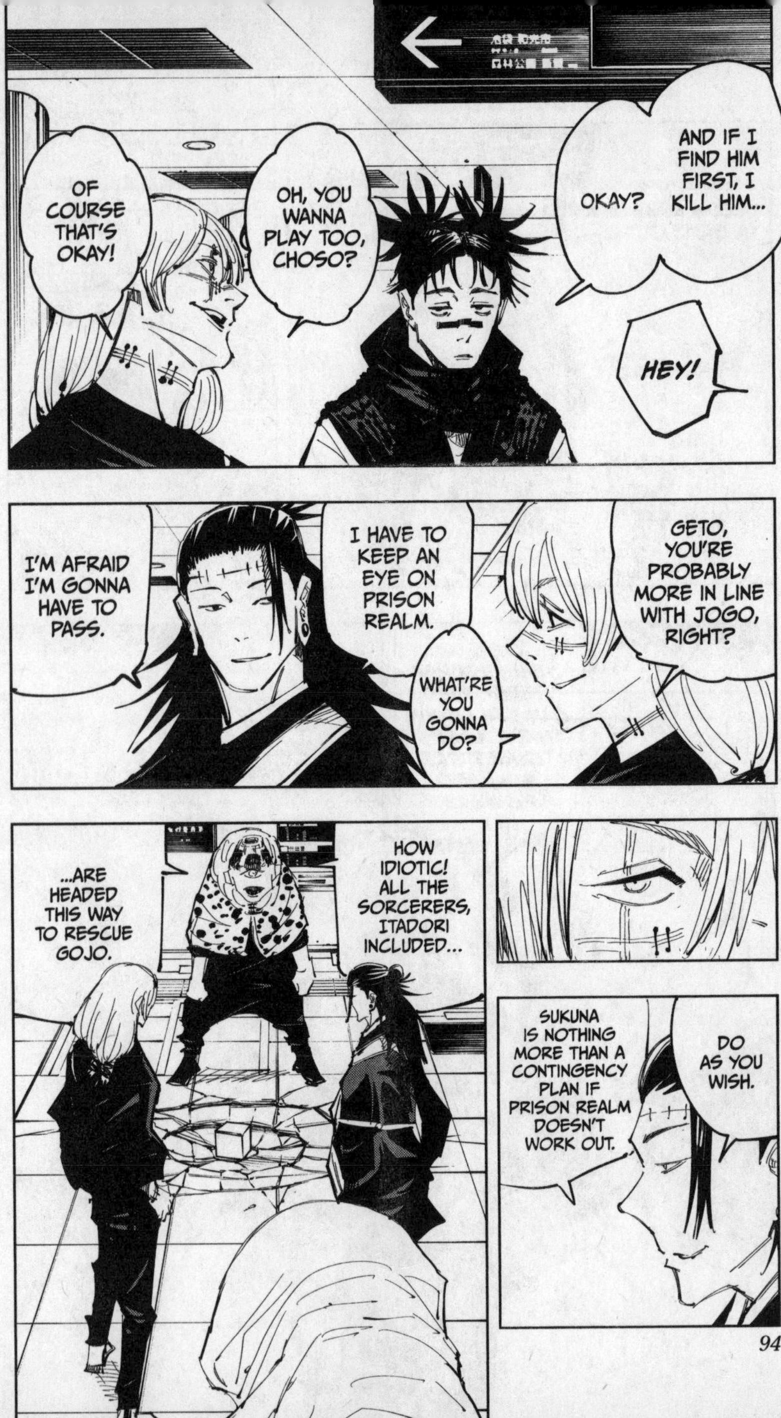
AND IF I FIND HIM FIRST, I KILL HIM... OKAY?
HEY!
OH, YOU WANNA PLAY TOO, CHOSO?
OF COURSE THAT'S OKAY!
GETO, YOU'RE PROBABLY MORE IN LINE WITH JOGO, RIGHT?
WHAT'RE YOU GONNA DO?
I HAVE TO KEEP AN EYE ON PRISON REALM.
I'M AFRAID I'M GONNA HAVE TO PASS.
DO AS YOU WISH.
SUKUNA IS NOTHING MORE THAN A CONTINGENCY PLAN IF PRISON REALM DOESN'T WORK OUT.
HOW IDIOTIC! ALL THE SORCERERS, ITADORI INCLUDED...
...ARE HEADED THIS WAY TO RESCUE GOJO.

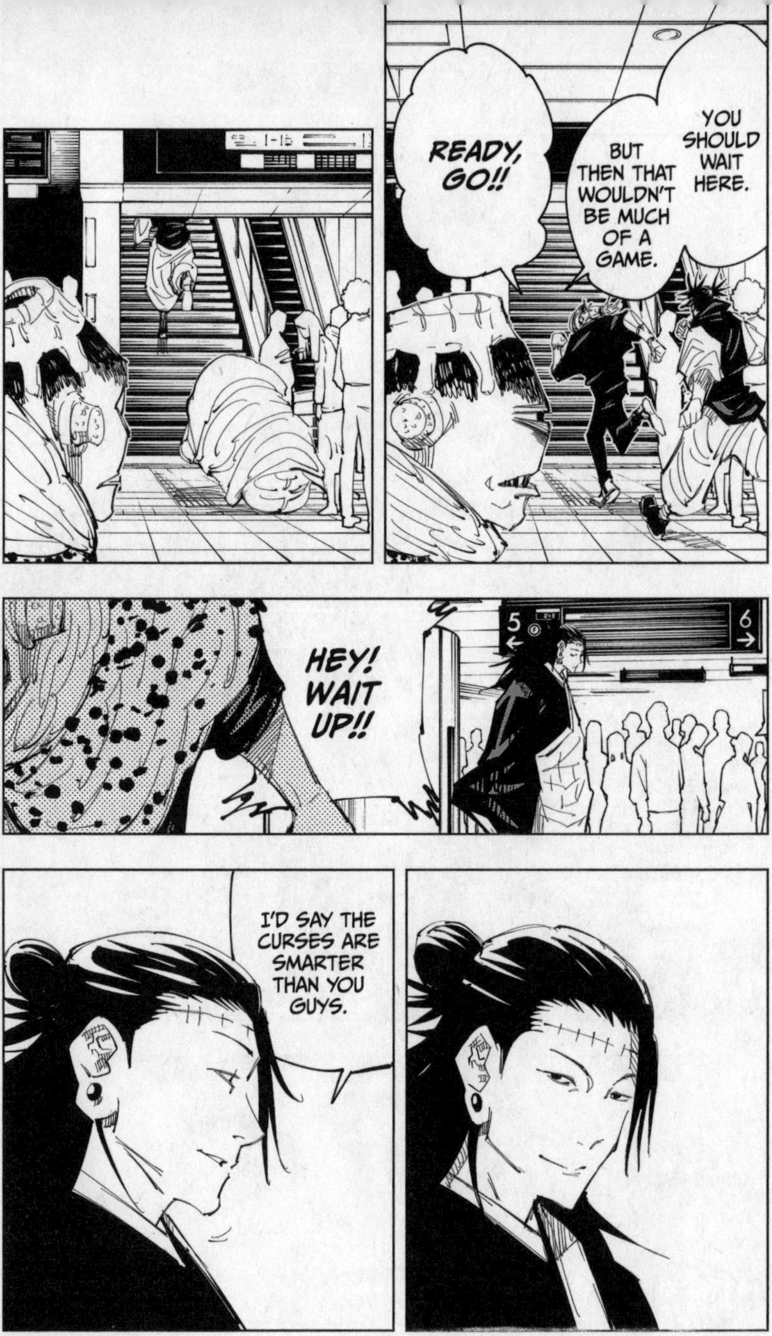
YOU SHOULD WAIT HERE.
BUT THEN THAT WOULDN'T BE MUCH OF A GAME.
READY, GO!!
HEY! WAIT UP!!
I'D SAY THE CURSES ARE SMARTER THAN YOU GUYS.

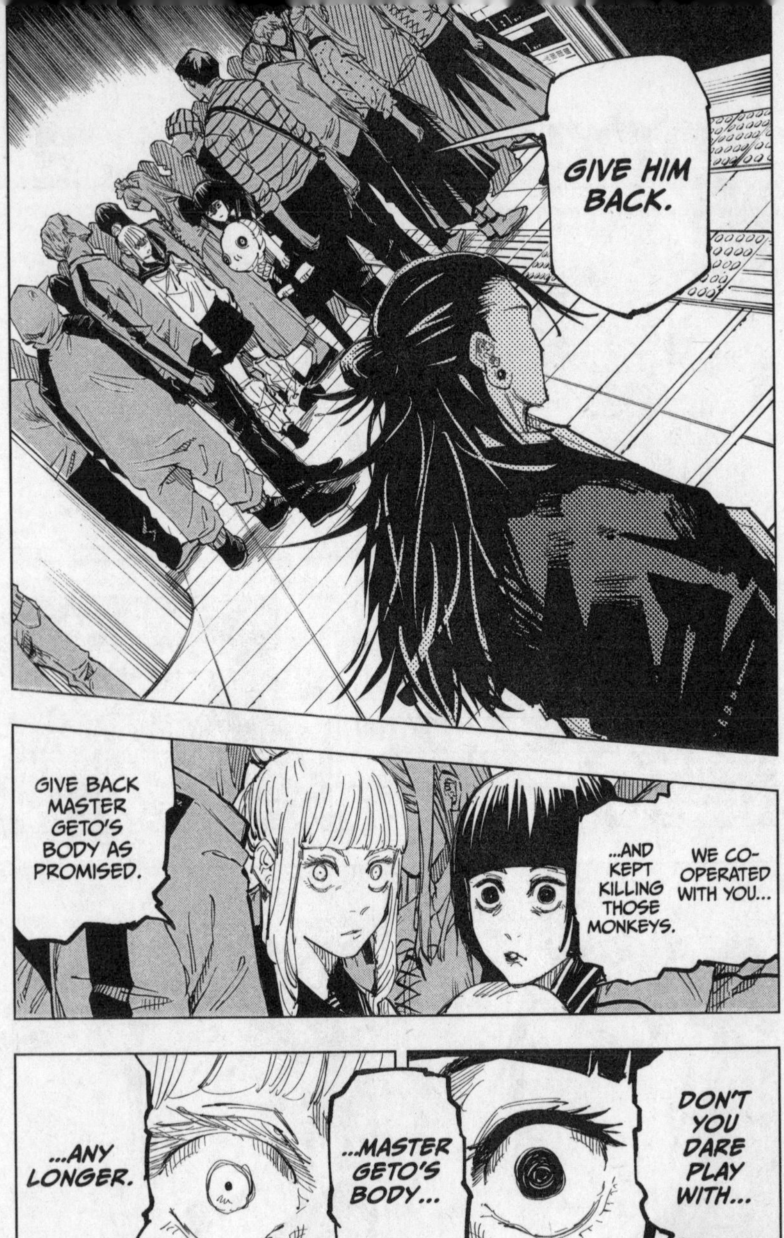
GIVE HIM BACK.
WE CO-OPERATED WITH YOU...
...AND KEPT KILLING THOSE MONKEYS.
GIVE BACK MASTER GETO'S BODY AS PROMISED.
DON'T YOU DARE PLAY WITH...
...MASTER GETO'S BODY...
...ANY LONGER.

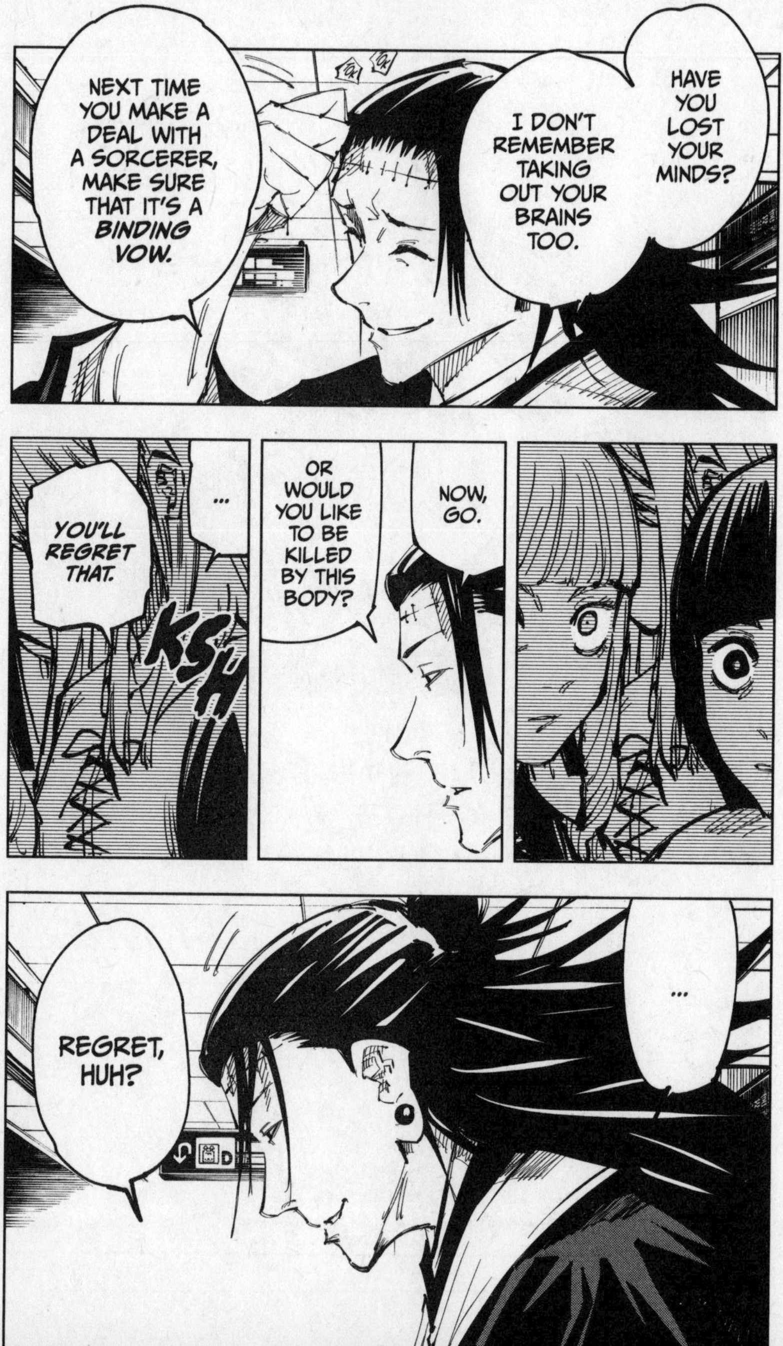
HAVE YOU LOST YOUR MINDS?
I DON'T REMEMBER TAKING OUT YOUR BRAINS TOO.
TOK TOK
NEXT TIME YOU MAKE A DEAL WITH A SORCERER, MAKE SURE THAT IT'S A *BINDING VOW.*
NOW, GO.
OR WOULD YOU LIKE TO BE KILLED BY THIS BODY?
...
YOU'LL REGRET THAT.
KSH
...
REGRET, HUH?

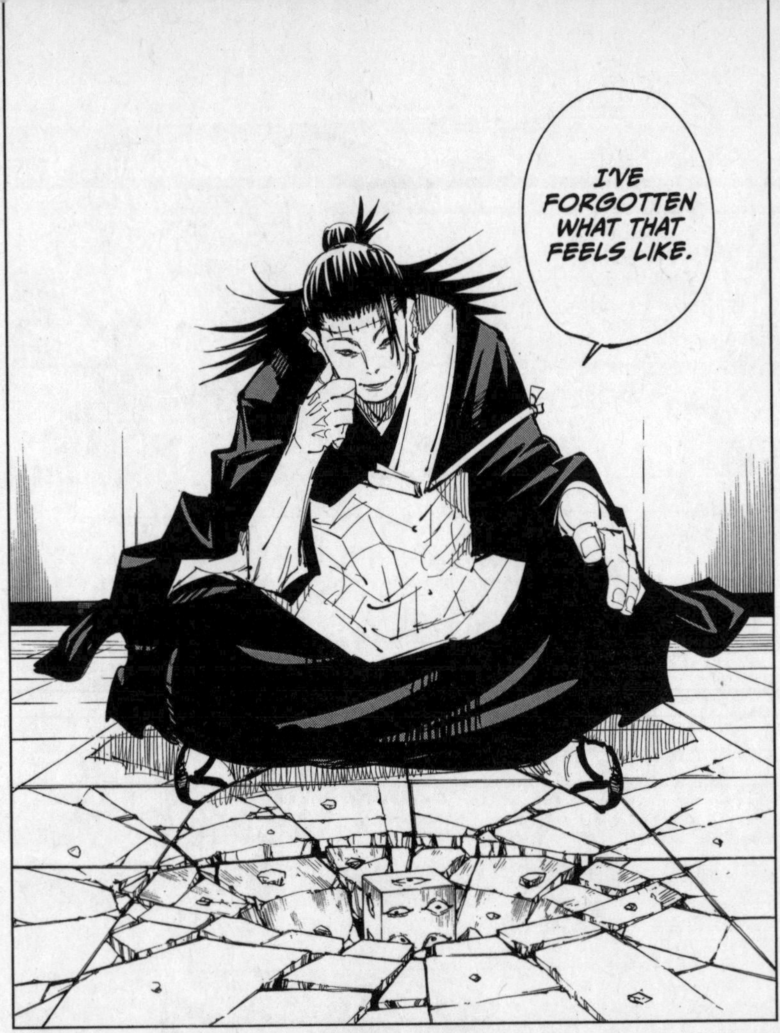
I'VE FORGOTTEN WHAT THAT FEELS LIKE.
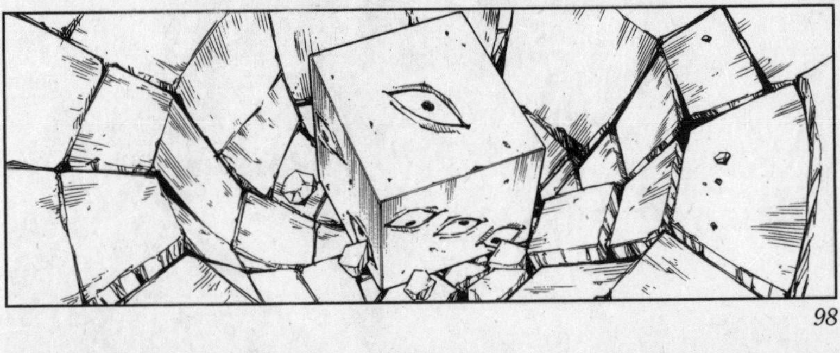

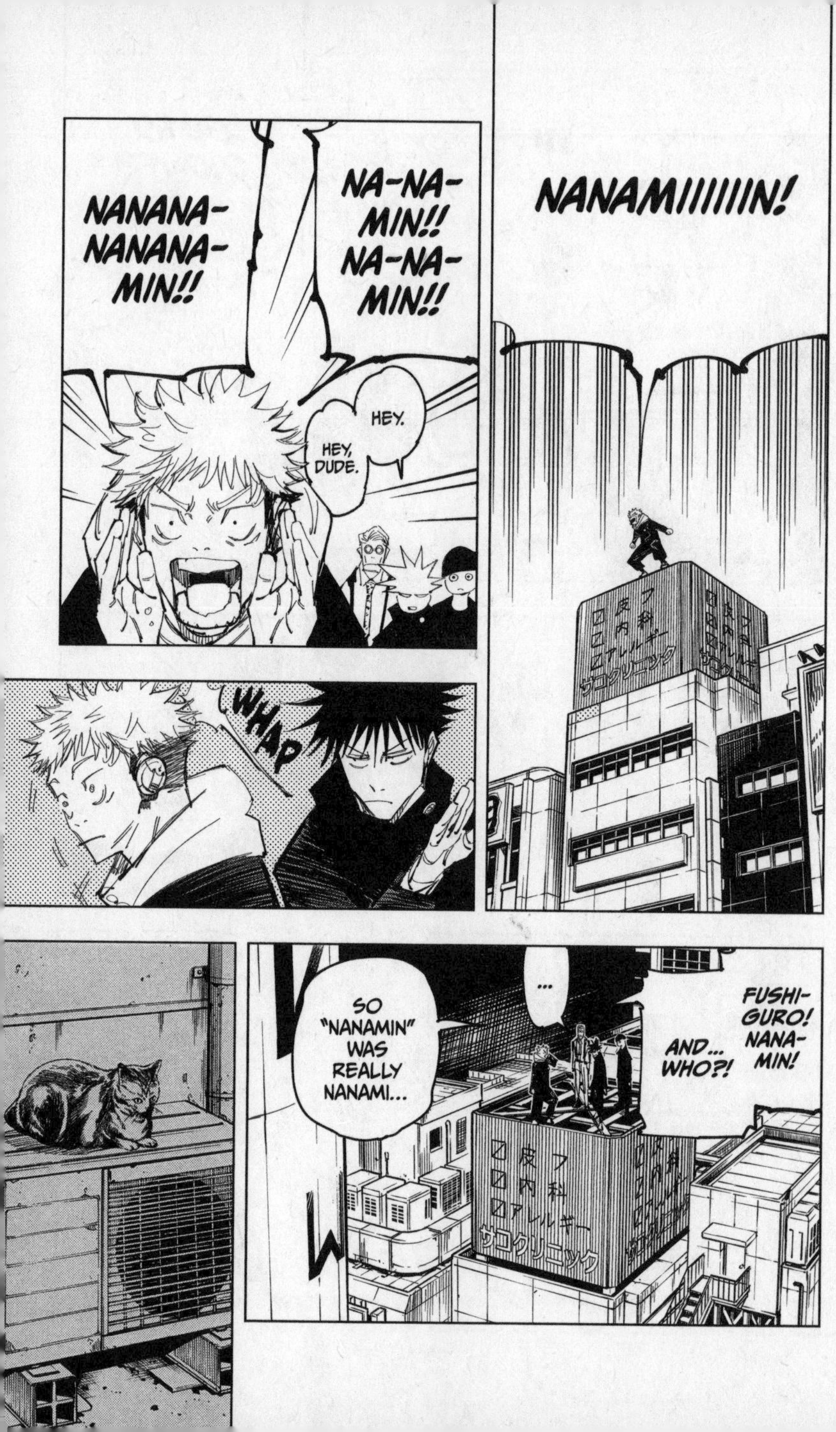
NANAMIIIIIIN!
NA-NA-MIN!! NA-NA-MIN!!
NANANA-NANANA-MIN!!
HEY.
HEY, DUDE.
WHAP
FUSHIGURO! NANAMIN!
AND... WHO?!
...
SO "NANAMIN" WAS REALLY NANAMI...

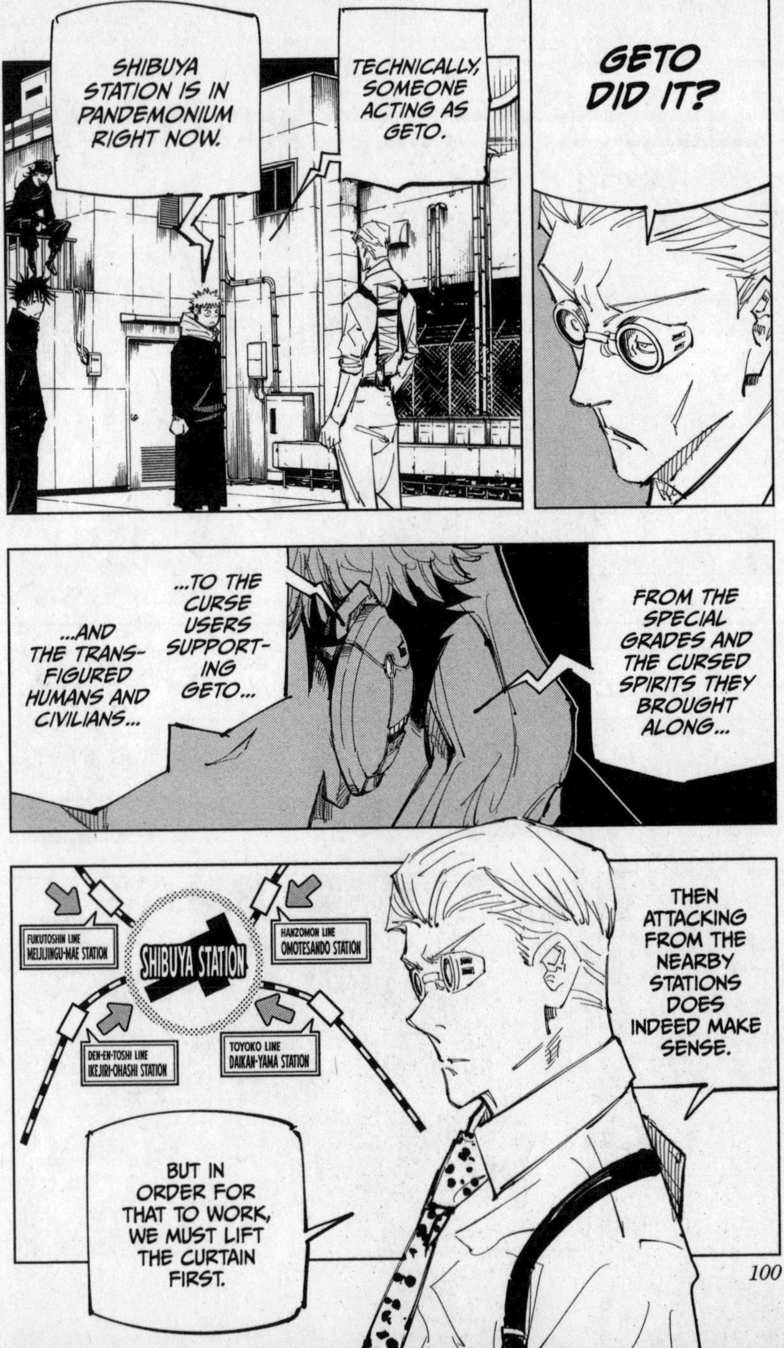
GETO DID IT?
TECHNICALLY, SOMEONE ACTING AS GETO.
SHIBUYA STATION IS IN PANDEMONIUM RIGHT NOW.
FROM THE SPECIAL GRADES AND THE CURSED SPIRITS THEY BROUGHT ALONG...
...TO THE CURSE USERS SUPPORT-ING GETO...
...AND THE TRANS-FIGURED HUMANS AND CIVILIANS...
THEN ATTACKING FROM THE NEARBY STATIONS DOES INDEED MAKE SENSE.
HANZOMON LINE OMOTESANDO STATION
SHIBUYA STATION
FUKUTOSHIN LINE MEIJIJINGU-MAE STATION
TOYOKO LINE DAIKAN-YAMA STATION
DEN-EN-TOSHI LINE IKEJIRI-OHASHI STATION
BUT IN ORDER FOR THAT TO WORK, WE MUST LIFT THE CURTAIN FIRST.

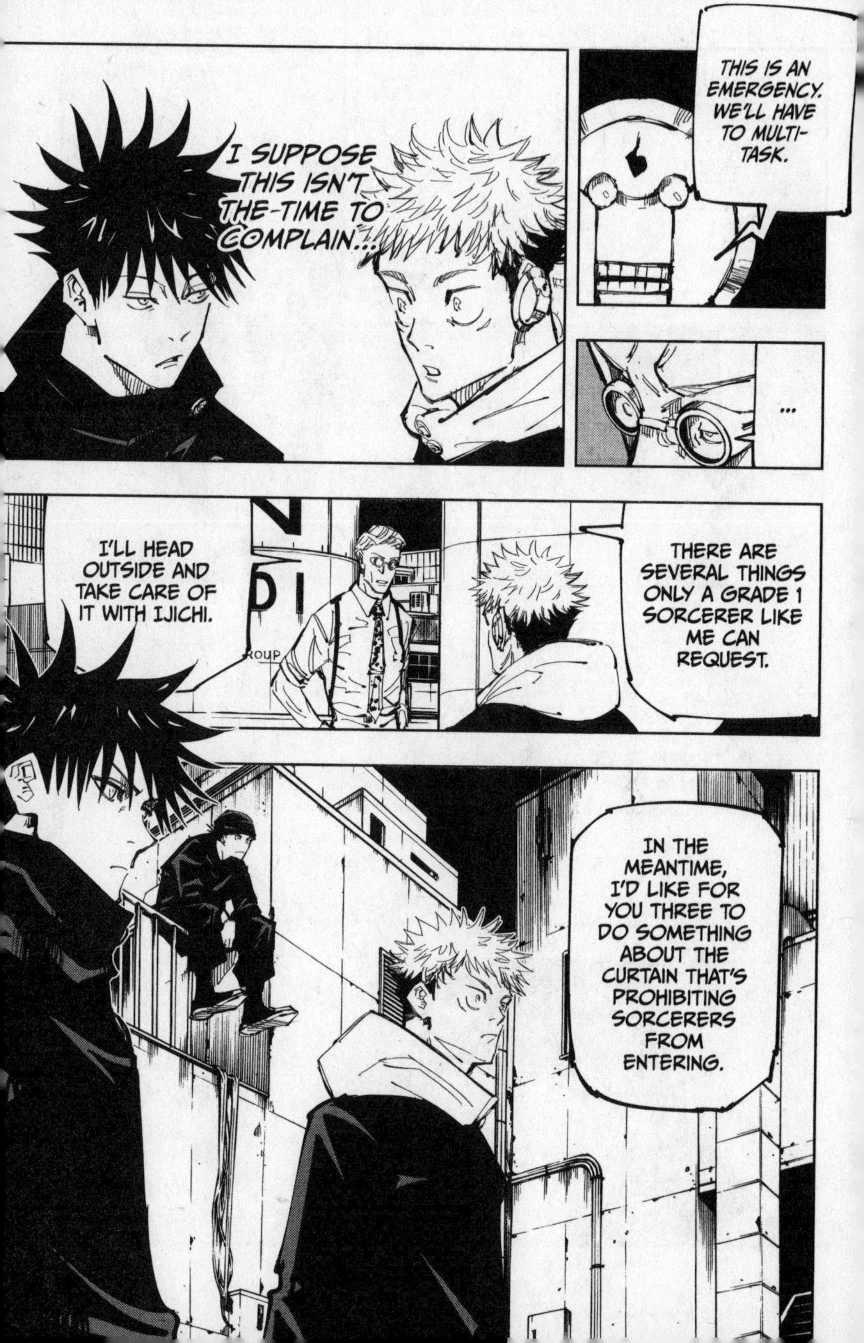
THIS IS AN EMERGENCY. WE'LL HAVE TO MULTI-TASK.
...
I SUPPOSE THIS ISN'T THE TIME TO COMPLAIN...
THERE ARE SEVERAL THINGS ONLY A GRADE 1 SORCERER LIKE ME CAN REQUEST.
I'LL HEAD OUTSIDE AND TAKE CARE OF IT WITH IJICHI.
IN THE MEANTIME, I'D LIKE FOR YOU THREE TO DO SOMETHING ABOUT THE CURTAIN THAT'S PROHIBITING SORCERERS FROM ENTERING.

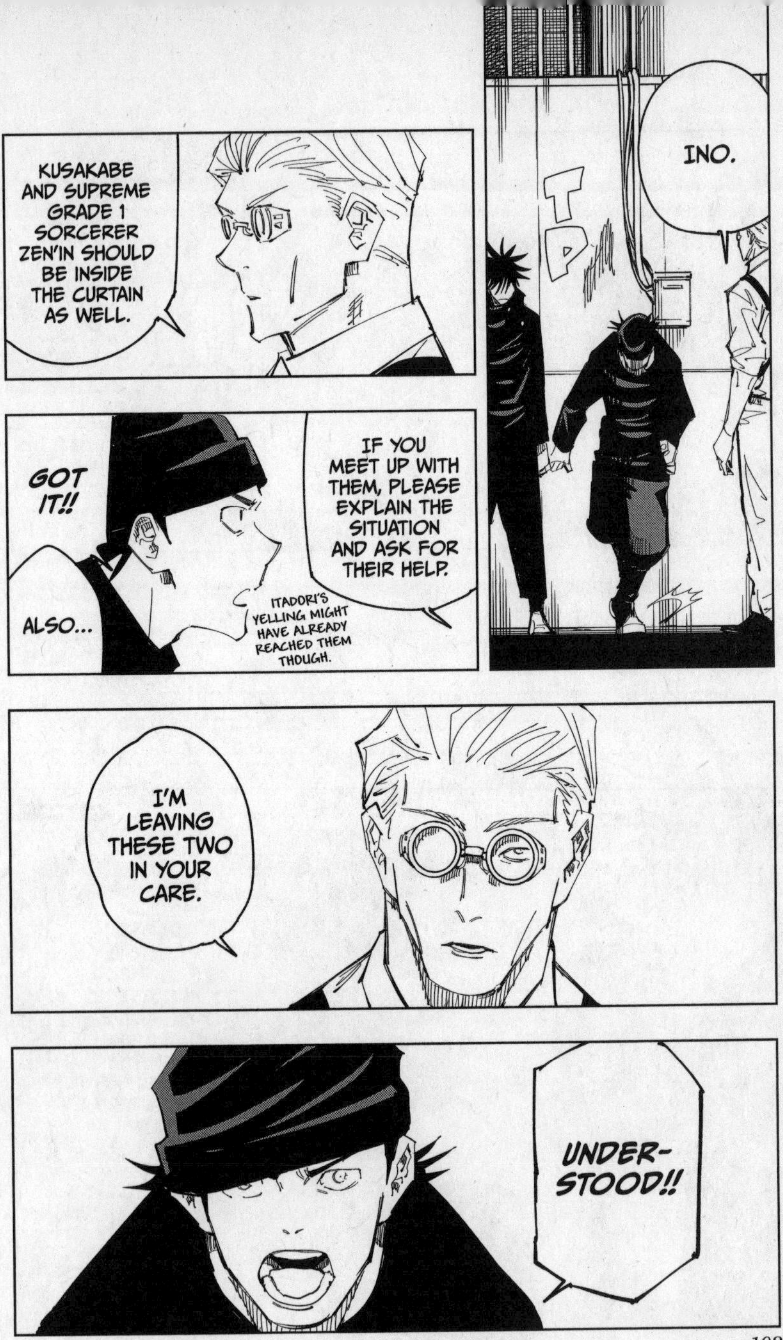
INO.
TP
KUSAKABE AND SUPREME GRADE 1 SORCERER ZEN'IN SHOULD BE INSIDE THE CURTAIN AS WELL.
IF YOU MEET UP WITH THEM, PLEASE EXPLAIN THE SITUATION AND ASK FOR THEIR HELP.
GOT IT!!
ITADORI'S YELLING MIGHT HAVE ALREADY REACHED THEM THOUGH.
ALSO...
I'M LEAVING THESE TWO IN YOUR CARE.
UNDER-STOOD!!

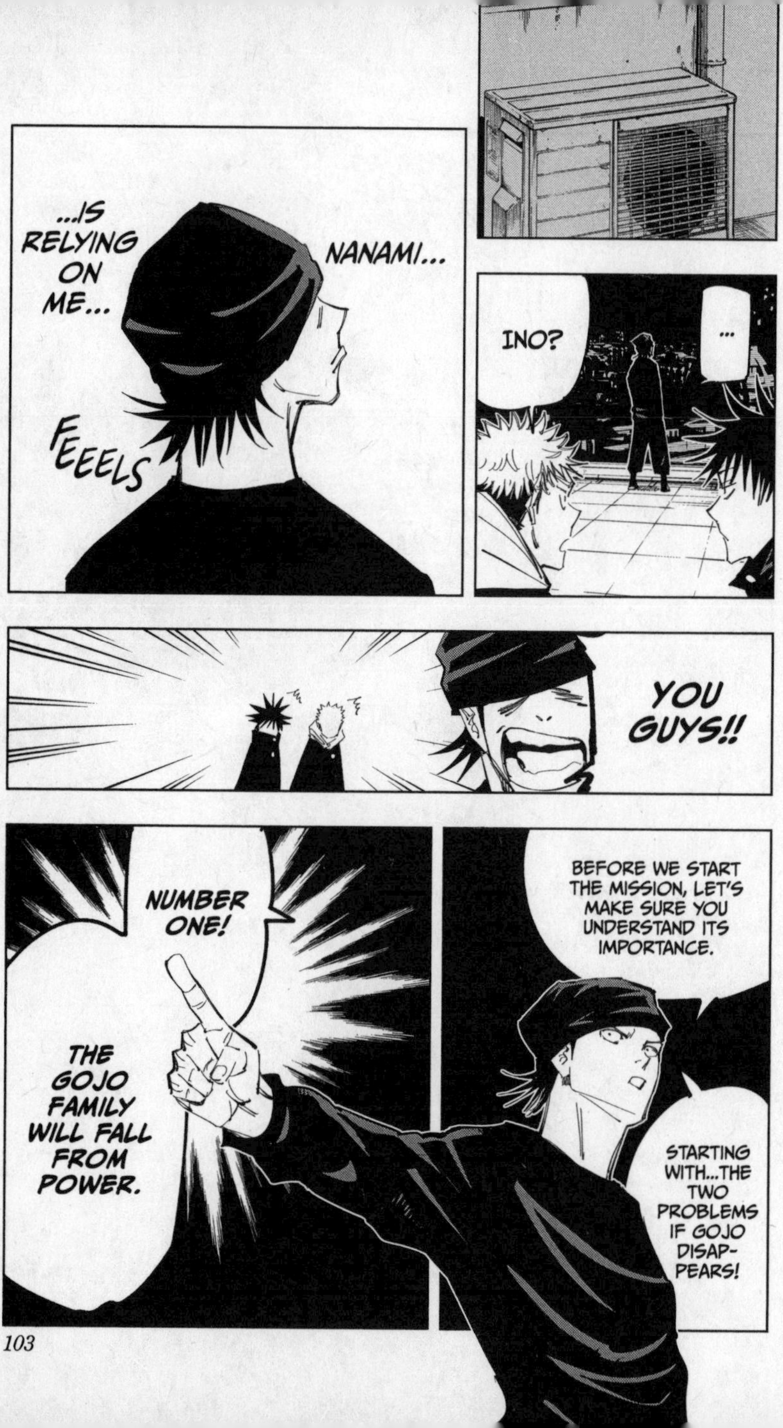
INO?
...
NANAMI...
...IS RELYING ON ME...
FEEELS
YOU GUYS!!
BEFORE WE START THE MISSION, LET'S MAKE SURE YOU UNDERSTAND ITS IMPORTANCE.
STARTING WITH...THE TWO PROBLEMS IF GOJO DISAPPEARS!
NUMBER ONE!
THE GOJO FAMILY WILL FALL FROM POWER.

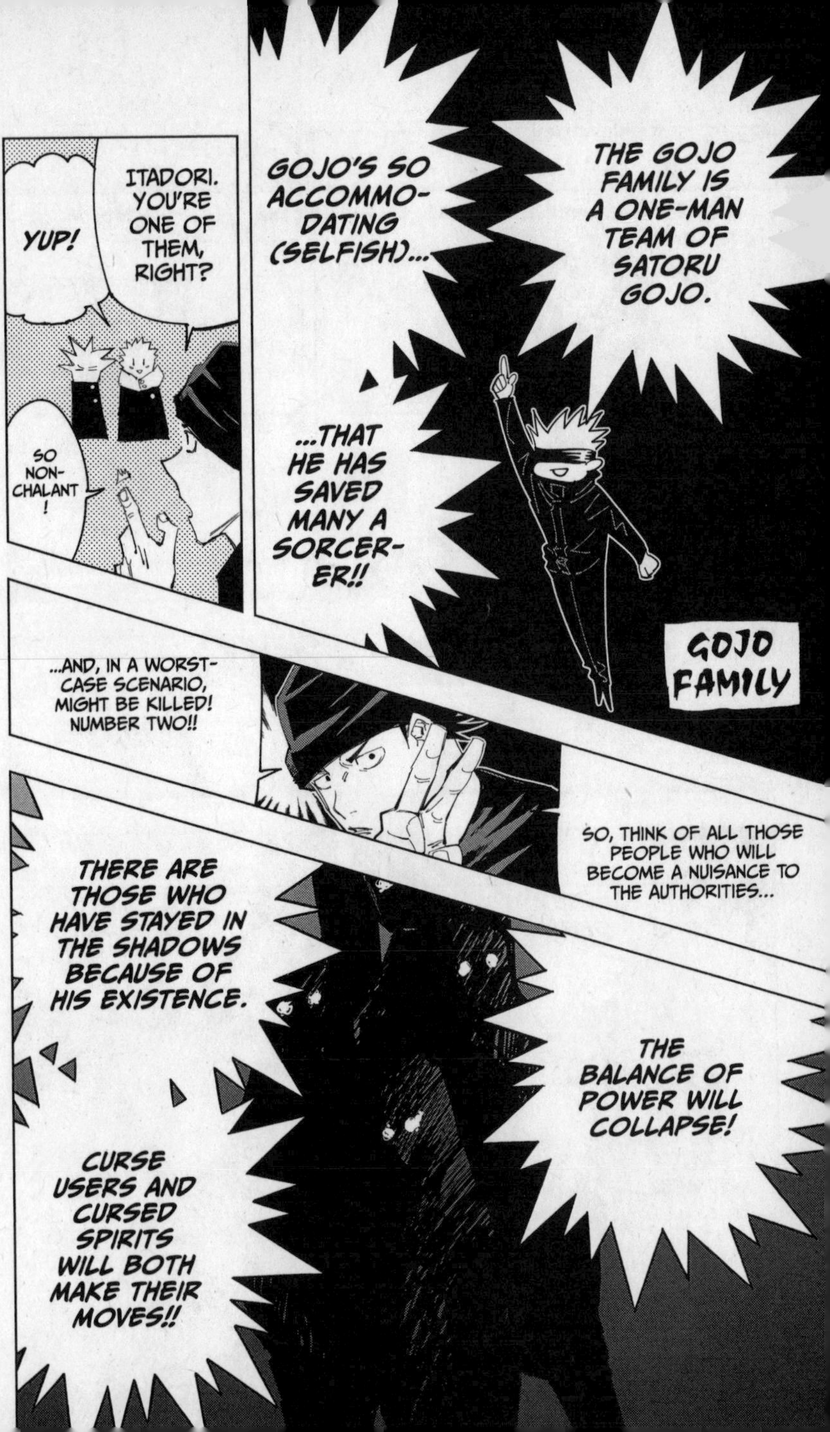
THE GOJO FAMILY IS A ONE-MAN TEAM OF SATORU GOJO.
GOJO'S SO ACCOMMODATING (SELFISH)...
...THAT HE HAS SAVED MANY A SORCERER!!
GOJO FAMILY
ITADORI. YOU'RE ONE OF THEM, RIGHT?
YUP!
SO NONCHALANT!
...AND, IN A WORST-CASE SCENARIO, MIGHT BE KILLED! NUMBER TWO!!
SO, THINK OF ALL THOSE PEOPLE WHO WILL BECOME A NUISANCE TO THE AUTHORITIES...
THE BALANCE OF POWER WILL COLLAPSE!
THERE ARE THOSE WHO HAVE STAYED IN THE SHADOWS BECAUSE OF HIS EXISTENCE.
CURSE USERS AND CURSED SPIRITS WILL BOTH MAKE THEIR MOVES!!

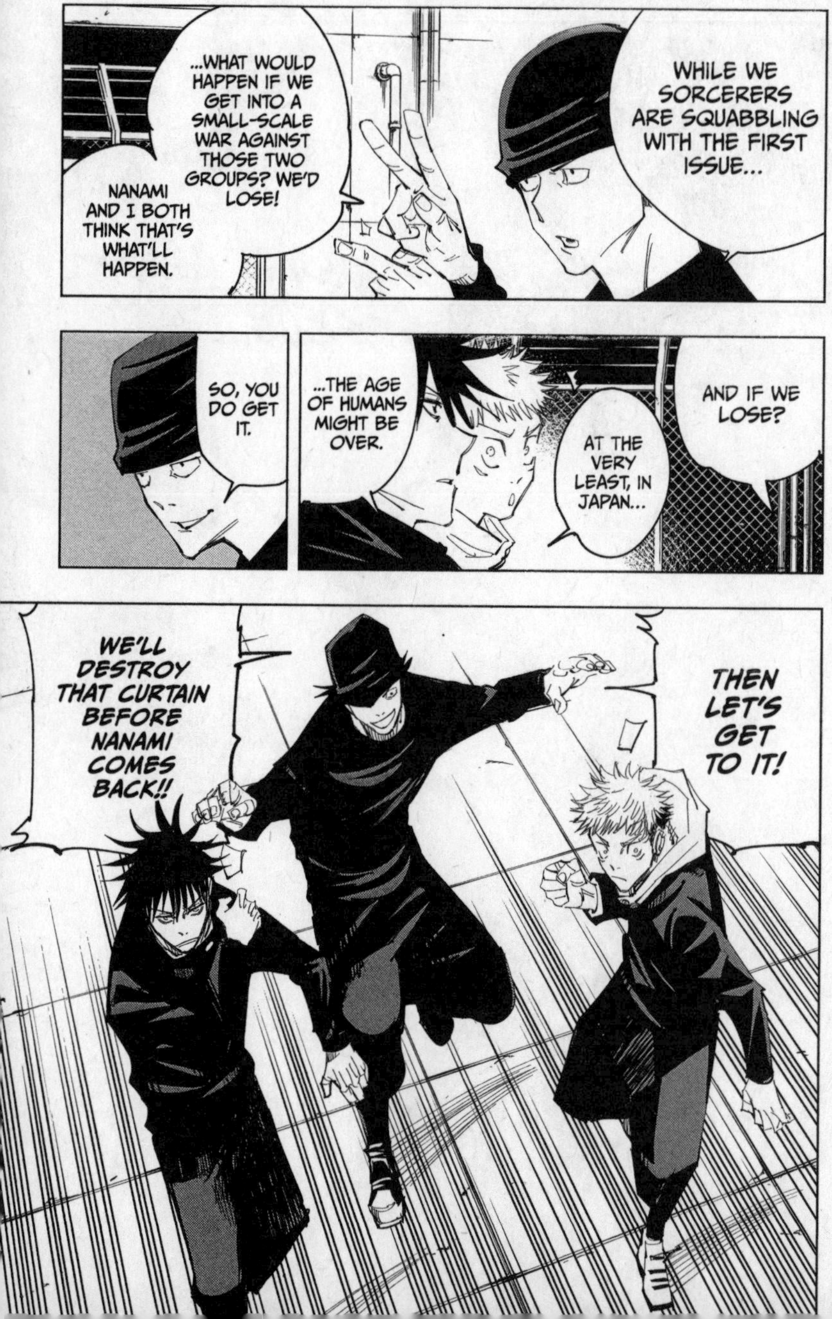
WHILE WE SORCERERS ARE SQUABBLING WITH THE FIRST ISSUE...
...WHAT WOULD HAPPEN IF WE GET INTO A SMALL-SCALE WAR AGAINST THOSE TWO GROUPS? WE'D LOSE!
NANAMI AND I BOTH THINK THAT'S WHAT'LL HAPPEN.
AND IF WE LOSE?
AT THE VERY LEAST, IN JAPAN...
...THE AGE OF HUMANS MIGHT BE OVER.
SO, YOU DO GET IT.
THEN LET'S GET TO IT!
WE'LL DESTROY THAT CURTAIN BEFORE NANAMI COMES BACK!!

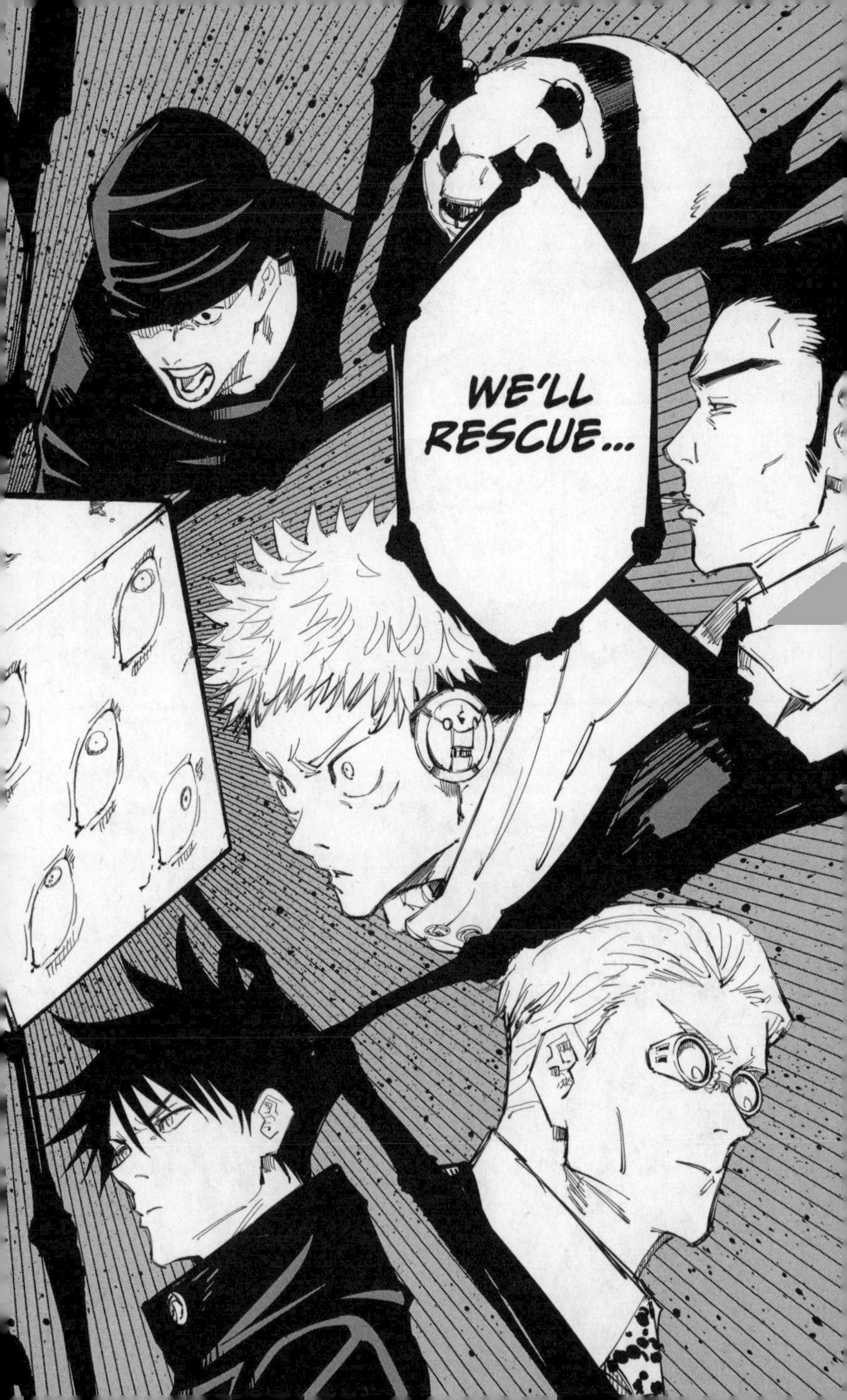
WE'LL RESCUE...

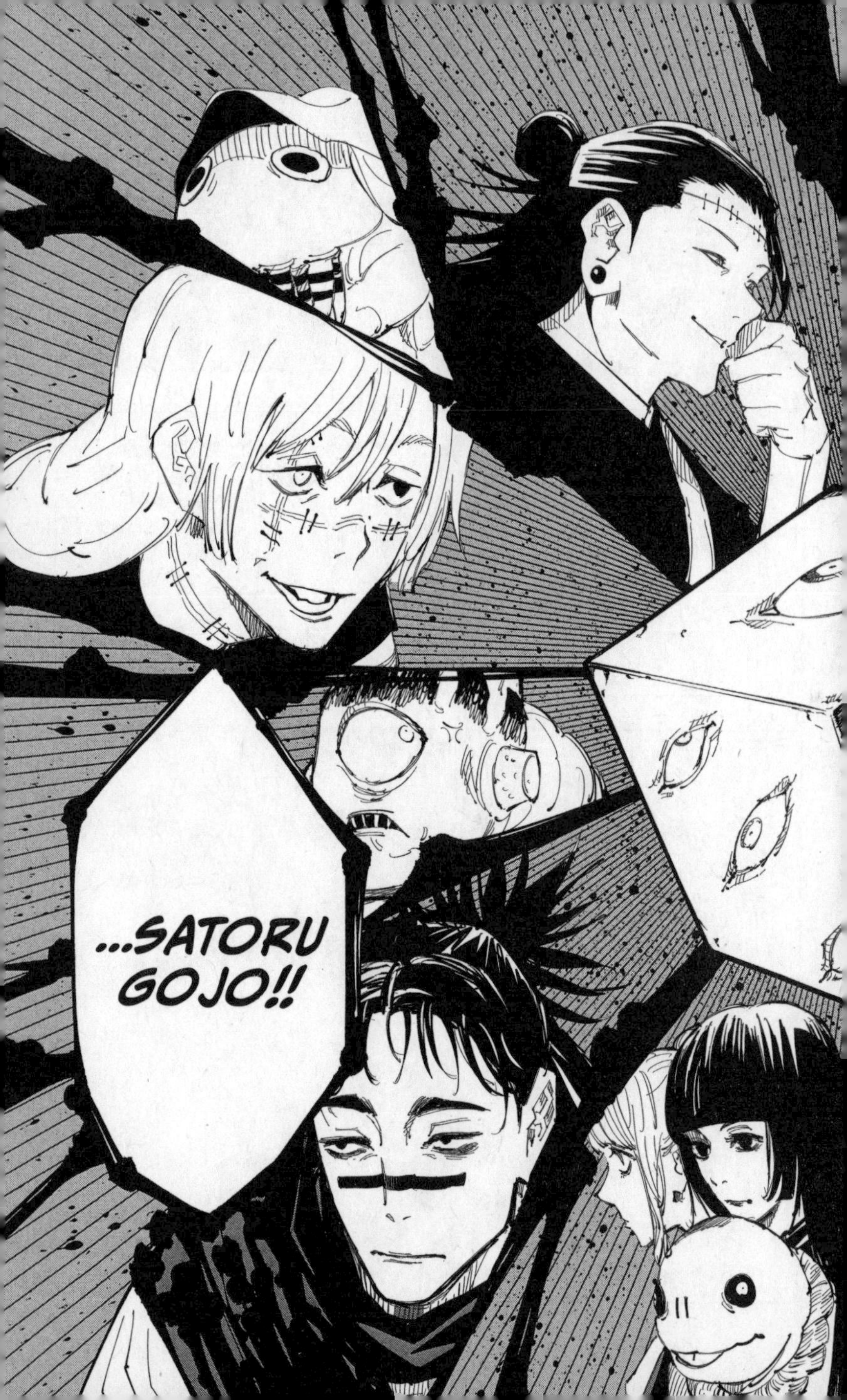
...SATORU GOJO!!

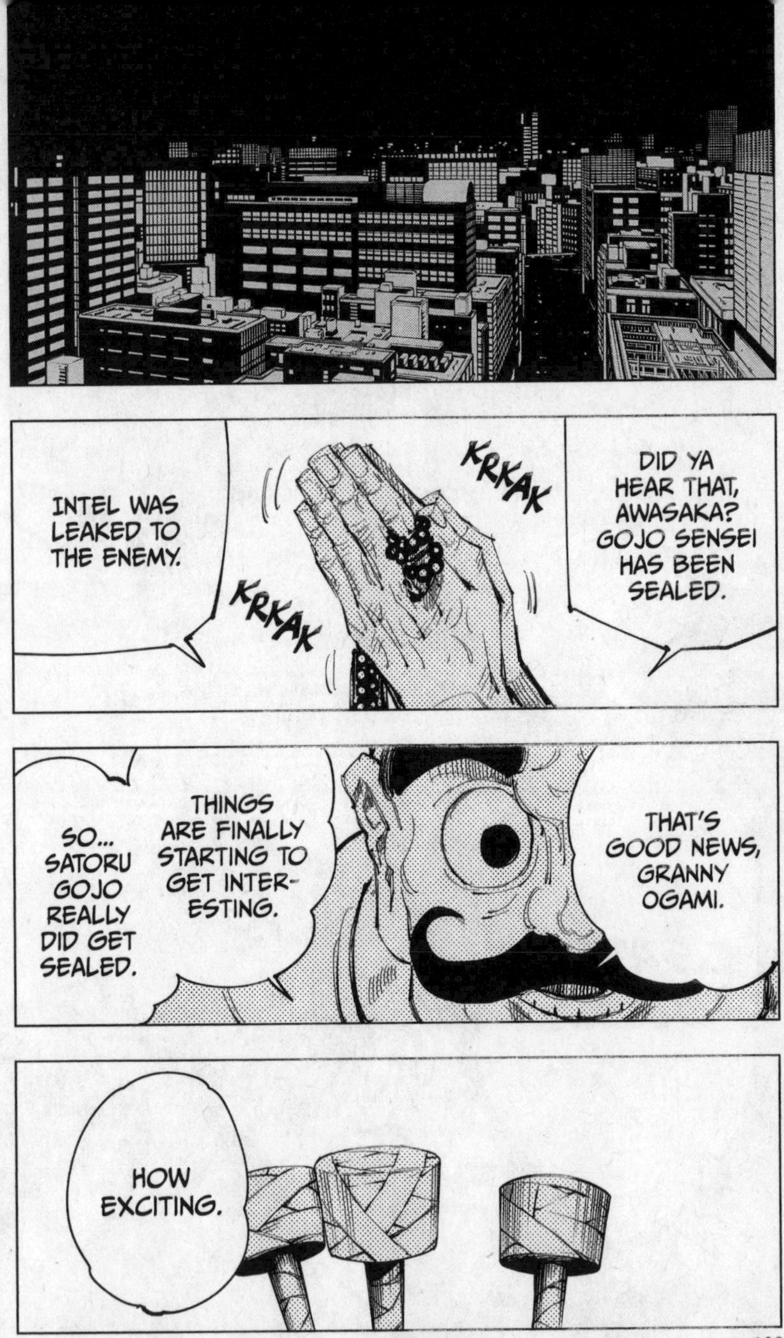
DID YA HEAR THAT, AWASAKA? GOJO SENSEI HAS BEEN SEALED.
KRKAK
KRKAK
INTEL WAS LEAKED TO THE ENEMY.
THAT'S GOOD NEWS, GRANNY OGAMI.
THINGS ARE FINALLY STARTING TO GET INTER-ESTING.
SO... SATORU GOJO REALLY DID GET SEALED.
HOW EXCITING.

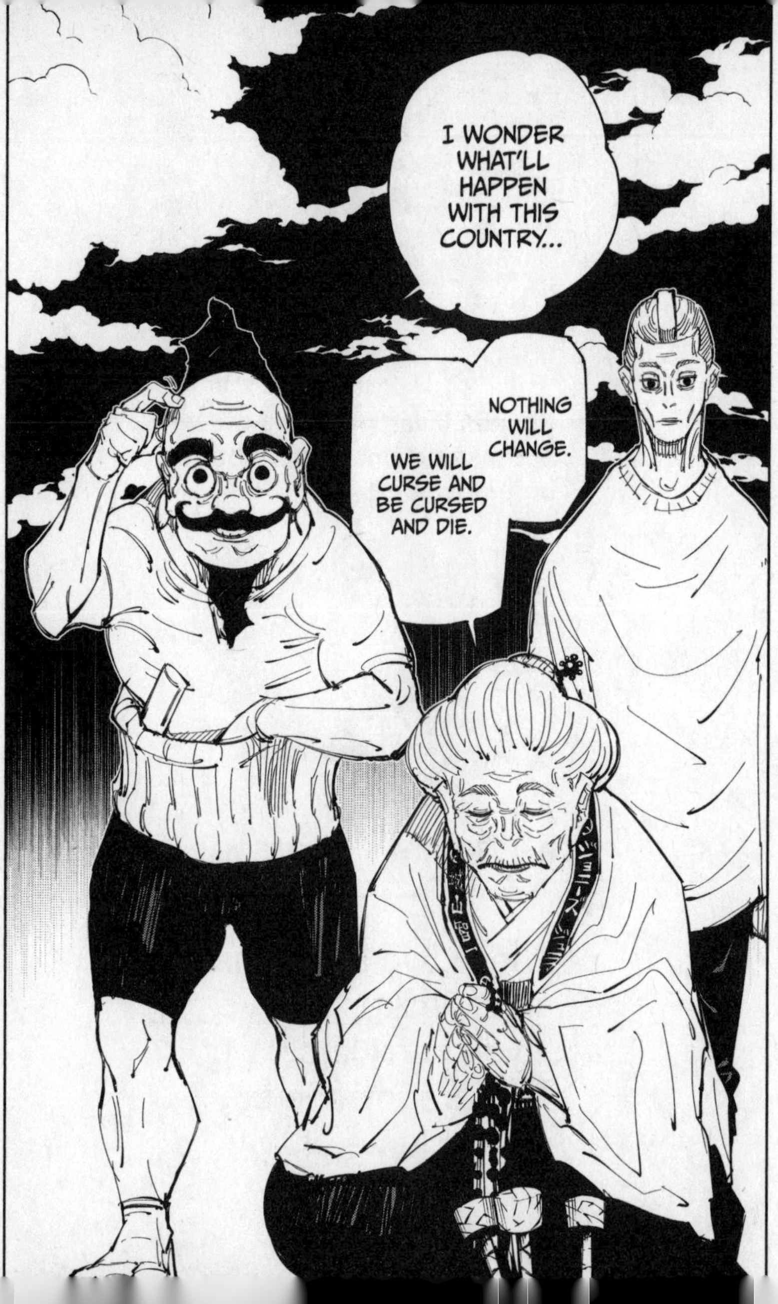
I WONDER WHAT'LL HAPPEN WITH THIS COUNTRY...
NOTHING WILL CHANGE.
WE WILL CURSE AND BE CURSED AND DIE.

Scenes I was planning on addressing but forgot about until now, part 4

• Twins

These two are Nanako and Mimiko.
If you don't know who they are, please ~~buy~~ read volume 0!

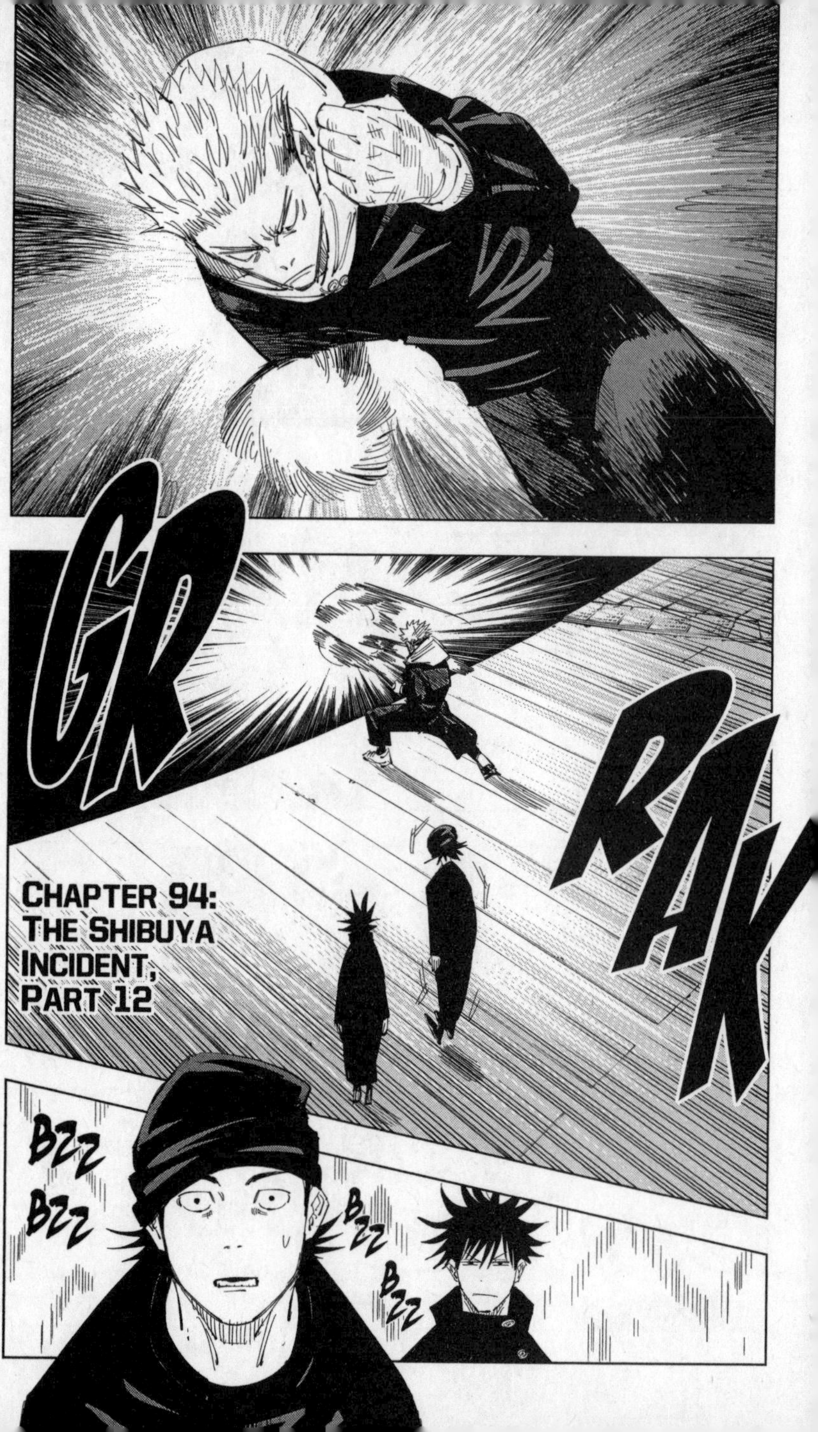
GR
RAK
CHAPTER 94: THE SHIBUYA INCIDENT, PART 12
BZZ
BZZ
BZZ
BZZ

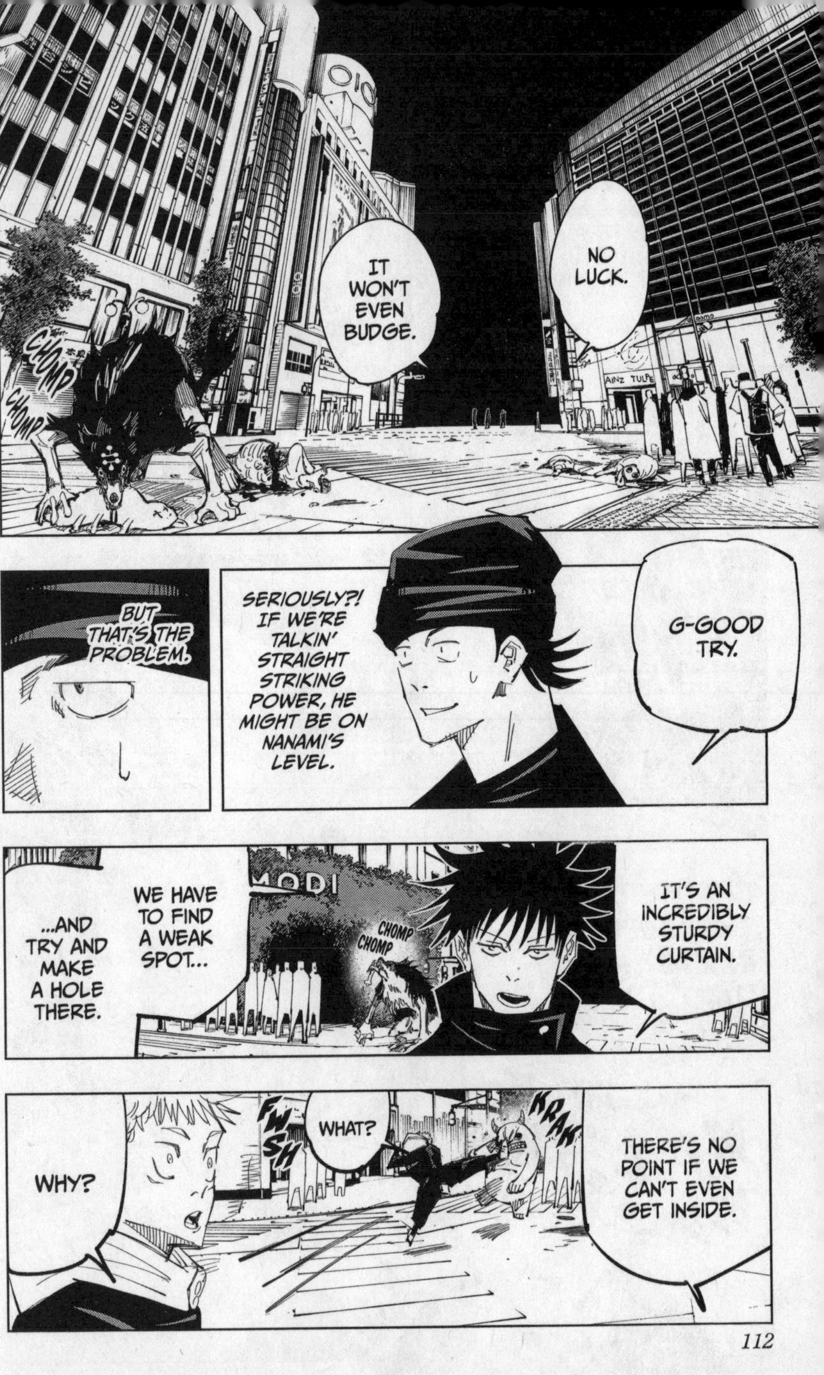
NO LUCK.
IT WON'T EVEN BUDGE.
CHOMP
CHOMP
AINZ TULPE
G-GOOD TRY.
SERIOUSLY?! IF WE'RE TALKIN' STRAIGHT STRIKING POWER, HE MIGHT BE ON NANAMI'S LEVEL.
BUT THAT'S THE PROBLEM.
IT'S AN INCREDIBLY STURDY CURTAIN.
MODI
CHOMP
CHOMP
WE HAVE TO FIND A WEAK SPOT...
...AND TRY AND MAKE A HOLE THERE.
THERE'S NO POINT IF WE CAN'T EVEN GET INSIDE.
KRAK
WHAT?
FWSH
WHY?

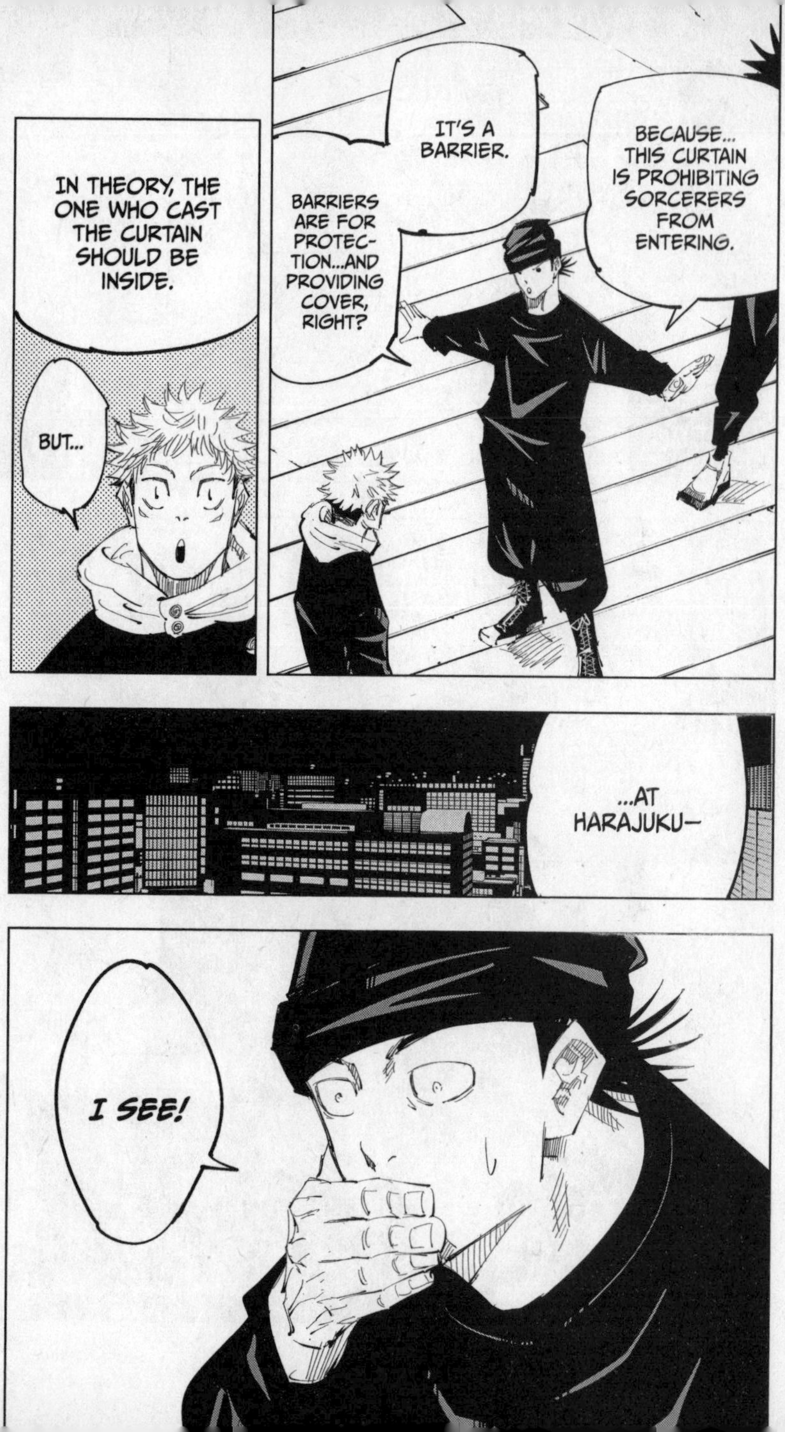
BECAUSE... THIS CURTAIN IS PROHIBITING SORCERERS FROM ENTERING.
IT'S A BARRIER.
BARRIERS ARE FOR PROTECTION...AND PROVIDING COVER, RIGHT?
IN THEORY, THE ONE WHO CAST THE CURTAIN SHOULD BE INSIDE.
BUT...
...AT HARAJUKU—
I SEE!

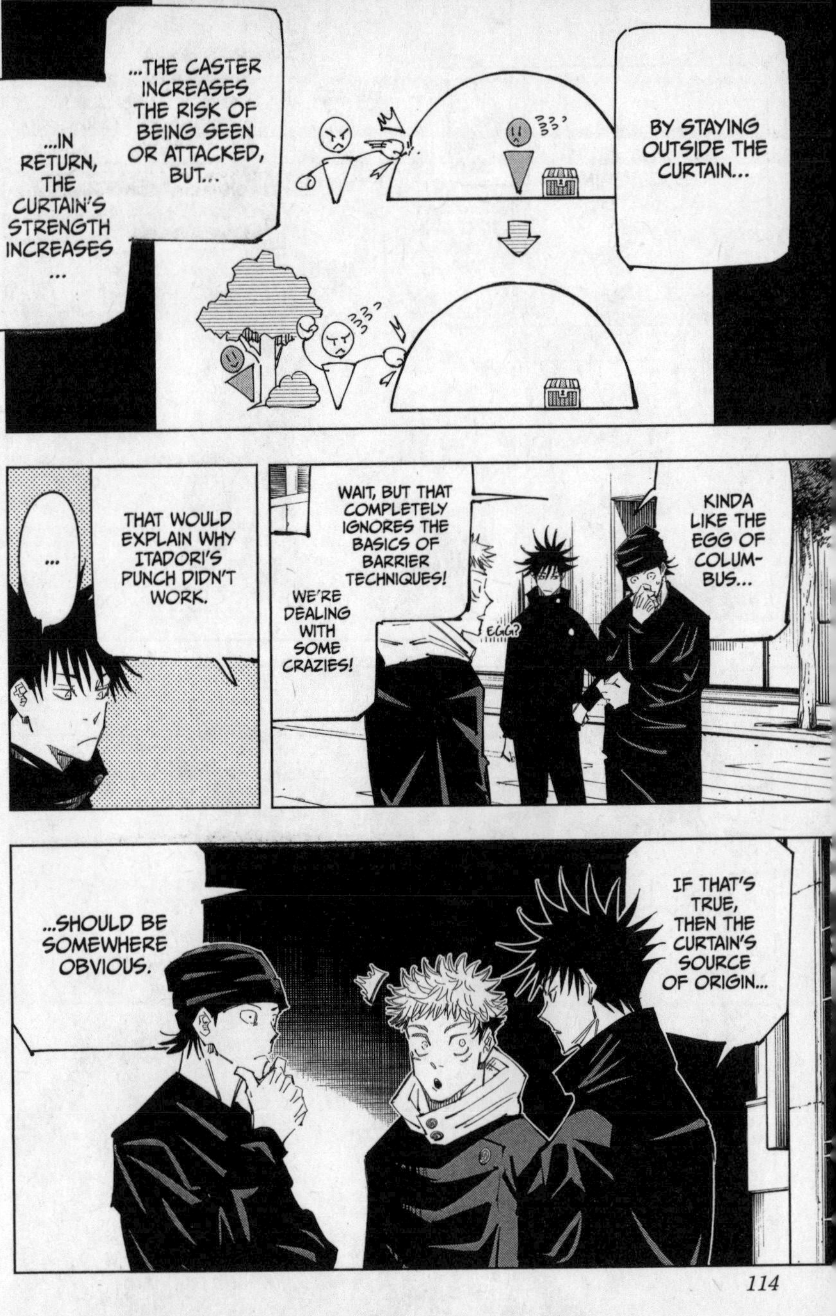
BY STAYING OUTSIDE THE CURTAIN...
...THE CASTER INCREASES THE RISK OF BEING SEEN OR ATTACKED, BUT...
...IN RETURN, THE CURTAIN'S STRENGTH INCREASES...
KINDA LIKE THE EGG OF COLUMBUS...
EGG?
WAIT, BUT THAT COMPLETELY IGNORES THE BASICS OF BARRIER TECHNIQUES!
WE'RE DEALING WITH SOME CRAZIES!
THAT WOULD EXPLAIN WHY ITADORI'S PUNCH DIDN'T WORK.
...
IF THAT'S TRUE, THEN THE CURTAIN'S SOURCE OF ORIGIN...
...SHOULD BE SOMEWHERE OBVIOUS.

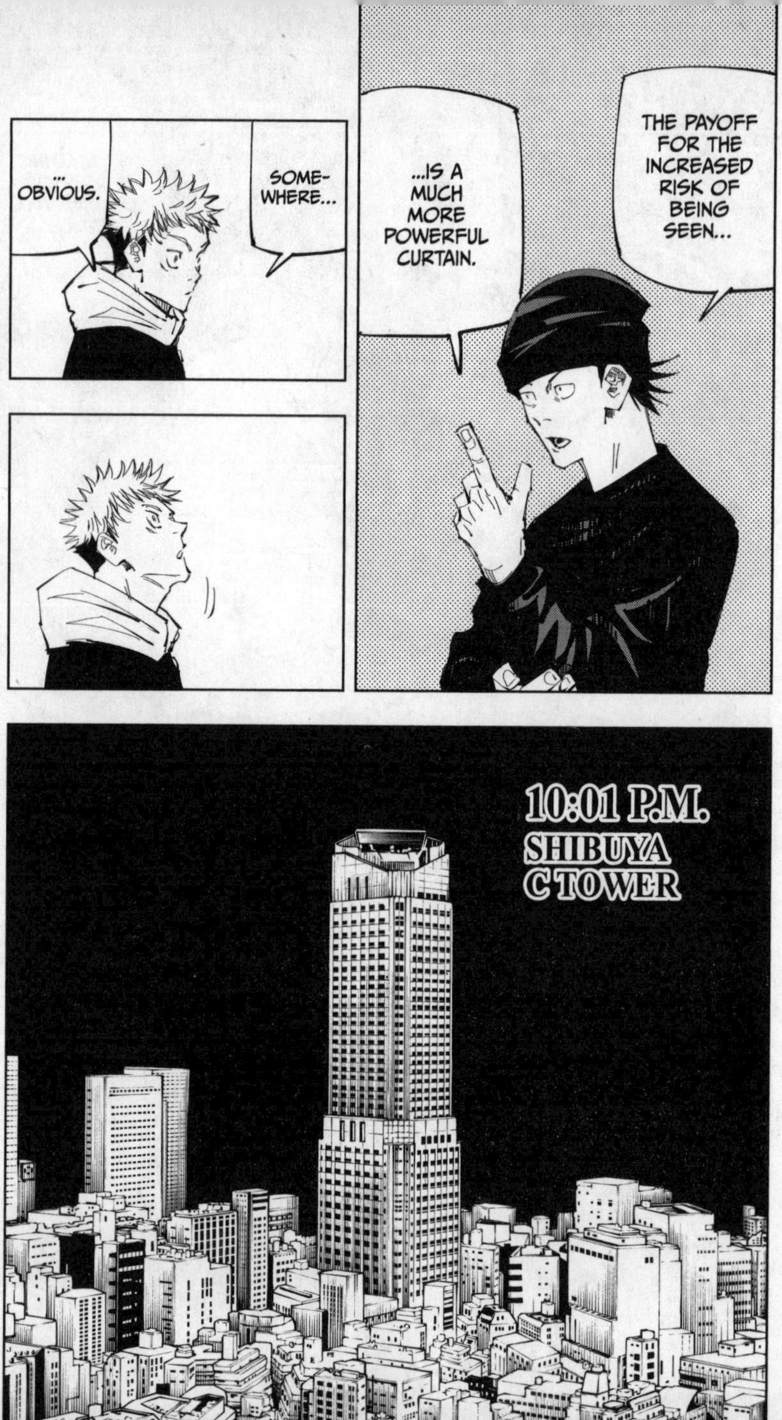
THE PAYOFF FOR THE INCREASED RISK OF BEING SEEN...
...IS A MUCH MORE POWERFUL CURTAIN.
SOME-WHERE...
... OBVIOUS.
10:01 P.M.
SHIBUYA C TOWER

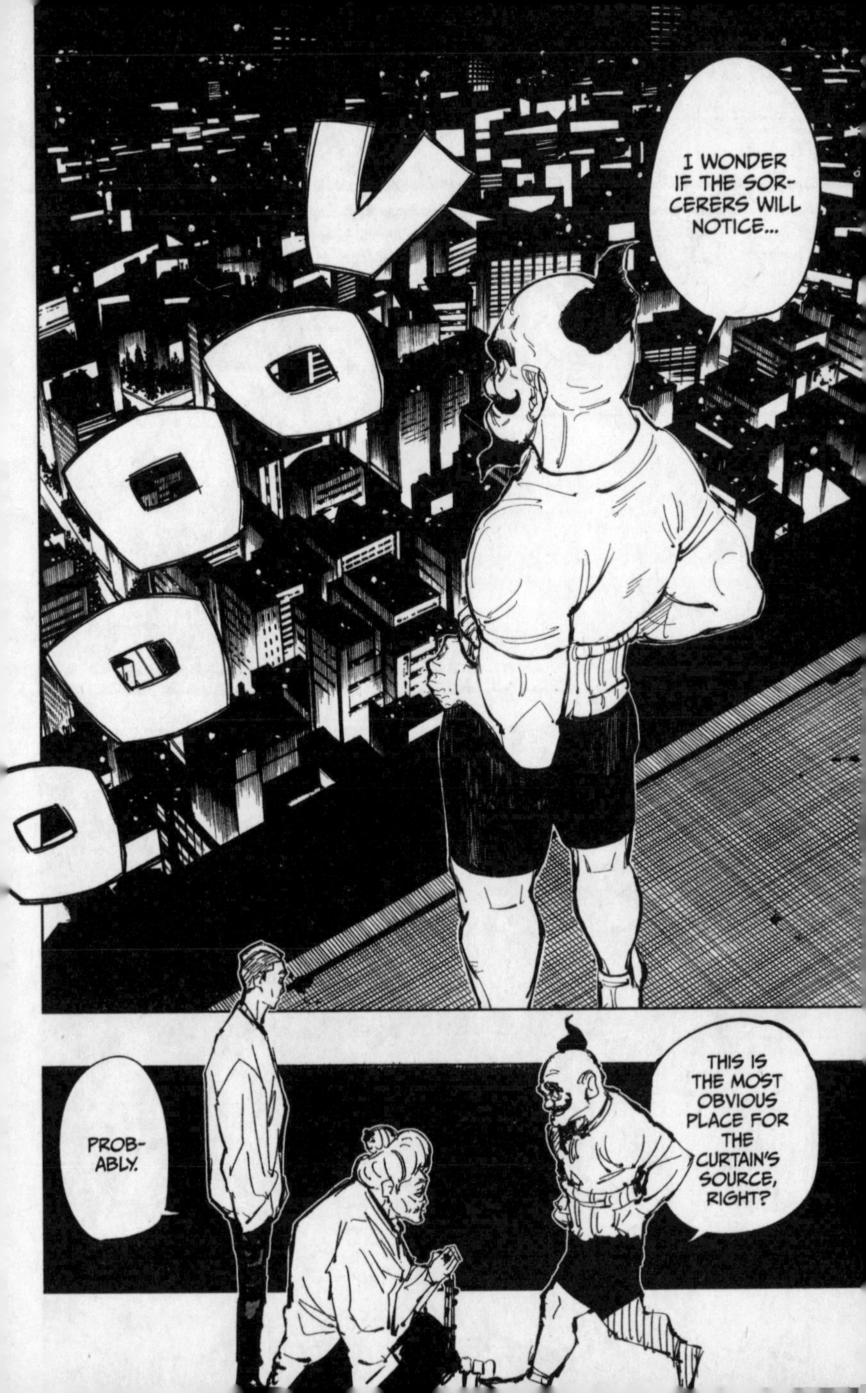
I WONDER IF THE SORCERERS WILL NOTICE...
THIS IS THE MOST OBVIOUS PLACE FOR THE CURTAIN'S SOURCE, RIGHT?
PROBABLY.

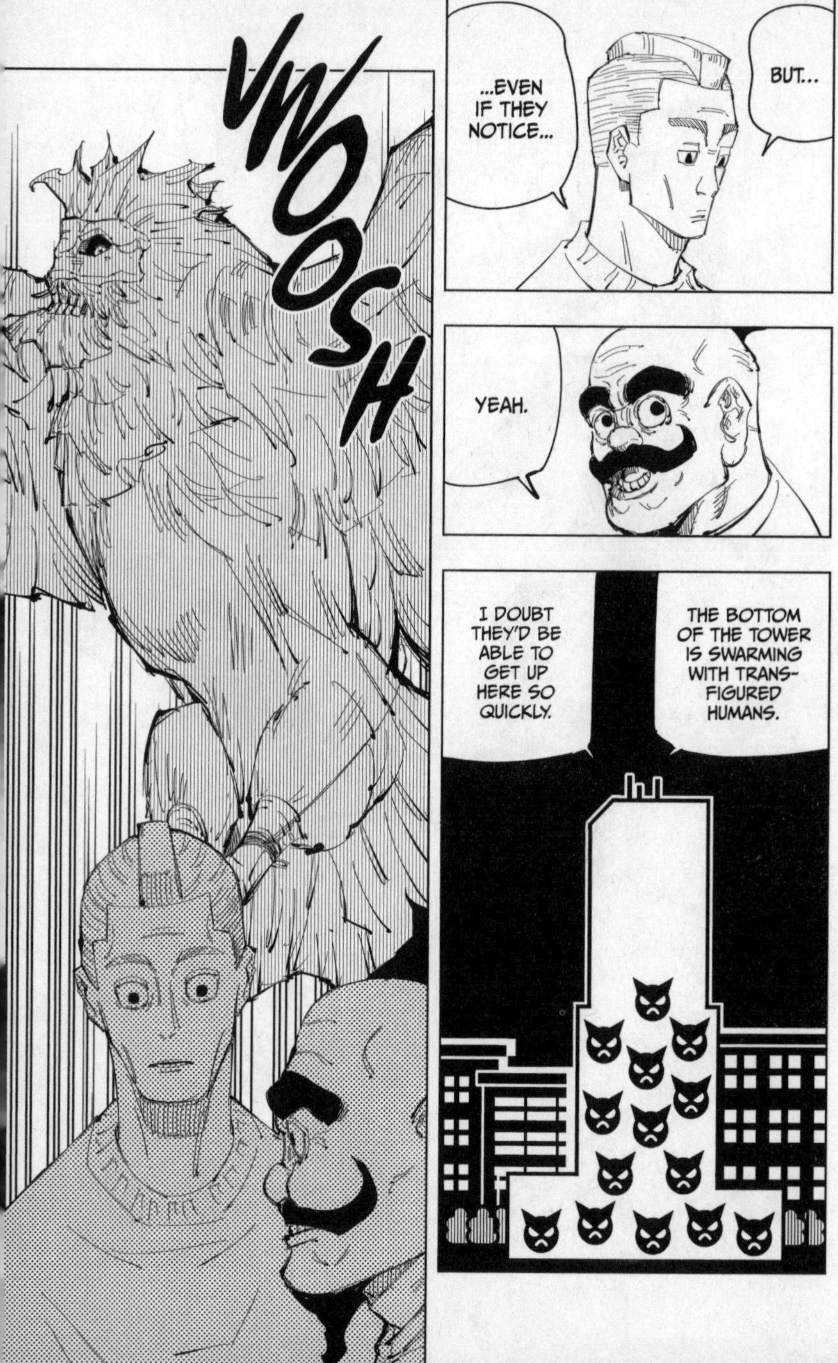
BUT...
...EVEN IF THEY NOTICE...
YEAH.
THE BOTTOM OF THE TOWER IS SWARMING WITH TRANS-FIGURED HUMANS.
I DOUBT THEY'D BE ABLE TO GET UP HERE SO QUICKLY.
WHOOSH

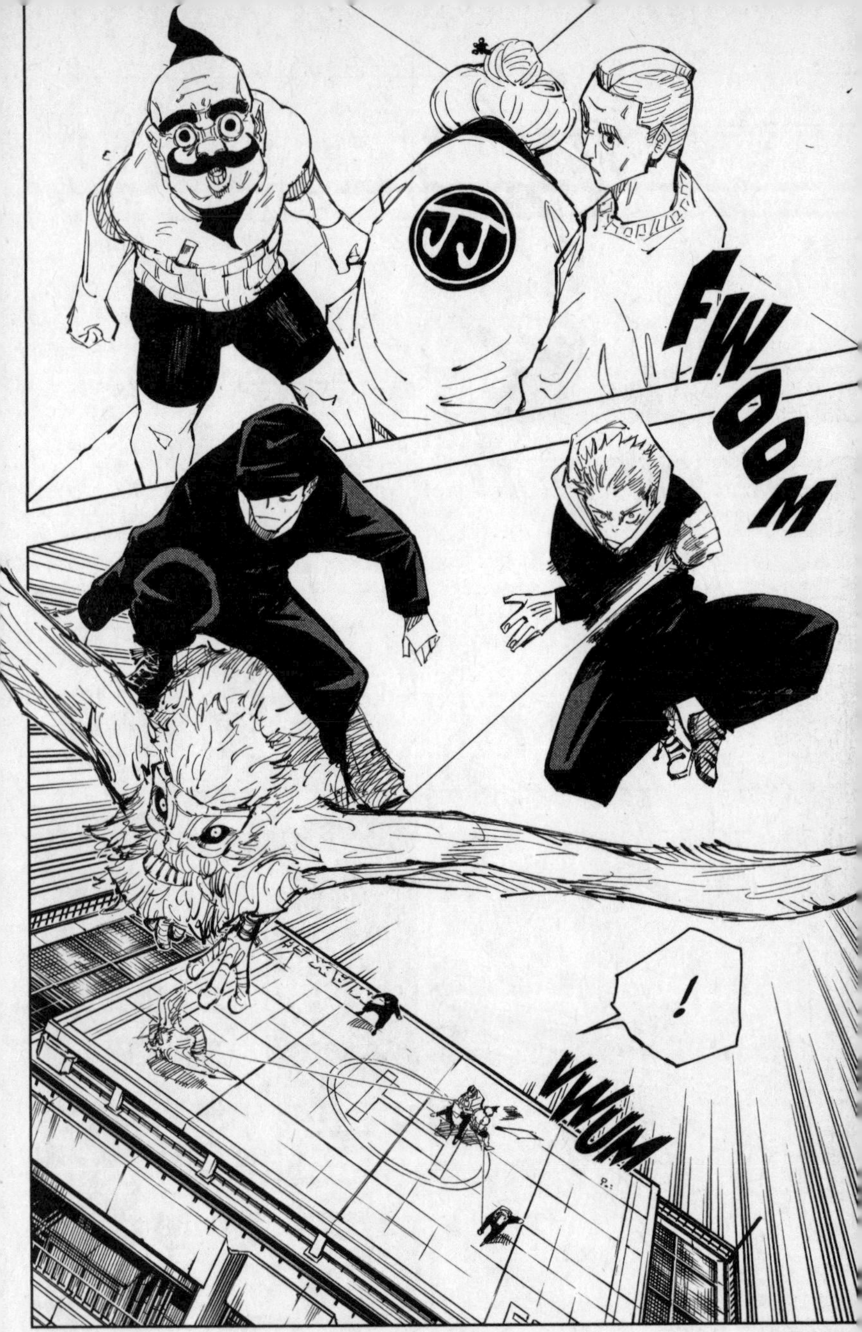
FWOOM
!
VWUM

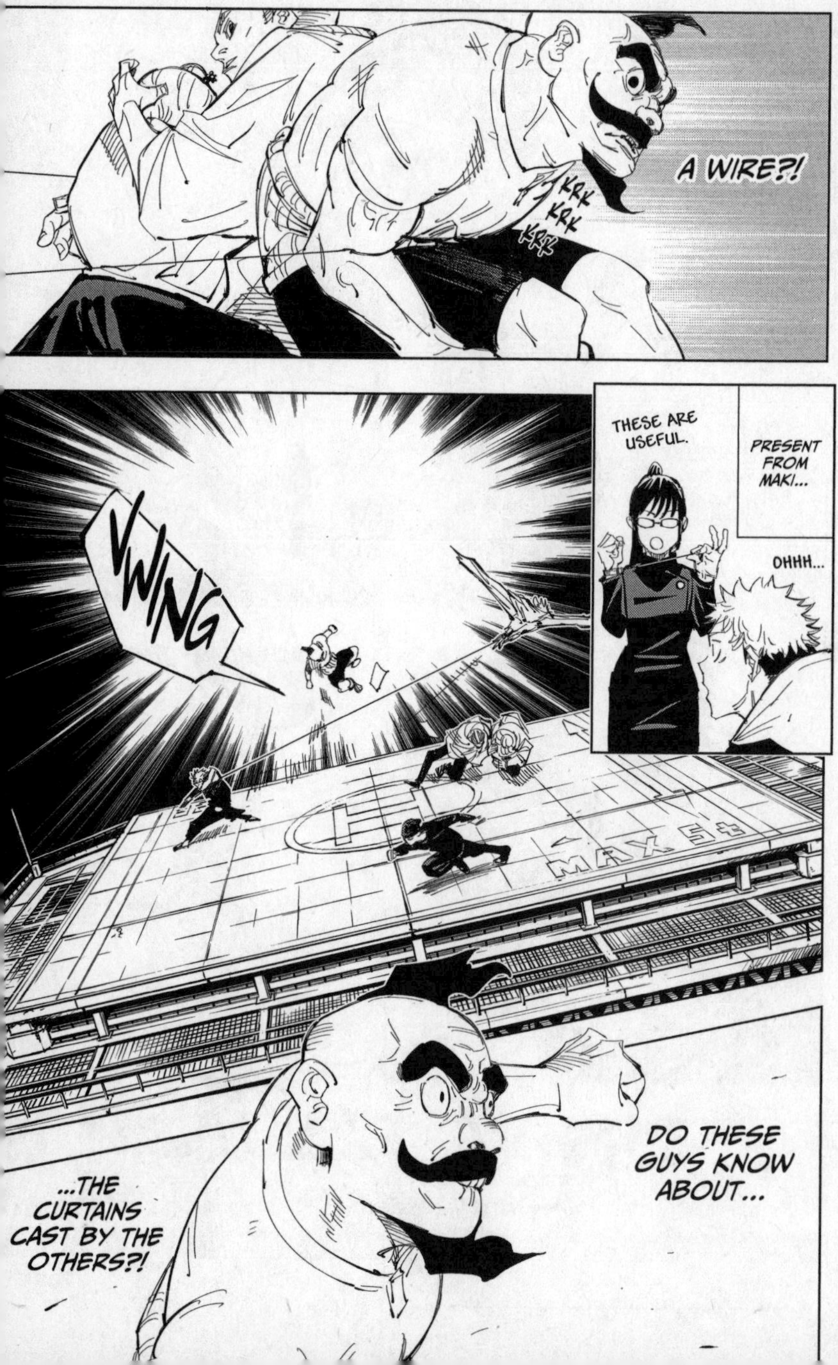
A WIRE?!
KRK KRK KRK
PRESENT FROM MAKI...
THESE ARE USEFUL.
OHHH...
VWING
DO THESE GUYS KNOW ABOUT...
...THE CURTAINS CAST BY THE OTHERS?!

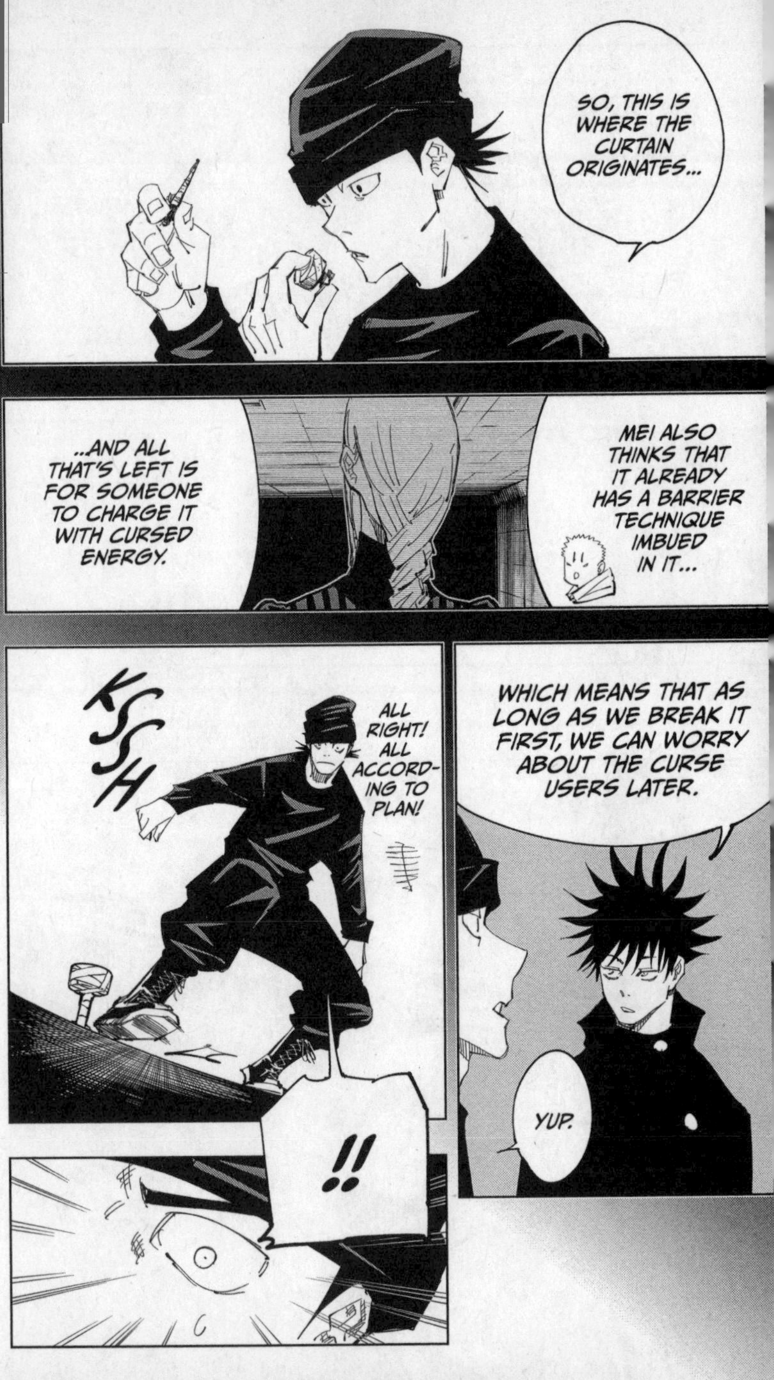
SO, THIS IS WHERE THE CURTAIN ORIGINATES...
MEI ALSO THINKS THAT IT ALREADY HAS A BARRIER TECHNIQUE IMBUED IN IT...
...AND ALL THAT'S LEFT IS FOR SOMEONE TO CHARGE IT WITH CURSED ENERGY.
WHICH MEANS THAT AS LONG AS WE BREAK IT FIRST, WE CAN WORRY ABOUT THE CURSE USERS LATER.
YUP.
ALL RIGHT! ALL ACCORDING TO PLAN!
KSSH
!!

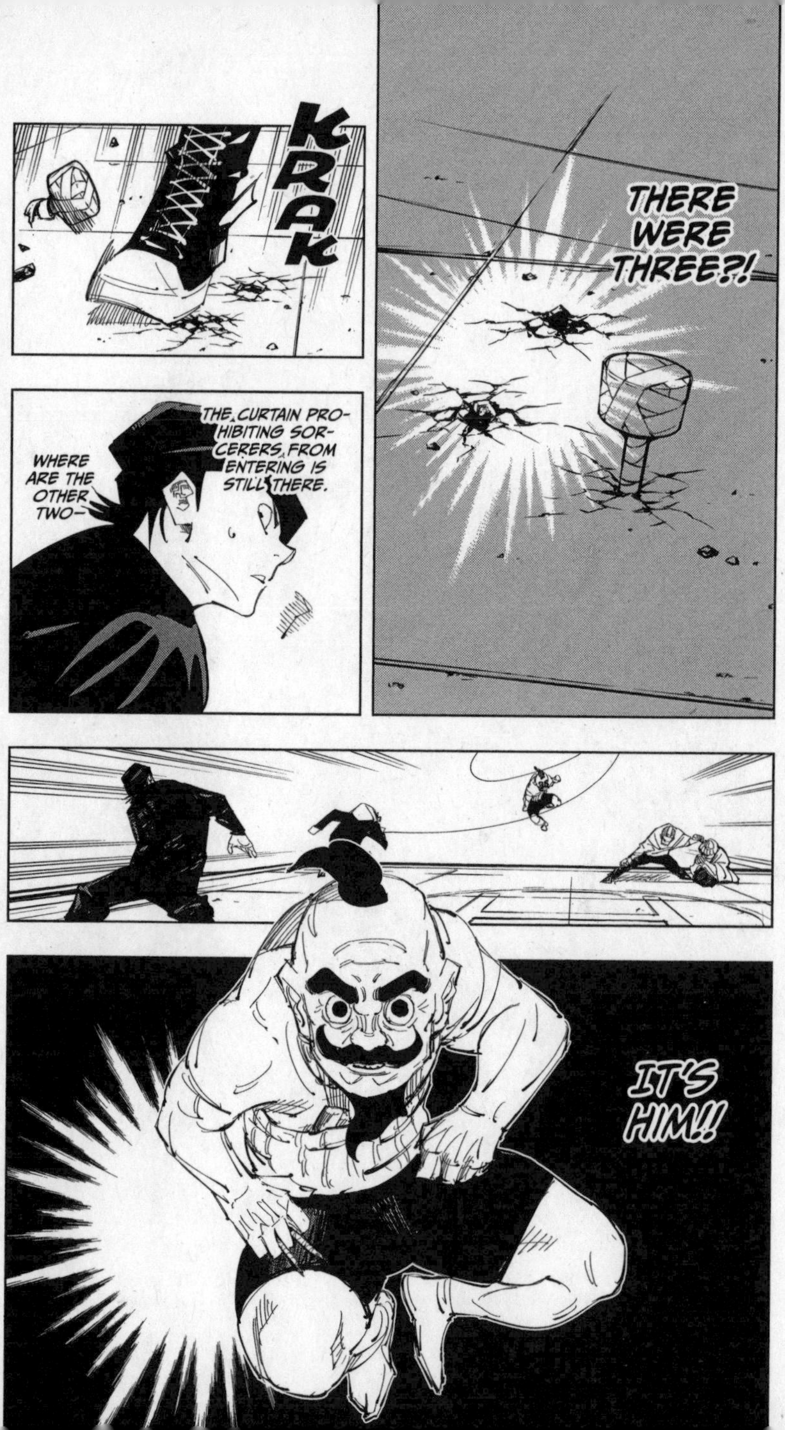
THERE WERE THREE?!
KRAK
THE CURTAIN PROHIBITING SORCERERS FROM ENTERING IS STILL THERE.
WHERE ARE THE OTHER TWO—
IT'S HIM!!

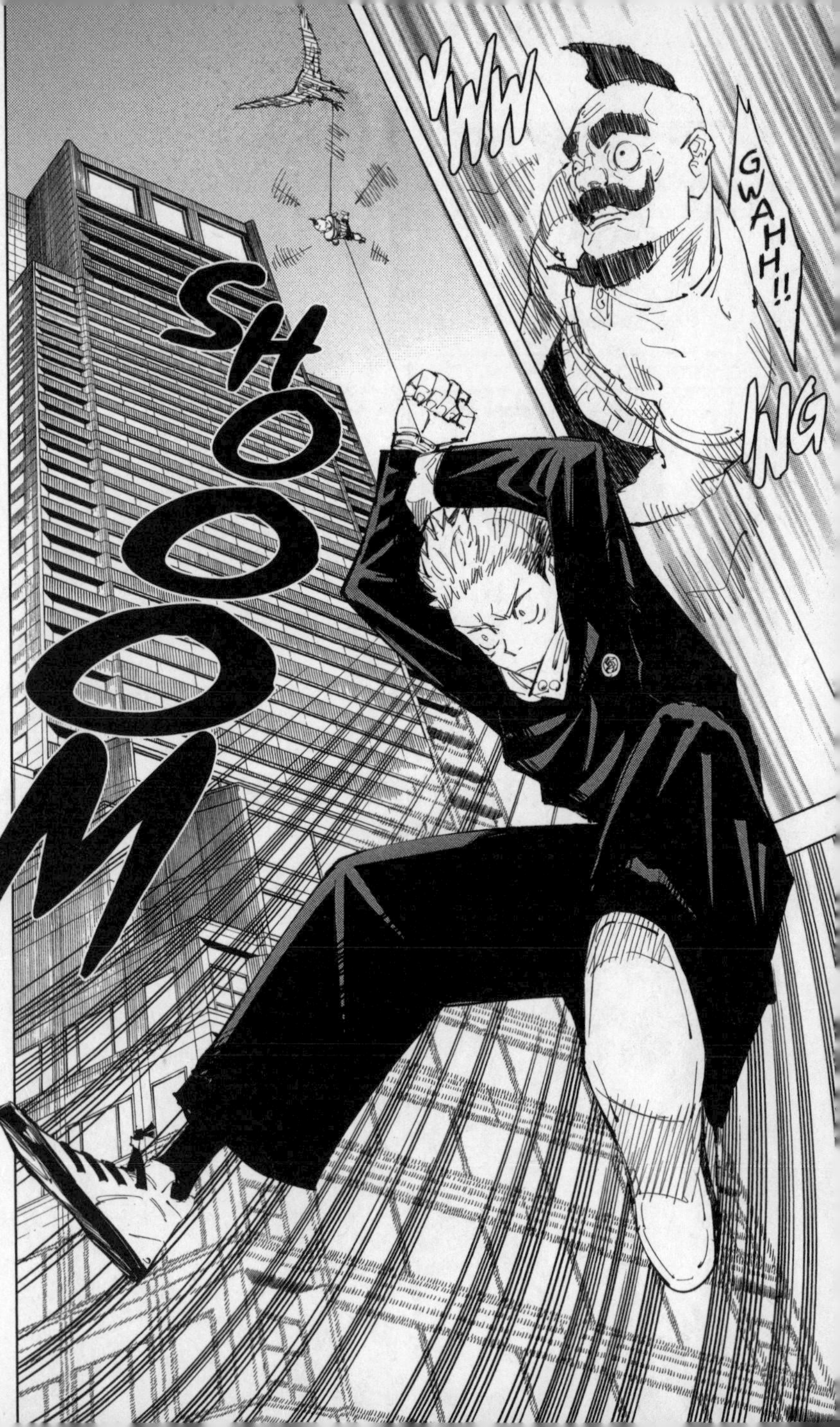
VWW
GWAHH!!
ING
SHOOOM

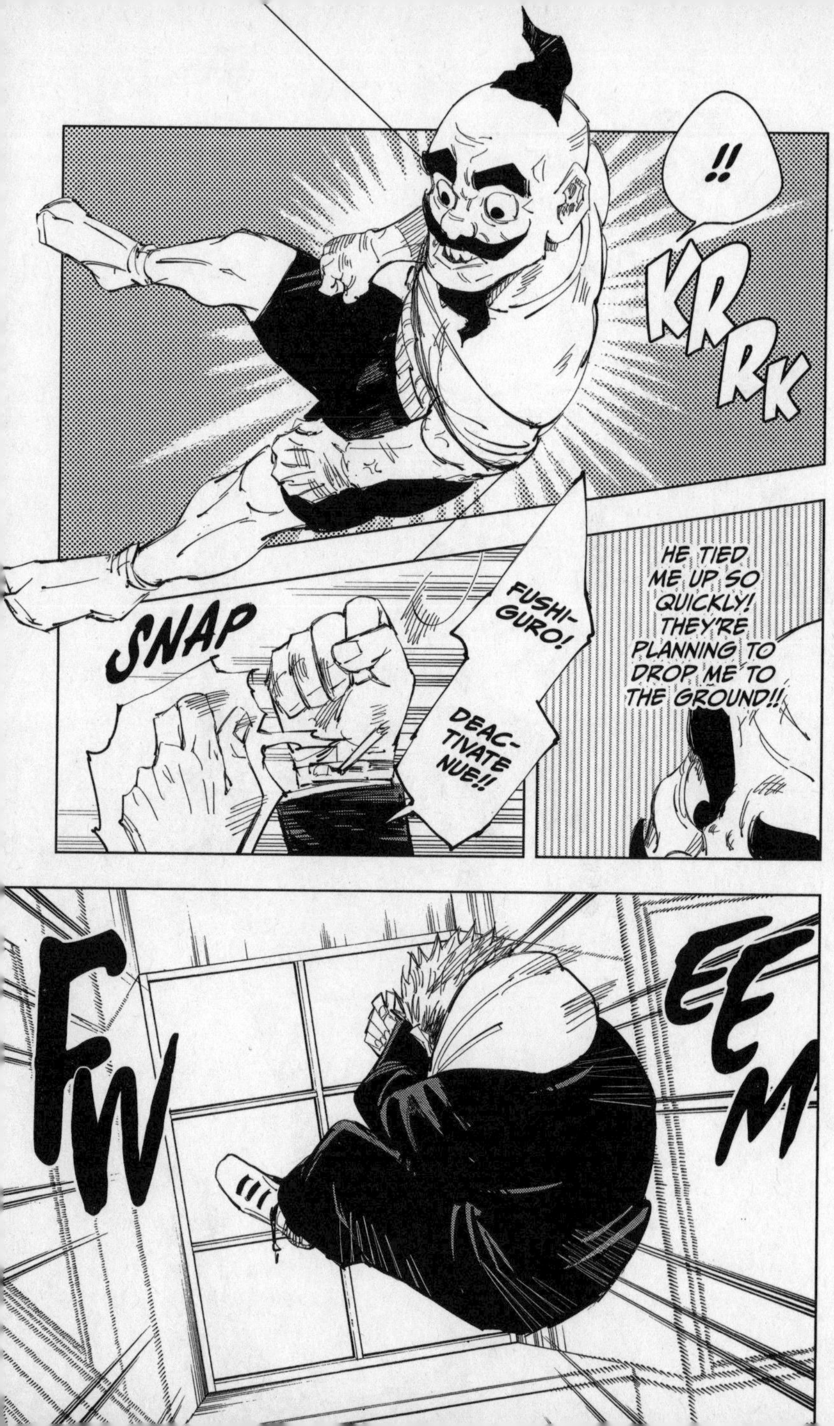
!!
KRRK
HE TIED ME UP SO QUICKLY! THEY'RE PLANNING TO DROP ME TO THE GROUND!!
FUSHIGURO!
DEACTIVATE NUE!!
SNAP
EEM
FW

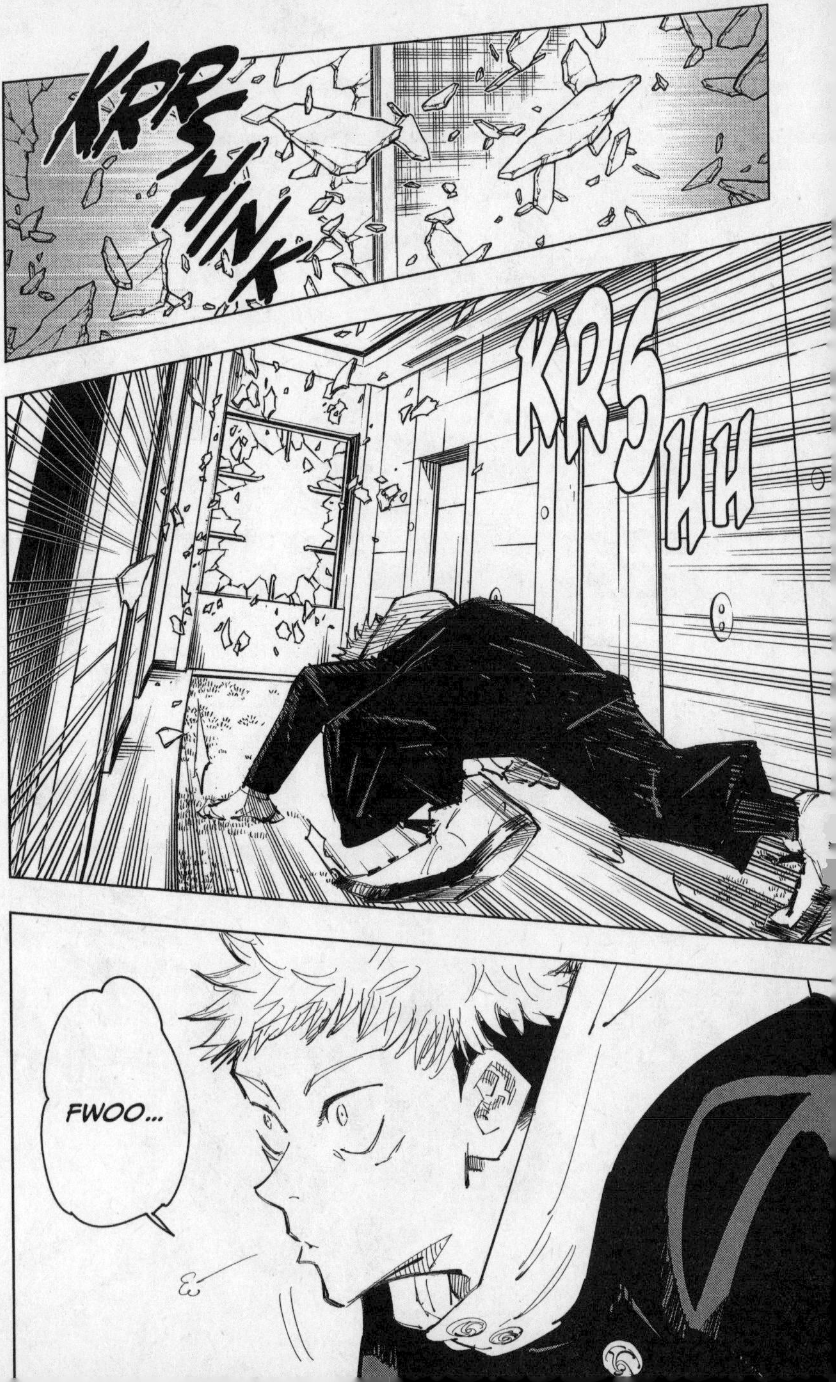
KRR SHINK
KRS HH
FWOO...

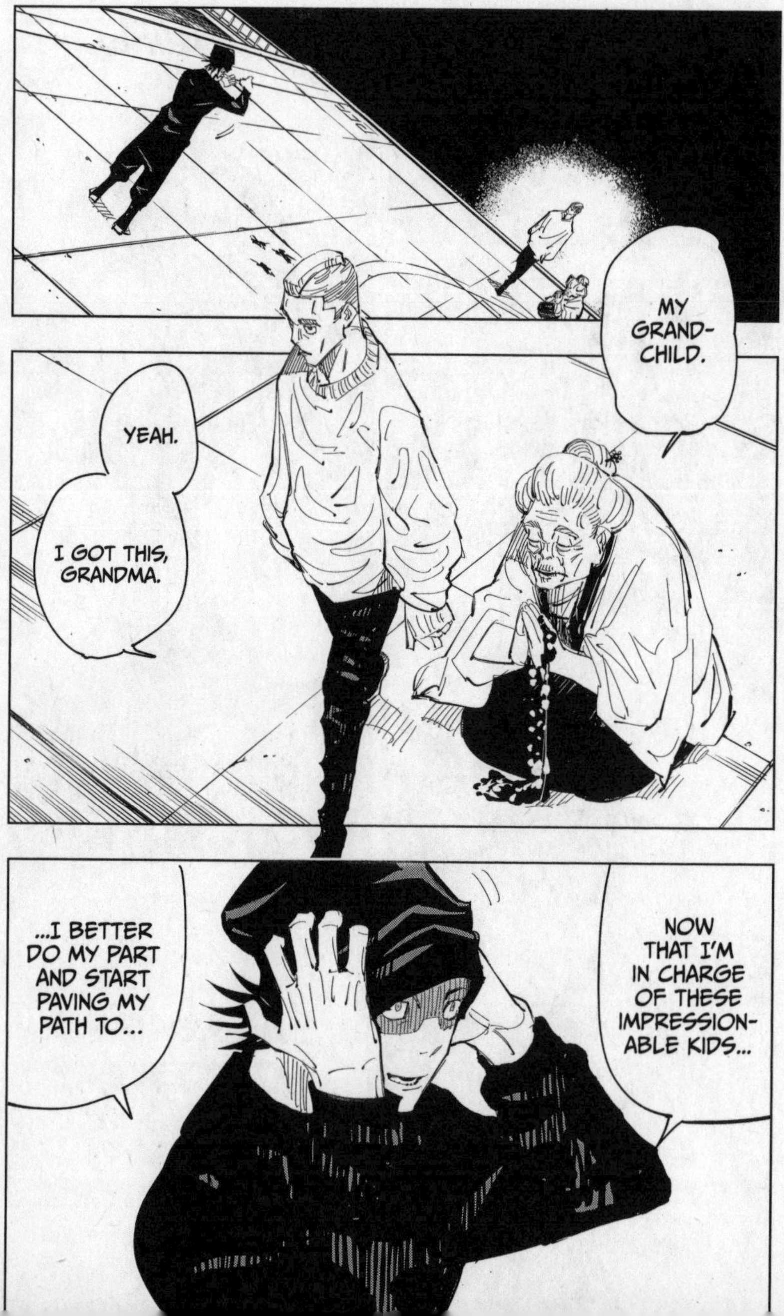
MY GRAND-CHILD.
YEAH.
I GOT THIS, GRANDMA.
NOW THAT I'M IN CHARGE OF THESE IMPRESSION-ABLE KIDS...
...I BETTER DO MY PART AND START PAVING MY PATH TO...

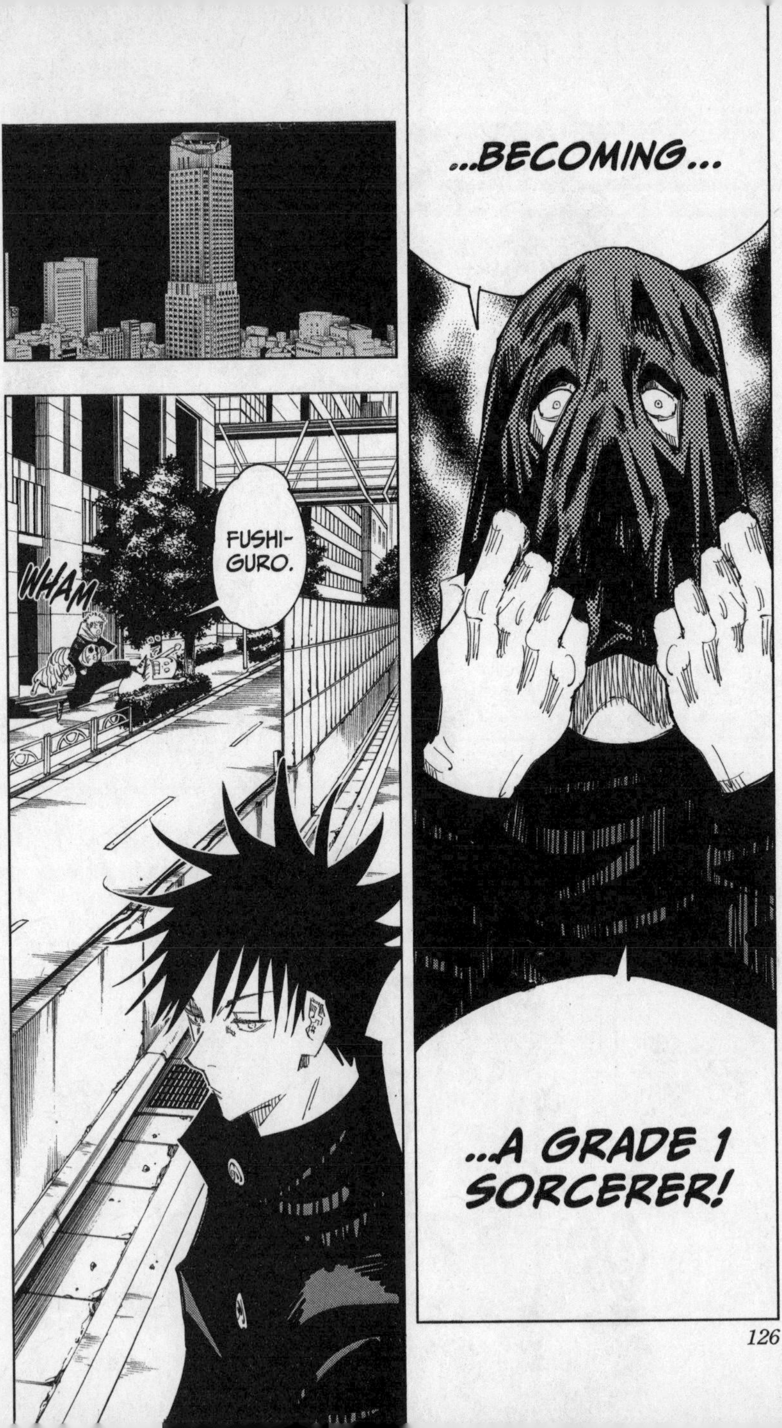
...BECOMING...
...A GRADE 1 SORCERER!
FUSHI-GURO.
WHAM

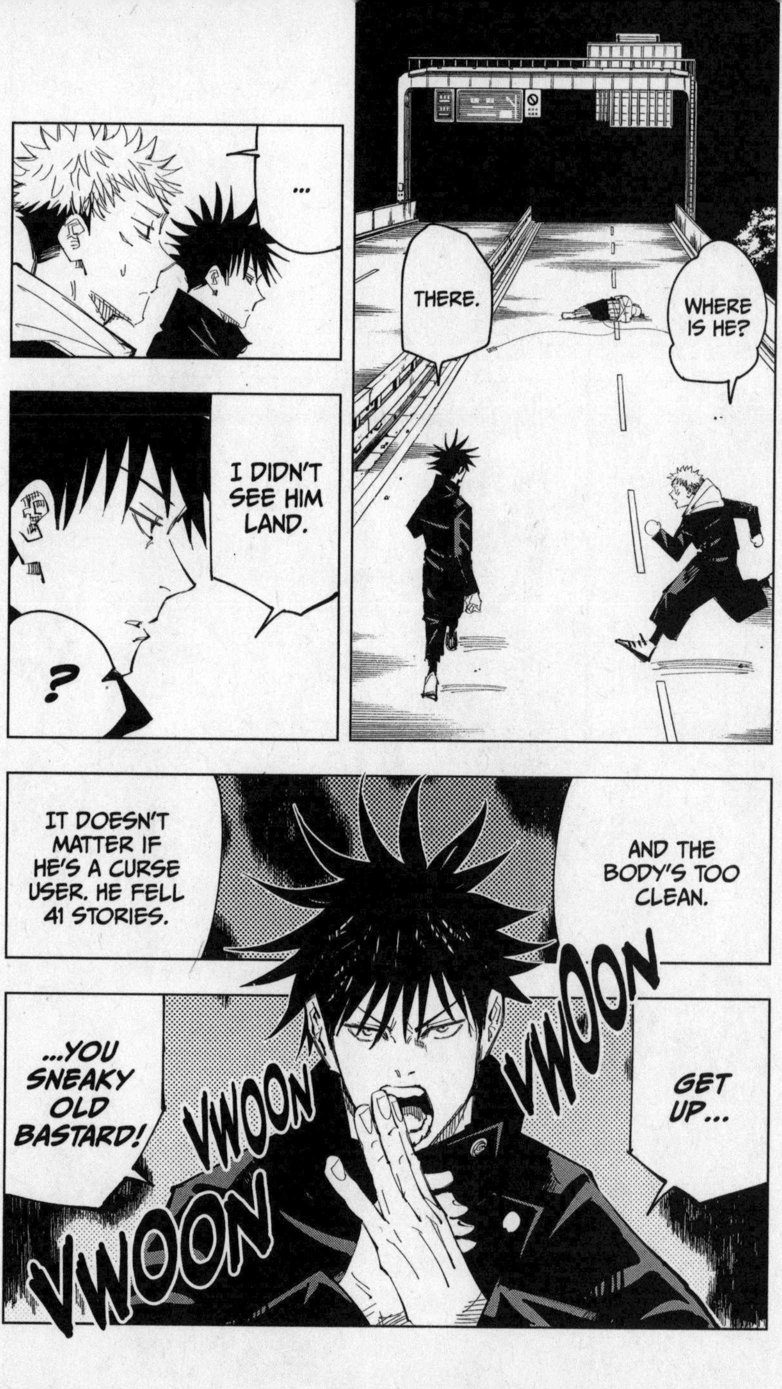
WHERE IS HE?
THERE.
...
I DIDN'T SEE HIM LAND.
?
AND THE BODY'S TOO CLEAN.
IT DOESN'T MATTER IF HE'S A CURSE USER. HE FELL 41 STORIES.
GET UP...
VWOON
VWOON
VWOON
VWOON
...YOU SNEAKY OLD BASTARD!

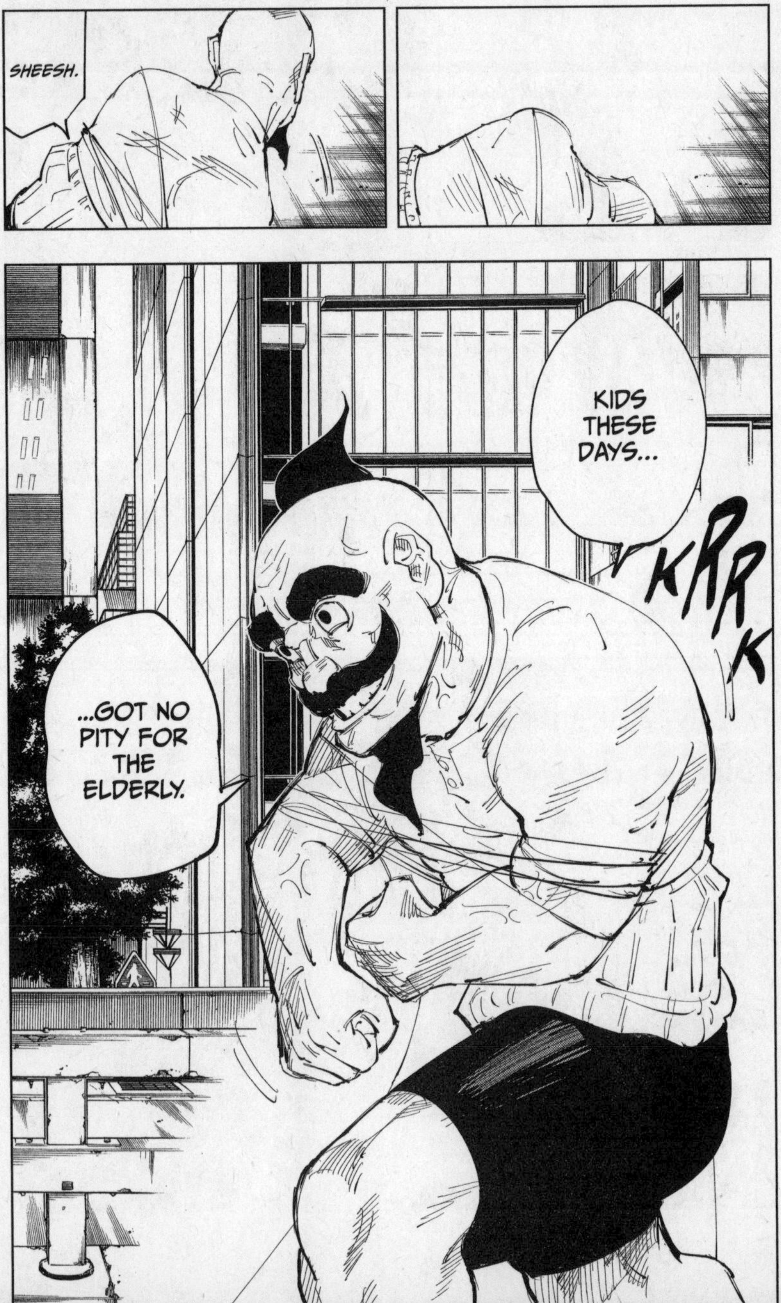
SHEESH.
KIDS THESE DAYS...
KRRK
...GOT NO PITY FOR THE ELDERLY.

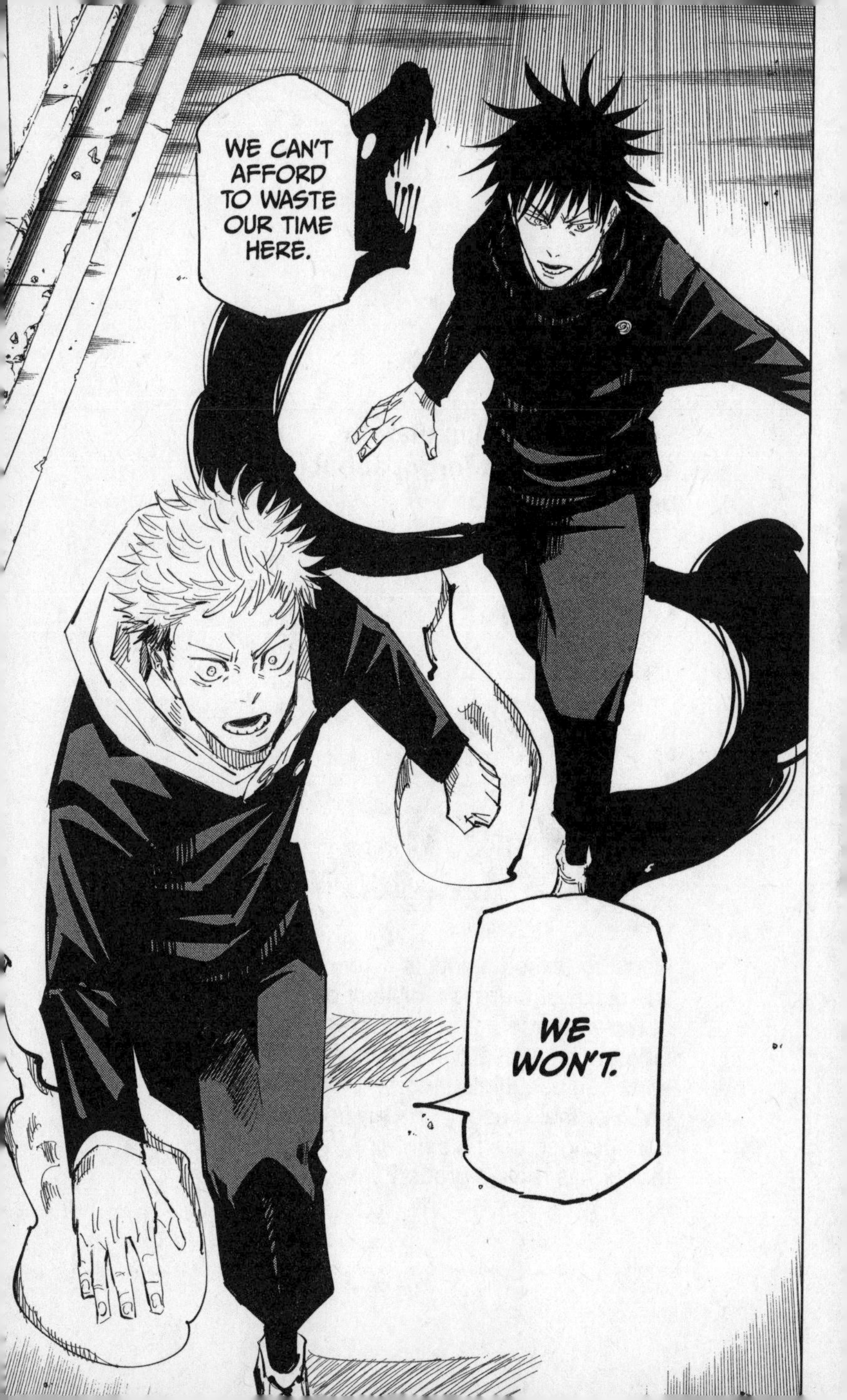
WE CAN'T AFFORD TO WASTE OUR TIME HERE.
WE WON'T.

Scenes I was planning on addressing but forgot about until now, part 5

• Ko-Guy's rank

Ranking cursed spirits is a very wishy-washy science, but there is a distinct difference between grade 2 and semi-grade 1. The difference is based on whether the cursed spirit can use jujutsu (cursed techniques) or not. For that reason, Ko-Guy is as strong, if not stronger, than a semi-grade 1, even though his rank is grade 2.

CHAPTER 95: THE SHIBUYA INCIDENT, PART 13

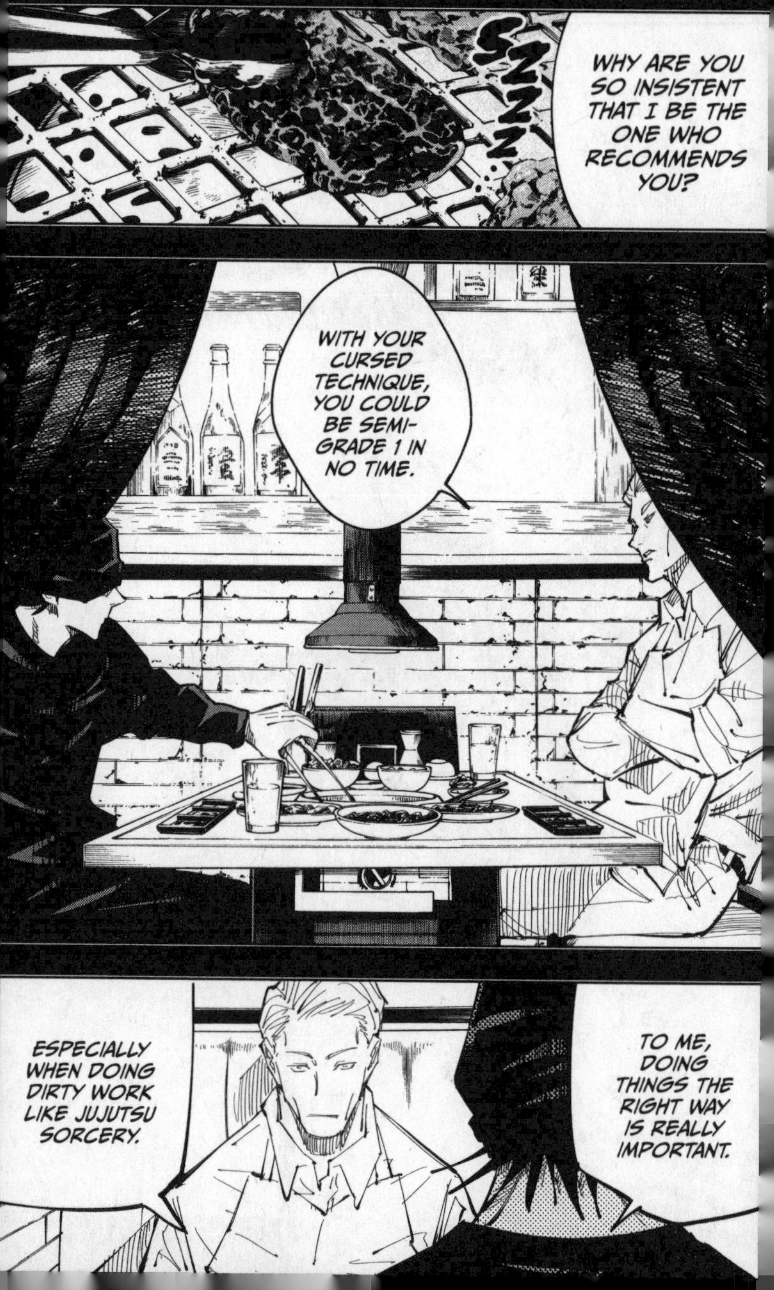
WHY ARE YOU SO INSISTENT THAT I BE THE ONE WHO RECOMMENDS YOU?
WITH YOUR CURSED TECHNIQUE, YOU COULD BE SEMI-GRADE 1 IN NO TIME.
TO ME, DOING THINGS THE RIGHT WAY IS REALLY IMPORTANT.
ESPECIALLY WHEN DOING DIRTY WORK LIKE JUJUTSU SORCERY.

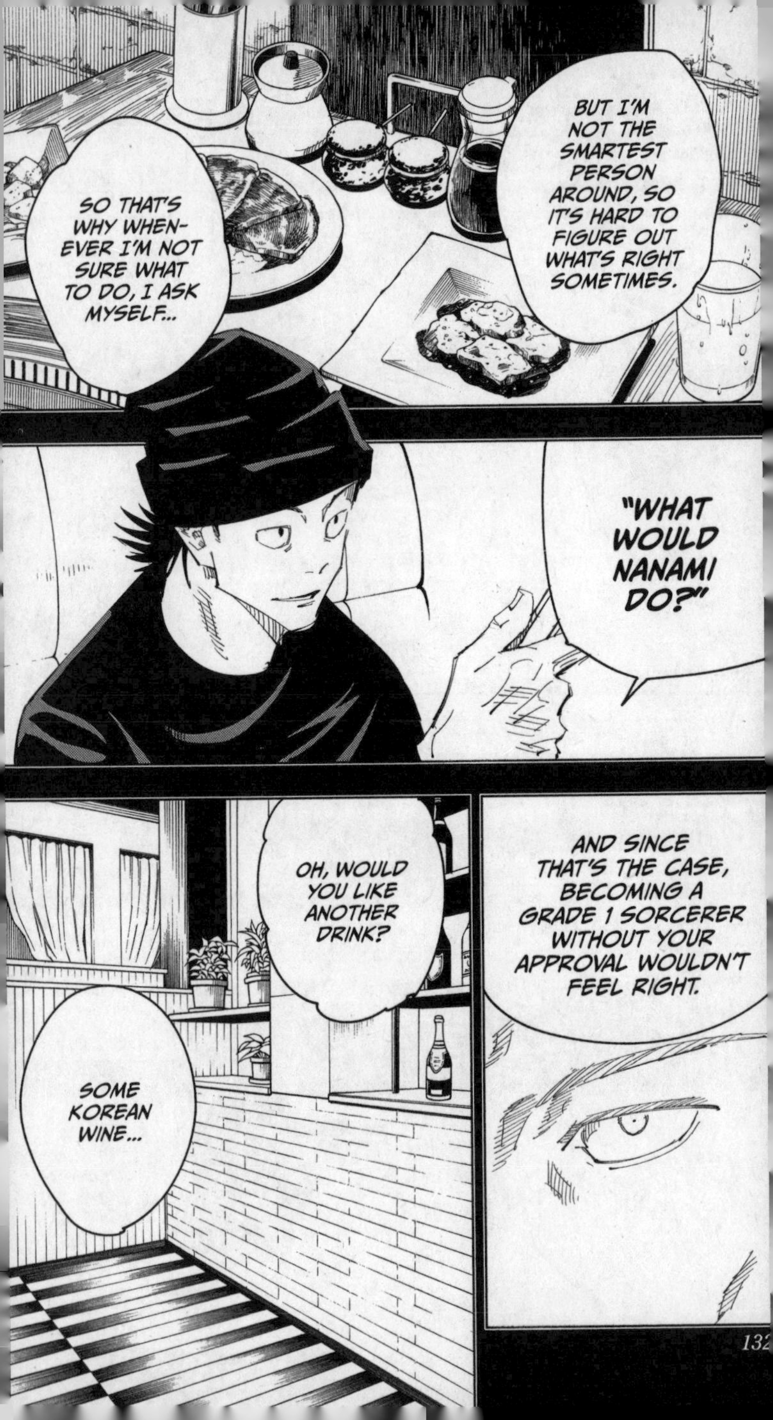
BUT I'M NOT THE SMARTEST PERSON AROUND, SO IT'S HARD TO FIGURE OUT WHAT'S RIGHT SOMETIMES.
SO THAT'S WHY WHENEVER I'M NOT SURE WHAT TO DO, I ASK MYSELF...
"WHAT WOULD NANAMI DO?"
AND SINCE THAT'S THE CASE, BECOMING A GRADE 1 SORCERER WITHOUT YOUR APPROVAL WOULDN'T FEEL RIGHT.
OH, WOULD YOU LIKE ANOTHER DRINK?
SOME KOREAN WINE...

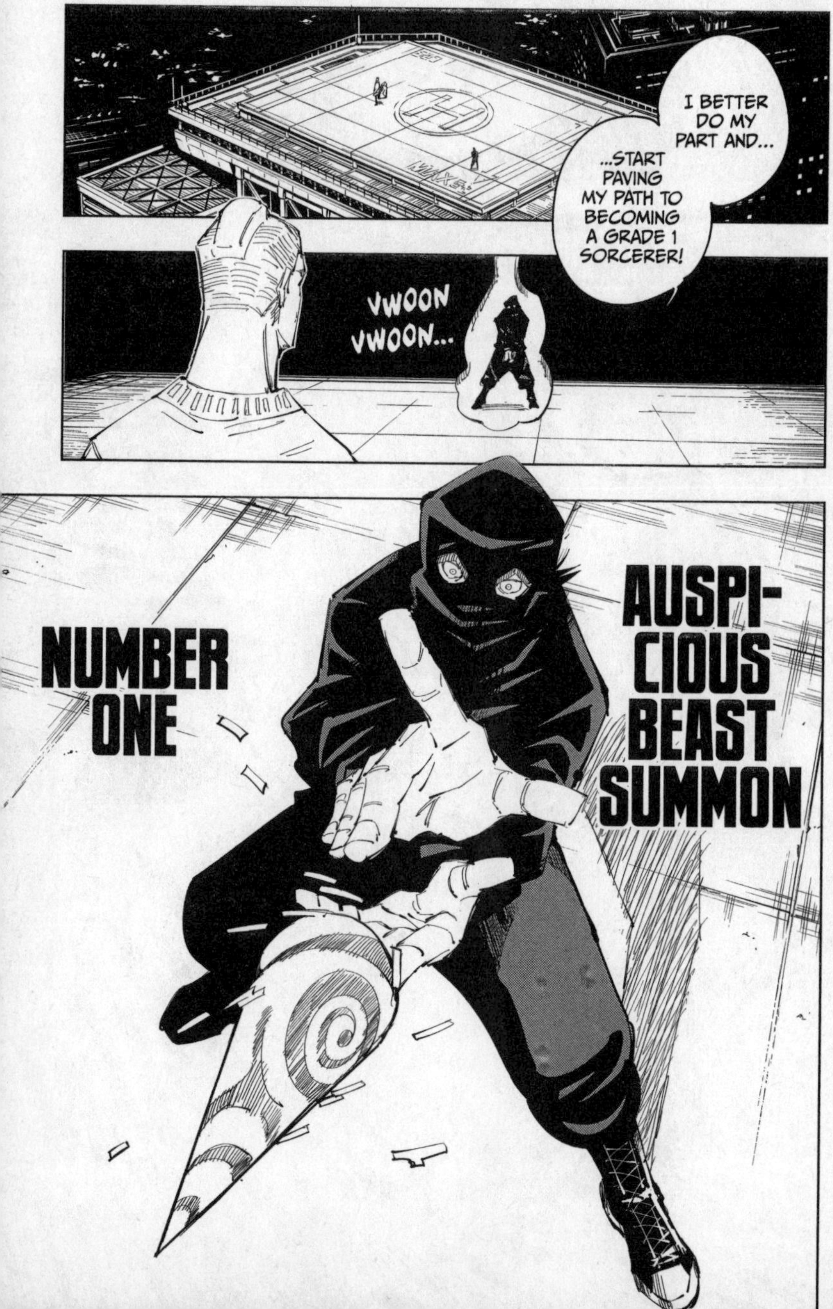
I BETTER DO MY PART AND...
...START PAVING MY PATH TO BECOMING A GRADE 1 SORCERER!
VWOON VWOON...
AUSPICIOUS BEAST SUMMON
NUMBER ONE

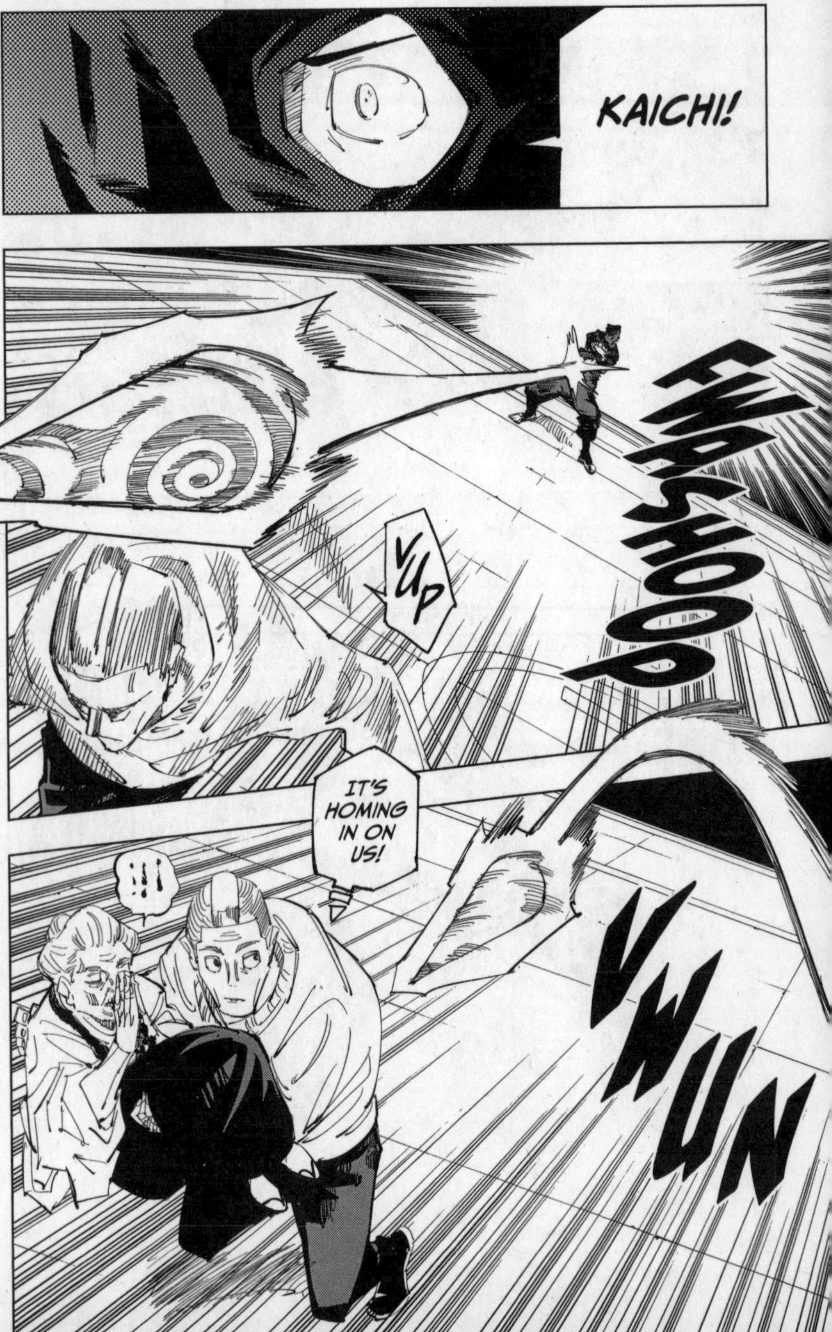
KAICHI!
FWASHOOP
VUP
IT'S HOMING IN ON US!
!!
VWUN

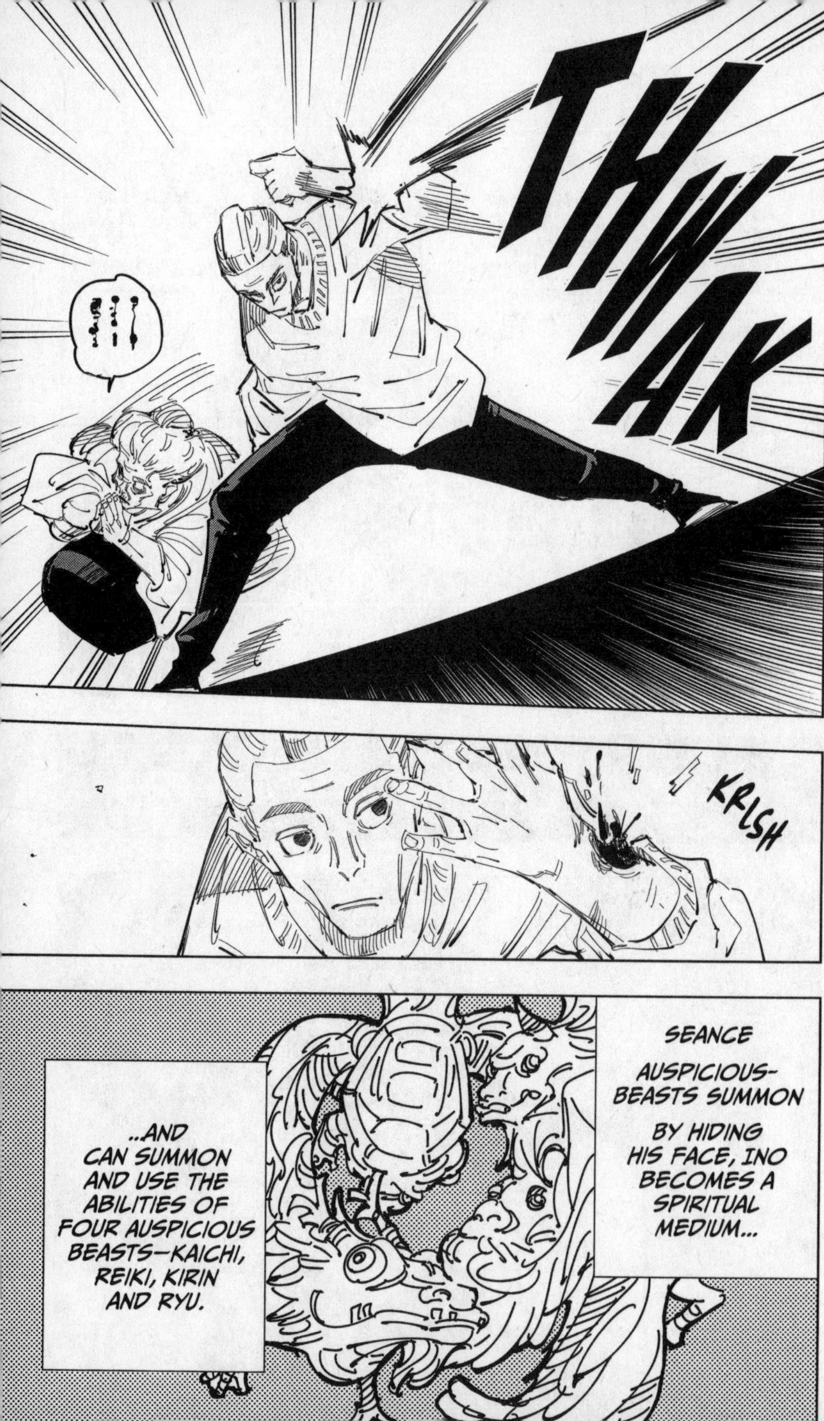
THWAK
KRISH
SEANCE
AUSPICIOUS-BEASTS SUMMON
BY HIDING HIS FACE, INO BECOMES A SPIRITUAL MEDIUM...
...AND CAN SUMMON AND USE THE ABILITIES OF FOUR AUSPICIOUS BEASTS—KAICHI, REIKI, KIRIN AND RYU.

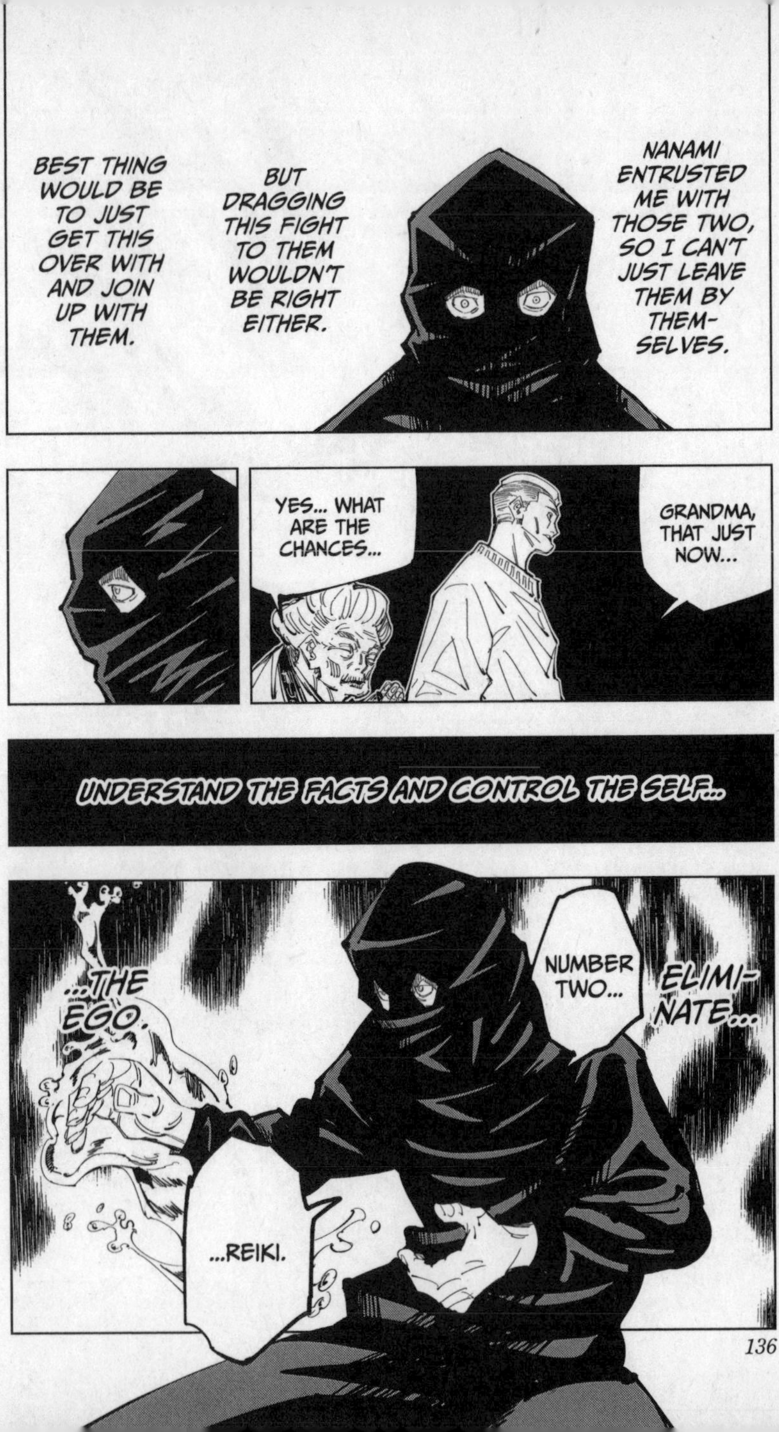
NANAMI ENTRUSTED ME WITH THOSE TWO, SO I CAN'T JUST LEAVE THEM BY THEM-SELVES.
BUT DRAGGING THIS FIGHT TO THEM WOULDN'T BE RIGHT EITHER.
BEST THING WOULD BE TO JUST GET THIS OVER WITH AND JOIN UP WITH THEM.
GRANDMA, THAT JUST NOW...
YES... WHAT ARE THE CHANCES...
UNDERSTAND THE FACTS AND CONTROL THE SELF...
ELIMI-NATE...
NUMBER TWO...
...THE EGO.
...REIKI.

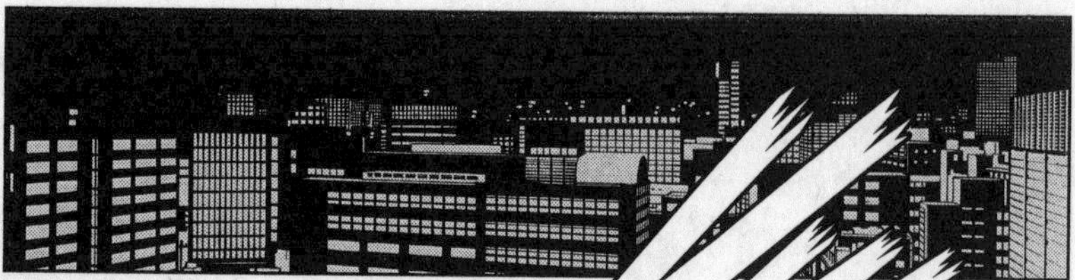

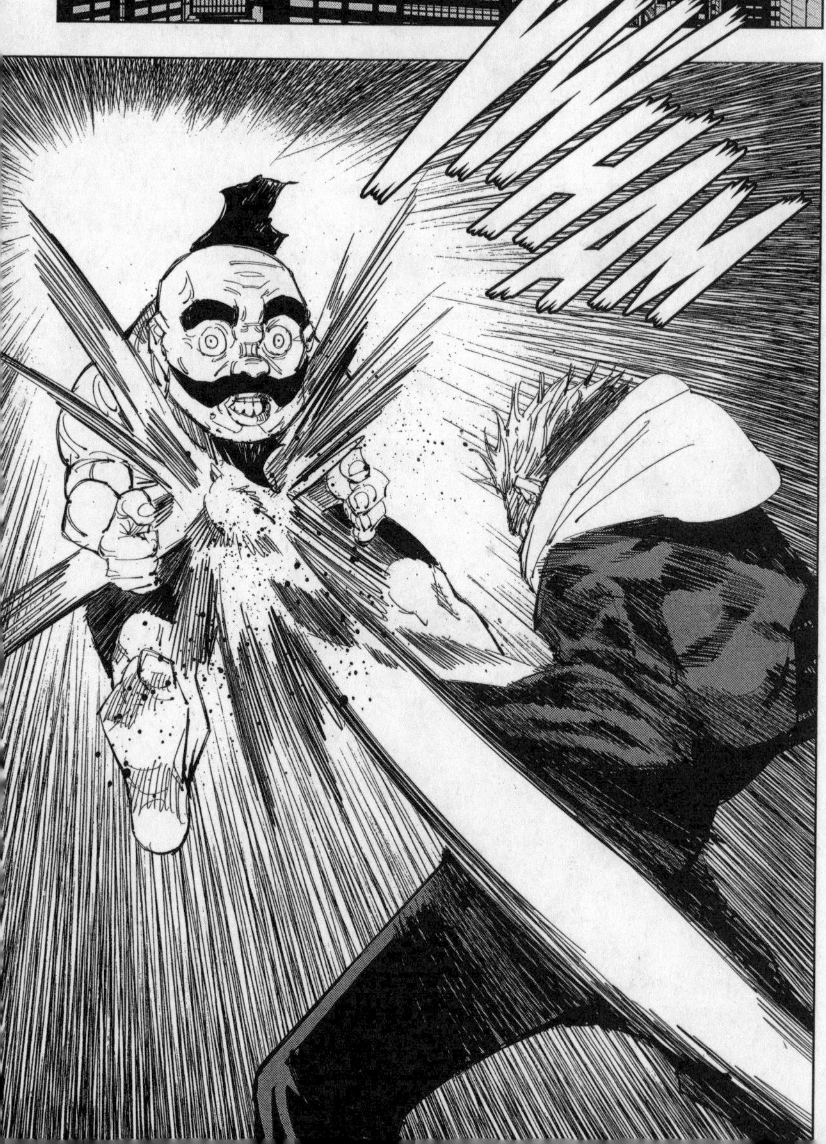
WHAM

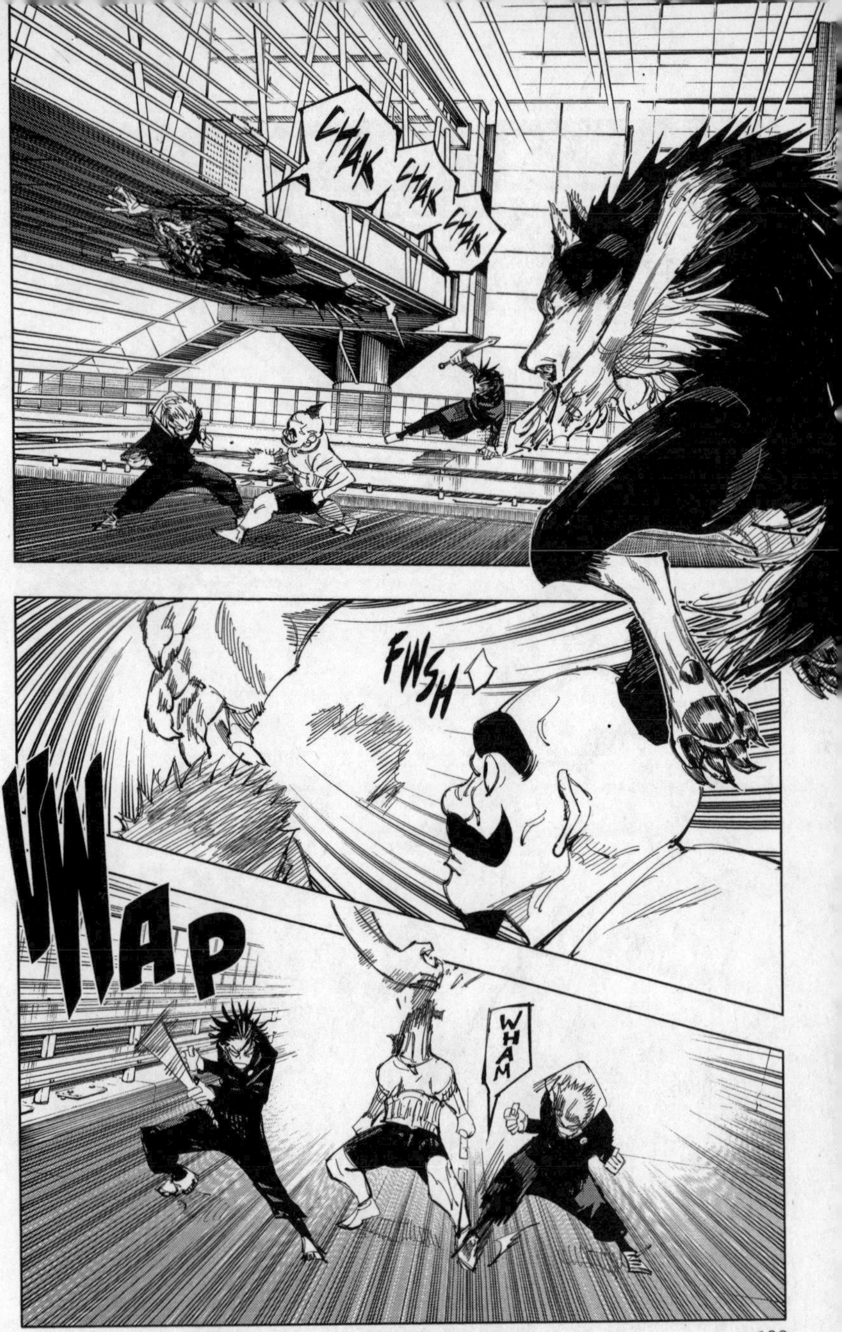
CHAK CHAK CHAK
FWSH
WHAP
WHAM

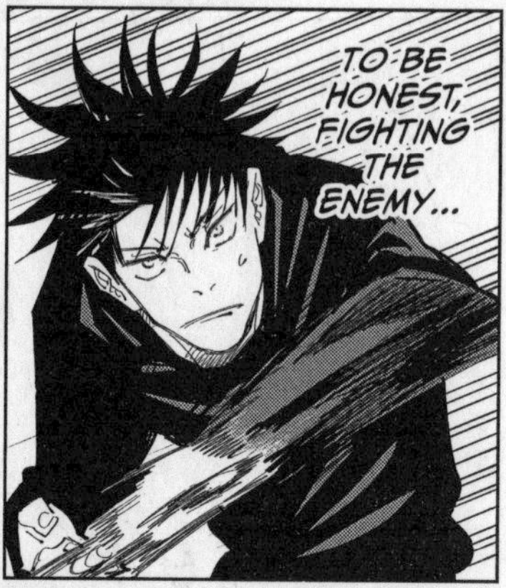
TO BE HONEST, FIGHTING THE ENEMY...

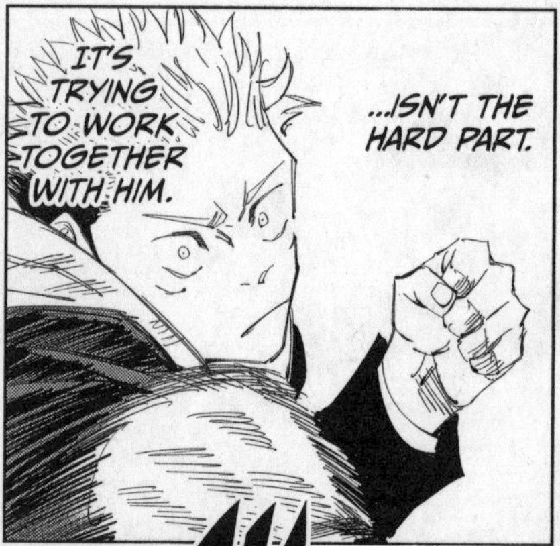
...ISN'T THE HARD PART.
IT'S TRYING TO WORK TOGETHER WITH HIM.

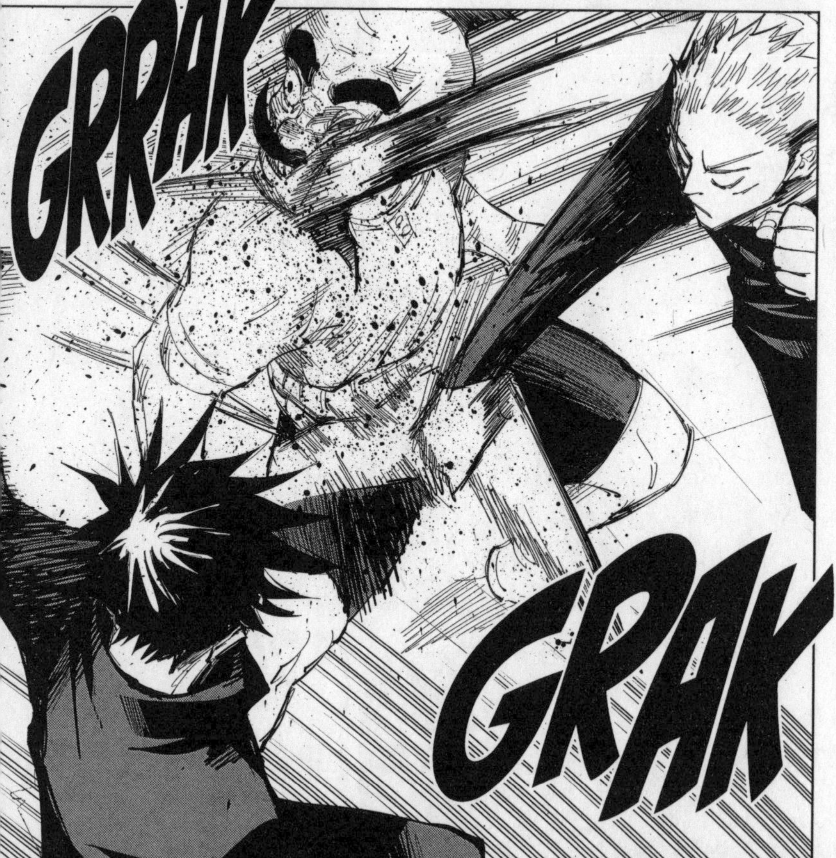
GRRAK
GRAK

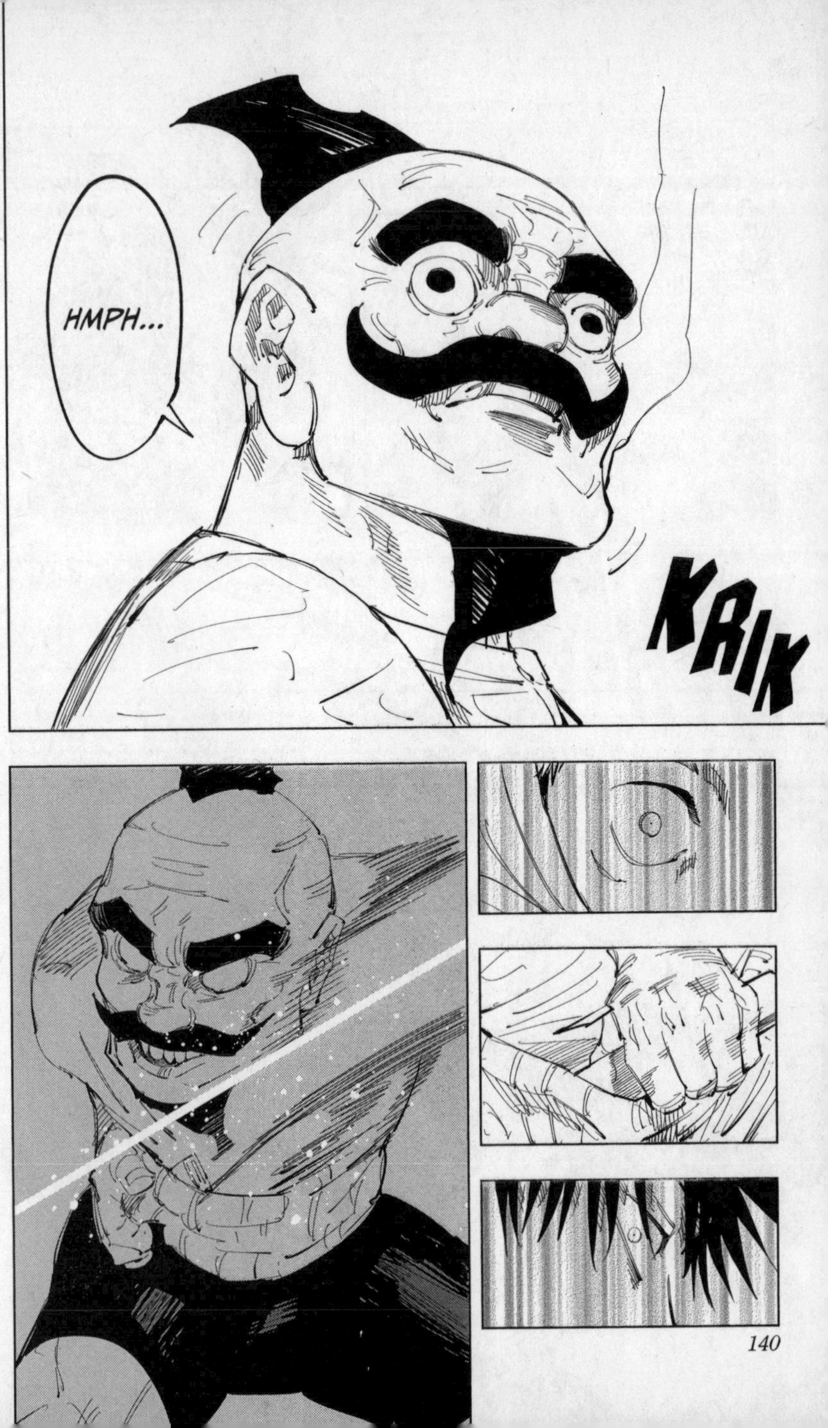
KRIK
HMPH...

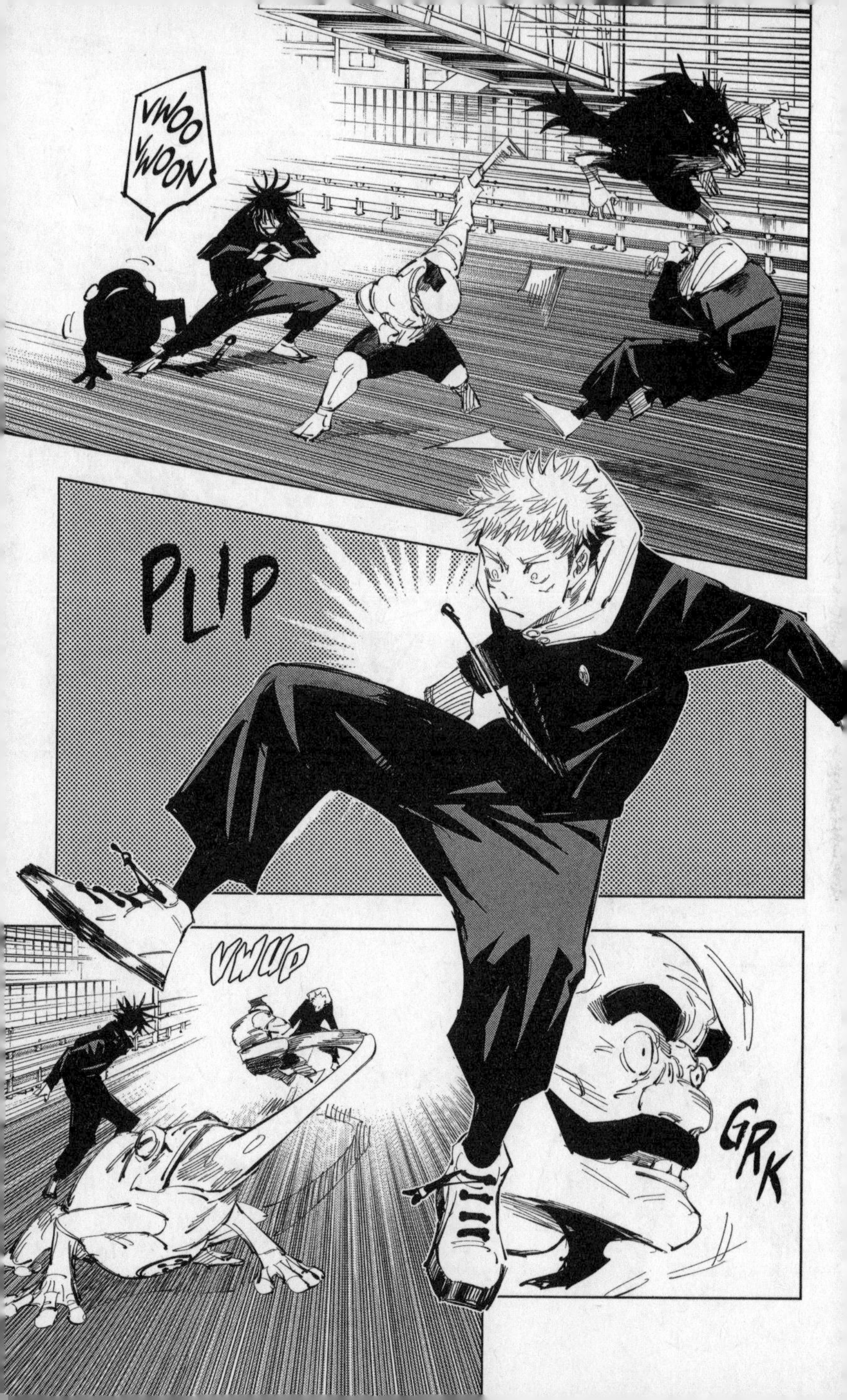
VWOO VWOON
PLIP
GRK
VWUP

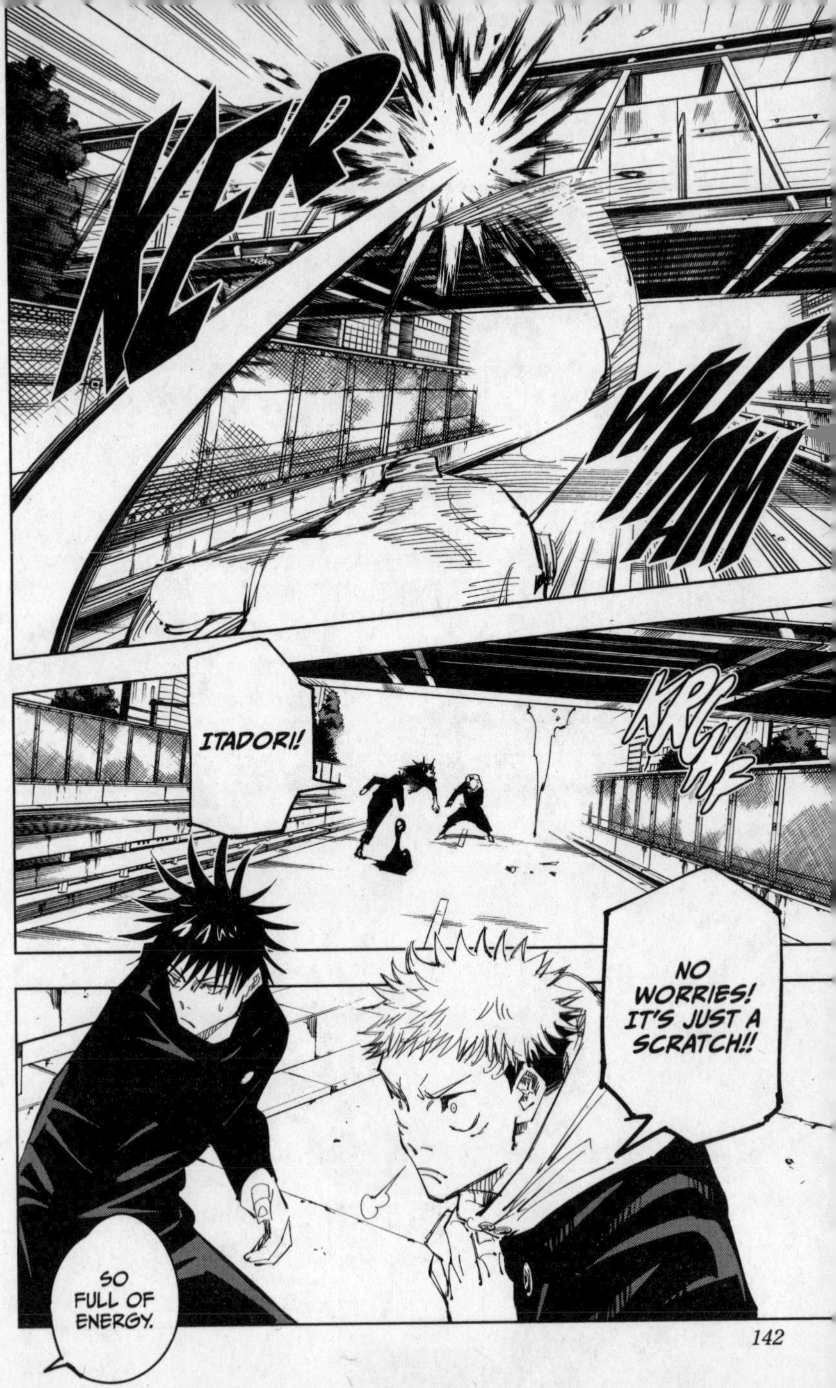
WHAM
ITADORI!
NO WORRIES! IT'S JUST A SCRATCH!!
SO FULL OF ENERGY.

DIVINE DOG'S CLAWS CAN DAMAGE EVEN A SPECIAL GRADE.
I HIT HIM WITH ALL I GOT TOO.
THEN WHY...
...IS HE NOT HURT?!
FUTURES FULL OF MUCH PROMISE.
TP
DEFINITELY WORTH KILLING.

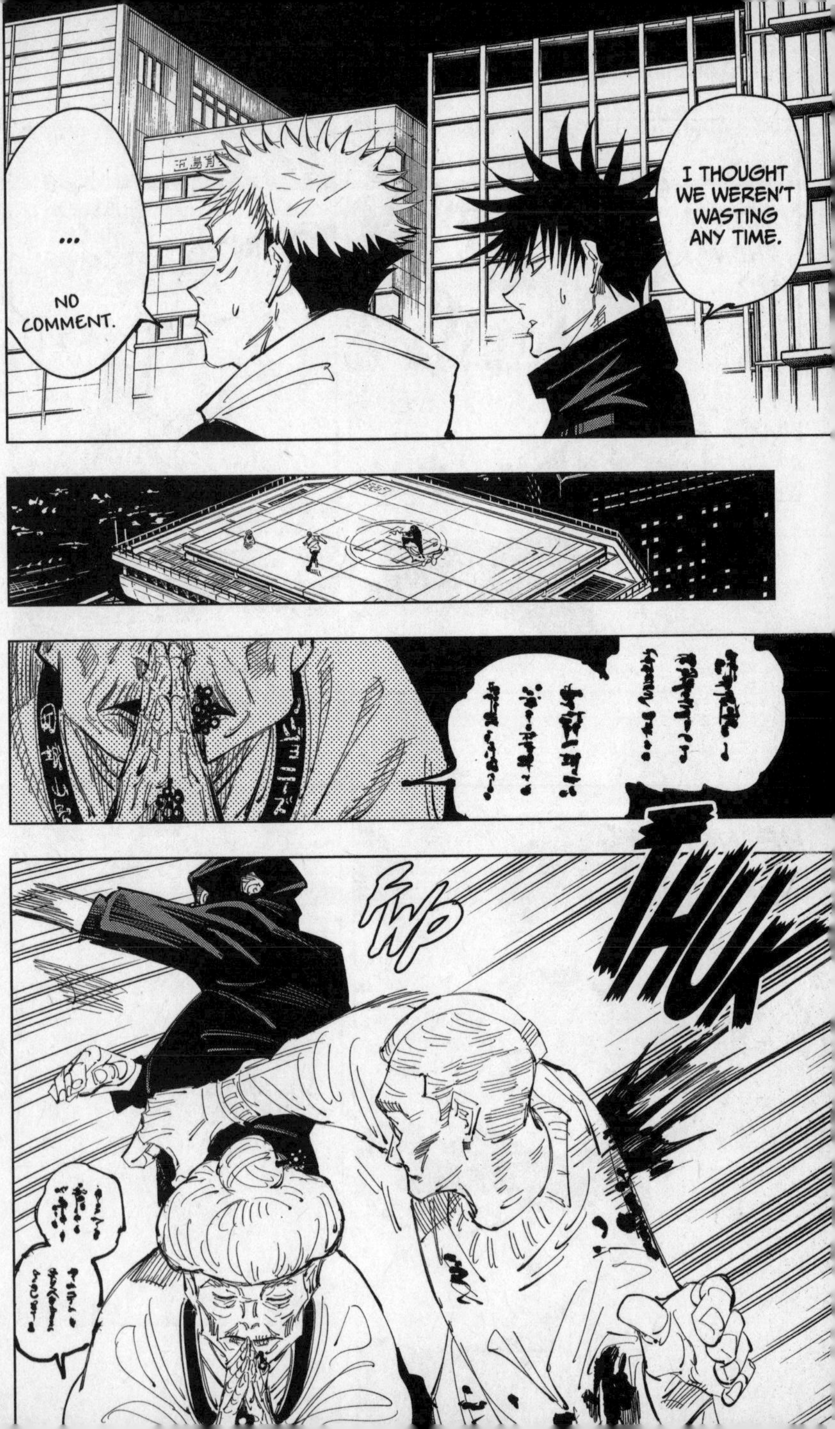
I THOUGHT WE WEREN'T WASTING ANY TIME.
... NO COMMENT.
THUK
FWP

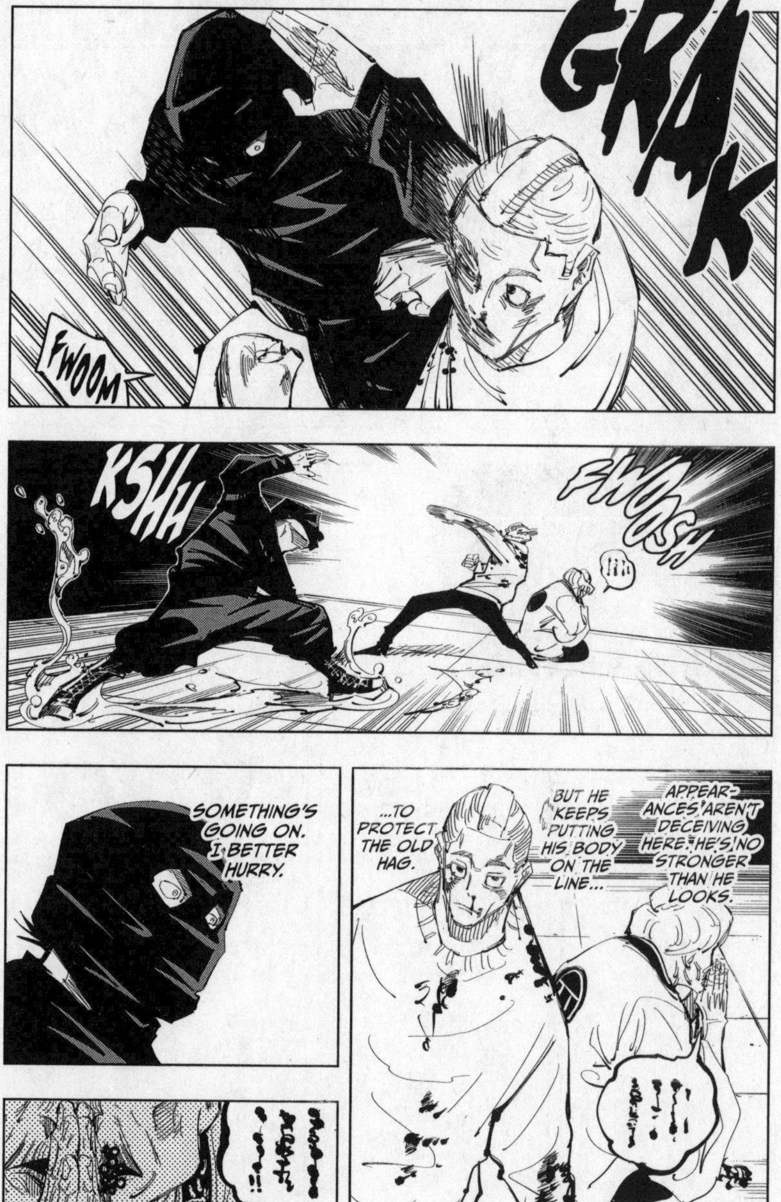
GRAK
FWOOM
FWOOSH
KSHH
APPEAR-ANCES AREN'T DECEIVING HERE. HE'S NO STRONGER THAN HE LOOKS.
BUT HE KEEPS PUTTING HIS BODY ON THE LINE...
...TO PROTECT THE OLD HAG.
SOMETHING'S GOING ON. I BETTER HURRY.

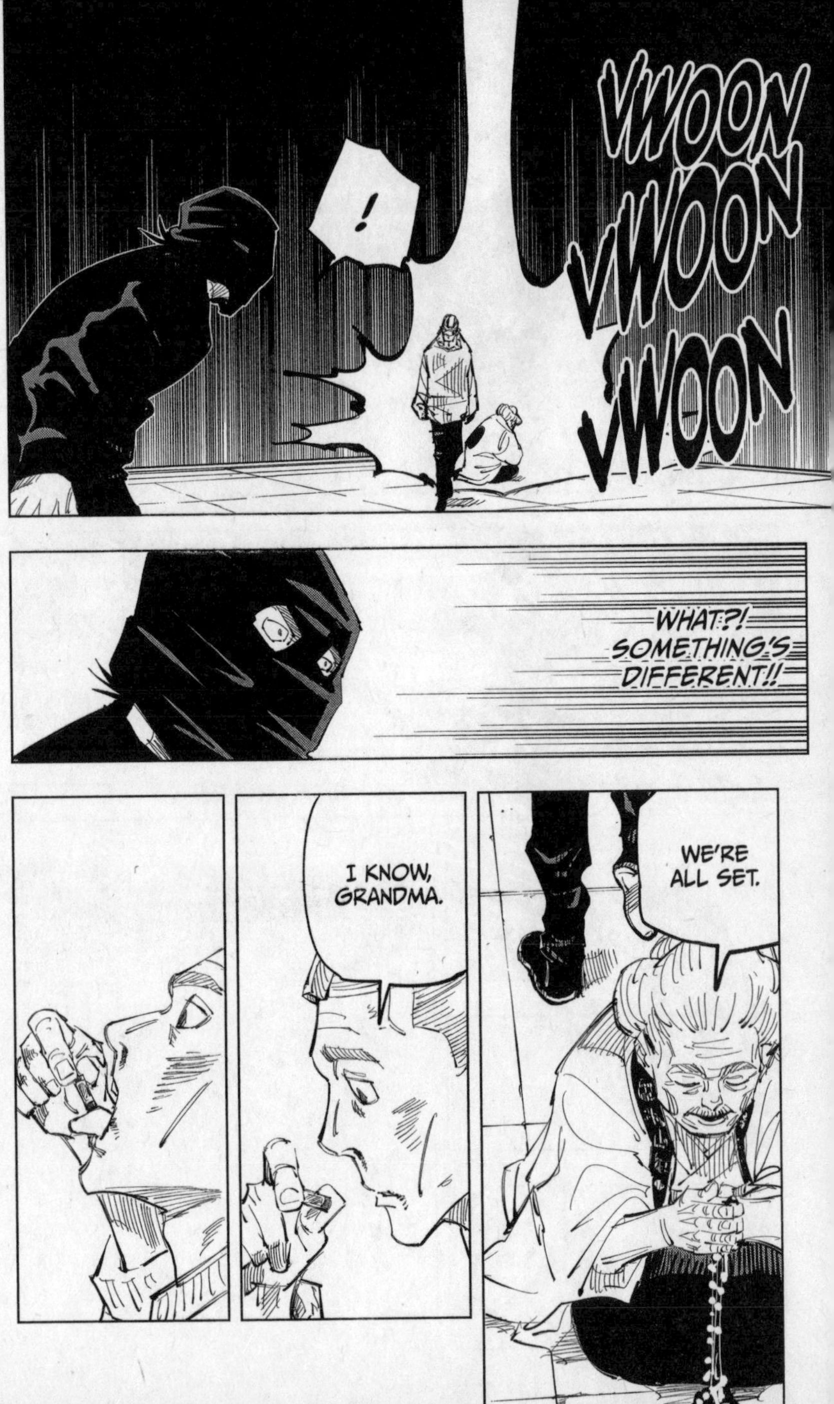
VWOON VWOON VWOON
!
WHAT?! SOMETHING'S DIFFERENT!!
WE'RE ALL SET.
I KNOW, GRANDMA.

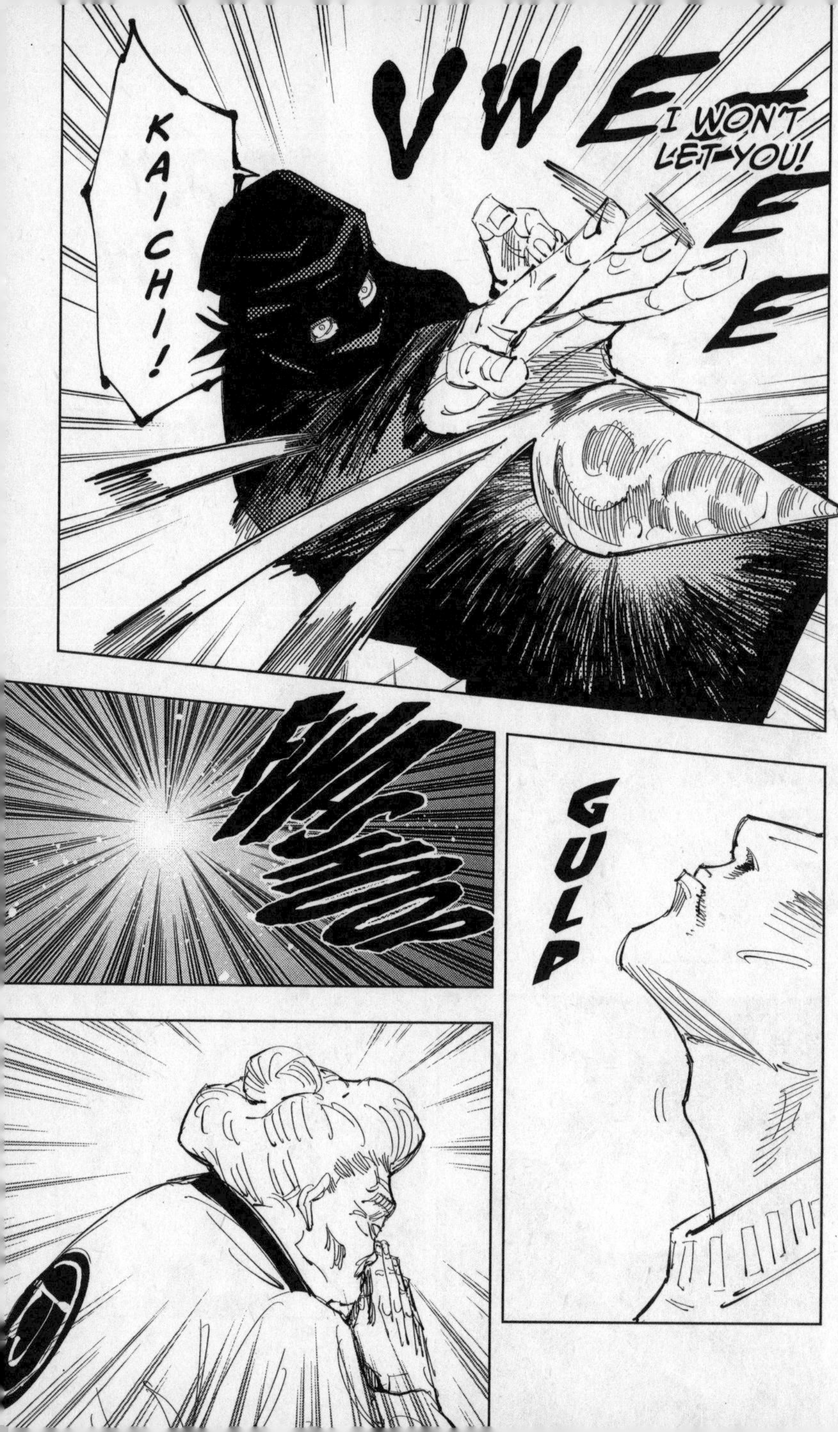
VWEEEE
I WON'T LET YOU!
KAICHI!
GULP
FWSHOOP

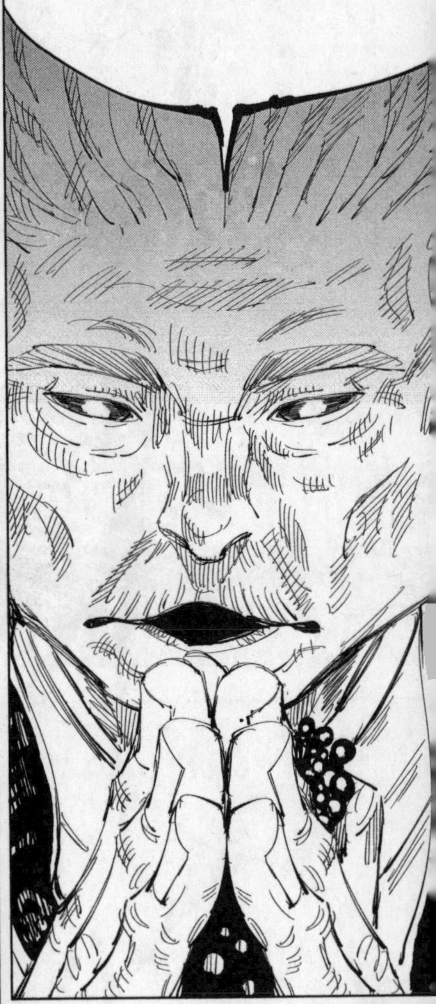
TOJI
ZEN'IN.
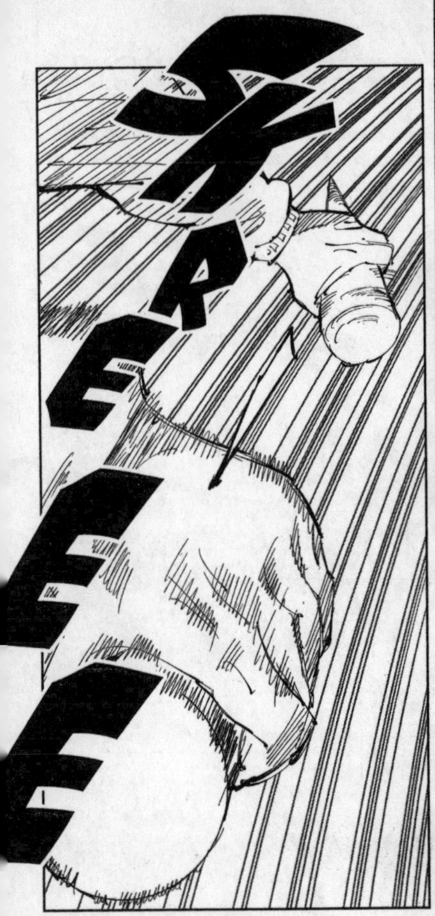
SKREEE
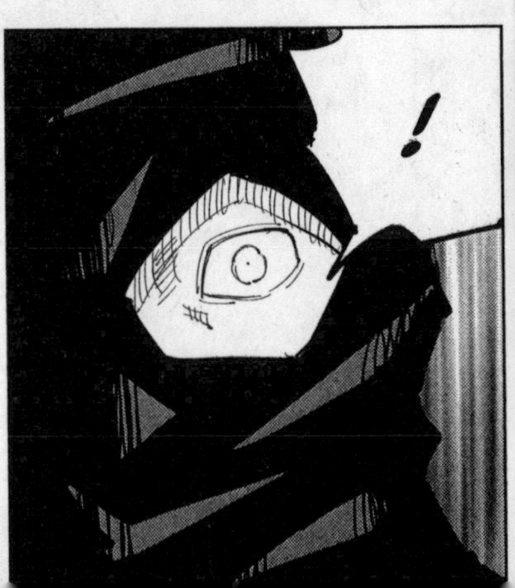
!

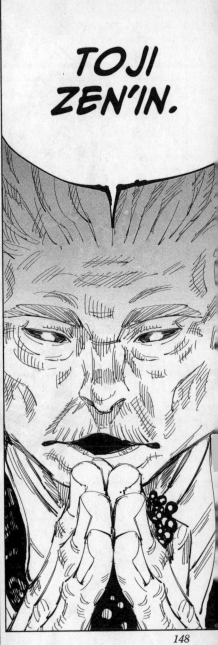

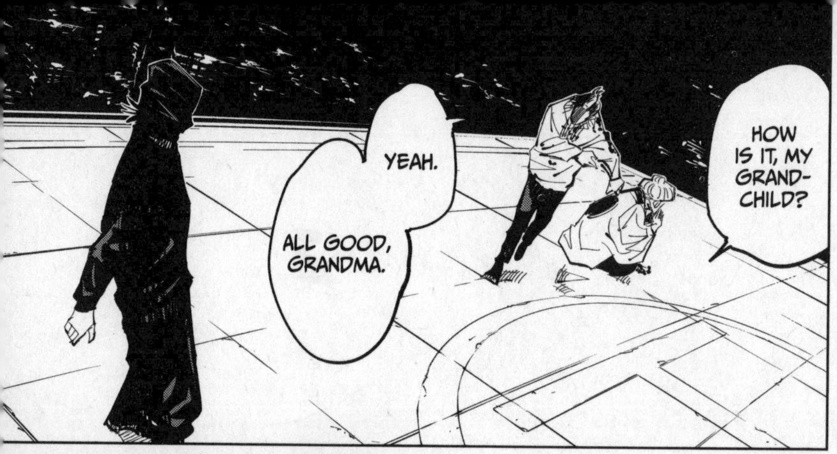
HOW IS IT, MY GRAND-CHILD?
YEAH.
ALL GOOD, GRANDMA.
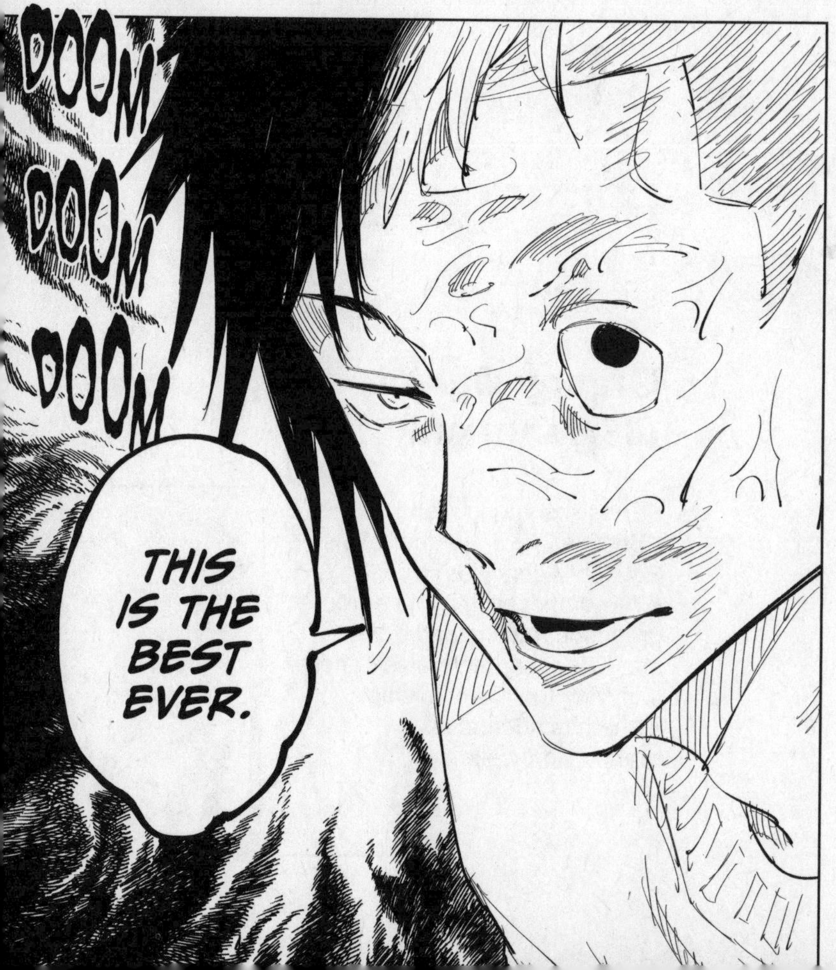
DOOM DOOM DOOM
THIS IS THE BEST EVER.

Granny Ogami
(87 years old)

• She likes young men.
• She's a junior member of the Boy Idol Agency fan club.
• The grandchild is not her real grandson, but instead a boy she kidnapped and raised after falsifying their relationship.
• She has numerous grandchildren like this.

December 7, 1989

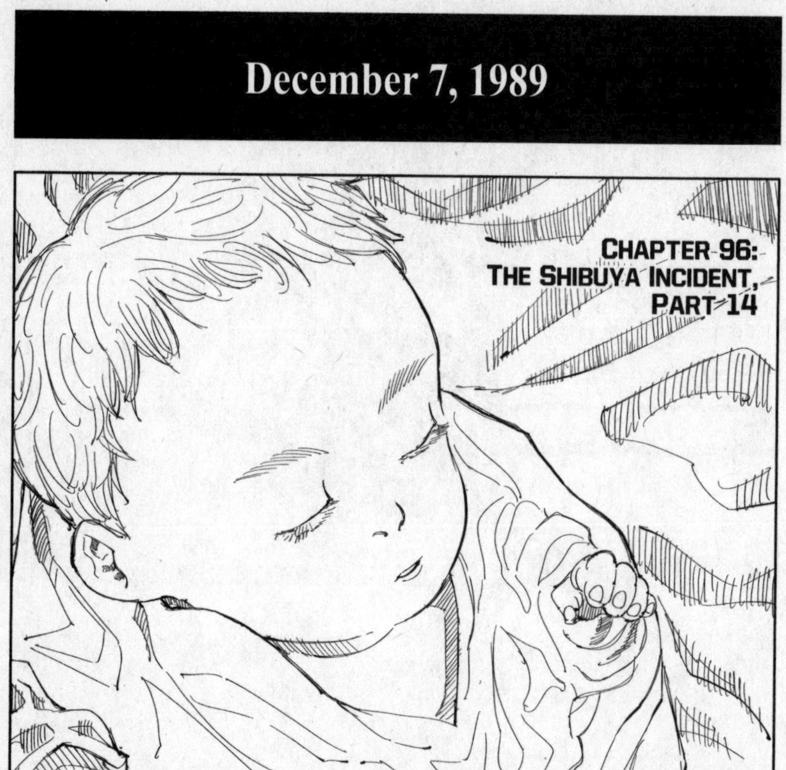
Chapter 96:
The Shibuya Incident,
Part 14

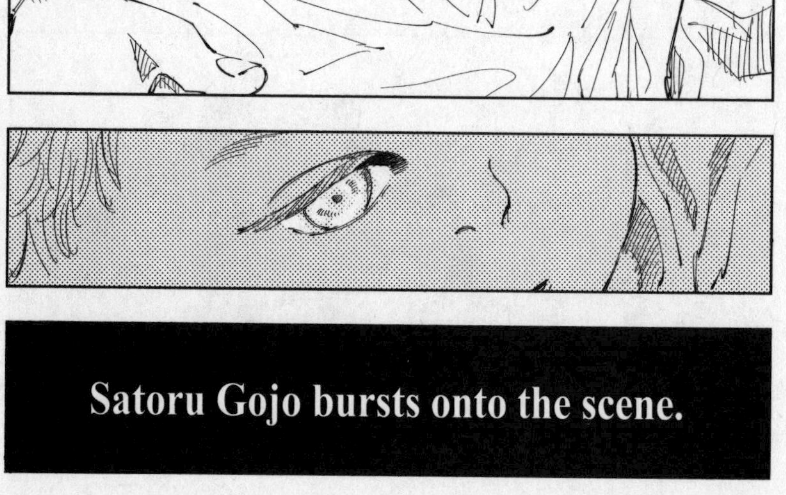

Satoru Gojo bursts onto the scene.

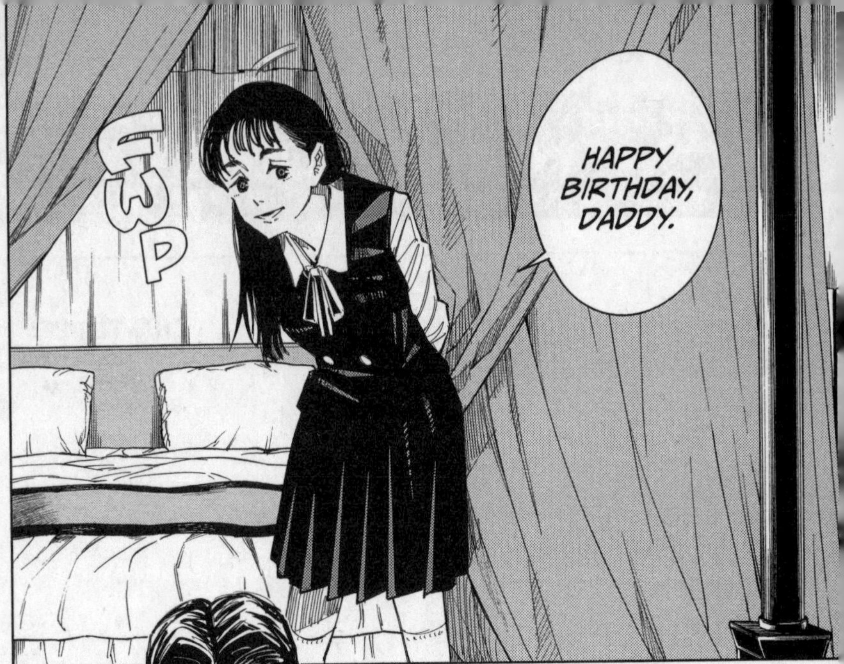
HAPPY BIRTHDAY, DADDY.

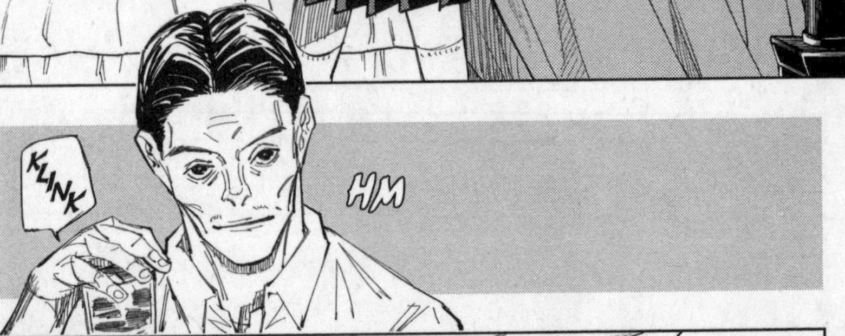
HM
KLINK

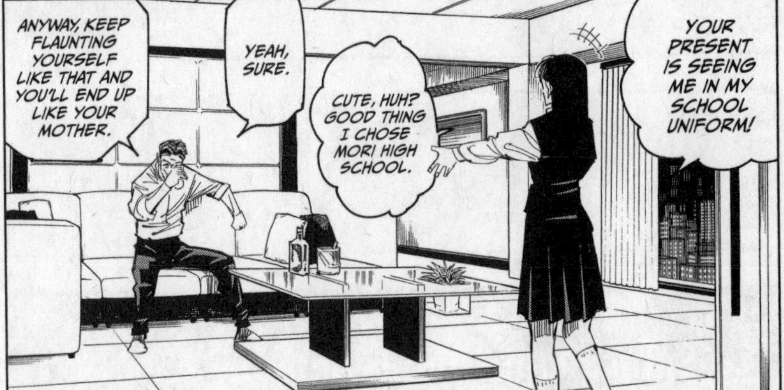
YOUR PRESENT IS SEEING ME IN MY SCHOOL UNIFORM!
CUTE, HUH? GOOD THING I CHOSE MORI HIGH SCHOOL.
YEAH, SURE.
ANYWAY, KEEP FLAUNTING YOURSELF LIKE THAT AND YOU'LL END UP LIKE YOUR MOTHER.

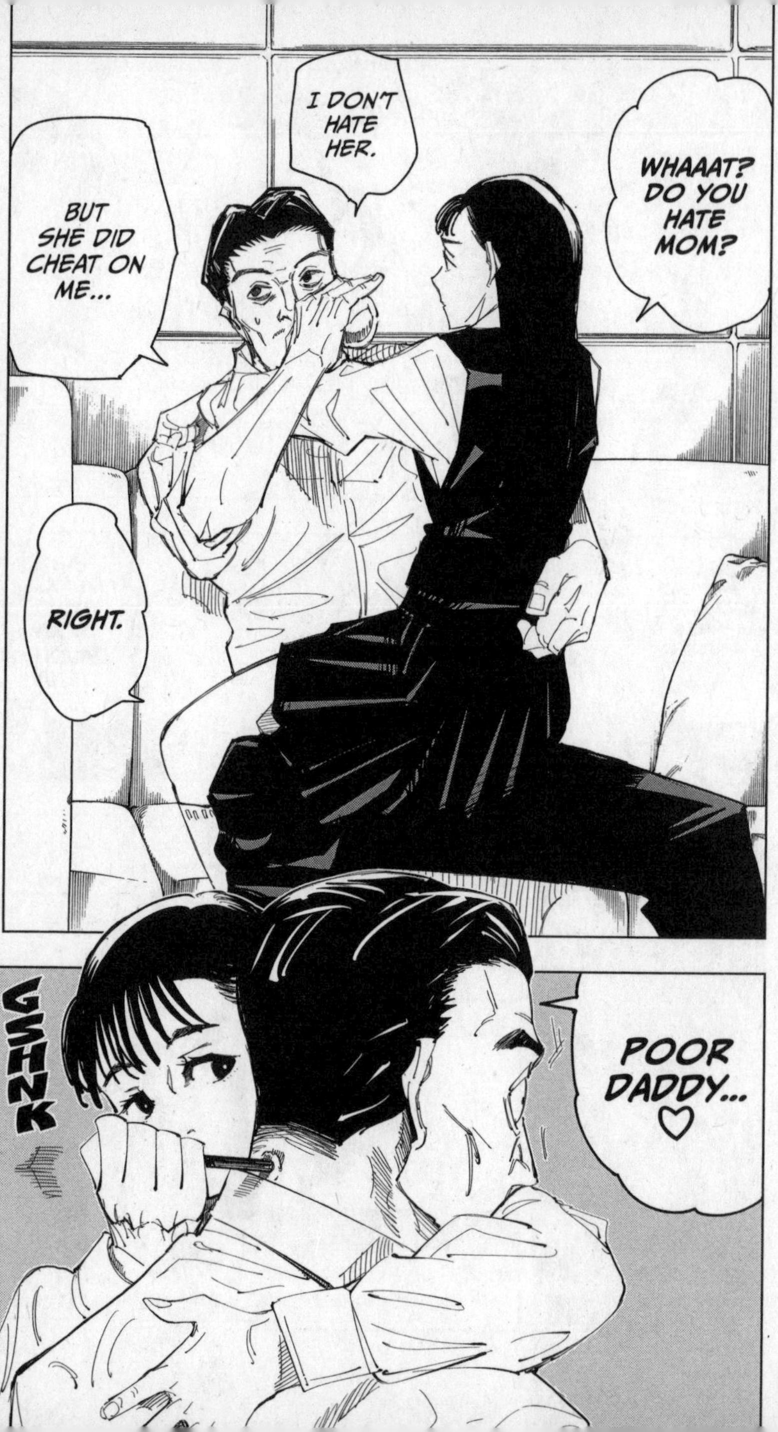
WHAAAT? DO YOU HATE MOM?
I DON'T HATE HER.
BUT SHE DID CHEAT ON ME...
RIGHT.
POOR DADDY... ♡
GSHNK

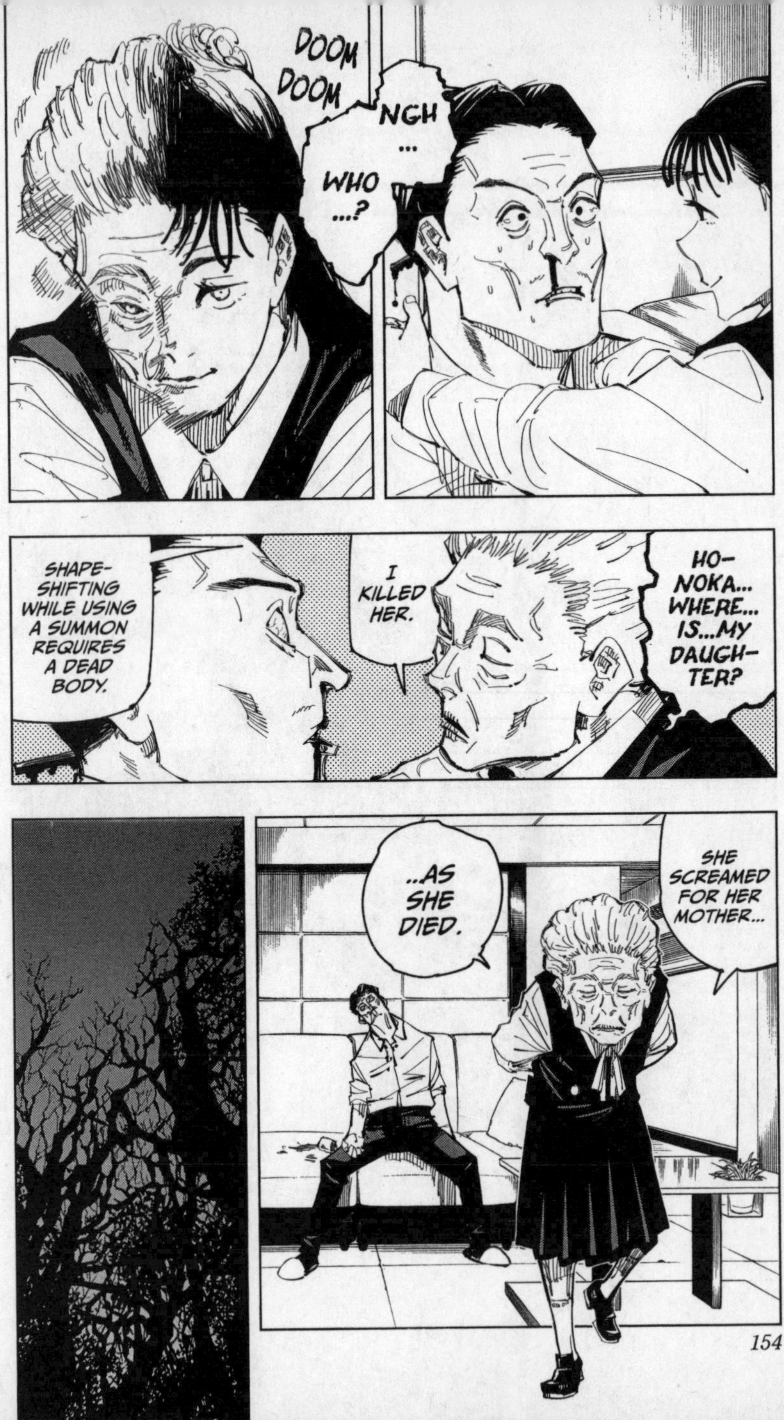
NGH ... WHO ...?
DOOM DOOM
HO-NOKA... WHERE... IS...MY DAUGH-TER?
I KILLED HER.
SHAPE-SHIFTING WHILE USING A SUMMON REQUIRES A DEAD BODY.
SHE SCREAMED FOR HER MOTHER...
...AS SHE DIED.

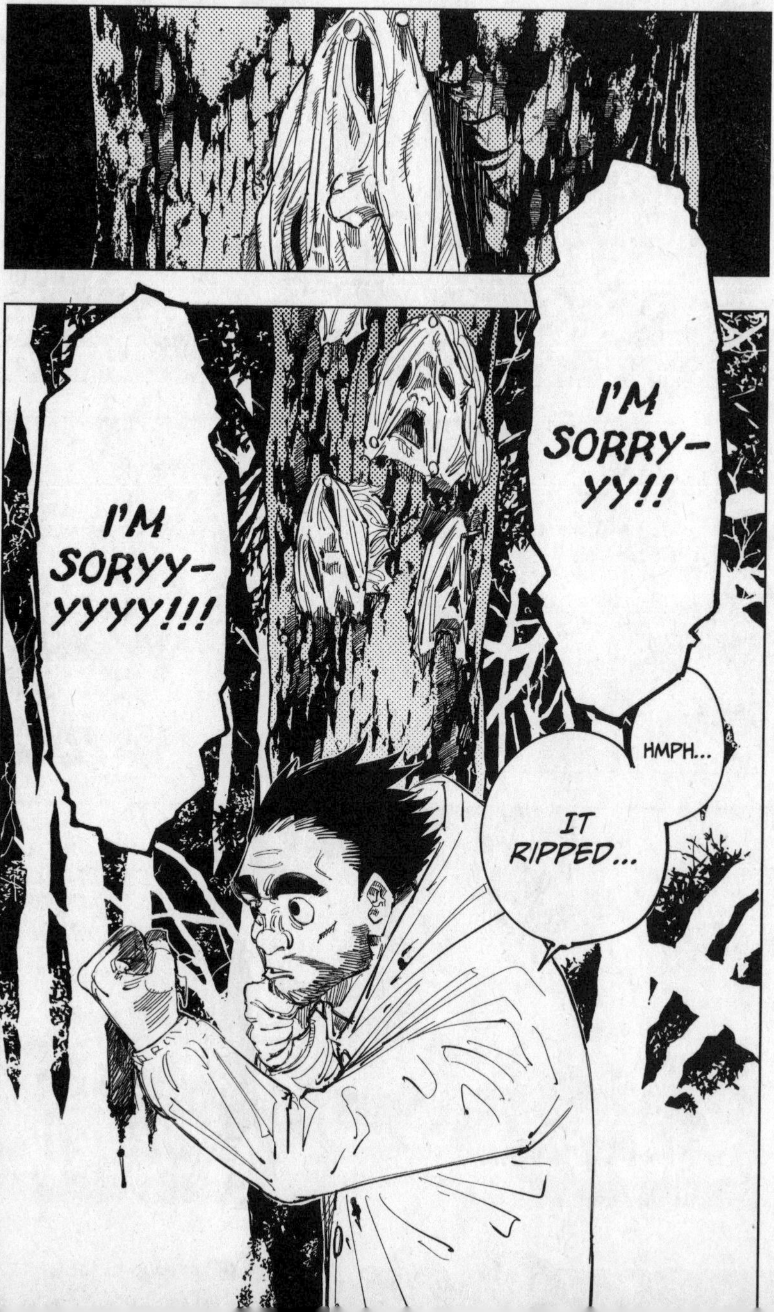
I'M SORRY-YY!!
I'M SORYY-YYYY!!!
HMPH... IT RIPPED...

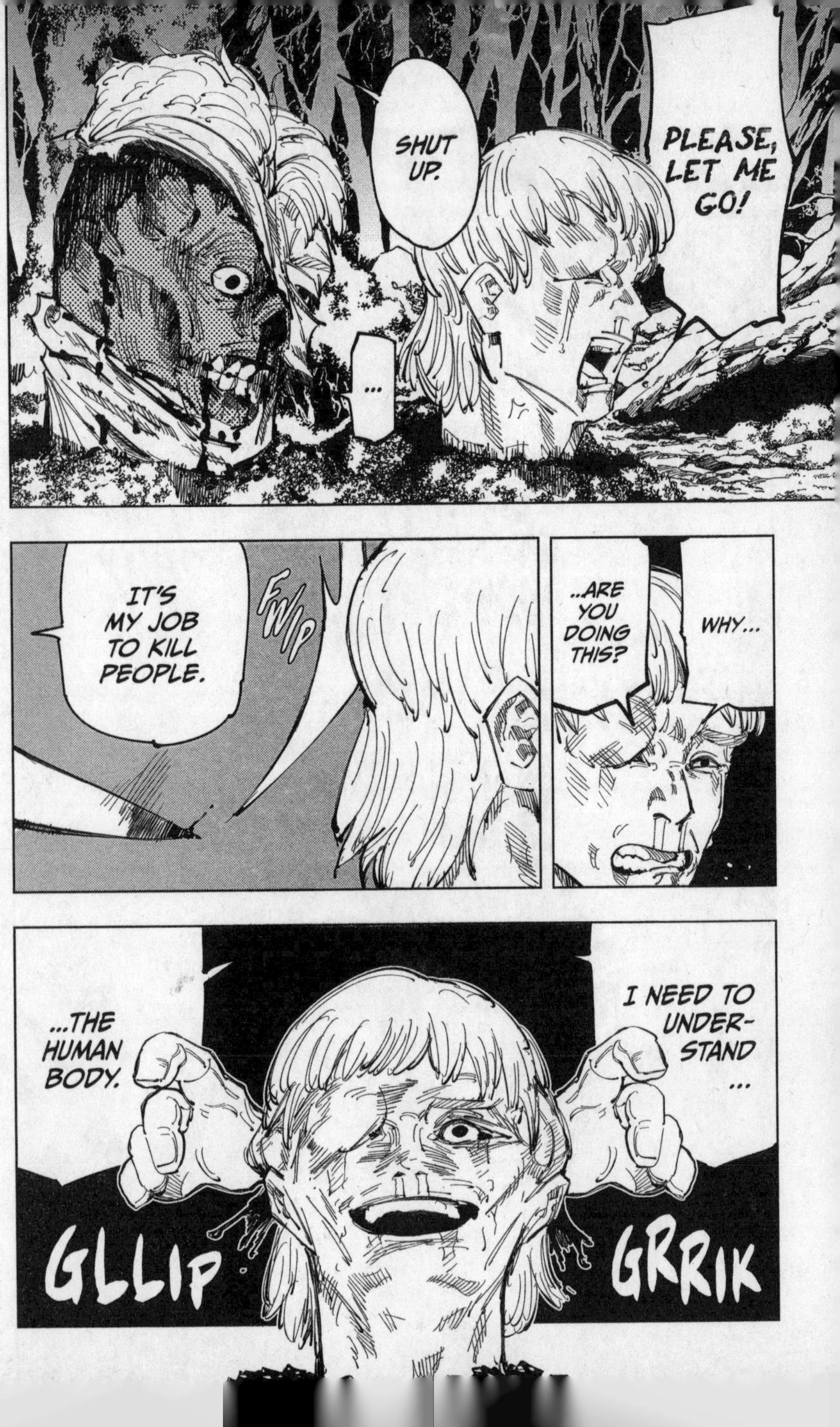
PLEASE, LET ME GO!
SHUT UP.
...
WHY...
..ARE YOU DOING THIS?
FWIP
IT'S MY JOB TO KILL PEOPLE.
I NEED TO UNDER-STAND ...
...THE HUMAN BODY.
GRRIK
GLLIP

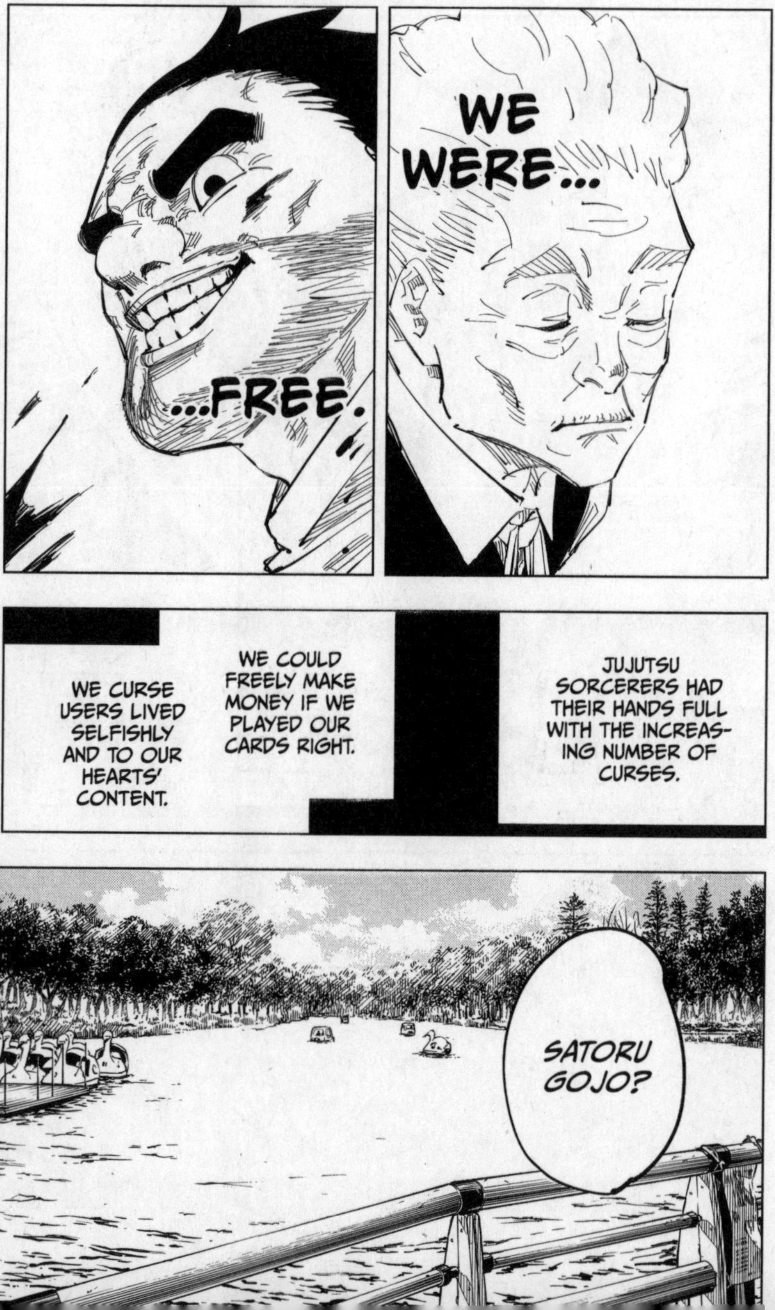
WE WERE...
...FREE.
JUJUTSU SORCERERS HAD THEIR HANDS FULL WITH THE INCREASING NUMBER OF CURSES.
WE COULD FREELY MAKE MONEY IF WE PLAYED OUR CARDS RIGHT.
WE CURSE USERS LIVED SELFISHLY AND TO OUR HEARTS' CONTENT.
SATORU GOJO?

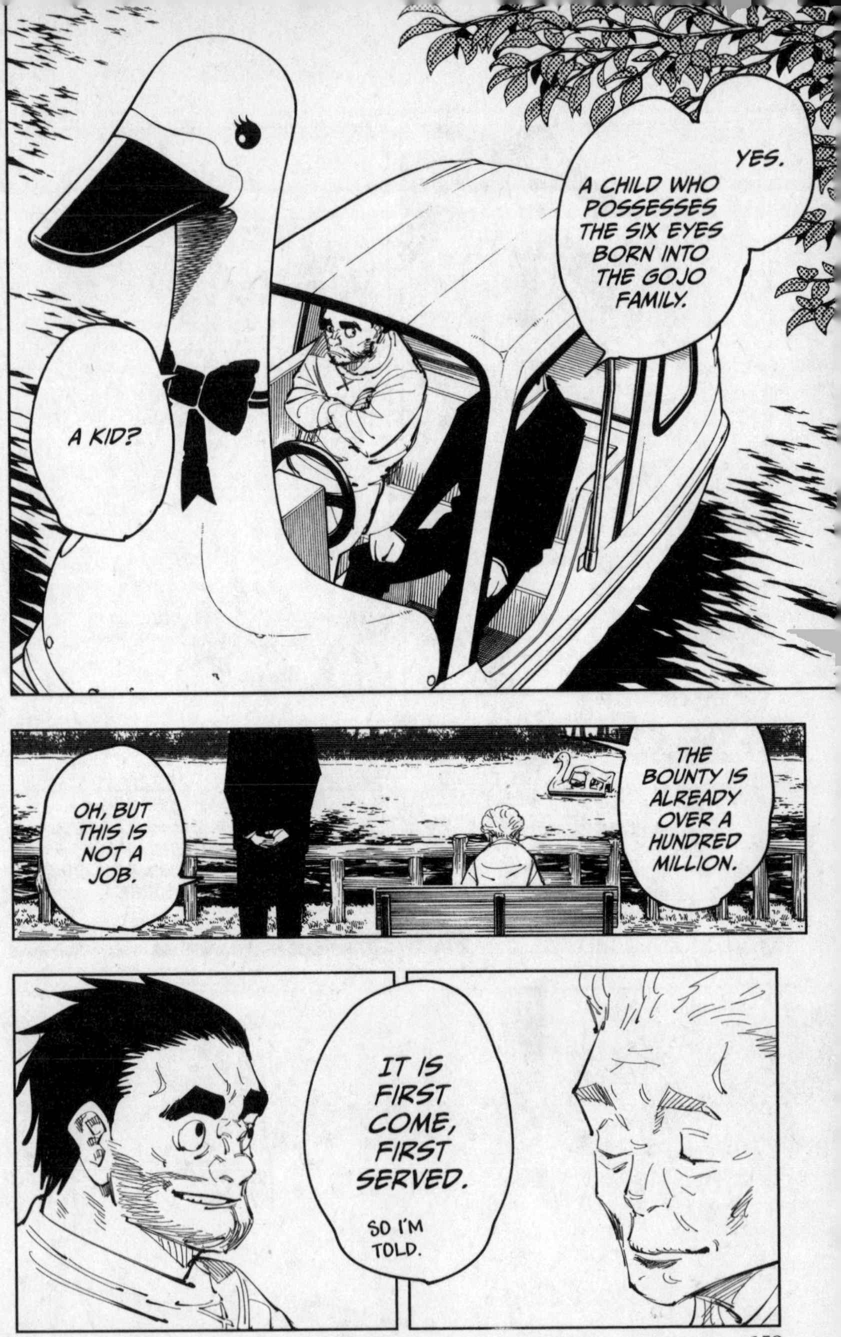
YES.
A CHILD WHO POSSESSES THE SIX EYES BORN INTO THE GOJO FAMILY.
A KID?
THE BOUNTY IS ALREADY OVER A HUNDRED MILLION.
OH, BUT THIS IS NOT A JOB.
IT IS FIRST COME, FIRST SERVED.
SO I'M TOLD.

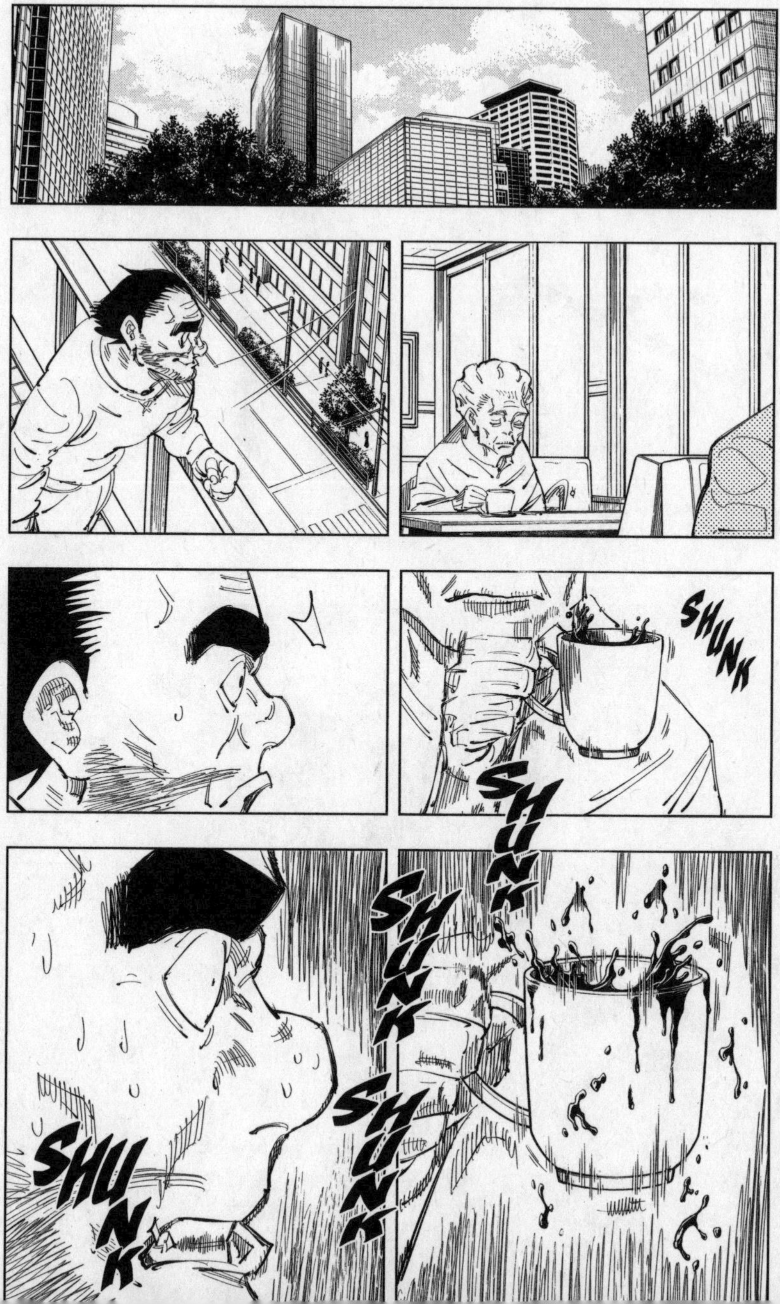
SHUNK
SHUNK
SHUNK
SHUNK
SHUNK

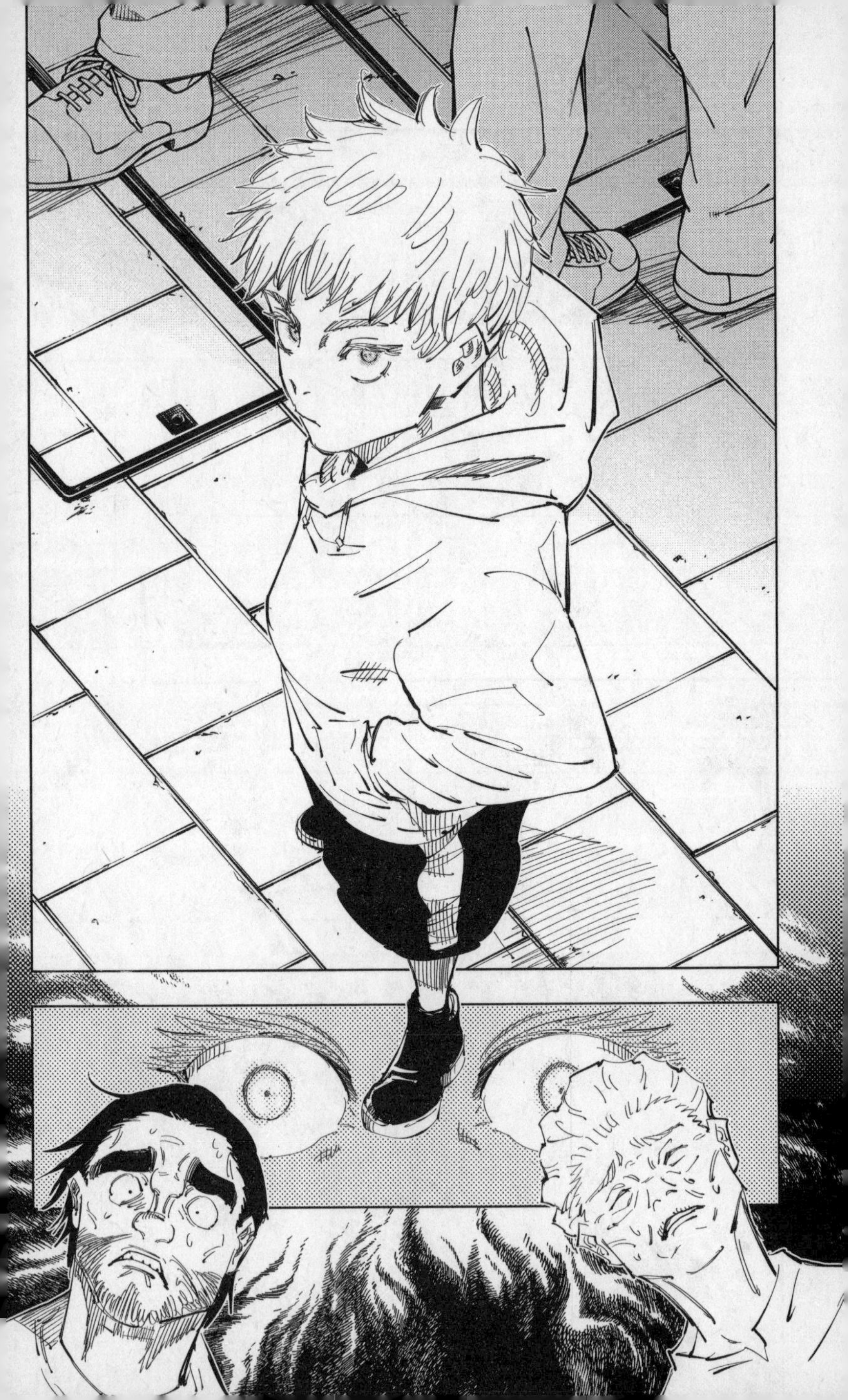

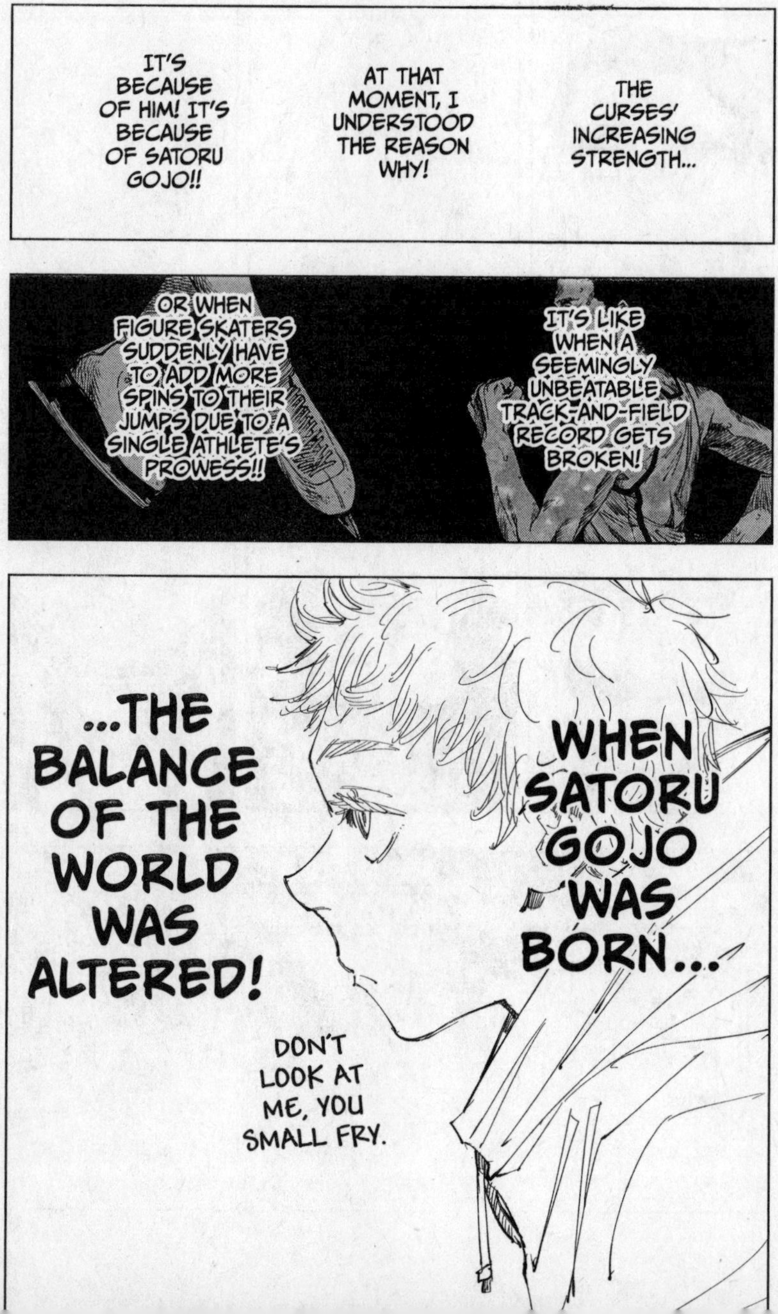
THE CURSES' INCREASING STRENGTH...
AT THAT MOMENT, I UNDERSTOOD THE REASON WHY!
IT'S BECAUSE OF HIM! IT'S BECAUSE OF SATORU GOJO!!
IT'S LIKE WHEN A SEEMINGLY UNBEATABLE TRACK-AND-FIELD RECORD GETS BROKEN!
OR WHEN FIGURE SKATERS SUDDENLY HAVE TO ADD MORE SPINS TO THEIR JUMPS DUE TO A SINGLE ATHLETE'S PROWESS!!
WHEN SATORU GOJO WAS BORN...
...THE BALANCE OF THE WORLD WAS ALTERED!
DON'T LOOK AT ME, YOU SMALL FRY.

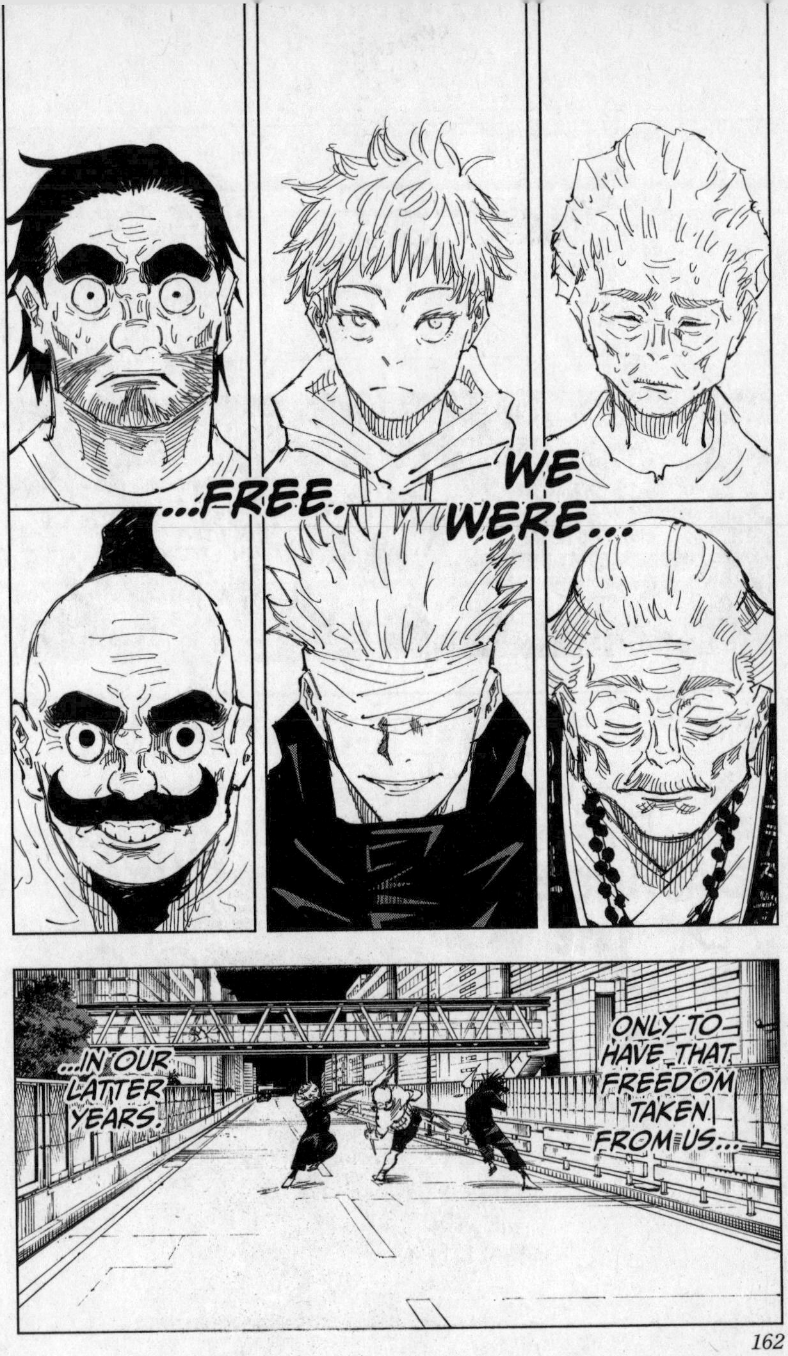
WE WERE...
...FREE.
ONLY TO HAVE THAT FREEDOM TAKEN FROM US...
...IN OUR LATTER YEARS.

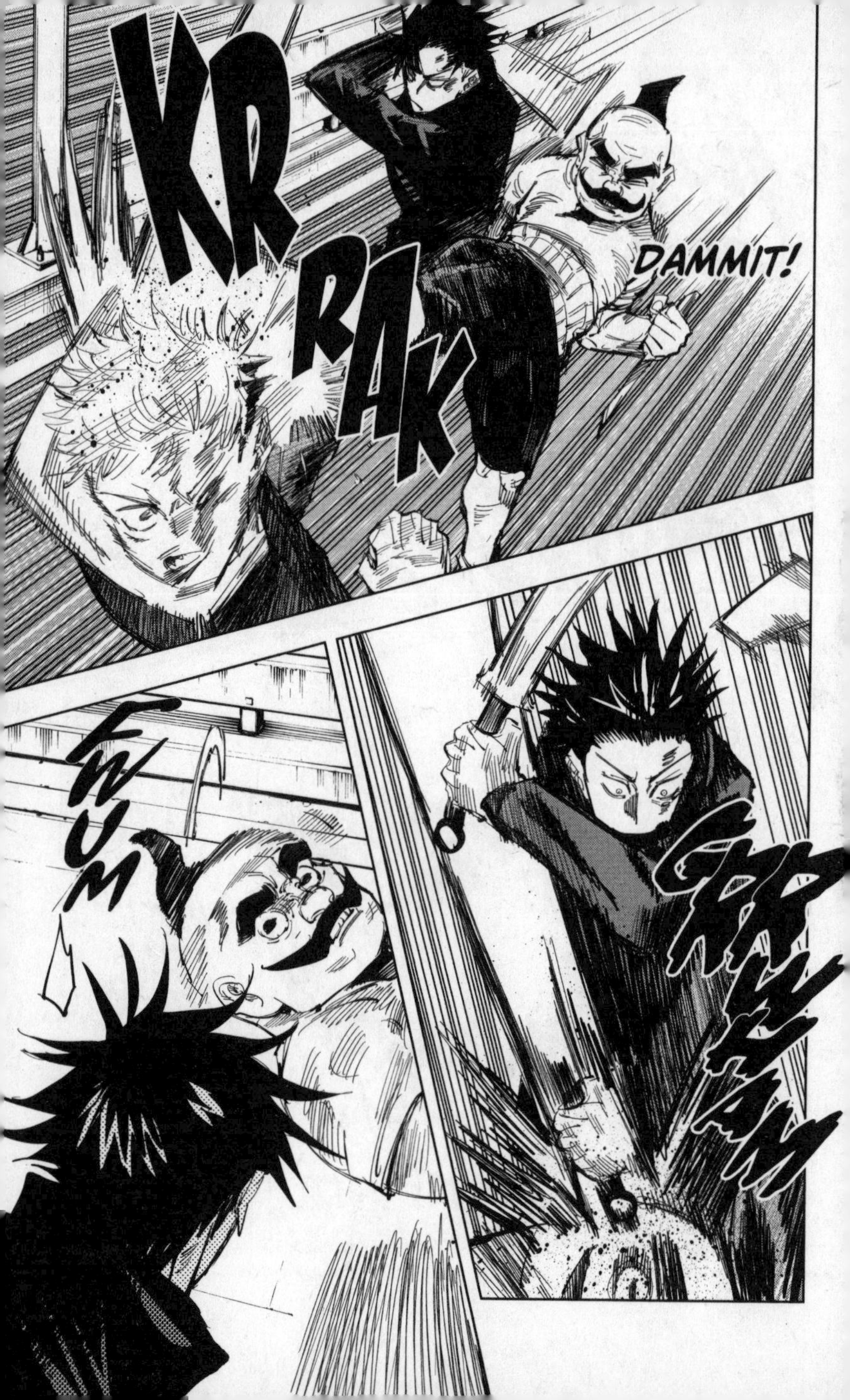
KRRAK
DAMMIT!
FWUM

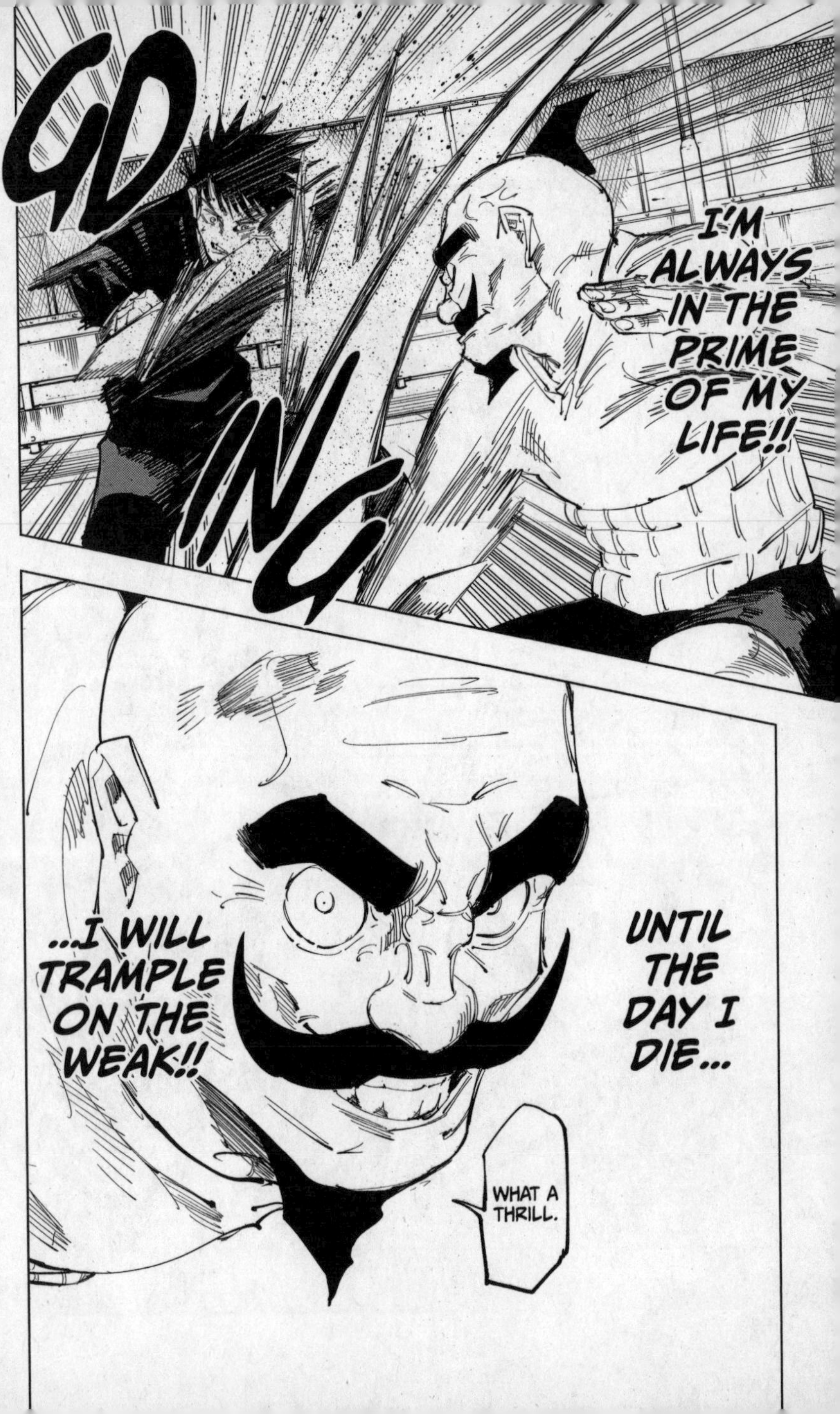
GOING
I'M ALWAYS IN THE PRIME OF MY LIFE!!
UNTIL THE DAY I DIE...
...I WILL TRAMPLE ON THE WEAK!!
WHAT A THRILL.

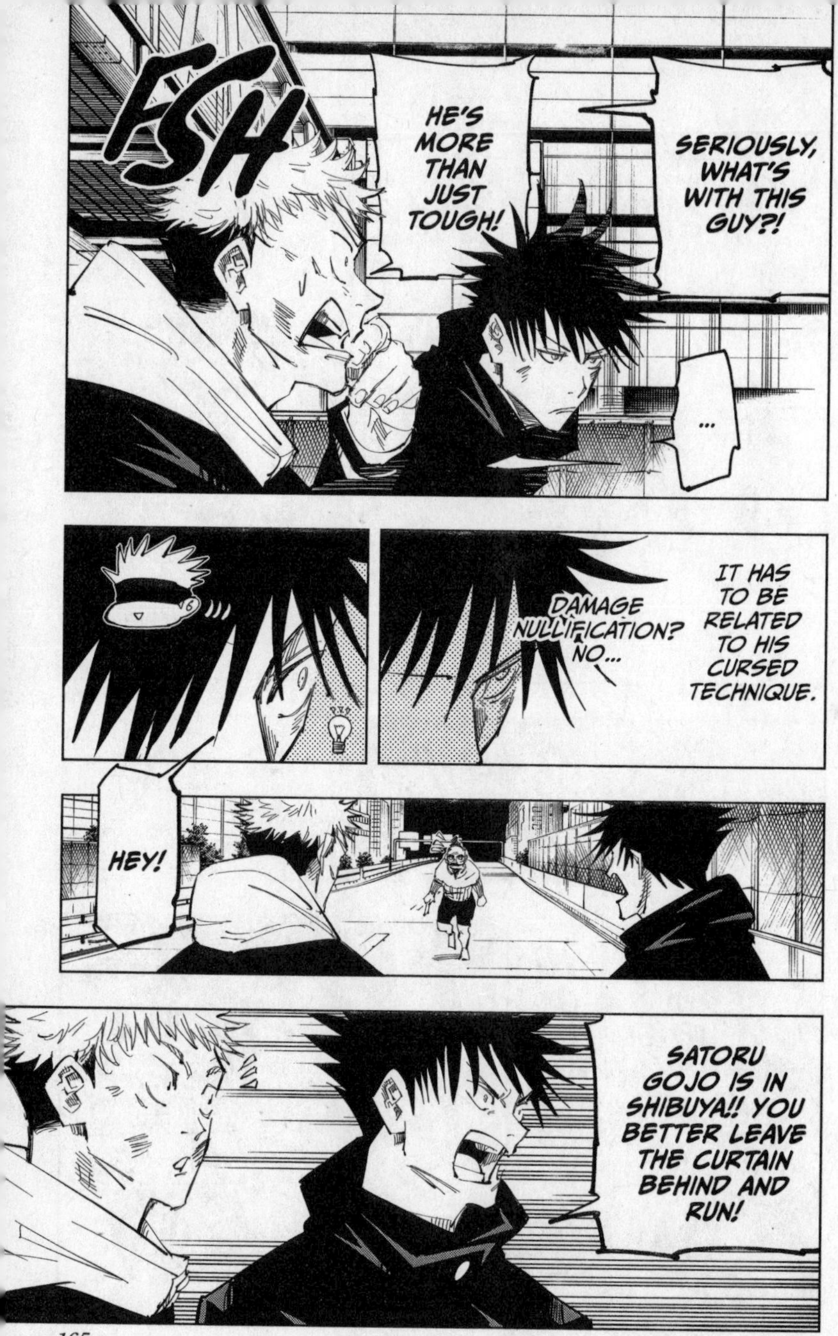
SERIOUSLY, WHAT'S WITH THIS GUY?!
HE'S MORE THAN JUST TOUGH!
FSH
...
IT HAS TO BE RELATED TO HIS CURSED TECHNIQUE.
DAMAGE NULLIFICATION? NO...
HEY!
SATORU GOJO IS IN SHIBUYA!! YOU BETTER LEAVE THE CURTAIN BEHIND AND RUN!

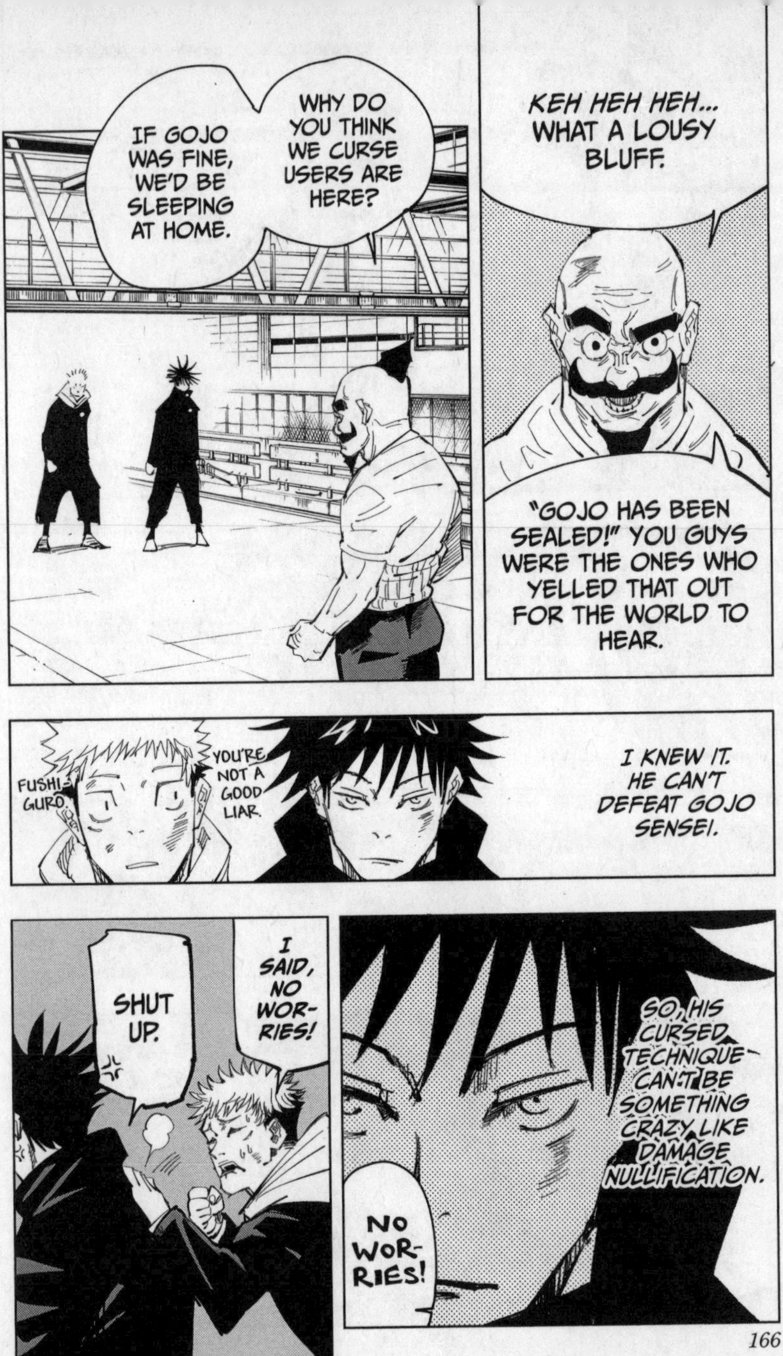
KEH HEH HEH... WHAT A LOUSY BLUFF.
"GOJO HAS BEEN SEALED!" YOU GUYS WERE THE ONES WHO YELLED THAT OUT FOR THE WORLD TO HEAR.
WHY DO YOU THINK WE CURSE USERS ARE HERE?
IF GOJO WAS FINE, WE'D BE SLEEPING AT HOME.
I KNEW IT. HE CAN'T DEFEAT GOJO SENSEI.
YOU'RE NOT A GOOD LIAR.
FUSHI-GURO.
SO, HIS CURSED TECHNIQUE CAN'T BE SOMETHING CRAZY LIKE DAMAGE NULLIFICATION.
NO WOR-RIES!
I SAID, NO WOR-RIES!
SHUT UP.

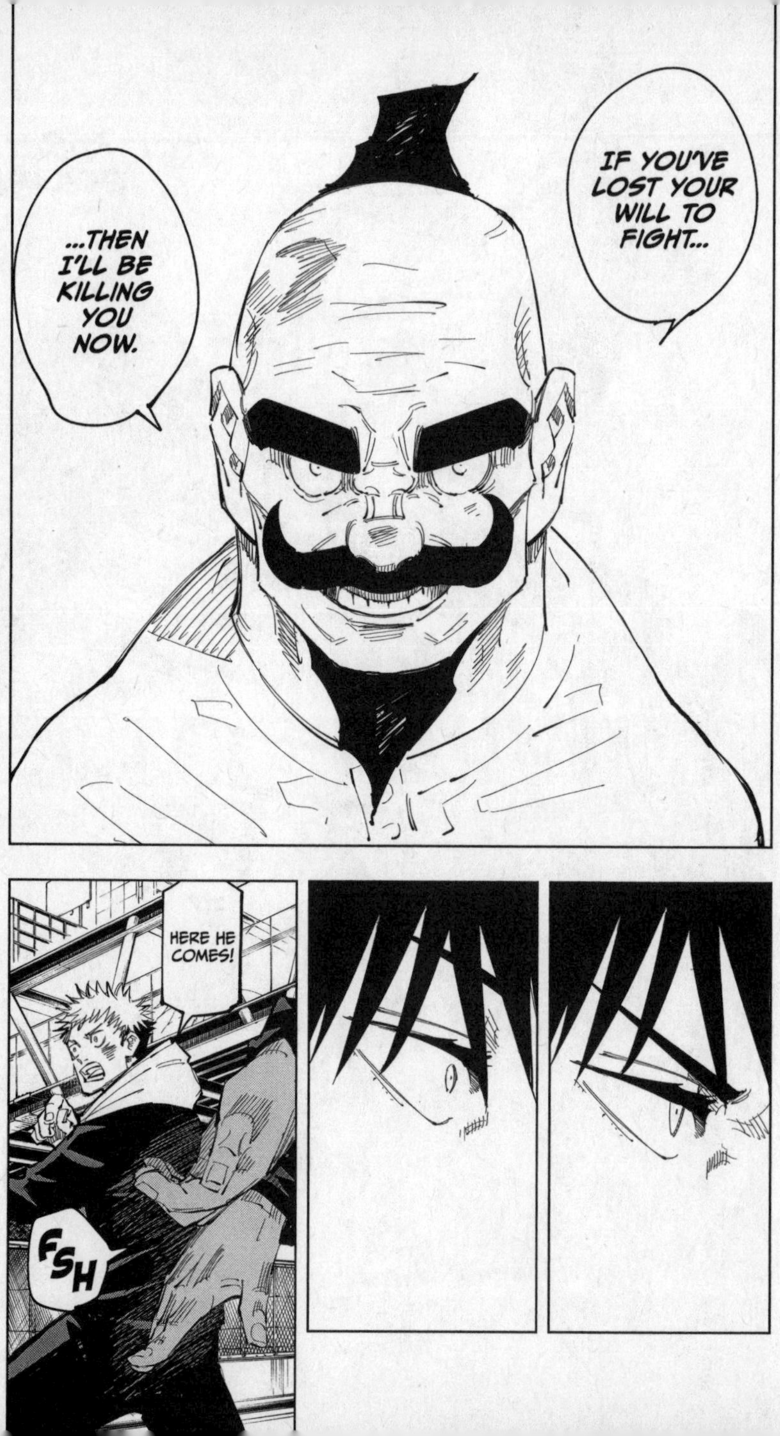
IF YOU'VE LOST YOUR WILL TO FIGHT...
...THEN I'LL BE KILLING YOU NOW.
HERE HE COMES!
FSH

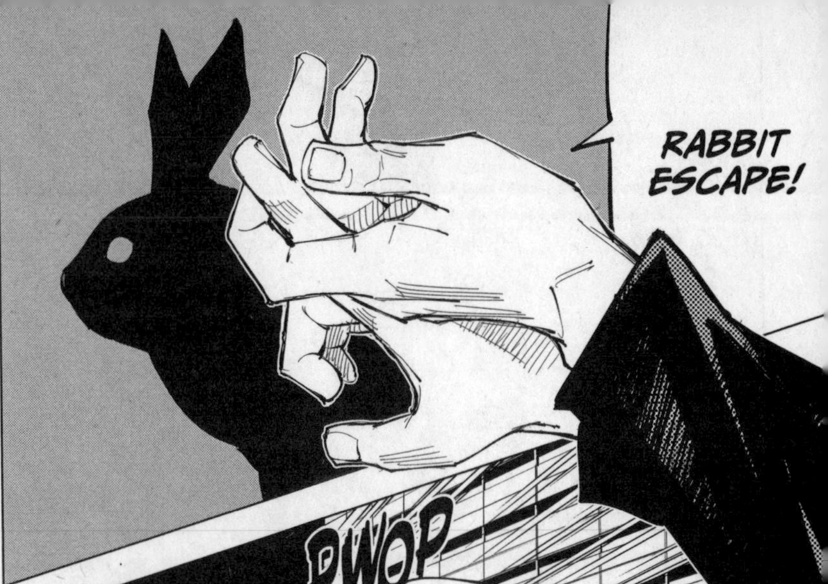
RABBIT ESCAPE!

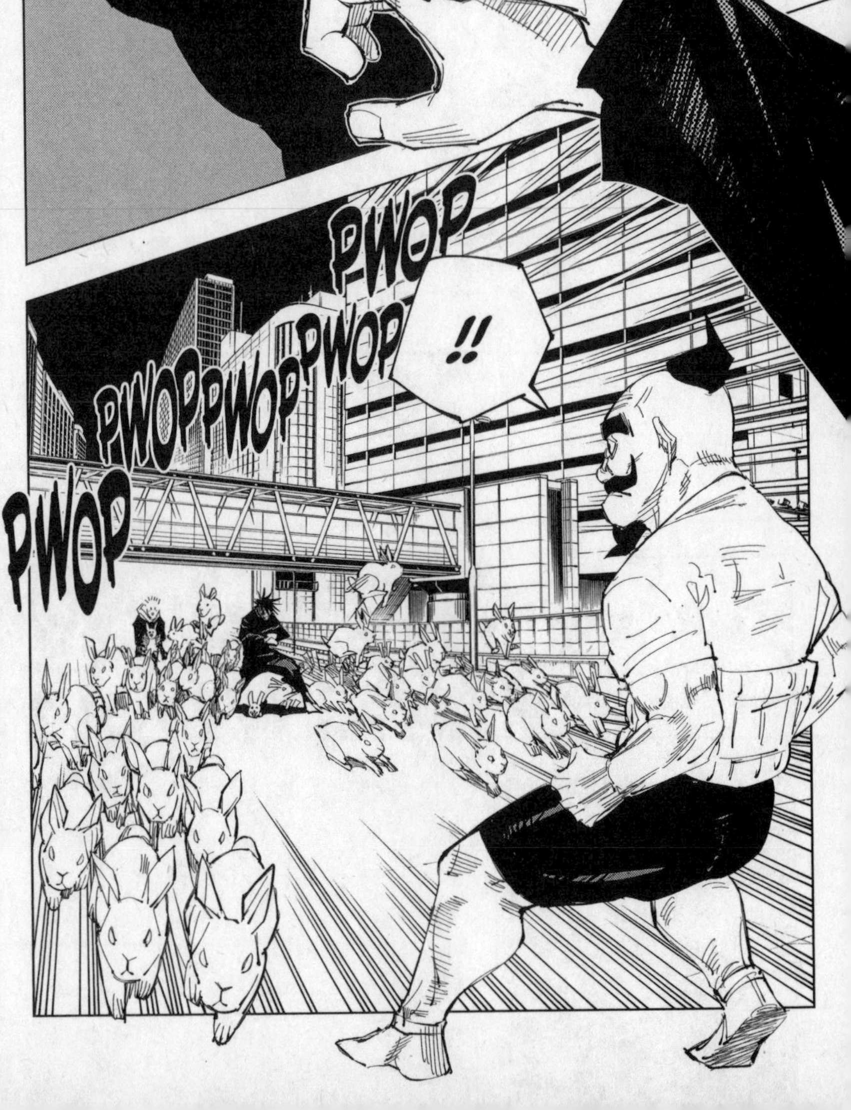
PWOP
PWOP
PWOP
PWOP
PWOP
!!

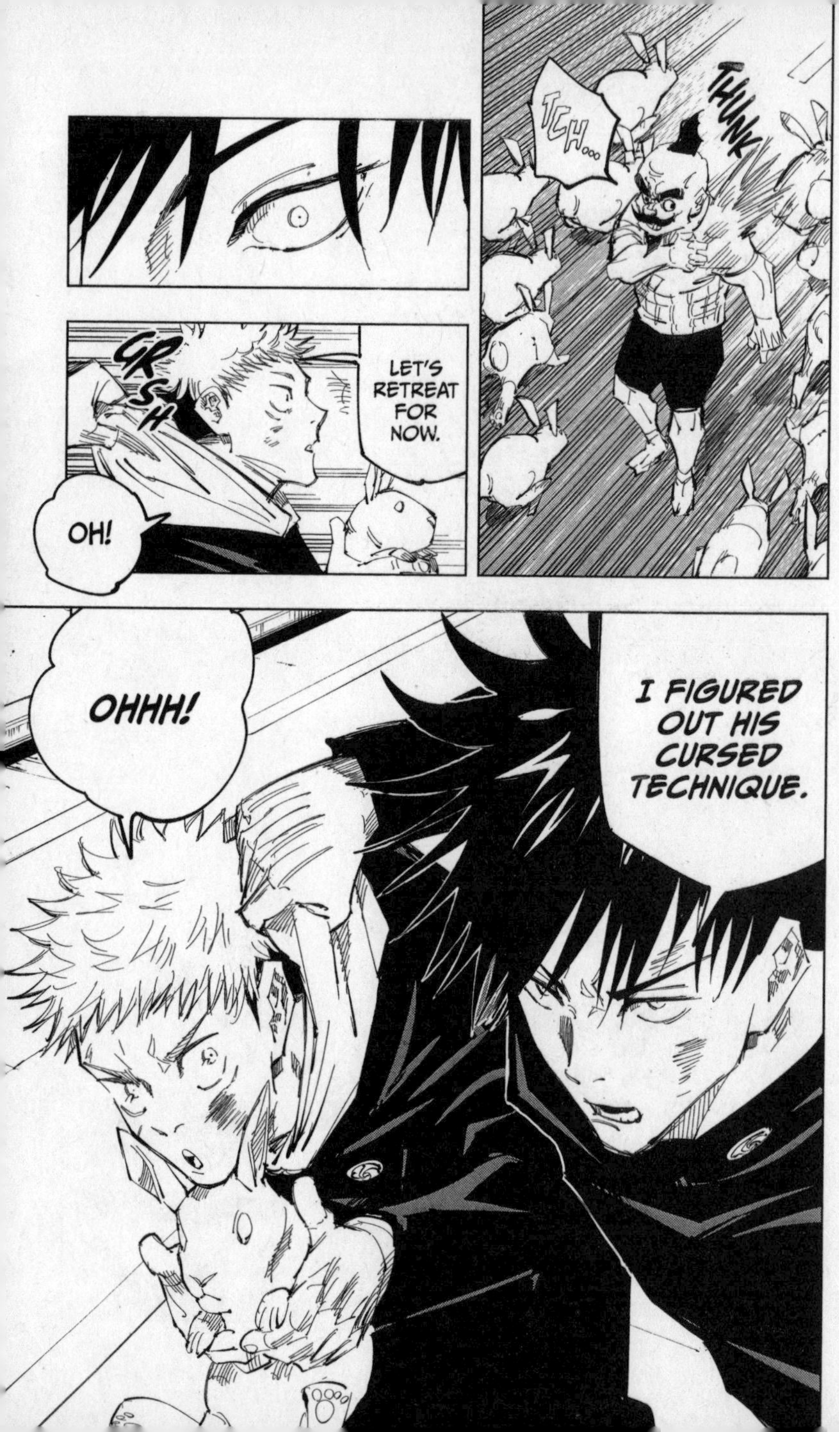
TCH...
THUNK
LET'S RETREAT FOR NOW.
GRSH
OH!
I FIGURED OUT HIS CURSED TECHNIQUE.
OHHH!

Jiro Awasaka
(61 years old)

• Jiro is an only child.
• He became a curse user so
he could make money to treat
his sick mother to a lavish life.
• That's the kind of lie he tells
without a second thought.

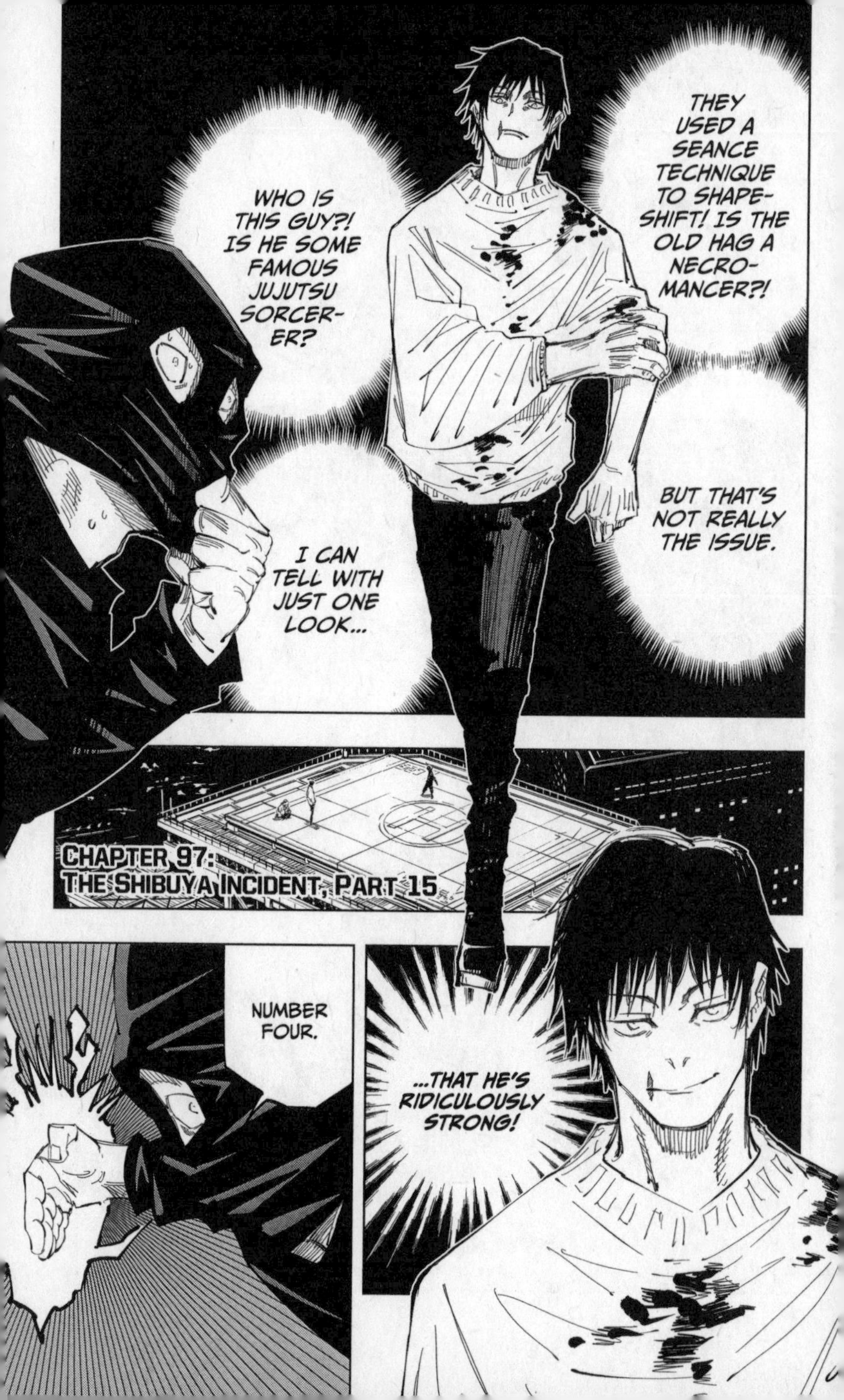
THEY USED A SEANCE TECHNIQUE TO SHAPE-SHIFT! IS THE OLD HAG A NECRO-MANCER?!
WHO IS THIS GUY?! IS HE SOME FAMOUS JUJUTSU SORCER-ER?
BUT THAT'S NOT REALLY THE ISSUE.
I CAN TELL WITH JUST ONE LOOK...
CHAPTER 97: THE SHIBUYA INCIDENT, PART 15
...THAT HE'S RIDICULOUSLY STRONG!
NUMBER FOUR.

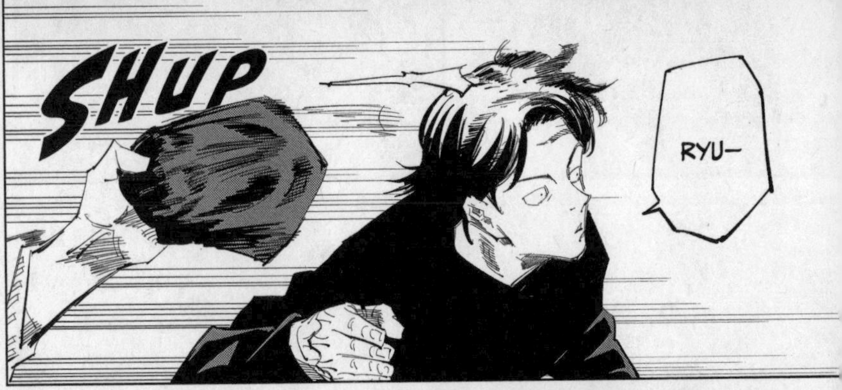
RYU—
SHUP

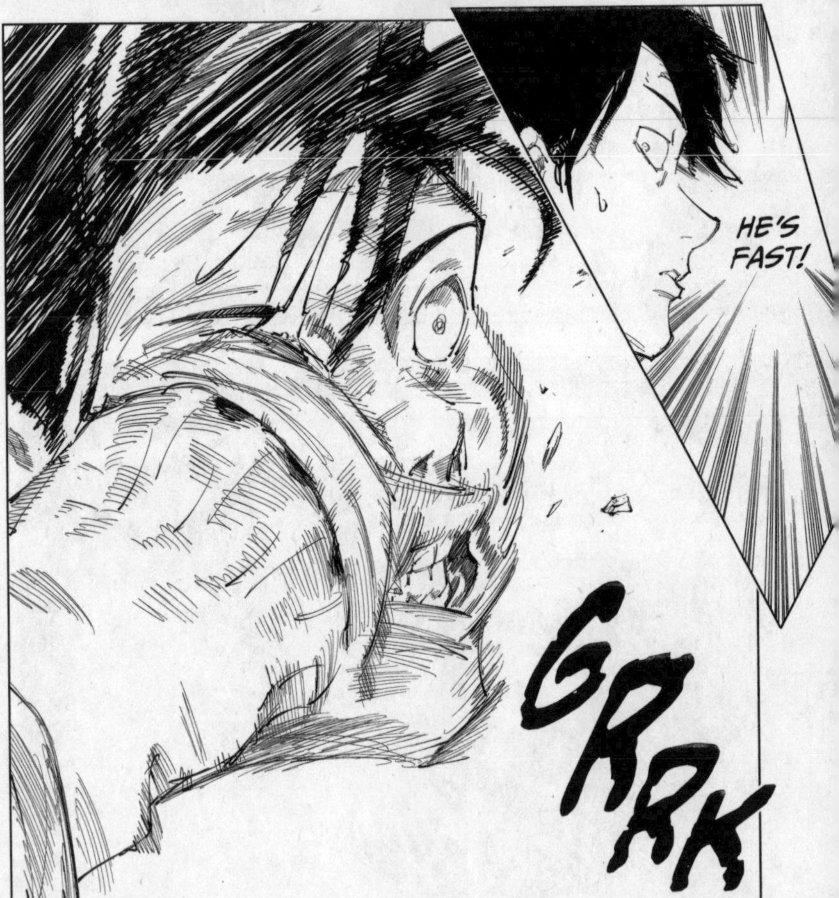
HE'S FAST!
GRRK

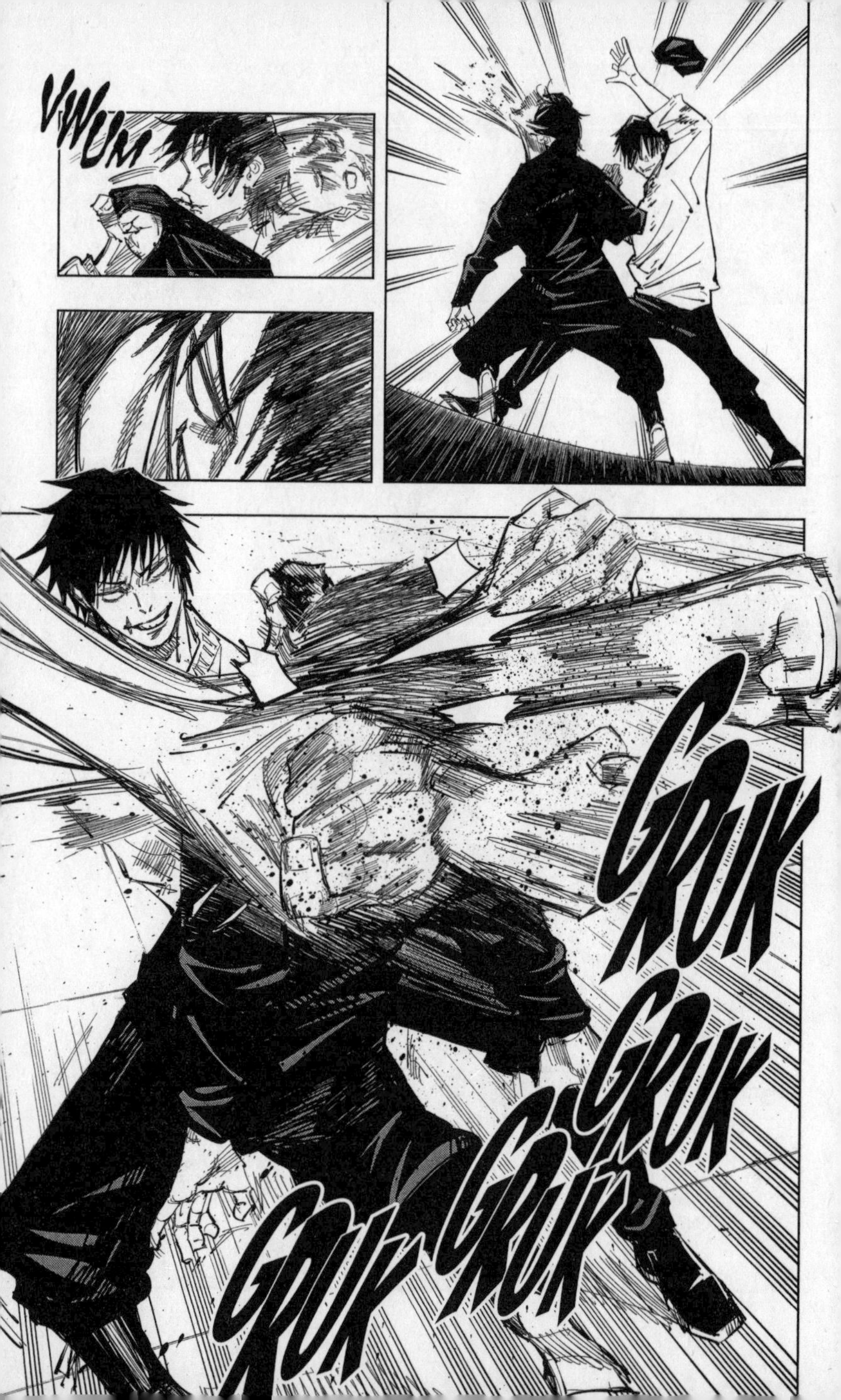
VWUM
GRUK
GRUK
GRUK
GRUK

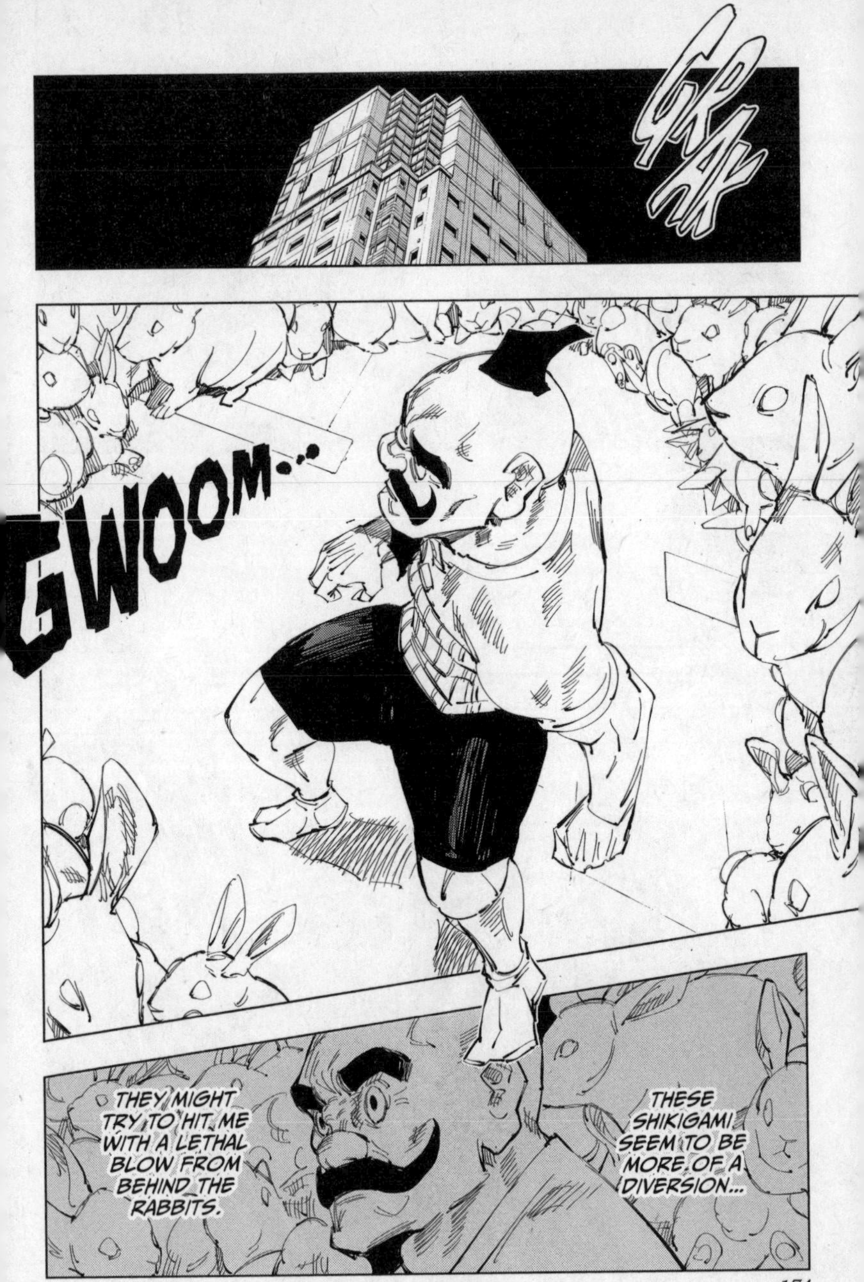
CRAK
GWOOM...
THESE SHIKIGAMI SEEM TO BE MORE OF A DIVERSION...
THEY MIGHT TRY TO HIT ME WITH A LETHAL BLOW FROM BEHIND THE RABBITS.

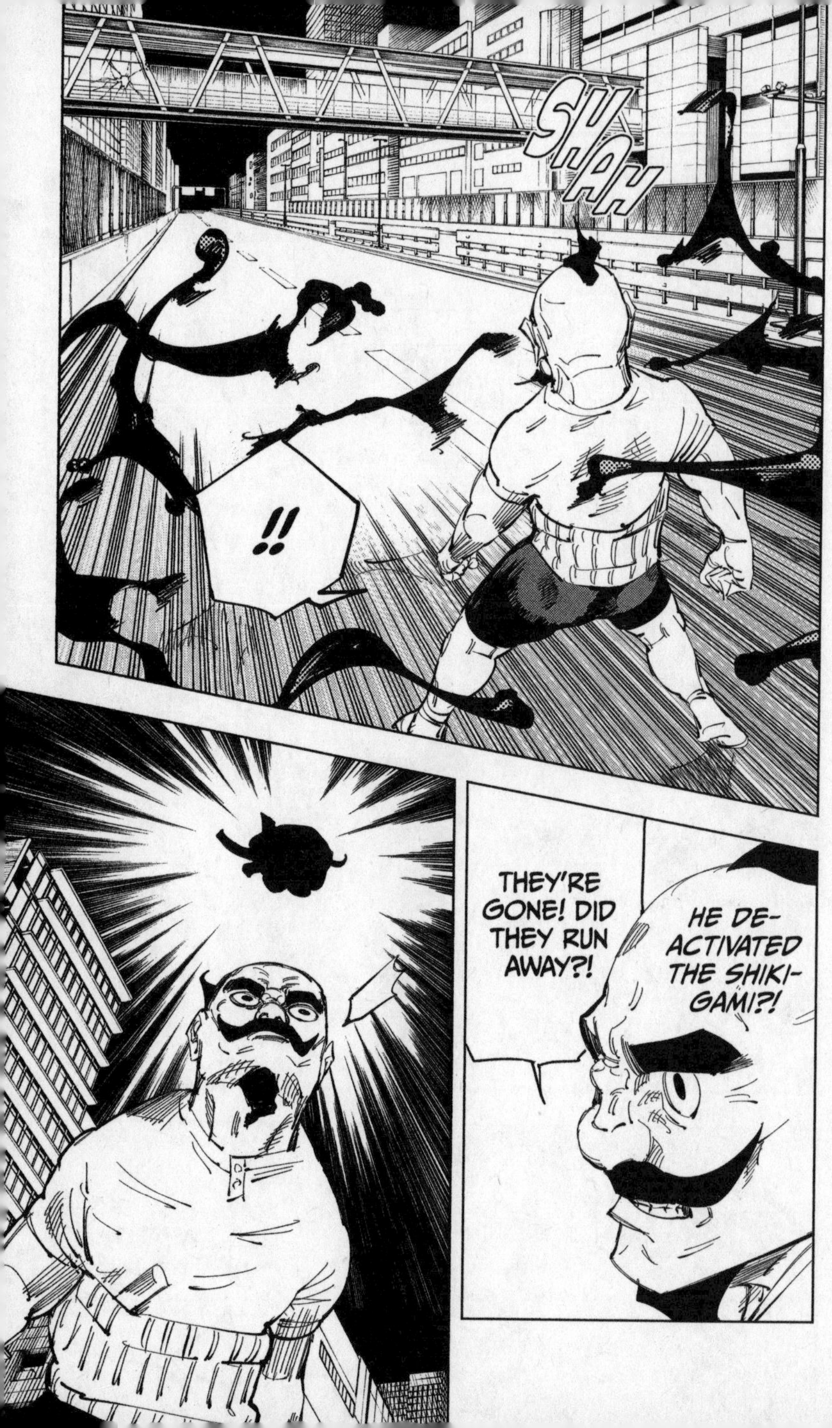
SHAH
!!
HE DE-ACTIVATED THE SHIKI-GAMI?!
THEY'RE GONE! DID THEY RUN AWAY?!

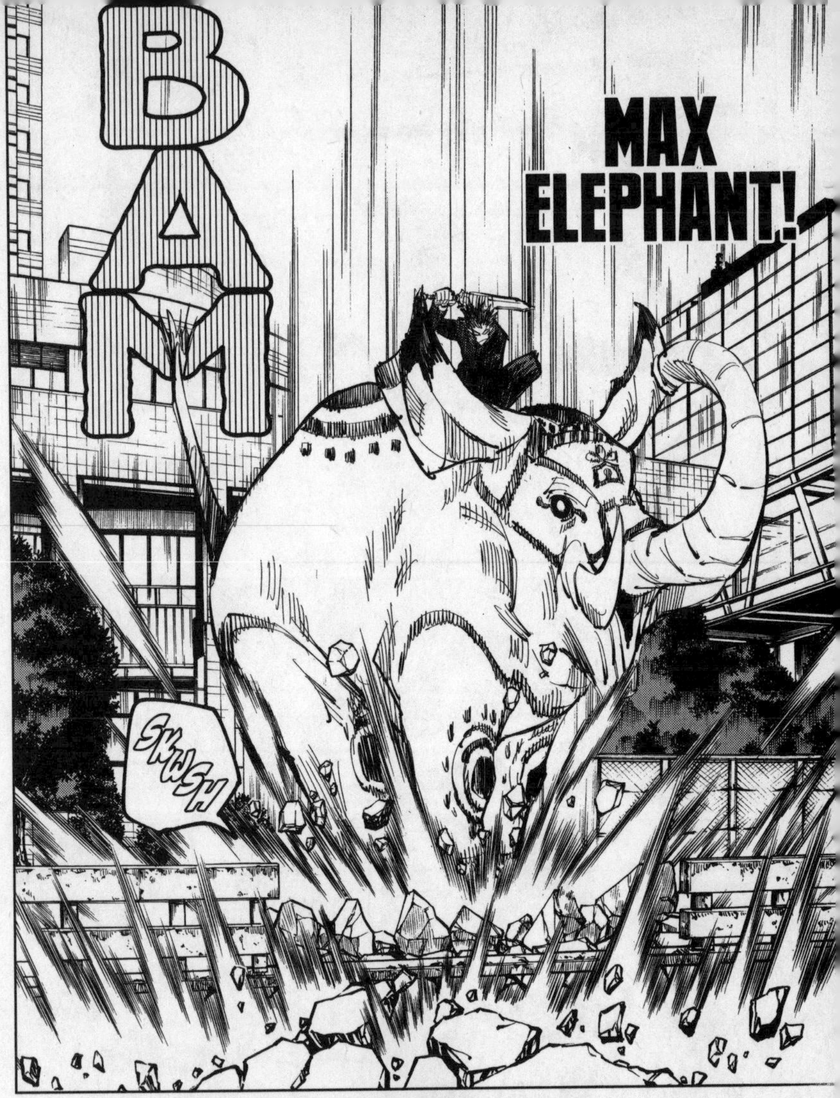
MAX ELEPHANT!
BAM
SKWSH
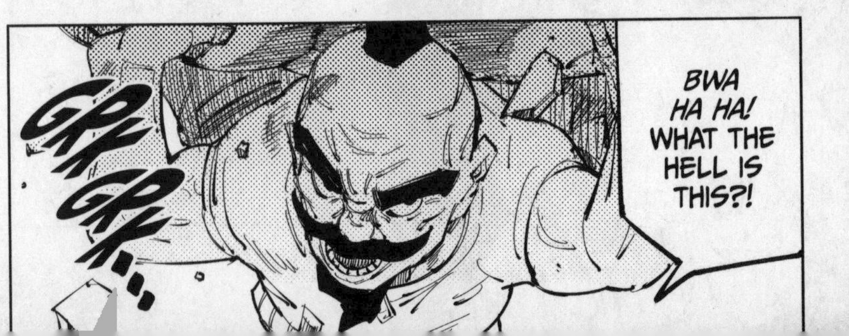
BWA HA HA! WHAT THE HELL IS THIS?!
GRK GRK...

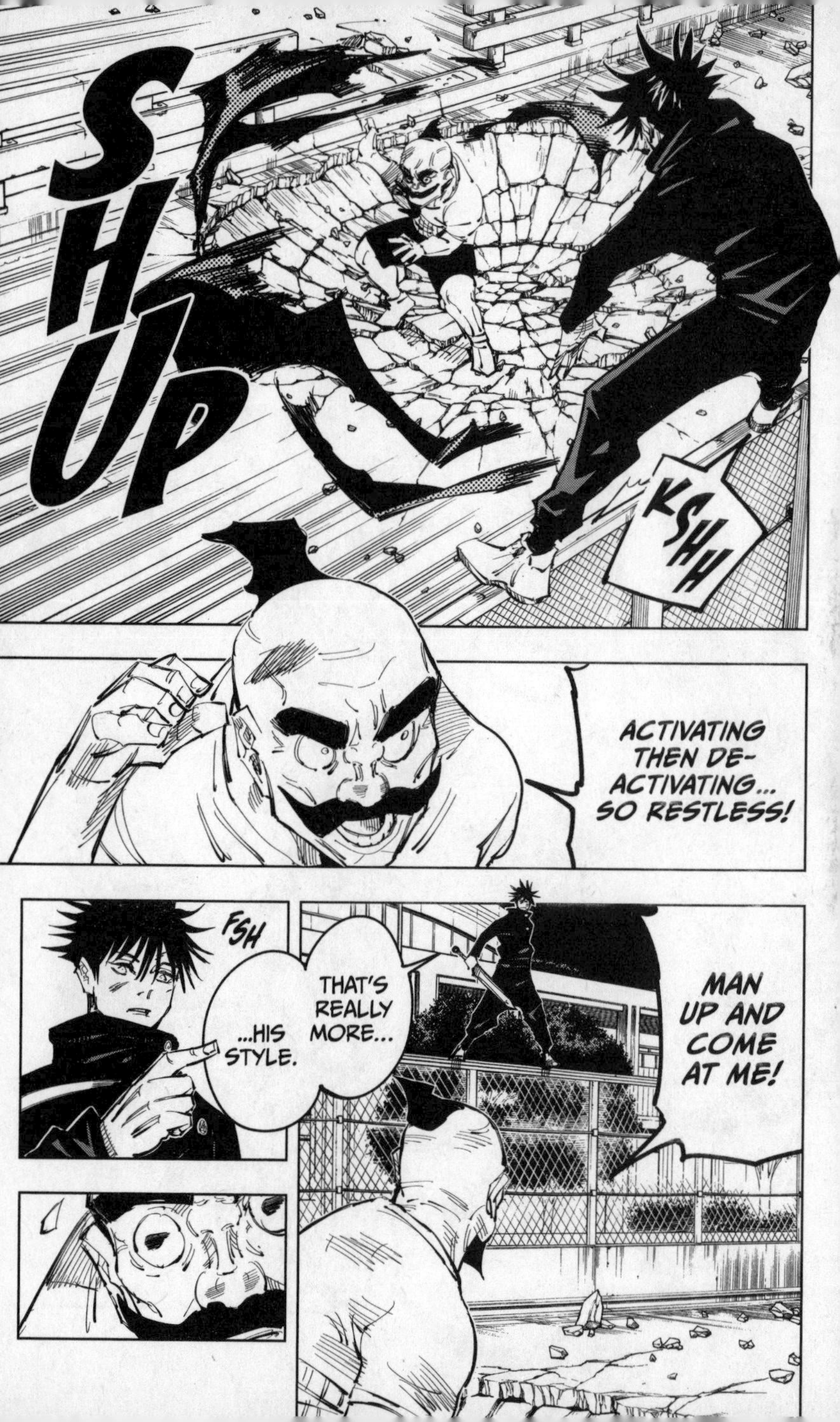
KSHH
SHUP
ACTIVATING THEN DE-ACTIVATING... SO RESTLESS!
MAN UP AND COME AT ME!
FSH
THAT'S REALLY MORE...
...HIS STYLE.

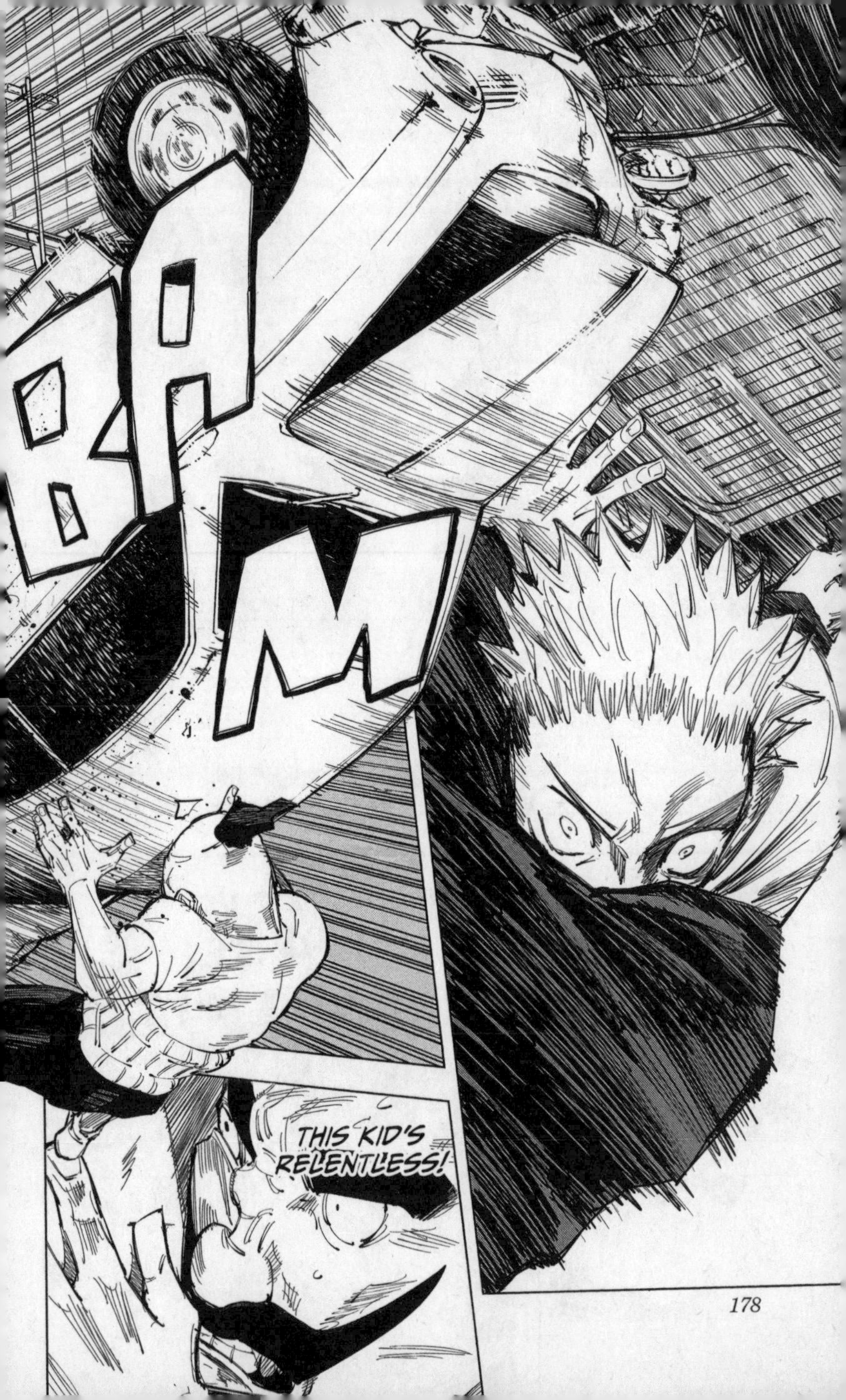
BAM
THIS KID'S RELENTLESS!

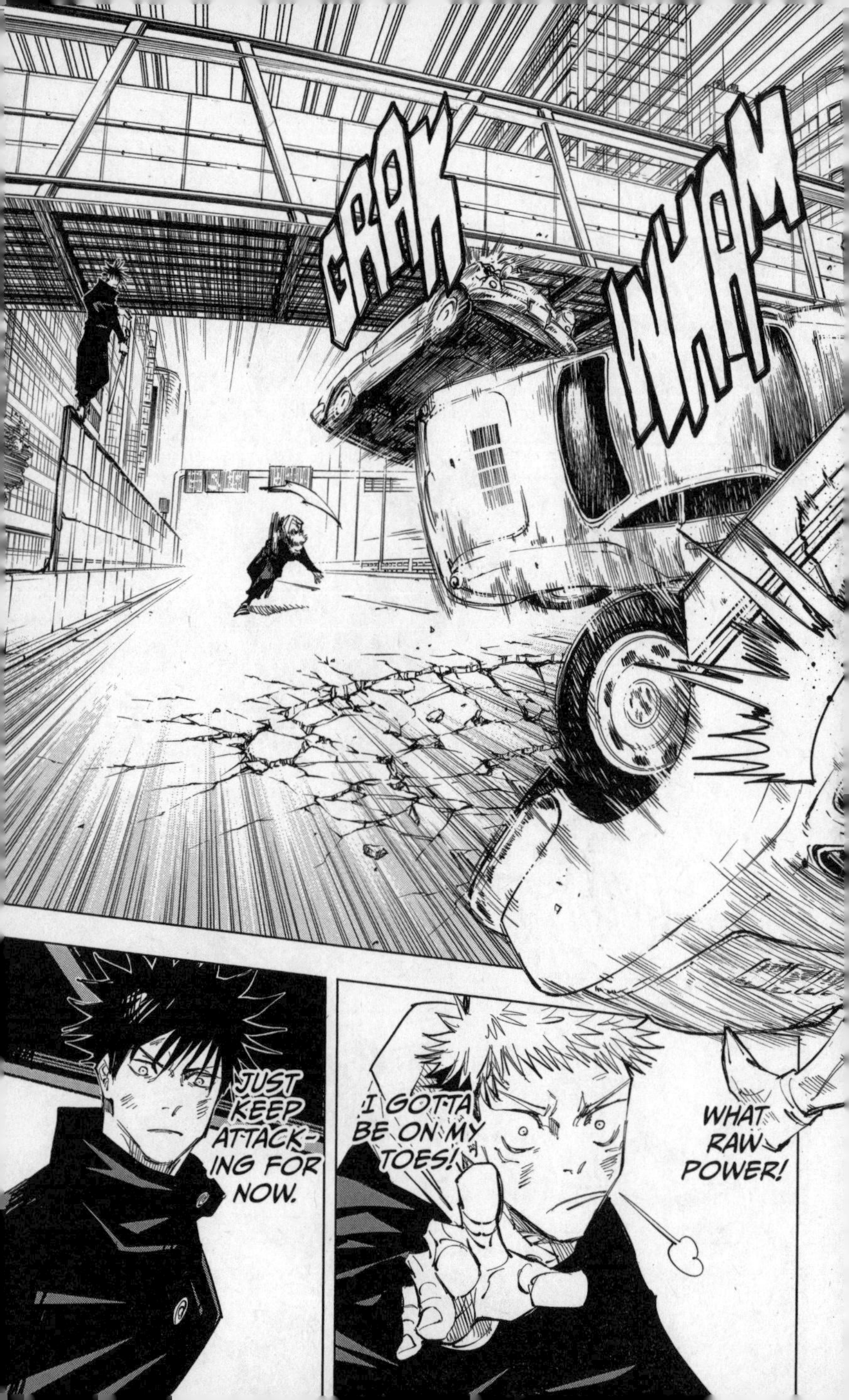
WHAM
CRAK
WHAT RAW POWER!
I GOTTA BE ON MY TOES!
JUST KEEP ATTACK-ING FOR NOW.

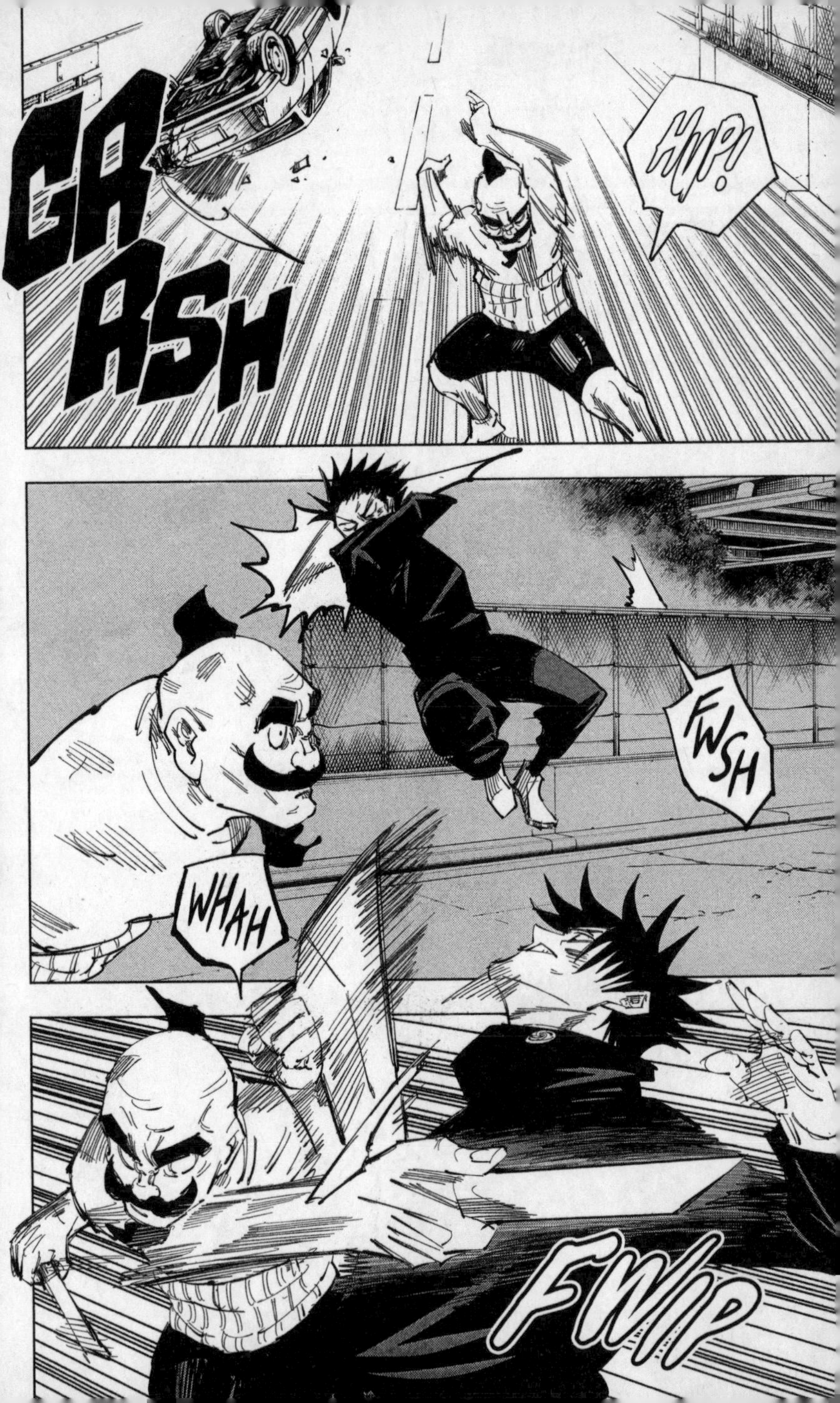
HUP!
CRASH
FWSH
WHAH
FWIP

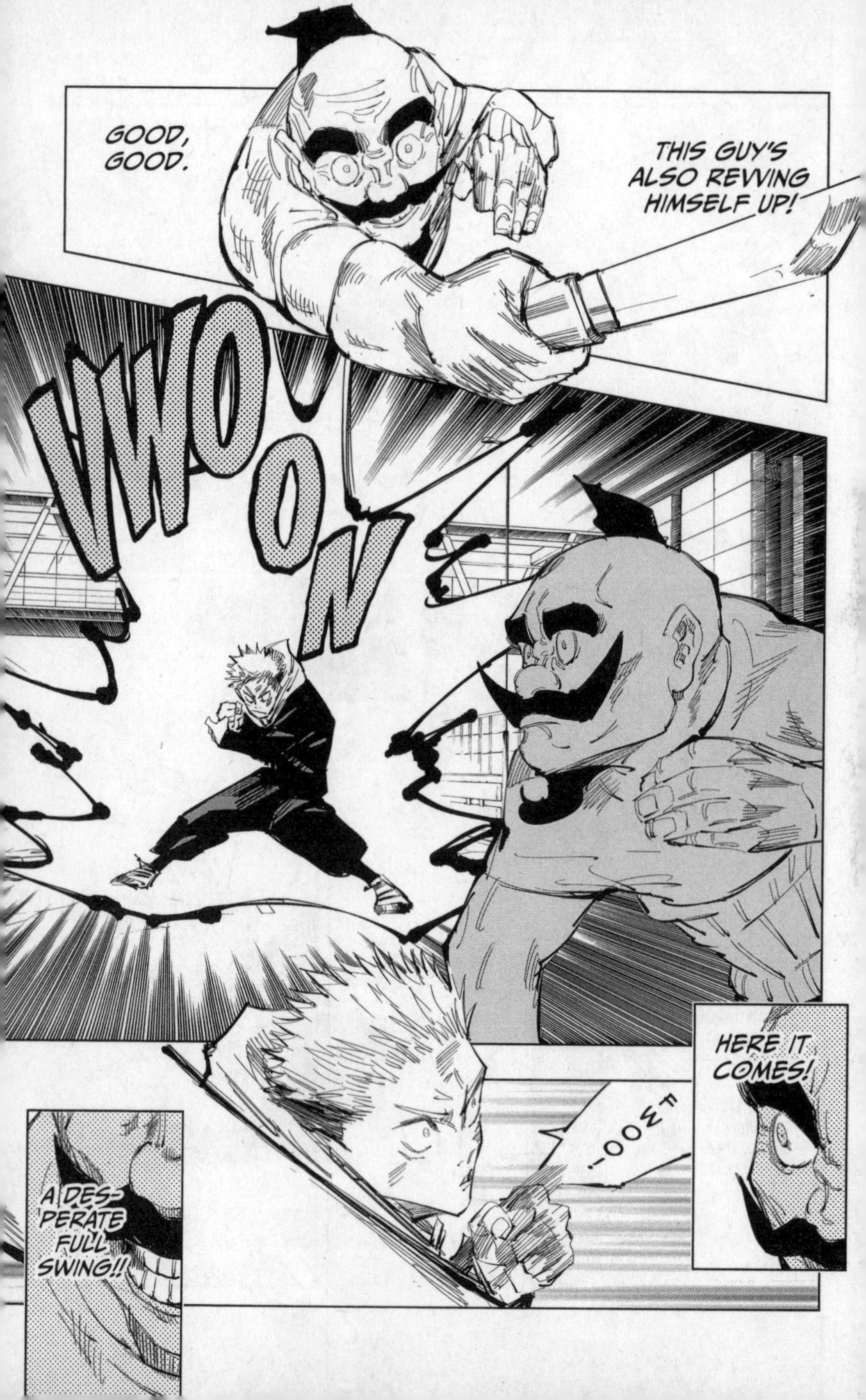
THIS GUY'S ALSO REVVING HIMSELF UP!
GOOD, GOOD.
VWOOON
HERE IT COMES!
FWOO-!
A DES-PERATE FULL SWING!!

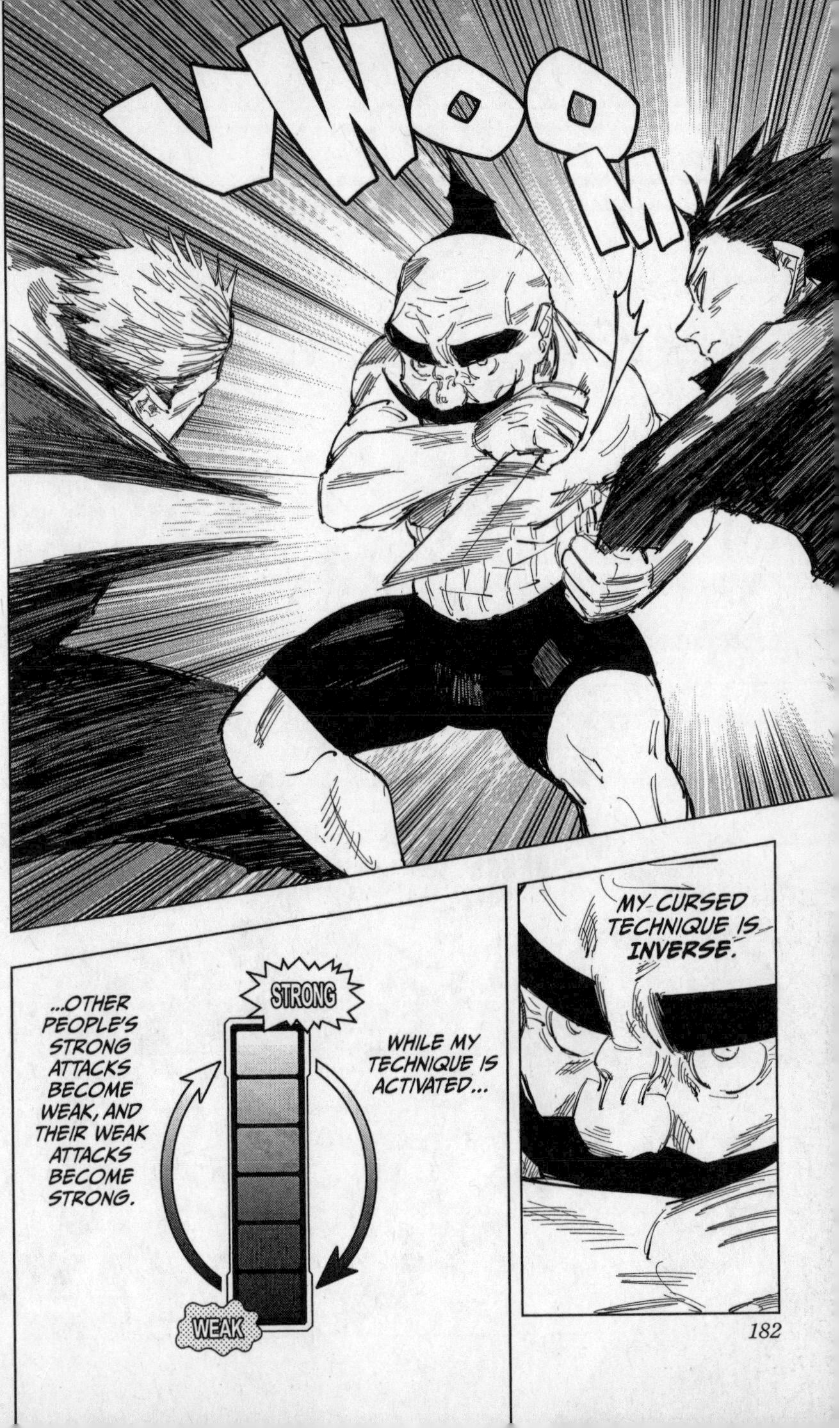
VWOOM
MY CURSED TECHNIQUE IS INVERSE.
STRONG
WHILE MY TECHNIQUE IS ACTIVATED...
...OTHER PEOPLE'S STRONG ATTACKS BECOME WEAK, AND THEIR WEAK ATTACKS BECOME STRONG.
WEAK

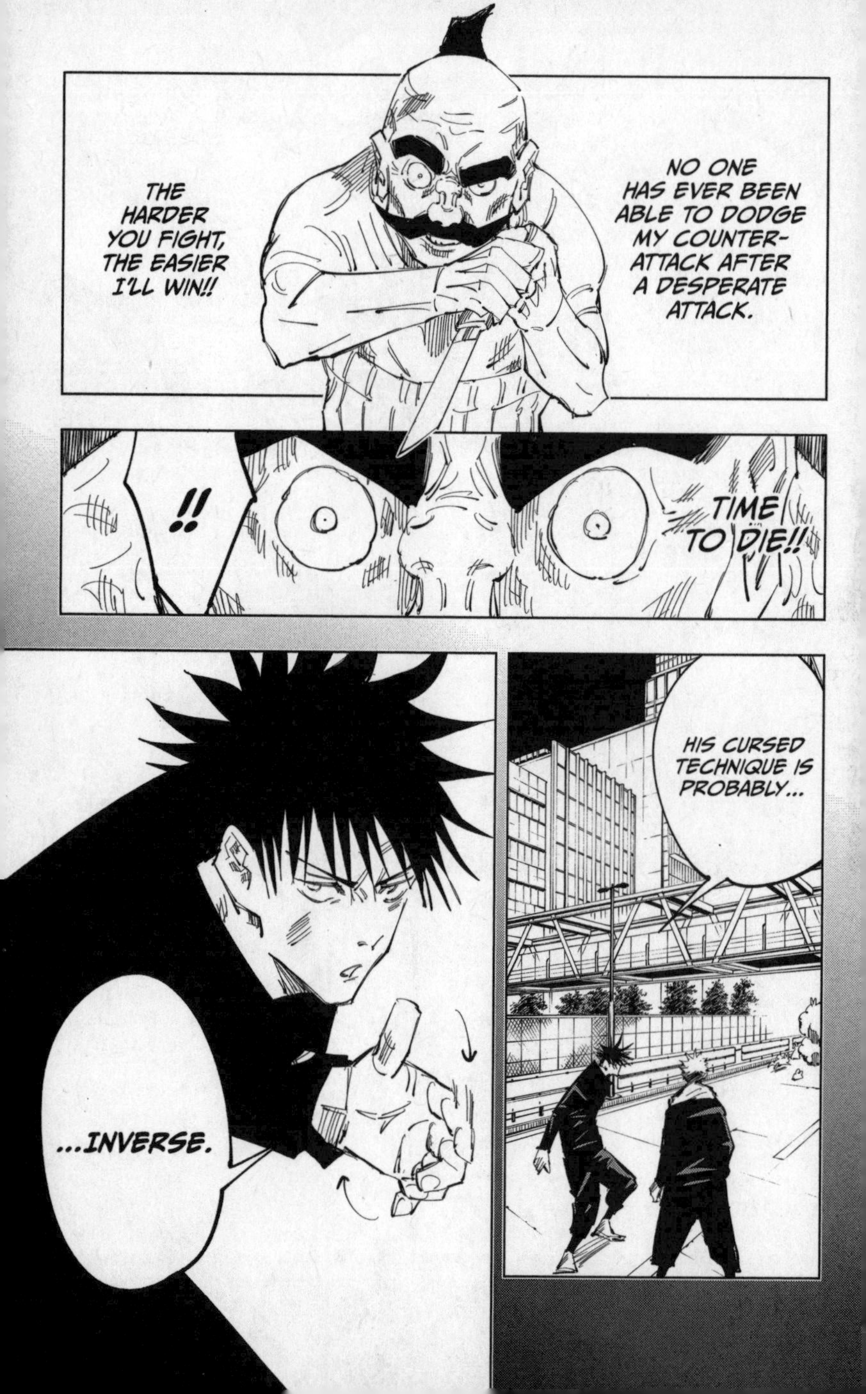
NO ONE HAS EVER BEEN ABLE TO DODGE MY COUNTER-ATTACK AFTER A DESPERATE ATTACK.
THE HARDER YOU FIGHT, THE EASIER I'LL WIN!!
TIME TO DIE!!
!!
HIS CURSED TECHNIQUE IS PROBABLY...
...INVERSE.

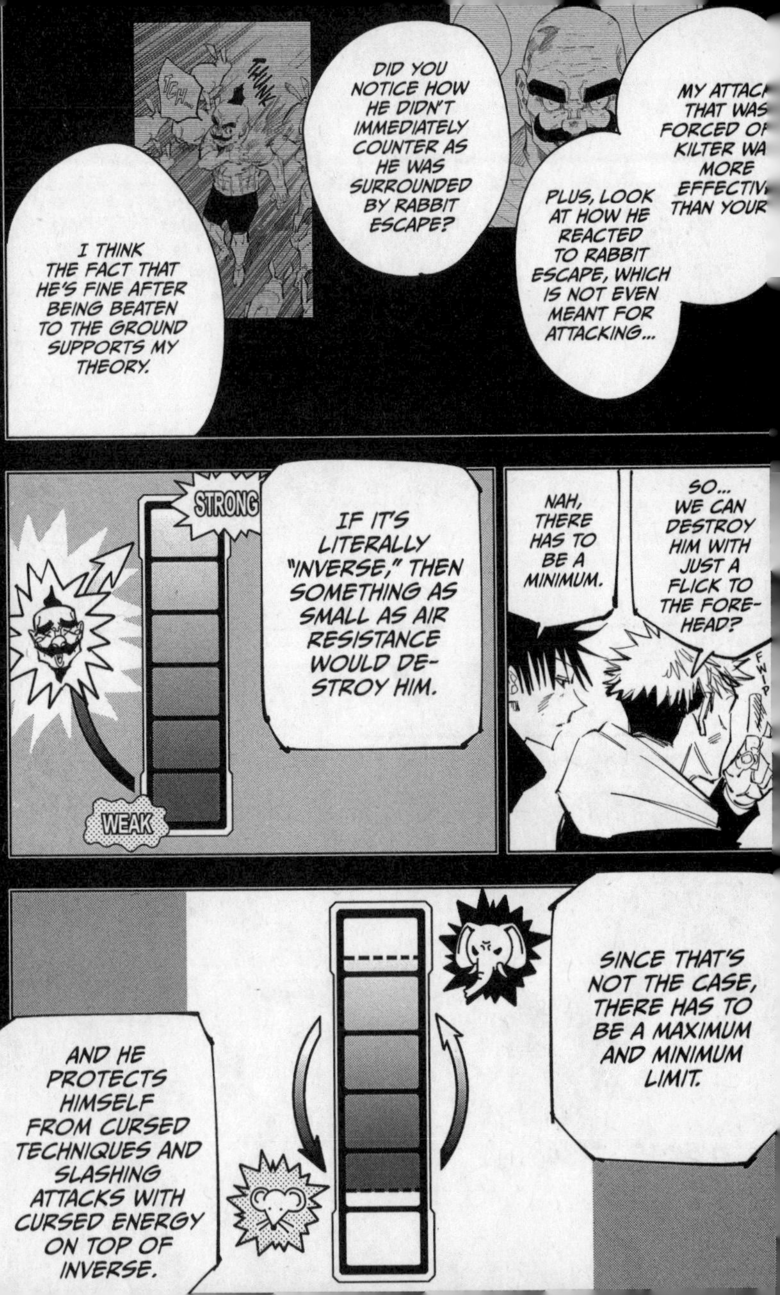
MY ATTAC THAT WAS FORCED OF KILTER WA MORE EFFECTIV THAN YOUR
PLUS, LOOK AT HOW HE REACTED TO RABBIT ESCAPE, WHICH IS NOT EVEN MEANT FOR ATTACKING...
DID YOU NOTICE HOW HE DIDN'T IMMEDIATELY COUNTER AS HE WAS SURROUNDED BY RABBIT ESCAPE?
THUNK
TCH
I THINK THE FACT THAT HE'S FINE AFTER BEING BEATEN TO THE GROUND SUPPORTS MY THEORY.
SO... WE CAN DESTROY HIM WITH JUST A FLICK TO THE FOREHEAD?
FWIP
NAH, THERE HAS TO BE A MINIMUM.
IF IT'S LITERALLY "INVERSE," THEN SOMETHING AS SMALL AS AIR RESISTANCE WOULD DESTROY HIM.
STRONG
WEAK
SINCE THAT'S NOT THE CASE, THERE HAS TO BE A MAXIMUM AND MINIMUM LIMIT.
AND HE PROTECTS HIMSELF FROM CURSED TECHNIQUES AND SLASHING ATTACKS WITH CURSED ENERGY ON TOP OF INVERSE.

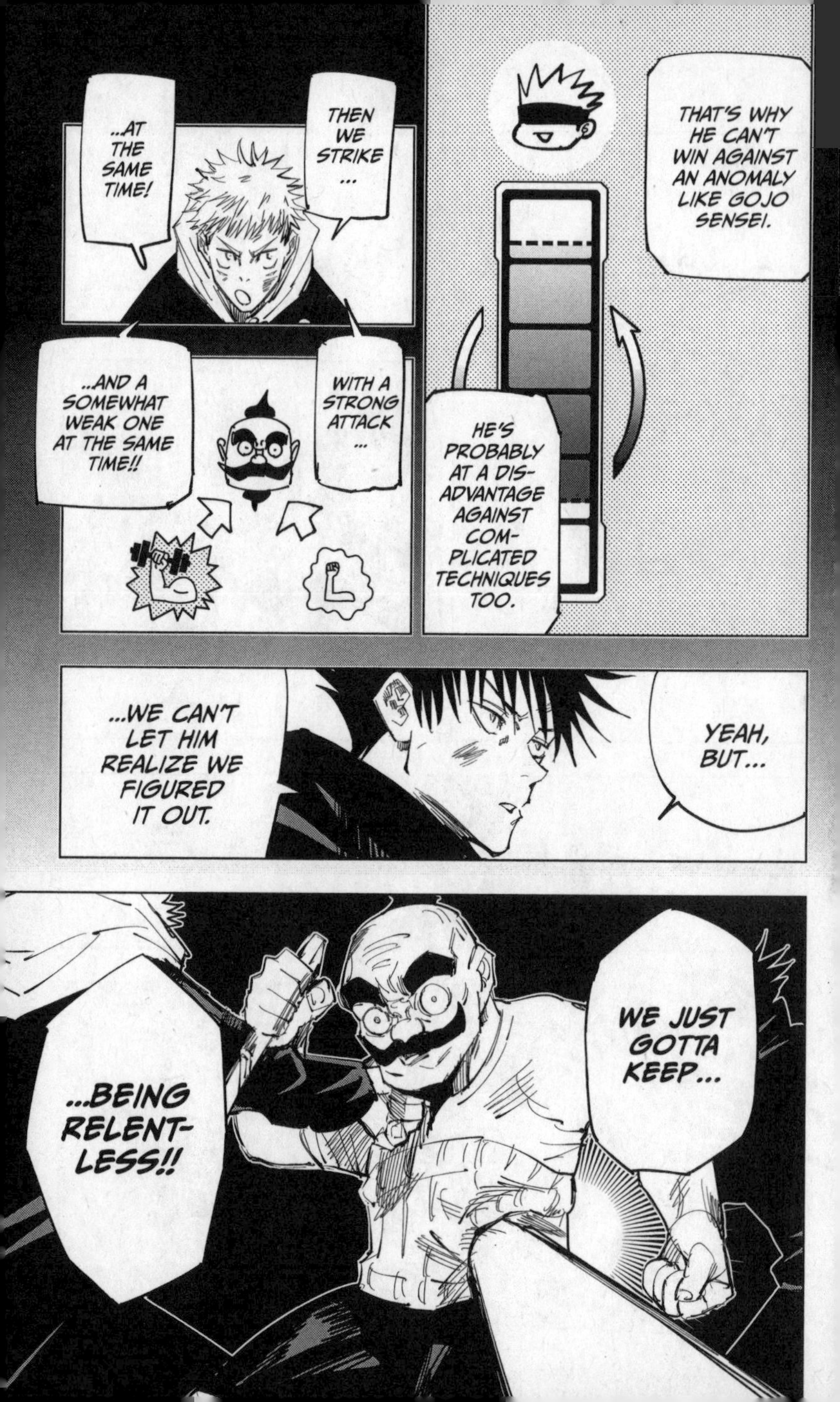
THAT'S WHY HE CAN'T WIN AGAINST AN ANOMALY LIKE GOJO SENSEI.
HE'S PROBABLY AT A DIS-ADVANTAGE AGAINST COM-PLICATED TECHNIQUES TOO.
THEN WE STRIKE...
...AT THE SAME TIME!
WITH A STRONG ATTACK...
...AND A SOMEWHAT WEAK ONE AT THE SAME TIME!!
YEAH, BUT...
...WE CAN'T LET HIM REALIZE WE FIGURED IT OUT.
WE JUST GOTTA KEEP...
...BEING RELENT-LESS!!

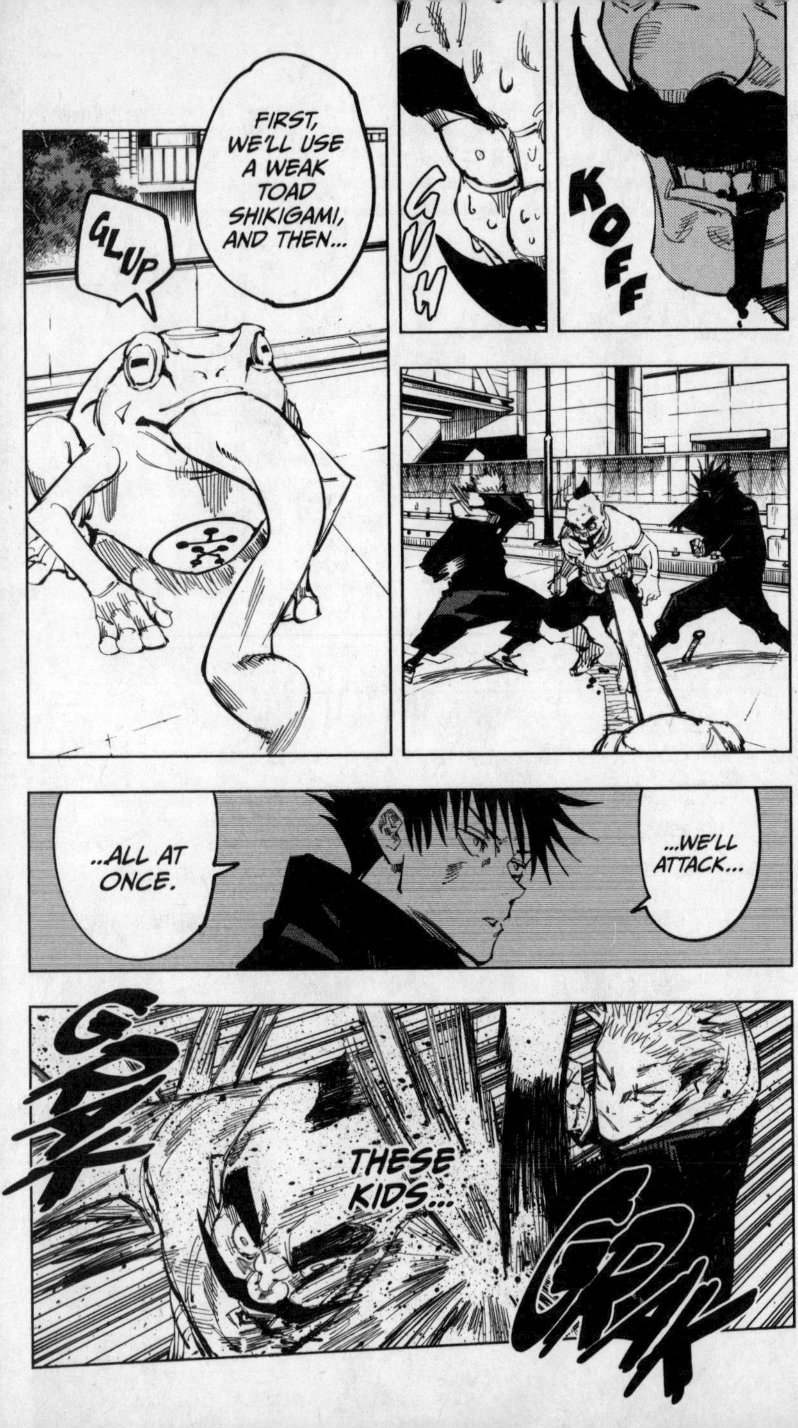
KOFF
GUH
FIRST, WE'LL USE A WEAK TOAD SHIKIGAMI, AND THEN...
GLUP
...WE'LL ATTACK...
...ALL AT ONCE.
GRAK
THESE KIDS...
GRAK

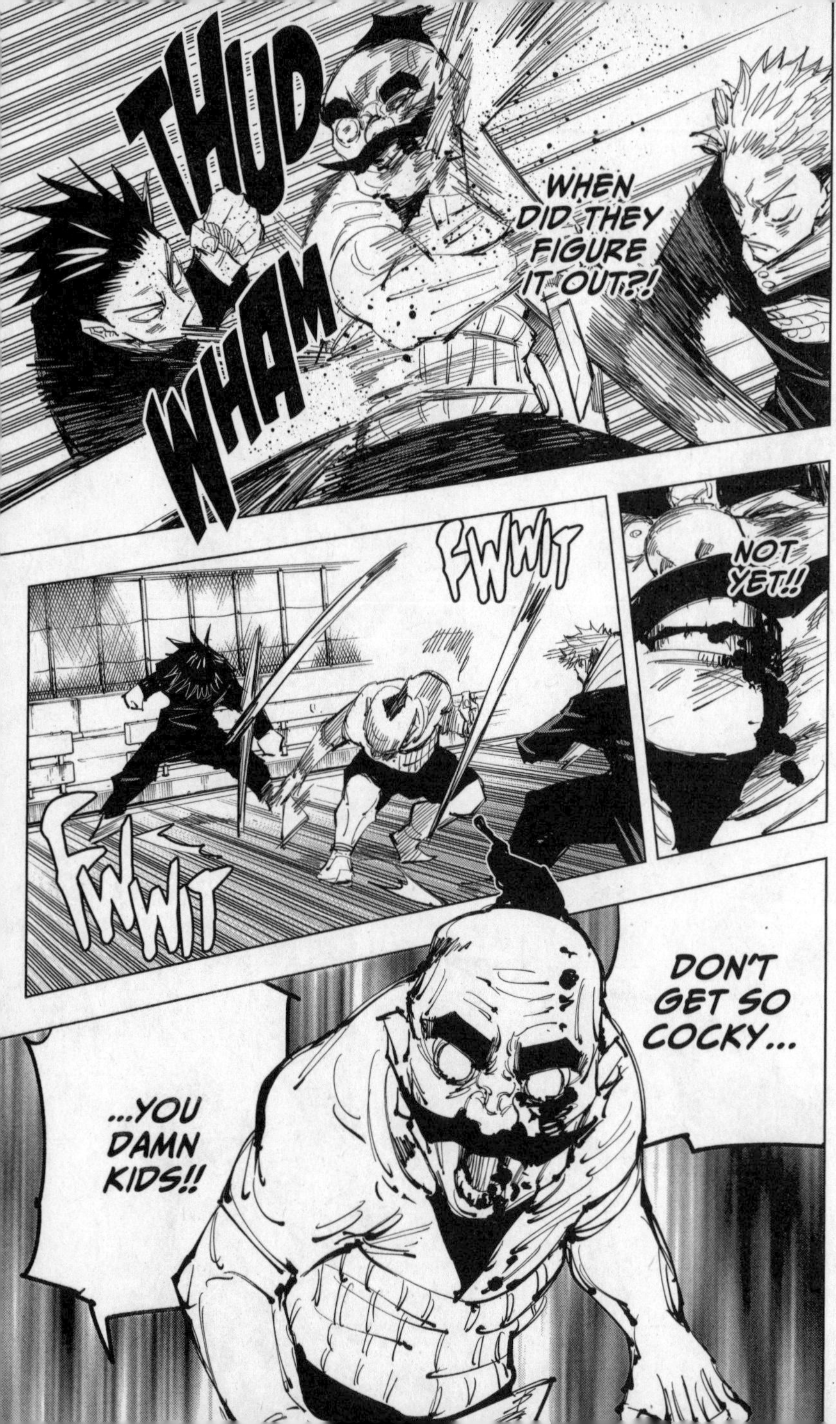
WHEN DID THEY FIGURE IT OUT?!
THUD
WHAM
NOT YET!!
FWWIT
FWWIT
DON'T GET SO COCKY...
...YOU DAMN KIDS!!

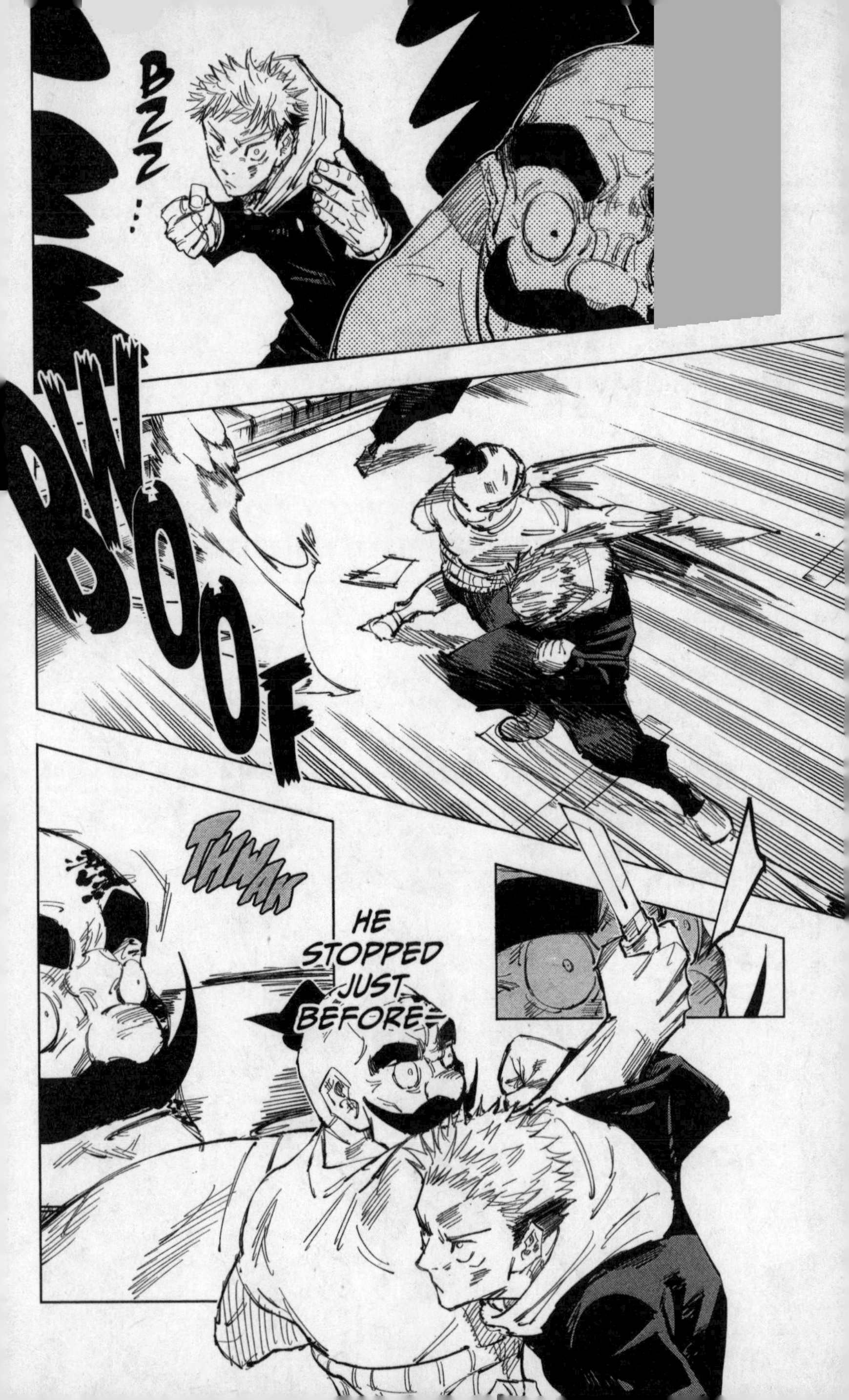
BZZ...
BWOOOF
THWAK
HE STOPPED JUST BEFORE

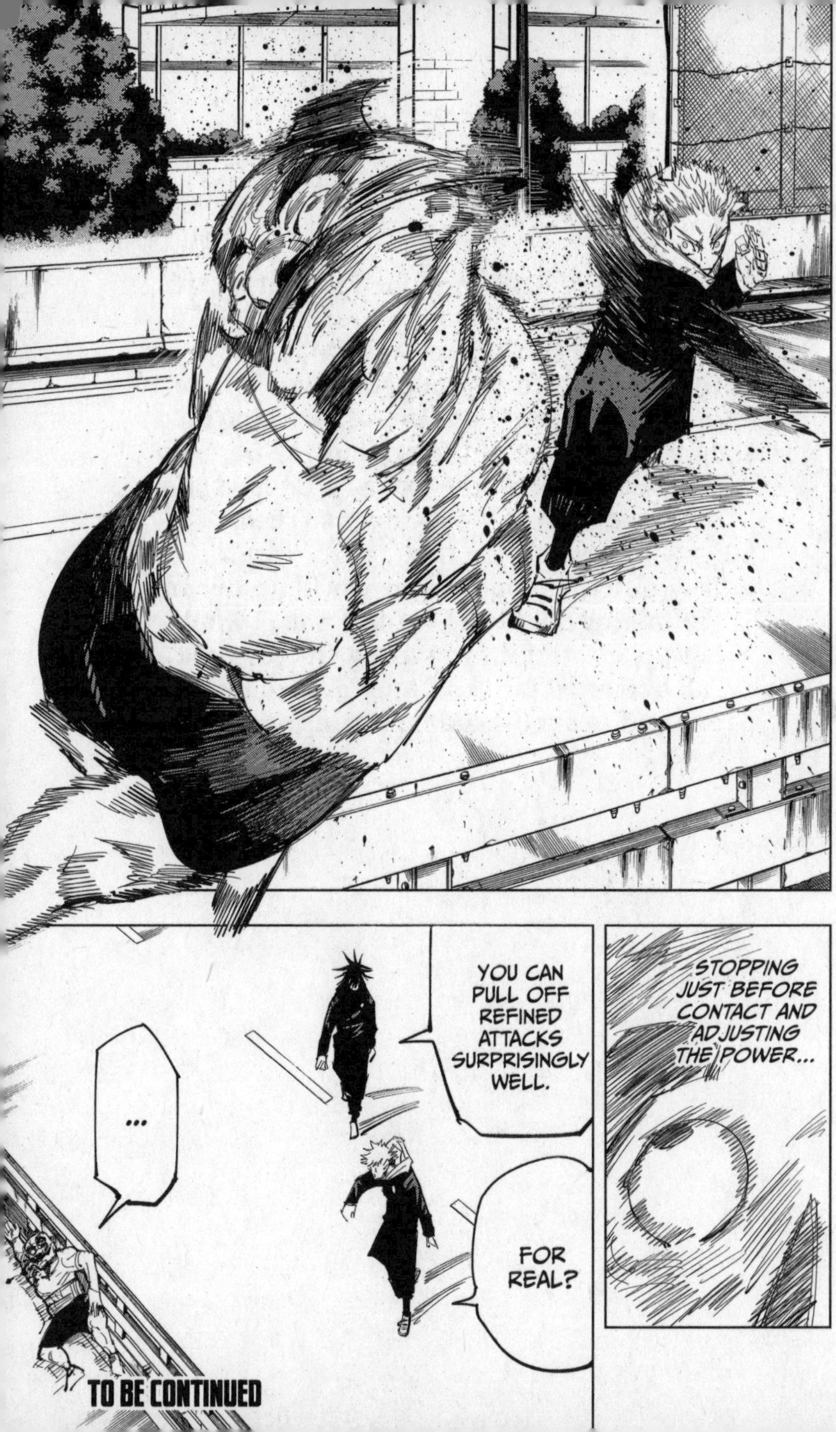
STOPPING JUST BEFORE CONTACT AND ADJUSTING THE POWER...
YOU CAN PULL OFF REFINED ATTACKS SURPRISINGLY WELL.
FOR REAL?
...
TO BE CONTINUED

Afterword

It is April 2020 at the time I'm writing this.

It's actually the beginning of May, but those in charge of production would hate me if they found out I put off working on a June volume in mid-May, thus the lie. This is also the reason the extras are typed and not handwritten. (Is it easier to read?)

It's quite the troublesome world we live in. I'm talking about the coronavirus. I would have preferred it for a manga like *Jujutsu*, full of words like "kill" and "die," to be enjoyed in a more stable world.

That said, there's really not much I can do to contribute to society. I find myself continuing to work on a manga that is dark and bizarre, adding to the dark and bizarre news of late... But I hope everyone can still enjoy it despite that fact.

This is completely irrelevant, but please pretend that you are me (Akutami) for a moment. My father, who recently started reading *Jujutsu*, asked, "Are Fushiguro's dad and Okkotsu modeled after me?" How would you respond? What should I have said?

—Gege Akutami

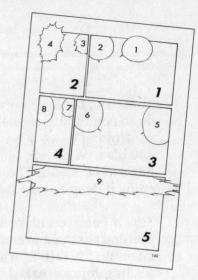

JUJUTSU KAISEN

reads from right to left,
starting in the upper-right
corner. Japanese is read
from right to left, meaning
that action, sound effects
and word-balloon order
are completely reversed
from English order.